WAYS OF DYING

SOUTH ASIA INSTITUTE, NEW DELHI BRANCH
HEIDELBERG UNIVERSITY
SOUTH ASIAN STUDIES NO. XXXIII

WAYS OF DYING

Death and its Meanings in South Asia

edited by

ELISABETH SCHÖMBUCHER

CLAUS PETER ZOLLER

MANOHAR

2020

First published 1999
Reprinted 2020

ISBN 978-81-7304-243-0

Published by
Ajay Kumar Jain *for*
Manohar Publishers & Distributors
4753/23 Ansari Road, Daryaganj
New Delhi 110 002

Printed at
Replika Press Pvt. Ltd.

Contents

List of Illustrations 7

Acknowledgements 9

Note on Transliteration and Transcription 11

INTRODUCTION

Death and its Meanings in South Asia
Claus Peter Zoller and Elisabeth Schömbucher 15

Death as Experience and Institution in Anthropological Theory
Klaus-Peter Köpping 36

PART I: THE CREATION OF ANCESTORS

The Making of Good Ancestors: Separation, Transformation and Exchange in Mewahang Rai Funerary Rites
Martin Gaenszle 49

How to Make the Spirit of the Dead Happy: The Rhetoric of Words and Deeds in a Jēnu Kuṟumba Death Ritual
Ulrich Demmer 68

Mourning, Mortuary Exchange and Memorialization: The Creation of Local Communities among Dalits in Gujarat
Shalini Randeria 88

Ancestors, Demons and the Ritual Impossibility of Death in Brahmanical Hinduism: Bālā's Fourteenth in Deopatan (Nepal)
Axel Michaels 112

Le sacrifice des os
Charles Malamoud 135

PART II: THE EXTRAORDINARY DEATH

Rivers and the Death of Children
Anne Feldhaus 153

Death as the Beginning of a New Life:
Hero-Worship among a South Indian Fishing Caste
Elisabeth Schömbucher 162

No Heroes in Kaliṅga? On Death in Kaliṅga Inscriptions
Georg Berkemer 179

A Note on Death and the Holy Man in South Asia
Hugh van Skyhawk 190

PART III: THE NARRATION AND PERFORMANCE OF DEATH

An Indian Myth of the Creation of Death and Life
Claus Peter Zoller 205

Stringing a Necklace of Heads: Sacrifice and Death in the Cult of Devnārāyaṇ
Aditya Malik 233

Narrated and Dramatized Death in Tuḷu Culture
Heidrun Brückner 249

Kūttāṇṭavar: The Divine Lives of a Severed Head
Alf Hiltebeitel 275

Contributors 327

Illustrations

1. Bālācaturdaśī—Family groups on Kailāsa hill in the morning after the night of Bālācaturdaśī. (Michaels) 313
2. Bālācaturdaśī—Torches (mahādīpa) to be lit in memory of the deceased. (Michaels) 314
3. Bālācaturdaśī—Chetrīs (Thāpā) performing *homa*. In white clothes: the chief mourner; with a shawl: the Brahmin priest. (Michaels) 315
4. Bālācaturdaśī—Pilgrims taking a (symbolic) bath at the cremation *ghāṭs* (Āryaghāṭ). (Michaels) 316
5. Bālācaturdaśī—All the grain collected by Poḍes (sweepers) near the Jayavāgīśvarī temple and Amālkoṭ Kacaharī. (Michaels) 317
6. Bālāguṭhīpūjā—To the back: a *kahaḥ* (trumpet) player and the secret entrance into Mṛgasthalī (right side). (Michaels) 318
7. Bālāguṭhīpūjā—Sacrificial arena at Dharmeśvara, with places set aside for the *homa* (left; in the middle a *vajra*) and a *kalaśa*, bell and conch. (Michaels) 319
8. Bālāguṭhīpūjā—One Mānandhar hands over a basket with two brass fishes and grains to two Rājopādhyāya priests. (Michaels) 320
9. A Vaṉṉiyar carpenter and painter work at night by petromax lantern to repaint Kūttāṇṭavar's head after the previous year's paint has been stripped from it. (Hiltebeitel) 321
10. Eye-opening ceremony for Kūttāṇṭavar's newly repainted head, placed for his first viewing on the *keṭāyam*, with village headmen in attendance. (Hiltebeitel) 322
11. Kūttāṇṭavar, reduced to a 'skeleton', at the 'weeping ground' (*aḻukaḷam*) beneath a large peepul tree, overlooking the tali-cutting and bangle-breaking of his devotees. (Hiltebeitel) 323
12. Open-air Kāḷiyammaṉ temple by the lake bund, where Kūttāṇṭavar's head regains his 'life' (*uyir*). (Hiltebeitel) 324

13. Diaggregation of Kūttāṇṭavar: his head is the last part of his body, other than straw, to be removed from his chariot. The cloth covering it has slipped off the head and is held above it. (Hiltebeitel) 325

14. *Uyir perutal,* 'the recovery of life'. Kūttāṇṭavar's head lies face-up, wrapped in red silk. Pāratiyār K. Muttuswami Pillai sings Pāratam with upraised hands. (Hiltebeitel) 326

Acknowledgements

The editors would like to thank the South Asia Institute for funding the Symposium on *Death in South Asia.* We are grateful to Ursula Rao and Ralf Ullrich for their help in preparing the computer-script for this volume. Anna Margaretha Hanser-Cole solved some major computer problems. We are grateful to her. Anne Feldhaus deserves thanks for correcting the English in several contributions. We would also like to thank those contributors who handed in their manuscripts early and who had to be patient with those who handed in theirs rather late. Finally, we would like to thank Klaus Kusterer for patiently solving our computer problems—even in the middle of the night.

ELISABETH SCHÖMBUCHER
CLAUS PETER ZOLLER

Note on Transliteration and Transcription

We have retained the various styles of transliteration and transcription adopted by the individual contributors. Where diacritical marks have been used, the standard academic conventions for Sanskrit have been followed.

INTRODUCTION

Death and its Meanings in South Asia

CLAUS PETER ZOLLER
ELISABETH SCHÖMBUCHER

This book is the outcome of a symposium held at the South Asia Institute in Heidelberg in the summer of 1993. It was planned by the Departments of Anthropology and Indology as an interdisciplinary approach to the meaning of death in South Asia. What death could mean to the bereaved became evident to the participants in a tragic way. Günther Sontheimer, Professor of Indology, died suddenly and unexpectedly on 1 June 1992, at the age of 58, just a few days after he and Richard Burghart, Professor of Anthropology, had decided to hold this symposium. Richard Burghart continued to plan the symposium, together with us, but he fell ill three months before its start. By the time the contributors to this volume met, it had become evident that he could not be cured of brain cancer. He died on 1 January 1994, at the age of 49. For Günther Sontheimer and Richard Burghart, death was not an arbitrary choice of themes to be selected for a symposium, but each of them had a certain closeness to, and a number of questions about death. For us, the symposium was far more than a purely academic exercise. Instead of merely collecting scholarly treatises on death in South Asia we found ourselves in a state of shock and bewilderment, and, for many of us, the symposium was part of the process of grieving.

Death is an all-pervasive phenomenon in every society. The questions death raises and the multiple answers to those questions touch upon the most intrinsic parts of human existence. However, reflections on death and mortality may occur on different levels. The level of personal experience and emotional involvement, so well documented in literature, seems to be generally absent in academic discourse (with the exception of Rosaldo 1984), whereas two other levels—ways of coping with death and dying through ritual practices, such as mourning rituals and cults of remembering, and conceptions of death and the discourse on life and afterlife—are part of academic discourse. Looking at the contributions to this volume, one might be tempted to ask whether the authors have been able to incorporate their emotional dismay into their scholarly elaborations, or rather whether the absence of emotional involvement in the contributions means that the two are incompatible? It seems to be one thing to write about death and reflect upon its implications on society, and another thing to experience personal loss, despair, grief, desolation and the failure to comprehend the death of a person near to oneself. An ethnography of dying—which has yet to be written—would have to include the emotional involvement of the dying and the bereaved, it would have to cope with the silence before death, besides considering concepts of death and the cultural practices related to it.

* * *

There exist several scholarly works which deal with dying, death and the dead in South Asia from a variety of perspectives. Some authors, like Parry (1994) and Vitebsky (1993), write from an ethnographic point of view and portray the social and ritual forms related to these spheres as expressions of human or superhuman agency. Others, like Heesterman, Schmithausen, Halbfass, Wezler and Oberhammer (in Oberhammer 1995), stress the conceptual aspects, and they seem to favour the idea of an agency of texts. It is the texts which mirror what people think. Again others, like Müller (1992), concentrate on rituals, which, under certain circumstances, too, may function as independent agencies. Other books, like Settar's two works (1986, 1990), or like the present one, try to take the ethnographic as well as the textual perspective into account.

Parry presents the views of Banaras Brahmins who are used to producing self-explanatory cosmologies and 'thanatologies', and who, as professionals serving a large clientele, have an answer for every question and a solution for every metaphysical problem. Müller presents one of the most widely used manuals, the *Antyeṣṭipaddhati*, which is employed in Brahmanical death rituals. An important insight of Müller is his demonstration of how specific performances of 'texts'—that is, the prescriptive rites as they are described in the *Antyeṣṭipaddhati*—have profound consequences for an understanding of the meaning of death. Since the ritual praxis allows that specific rituals can be omitted or shifted, or that two rituals can collapse into one (Müller 1992: 26), new meanings of rituals can emerge which *cannot* be hermeneutically extracted out of the texts as they are. We will take up this point again later. The book introduced and edited by Oberhammer is almost exclusively based on a hermeneutical approach; the contributors interpret and analyse highly articulate 'classical' speculations and teachings on death-related concepts and philosophical systems. Apart from the astute introduction ('Religionshermeneutische Bemerkungen zum Phänomen des Todes') by Oberhammer (1995: 9-26), which deals with the phenomenon of death from a culture-transcending perspective, the contributors to this book hardly investigate such questions as what relevance these speculations had for which people, and how the speculations were converted into practice. This lacuna cannot be justified by the fact that all contributions except the last deal with texts from old and medieval India. How the problem could be solved is suggested in the works of Settar (1985, 1990). He has attempted—though not completely successfully—to investigate the philosophy and practice of voluntary termination of life among the Jains as it is reflected in a huge number of philosophical, literary and other texts, and in art and architecture. This custom, which is conducted according to intricate instructions, was and is practiced by a minority. Nevertheless it is informed, as we will see, by central concepts of the South Asian civilizations.

All the contributions mentioned so far deal with textually represented cultural traditions. This bias neglects the fact that numerous cultural traditions in South Asia are not represented in the form of written texts. We hope that the present book helps to improve this situation slightly by giving a voice also to people who are usually not taken notice of. Vitebsky's book on the Sora tribals, who live around the borders of Orissa and Andhra Pradesh, is already an important contribution in this direction. The Soras' concepts and rituals connected with death are rather the opposite of being self-explanatory: by showing the inadequacy of translating crucial concepts of the Soras related to personhood, living and dying with familiar Western ones—for instance *sonum* with 'spirit, deity'—Vitebsky is able to point out how such translation practices lead simultaneously to an intellectual acquisition and an existential distancing, and to the construction of supposed dichotomies between 'primitive' and 'rational' thinking (1993: 13). Our own and other people's field experiences fully corroborate his concern.

We consider Dumont's monolithic and hierarchical model of Indian society (as well as all other universalistic theories) defective not only because of widespread countervailing egalitarian movements (Parry 1974, Lorenzen 1981, 1987) and because of 'counterdiscourses' among low-castes, women, and even higher castes in 'peripheral' regions. It is also defective because it does not take into account the very common phenomenon that people or groups of people think in, and make use of, a plurality of concepts and discourses, which frequently do not match with each other, and which can be imperfect and unstable. Moreover, it is defective because it does not take into account that various groups of people may, for instance, practice the same or similar rituals while attaching to them very different meanings or, *vice versa*, convert similar concepts into different rituals or other practices.

Thus, South Asia cannot be adequately grasped by means of a universalistic model or theory. It is a vast area of a multitude of cultures. On the other hand, it also cannot be grasped by the notion of composite culture, so much in vogue at present. The notion is too aesthetic, its meaning too passive to take into account the many contradictions, fractions and tensions that do exist in the relations between people and groups, in the endless disputes, conflicts and clashes which accompany the encounters between various communities and sub-cultures. These facts are reflected in this book. Thus, we would like to stress that the book's apparent 'incoherence', the sheer absence of a common bond (besides the general theme of death) is not accidental, but a reflection of South Asian realities. Conceptual systems, ritual prescriptions, and the actual thinking and acting of people, their stressing or neglecting of 'facts', their adaptation to precepts, and their manipulation or violation of rules, concepts and customs create dynamic fields of tension which may, but must not, culminate in crises and conflicts. Several contributions to this volume describe such fields of tension, which are controlled by a multitude of agencies.

However, besides or beneath such dynamic processes there seem to be a few practices and ideas which appear so widespread that they may be understood as a sort of 'primer', colouring as it were the regional cultures more or less intensely. One is the very widespread *practice* of cremation of the dead, another is the very widespread *concept* of an intimate relation between death or dying and violence (in the sense that death as a *natural* end to life appears not to be a dominant idea in South Asia), a third is the very widespread *concept* of a transformation the dead undergo after death, and a fourth is the *concept* that this world is not automatically followed by *one* other world, but that there are options. The following outline, which refers to these practices and ideas, must necessarily remain incomplete and frequently simplifying and curtailing. However, this is unavoidable if one tries to say a few general things about death in South Asia.

In Western scholarship on the phenomena of death and dying it is generally held that the awareness of death is a sequel to the development of self-awareness, and an intrinsic attribute of humankind (Palgi and Abramovitch 1984: 385): death as the end of one's existence can be intellectually anticipated at any moment. This 'analytical' position, stressing transience and the irrevocable end of individual existence, differs sharply from the 'existential' points of view based on 'hope', which generally advocate opinions that death leads toward perfection. Thus, there are, for instance, the classical Indian concepts of *mokṣa, apavarga,* etc. ('emancipation, liberation'), which only make sense before a background of death, and which promise an identity of the *ātman* 'self' and the *brahman.* Renouncing the world and finally physical death are widely considered to be necessary conditions for achieving this state. The point of view of Catholic theology, to give an example from a very different culture, is that the soul not only does not lose its 'substantiality' after death, but experiences more clearly to what extent it is in harmony and disharmony with the universe (Rahner 1958: 17-26).

The inseparable relation between the 'self' and death seems to allow at least three positions or perspectives: the first, which especially characterizes Western traditions, is to put life and death into an utmost contrast: death is the quintessential other—behind the horizon of existence and perception. This possibility of a radical and final non-existence for every person is, according to Heidegger, explained by the fact that being and nothingness (Sein und Nichts) fundamentally belong together: being and nothingness mutually reveal each other. Nothingness is especially experienced in the states of fear, when one loses one's grip over being or over oneself (in Stein 1950: 55, note 45). Such considerations appear closely related to a radical dualism of body and soul, where the meaning of death is equated with the visible end, decay and dissolution of the body, where death thus exclusively means radical loss and bereavement. Such a point of view is represented by the French philosopher Simone Weil, who claims that the belief in immortality is harmful because it is beyond our power to envisage the soul as truly disembodied ('wahrhaft entkörpert'). Such a belief would be the belief in a prolongation of (mundane) life (Weil 1989: 56). It is obvious that a theoretical-mystical position which derogates or even fully rejects speculations about the other world, as well as 'transcendental' human experiences, for theological reasons (Haas 1989: 123),[1] is not very far removed from a radical-secular position which denies a hereafter and the actual existence of a religious sphere.

The second position on the relation between 'self' and death comprises the whole range of 'conceptualizations' of death as a continuation, prolongation or transformation of (mundane) life, which all somehow rest upon the idea that the spheres of life and death, of this world and the other(s), cannot be so radically different.[2] This position rather assumes all sorts of structural similarities, and, especially, that the two spheres physically or spatially touch or even permeate each other. Such is certainly the view of the majority of people in South Asia. Most of the papers in this book deal with such a view. Here we do not come across highly abstract and decontextualized philosophies, but find concrete spheres of life which are shaped by an 'architecture' which—through the concrete actions of the people and through the discourses they use—encompasses this world *and* the other world(s). The hereafter has, in some way, always also a presence in the here and now. Within this sphere the abstract 'thanatologies' of Brahmanical erudition, which are characterized by static structures and unambiguous 'facts', are confined to a peripheral position. It is a sphere which is characterized by *agency*: neither does death here involve a radical break of relations with the living nor does it involve concepts of a mechanistic predetermination of the fates of the dead. On the contrary, here it is important to *cultivate* the relations between the living and the dead, for instance in the form of festivals. During such festivals, which are celebrated in different parts of

India, the dead (sometimes in form of an anonymous group) temporarily return to the realm of the living: they are invited, welcomed, regaled with offerings, they may become incarnated in media, and finally they will be dismissed. Within this sphere the living and the dead also frequently try to influence each other: the living may try to exploit the powers of deified dead for their personal advantage, or the dead may try to have the living do specific deeds or may even try to fetch the living into their world. Besides visits and interferences in one another's territories, relations can also be continued due to the fact that sometimes dead persons can leave behind something of their 'substance' in this world. This is the case with *dargāhs* (graves of Muslim saints) and *samādhis* (tombs of Hindu ascetics), but also with all those numerous and variegated 'memorials' which are said to be 'charged'.[3] Pointing out these facts, we would like to express our disagreement with current ideas that death is always a dramatic but sharply demarcated event which suddenly invades the harmonious realm of the living and has to be overcome as fast as possible in order to re-establish harmony. Despite the usefulness of the theory of the notions of 'separation-liminality-reintegration' (Turner 1969), the presence of death, the 'celebration of death', is certainly more relevant for most people than this theory suggests.[4] A final characteristic of the second position is that the actors in both spheres have a limited time during which they are effective: as a rule, one day deified people stop being active or are simply forgotten by the living, and new deified beings occupy their place.

All these interrelations are not only ordered by an abstract principle of this world and the other, but are frequently integrated into concrete landscapes: the subcontinent is covered with entrances into the netherworlds (König 1984) which have the form of burning grounds, ponds, wells, pits, caves, termite mounds, etc. Confluences of rivers, cliffs and mountains were places where religious suicide opened doors leading into higher other-worldly spheres. Sometimes this and the other world do not only have common points of contact, but there may be gradual transitions between the two or they may interpenetrate each other: in mountainous regions like the Himalaya it is not uncommon to find the high alpine regions and peaks associated with purity and other-worldliness, and the deep valleys with impurity and dull this - worldliness. We thus find that the lifestyles of most people in South Asia are deeply influenced by universes in which the other world is firmly anchored in this one.

Let us now turn to the third position. It is characterized by a desire for salvation, liberation, emancipation, release, disengagement, dis-entanglement, or detachment. It is a desire to overcome death—or, more precisely, death and life—and it aims at severing all ties, bonds and attachments, all that ensures communication and exchange. This goal is strived for through a multitude of forms of 'self-sacrifice', both in the

Vedic-Brahmanical traditions and in many ascetic groups which do not accept the authority of the Vedas. The third position develops out of the second: when there is no radical difference between this world and the other, and, consequently, between body and soul, then the body will continue exerting its influence on the soul.[5] Both body and soul are, as well as the spheres of this and the other world, results of creation. Thus they are seen to emerge out of the more basic dichotomy between the spheres of creation and non-creation.[6]

According to modern Brahmanical Hinduism dying and being born are basically two aspects of the one process of cosmic 'digestion' (Parry 1989: 510). Such a repeated change between this world and the other requires a 'propulsion', that is *karma.*[7] This 'propulsion', which is kept running by a permanent consumption and reaccumulation of *karma*, can be overcome either through ascetic-purificatory acts or, in the case of *bhakti*, through the grace of God. The original state of non-creation can be achieved, for instance, either by perfect control (and preservation) of the body (as practiced in various Yogic sects), or by a perfect 'self-sacrifice' (as practiced in Brahmanically informed Hinduism in the form of the last sacrament, the *antyeṣṭi* 'funeral sacrifice',[8] or by a perfect 'scratching out of the body', *sallekhana* [a severe ascetic practice formerly found among Jains (Settar 1990: 177)].[9]

In Brahmanic Hinduism there are two theories of what happens after the 'self-sacrifice' of cremation (Parry 1989: 509-10):

(*a*) The more chronologically distant the ancestors are, the more refined they become, until they completely lose their identities and become one with the *viśvedevāḥ* (see also Knipe 1977).
(*b*) When, after the *sapiṇḍīkaraṇa*-rite, the dead has gotten rid of his *preta*-body, he gets a new body (a punishment- or experience-body) and starts to use up his *karma* in hell or heaven until he is reborn on earth.[10]

We can see that (*b*) is an 'exaggerated' description of the second perspective, and that (*a*) explains how it is to be overcome. It is 'exaggerated' because it does not perceive any more a movement to and fro of *actions* between this and the other world, but a movement to and fro of *actors*. A compelling consequence of this *punarmṛtyu* 'redeath' is the idea that the events after death and before birth are basically the same. There is ample evidence for this. Here are two examples: during the ten months after death and before birth the departed spirit and the embryo both have to suffer hunger and deprivation, both have to cross a river full of garbage, and both have to traverse various hells.[11] Moreover, the pollution caused by death and birth is referred to by the same word, *sūtaka*, 'impurity caused by child birth' (Das 1976: 259).

The following point should by now be evident: whether or not *antyeṣṭi* and *sapiṇḍīkaraṇa* are rather meant to furnish the dead 'provisionally' with rebirth in a caste as high as possible or directly with a 'push' towards final emancipation, it is clear that both aim—like the more radical exercises of various ascetic sects and religions—at a severance of previous attachments and bonds. This appears to us to be an important reason for the conspicuous absence of ancestral worship in Brahmanical Hinduism and in the other schools and religions that aspire for salvation. This severance is achieved through *violent* but, ideally, *voluntary* acts of 'self-annihilation'. Additionally, they require the determination of the correct *moment* for their realization. For instance, in Brahmanical Hinduism a dying man '[h]aving previously predicted the time of his going . . . by an effort of concentrated will . . . abandons life' (Parry 1982: 359).[12] And one more example: various Jain texts make it very clear that '[w]ithout ensuring right causes, no aspirant is to embrace ritual-death' (Settar 1990: 25). Right causes were, for instance, when the person '(*a*) sensed the imminence of death; (*b*) suffered an accident, more or less fatal in nature; (*c*) realized the impossibility of sustaining the spiritual life; and (*d*) under-went emotional hurt or disillusionment in life' (Settar 1990: 26).

These concepts of 'self-sacrifice' and 'self-annihilation' thus can be characterized as voluntary acts of violence at the right time and under the right circumstances. They differ from the second perspective presented earlier in various ways: the second perspective (1) either has to do with 'natural' deaths[13] and stresses a smooth and unproblematic transfer into the other world, or (2) sees death also as an act of violence. However, contrary to the cases described earlier, here the act of violence is carried out, as a rule, against the will, or at least without the explicit consent of the person-to-die, or as a wilful violent act that is directed against somebody or something else. Consequently, this type of violence is *untimely* violence. Again, we may discern here two forms of violence: (i) one that is intentionally perpetrated by another person, and (ii) all the other cases where violent death occurs either unintentionally and unexpectedly or as the result of (uncontrolled) aggression against oneself or against somebody or something else.

(i) Death caused by another person of one's community: here, death is the result of a bad (magical) deed performed either by a member of the community or family (see the contribution of Demmer on the Jēnu Kuṟumba) or by a dead person from the other world (Vitebsky 1993 on the Sora).
(ii) Other untimely deaths: this comprises all those who find an end through an accident, a fight, suicide out of anger or desperation, a disaster, a war, or the malice of demons or fairies, and all those

for whom the proper post-mortem rituals could not be performed or who violated their social obligations.[14] In close vicinity with this complex are probably those types of socially or politically motivated suicides which are frequently reported in the Indian newspapers. It may be worthwhile to investigate whether this type of suicide is usually committed just as an act of protest or whether people associate with it religio-magical ideas. According to widespread beliefs found all over the subcontinent, these souls which have found such violent deaths remain in a limbo, they become *bhūt-pret*, until some of them get deified under favourable circumstances and thus reintegrated on a new level. The voluntary deaths, the involuntary ones, and the 'natural' ones also differ with regard to the length of time that the dead remain related to the sphere of the living: the extremes reach from immediate and irreversible disappearance (illustrated, for instance, in many Jain hagiographies) to a very prolonged association with this world in the case of the deified dead. The other cases described earlier could be located somewhere in between these poles.

The distinction of two poles suggested here—voluntary and timely 'self-sacrifice' or 'self-annihilation' *vs.* involuntary and untimely violent death (with the various 'natural' deaths in-between)—differs substantially from Blackburn's theory about death and deification in (south) India. Blackburn says (1985: 265): 'The natural dead become ancestors sustained through ritual and sacrifice until they are reborn, but the violently killed are never reborn.' He specifies that (p. 273): 'folk cults embrace violence, while the classical sacrifice and philosophy rejected it'. However, that is not exactly the case, because in the Brahmanical post-mortem rituals 'cremation is an act of violence perpetrated by one's son' (Parry 1989: 506), and in the course of the cremation-sacrifice 'sacrificer, victim and god are identified with each other' (Parry 1981: 361). We thus cannot see here a difference between classical and folk traditions but only one between different manifestations and conceptualizations of violence. Death, contrary to Western understandings, is not something that has to be passively sustained but is rather something that is carried out actively. Death, actively caused by oneself, ideally leads to permanent detachment. This is typically found in non-Brahmanical and Brahmanical ascetic contexts. Death, actively caused in other ways, ideally leads to long-term relations with the world of the living. This is typically found in those contexts in which asceticism is peripheral or absent. We thus detect violence as a basic agent at the heart of the transformations of death and birth, creation and destruction.

Ritual action such as funerary rites, rituals of mourning and rites of remembering as well as concepts of death and after-life are said to try to conquer death, to regenerate life, to achieve immortality and to continue life after death. However, death comes in many forms and has therefore various meanings. Responses to death and concepts of after-life vary accordingly. One aim of this book was to take into consideration not just 'death' but rather who dies what kind of death, is it an old person, a young person, is it a good or a bad death and what are the cultural practices related to these deaths. Another shortcoming in the interpretation of death is mentioned by Blackburn who rightly observed that 'the discussions of the problem of death are based almost exclusively on classical traditions, the mythological and philosophical texts' (1985: 256). For this reason, we not only wanted to include folk texts into the body of textual tradition but also various cultural practices (ritual action, performance of stories, epics) which are related to the theme of death. Taking into account the interrelatedness of text and practice, we wanted to know whether cultural practice merely aims at being a victory over death or defeating death, or whether it may also aim at accepting death and making use of the power of death.

* * *

The contributions have been organized into three sections. The papers in the first section deal with the 'good' death, the expected death after a fulfilled life, and they focus on the bereaved who are responsible for the transformation of the dead into ancestors. It has been argued by Knipe that at the time of death the procedures for cremation (*antyeṣṭi*) and the rites for the departed (*śrāddhas*) are fairly uniform throughout India and are performed according to Vedic models (1977: 111). To answer the question 'who is a Hindu after death?' he argues that in the course of the rite of *sapiṇḍīkaraṇa*, the deceased enters the world of ancestors. It is argued here that this is not an automatic process but that it refers only to those persons who die a good death. Moreover, ancestors are not a uniform category of beings, but the perception of the deceased as ancestors and their relation to the living can differ. According to Brahmanical conceptions ancestors are grouped into three categories, the (liminal) *preta*, the 'fathers' (*pitaraḥ*) and the remote dead (Knipe 1977: 118). Only the ancestors of the *pitaraḥ* category are accessible and can be ritually approached as a whole. In non-Brahmanical conceptions, by contrast, ancestors retain their individuality as long as they are remembered and they can be approached individually for rather concrete human needs.

One example of a non-Brahmanical concept of ancestors is provided by Martin Gaenszle's paper on the transformation of the deceased into ancestors among the Mewahang Rai in Nepal. Only 'good' ancestors are able to provide the living with 'life force' (M. '*saya*'), i.e. well-being, prosperity and even good marriages. However, even if a person dies a 'good' death after a fulfilled life, leaving behind a married son, it cannot be taken for granted that the deceased will be transformed into a 'good' ancestor. It is the responsibility of the bereaved to guarantee the process of transformation from a potentially dangerous spirit to a basically benevolent ancestor by propitiating and honouring the ancestral spirit adequately. As Gaenszle shows, good ancestors are actually 'made' in the course of funerary rites. In a succession of rituals which can be characterized as 'rites de passage' for the deceased, the dead person is separated from the living, the roaming soul is transformed into a 'pacified' ancestral spirit and finally it is integrated into the world of ancestors. It is the duty of a spirit after being satisfied with good food and after being honoured by the care of his relatives to give something in return. A 'good' ancestor whose dangerous power has been transformed into a positive, life-giving power, is characterized on the one hand by complete detachment from the world of the living, but on the other hand retains its individuality and may be approached by ordinary householders for the sake of regenerating social life.

Among the Jēnu Kuṟumba, a group of gatherer-hunters in the Nilgiris, it is again the duty of the living relatives to secure the well-being of the spirits, although in a different way. Here, the structure of the social world encompasses the after-life and gets extended to the world of spirits. A 'natural' or 'good' death being impossible, the Jēnu Kuṟumba perceive death as the result of moral failure on the part of the living. After death, the spirits of the deceased are not only in a state of confusion and in need of support from their living relatives to reach the deities, but the spirits also hold their relatives responsible for their death and for their suffering after death. Subsequently, the living are responsible to take care of the spirits and to make good what they have done wrong. Ulrich Demmer shows in his article that death is interpreted by the Jēnu Kuṟumba as a violation of the social and moral order of the community. Death leads to confusion, weakness and loneliness not only on the part of the living but also on the part of the deceased. In a series of rituals the bereaved not only have to negotiate with the spirit verbally but they have to do 'work', such as building a hut, in order to make the spirit happy. In the liminal period following the funeral, the spirit feels neglected, lonely and without support. He lacks social bonds and does not yet have divine bonds. In the dialogue with his living relatives through a medium, the spirit accuses his relatives of 'unsocial' behaviour, i.e. of neglecting him during his lifetime, and thus having provoked his death. Only when the spirit can be convinced by words and deeds that the living care for him will he be able to join the deity and the liminal phase of unrelatedness can be overcome. Among the Jēnu Kuṟumba, each death is a bad death per se and has to be converted by the living into a good death. Communication between the living and their pacified spirits does not end with the death-ritual but will be continued in other contexts, such as healing rituals, where again spirits are asked as individuals for protection and help.

In her paper on mortuary feasts among Dalit castes in Gujarat, Shalini Randeria focuses not on what the living have to do for the dead, but on what they have to do for themselves. Mortuary feasts, according to the Dalits themselves, are not held in the first instance to secure the deceased's transformation into an ancestor. Besides being an occasion to honour a parent who has died after a fulfilled life, mortuary rituals are occasions for the production of social order, for the creation of locality, and for the redefinition of the social group. The mortuary feast constitutes the climax of a series of mourning rituals. In the course of this event, the unity of the territorial subunits of the caste (*paragṇũ*) and of the co-residential community in the village (*vās*) is reasserted. Both units are constantly threatened by division. Locality among Dalits is a fluid and fragile social construction. Therefore, considerable uncertainty accompanies the preparations in the weeks between the burial and the feast. Smouldering conflicts between caste members, especially affines, may come to the surface and may eventually lead to the splitting of the social group. Mortuary feasts are occasions for the hosts to gain prestige by demonstrating generosity, serving lavish food and inviting large numbers of guests. On the other hand, the guests may honour the host and approve of existing social relations by accepting the invitation and providing generous gifts, but they may also demonstrate their disapproval of political authority or affinal relationships by staying away from the feast or by presenting inadequate gifts. Memorial feasts have been criticized recently (especially by younger caste members) for their lavishness and for their display of authority and political power. This again shows that funerary feasts are not only held in memory of the dead but are also celebrations for the living in which political authority within the caste is contested and bonds within the local community are redefined.

Axel Michaels investigates the complex structure of the festival 'Bālācaturdaśī' in the Kathmandu valley, which is celebrated in the month of Maṅgsīr and marks the beginning of the cold season. The festival combines two, at first sight unrelated, major rites: worship of the ancestors and worship of the demon Bālā. In the first set of rites, activities like vigil, *homa* and the scattering of sesame seeds serve to deal with the dead, who have to be helped to reach their destination and prevented from returning to the sphere of the living. Only when the mourners succeed to transform the liminal state of a *preta* will the dead be able to become *pitaraḥ* and eventually *viśvedevāḥ*, from which state they can be reborn. But Bālācaturdaśī is more than an annual festival for ancestors, it is also a festival of the demon Bālā, who is mythologically killed and ritually pacified to ensure that the transformation of the dead into ancestors is not interrupted. Despite the festival's name, there is no clear relation between the myths related to Bālā and the worship of the dead. 'Bālāguṭhīpūjā' is a ritual known to only a few people, in which the demon Bālādaitya is worshipped, and which partially re-enacts the myths of Bālācaturdaśī. This ritual has to do with rain and fertility, and is generally associated with the regeneration of life. The two aspects of the festival were originally probably not related, but were later on combined because of the complementary relationship between ancestor and demon worship. Since Brahmanic death rituals are characterized by the absence of almost any individualistic features, festivals like Bālācaturdaśī fulfil a general need for an individualized worship of deceased persons either in the form of deified heroes or in the form of demons. Michaels suggests that, even if Brahmanical concepts and ritual action of the pilgrims do not seem to correspond, and even if the pilgrims are not aware of the Brahmanical myths of the demon Bālā and cannot therefore 'explain' their ritual action, the structural link between ancestor and demon worship may be seen in the fear of ritual fault during death rites and the endeavour to perform the rites properly, since the future of both the dead and the mourners is endangered if 'death is not pacified', i.e. if the rites are not properly performed.

Charles Malamoud's contribution provides an extreme example of death, one which—even after it has already occurred—is controlled and encompassed by society. The author shows that under certain circumstances death can be 'postponed'. In order to continue a Vedic *sattra* ritual once it has begun, all the sacrificers had to participate throughout the ritual process in order to guarantee its religious merit. A *sattra* lasted from a minimum of twelve days up to one year or even twelve years, and generally comprised seventeen (or up to twenty-four) sacrificers. All these persons acted collectively as sacrificers as well as ritual functionaries or priests. If one of the sacrificers-cum-priests died before the *sattra* was concluded, he had to survive in the context of the sacrifice, because otherwise neither he nor the rest of the group would benefit from the sacrifice. Therefore, the body of the dead man had to be cremated, his bones had to be collected into a bag made of black antilope leather, and they had to substitute for the person. At that point no funerary rites were conducted, no transformation into an ancestor (*pitṛ*) took place, and the bones of the dead man did not pollute the sacrificial site. A near relative was selected to substitute as ritual functionary, but, in his role as sacrificer, the deceased could not have died. As sacrificer, he could not be substituted for, but had to be present in the form of his bones and through his wife, who was not yet a widow. After one year or after the *sattra* had taken place (here, the texts are not precise) the *asthiyajña* (bone sacrifice) took place; this is described as a kind of *soma* offering. In the bone sacrifice, the bones, which are in fact the remains of the person, were the sacrificer, the one who benefited from the ritual. Thus, the success of the sacrifice, which depended on the continuous presence of all those who had committed themselves in the beginning, could be guaranteed even in the case of death.

As distinguished from section one, whose papers deal with a 'good' death, the contributions of section two deal with an 'untimely' or 'extraordinary' death, such as the death of children or a violent death in battle. Such a death is a dreadful experience for the bereaved and brings them indescribable sorrow. Whereas the death of those who died at the end of a fulfilled life is widely accepted and care has to be taken to transform the dead into ancestors, everything is done to prevent the premature death of a child or young adult, and, in case it cannot be averted, such a death may be defeated by deification, although it can hardly be accepted and is perhaps never understood. Persons dying violently or suddenly are unable to anticipate death (as demanded especially by Brahmanical conceptions). They die unconsciously and some of them become *bhūt-pret*, whereas others are deified. Contrary to persons who have died 'consciously' and who eventually enter the world of ancestors, those who are violently killed or who die too early retain their individual character and remain related to the social world.

In her paper on 'Rivers and the Death of Children', Anne Feldhaus presents three stories, all of which have to do with the death of children and make clear the ambivalent power of river and water deities. River and water deities have the power to give children and to protect their lives but they can also take them away. The aim of the parents in all three stories is to prevent the death of a child. The story of Varuṇa and Hariścandra (from the Gautamī Māhātmya) depicts Varuṇa's ambivalence. He enables Hariścandra to have a son, but then wants the son's life back in sacrifice. In the story of the folk goddess Bhivāī, the goddess fulfils the wish for a child on the condition that vows be performed. The child has to be floated on a raft on the river in front of the goddess's temple. The story of Bhivāī shows the ambivalent power of the goddess: she can give a child, protect it, but she can also take it away. In the third story, a Maharashtrian woman got afflicted by the Sātī Āsarā, invisible beings who live in or near water and who afflict women by making them infertile, causing them to have miscarriages and causing their children to die young. The Sātī Āsarā are not worshipped to get children, but rather placated by women to prevent them from taking their children away. Out of the nine pregnancies of Kalāvatī, whose story is narrated, five children were born premature and died and one was born premature and is of weak health, whereas only three children survived and are in good health. The parents (and even the doctor) were convinced that this could not have been due to medical treatment but solely to the offerings made to the Sātī Āsarā. Contrary to the 'good death', which should ideally be anticipated by the dying and which is as it were celebrated by the living, an untimely death, and especially the death of children, is regarded as something extremely undesirable which should be prevented by all means.

Whereas in the stories narrated by Feldhaus the death of children could be prevented somehow or other, Elisabeth Schömbucher's paper deals with children's death which could not be averted. Among the Vāḍabalija, a caste of fishermen in Andhra Pradesh, children may become divine beings, heroes (Telugu *vīrulu*), after their premature death. Living in the realm of deities, they may help and support their relatives. They can be invoked into the body of a medium if their family members face problems, such as illness, bad luck, or continuously poor yields from fishing. Although *vīrulu*, after their deification, are at the bottom of the divine hierarchy, the Vāḍabalija prefer to ask them for help instead of a more powerful deity. A comparison of texts spoken by the media during a state of possession shows principal differences in the utterances of the two divine entities. Whereas deities are usually inquisitive, demanding, and threatening, *vīrulu*, as members of the family, are good-natured and lenient about the 'sins' of their relatives, and their demands are rather modest. Thus, the untimely death of a child or young adult need not necessarily be a 'bad' death resulting in uncontrollable spirits and ghosts, but it may develop into a 'good' death, when the deceased child manifests itself as a divine being. Such a death may turn out to be of advantage for the bereaved, although the deification might be of little consolation for the mother.

A different hero concept, that of warriors who die on the battlefield, is the focus in Georg Berkemer's paper. He shows how the heroic theme was introduced into the regional culture of Kaliṅga and proposes a few answers to the question why there were no hero cults in Kaliṅga for a long time. Whereas hero stones abound in western India and the Deccan, and whereas hero cults have been politically sanctioned in Andhra since the thirteenth century and can be observed to this day, the inscriptional records of Kaliṅga avoid any allusion to the premature, violent death of a ruler or warrior. The absence of heroes (Sanskrit *vīra*) in Kaliṅga may be explained by the fact that the cult of Jagannāth was the dominant cult of the state deity and that there was no place for a cult of hero worship; such a cult was prevalent among Andhras, who were not only of low caste status but also the enemies of Kaliṅga. Berkemer concludes that only later, when new, politically dominant groups immigrated from Andhra, were hero cults introduced into Kaliṅga.

A rather different form of 'deification' and a different example of a victory over death is presented by Hugh van Skyhawk in his article on Ṣūfī saints. Ṣūfī saints are believed to have transcended death. At the moment of his death as an individual, the saint (*pīr*) gains a new life in the experience of divine unity. A *pīr* usually manifests himself in a benevolent form for the benefit of those who come to his shrine. Children are brought to the shrine to grow up healthy and live long and prosperous lives. Those who are born or die near the *pīr,* or those whose mortal remains are brought for burial to the shrine, may benefit from his divine power and his victory over death. By touching his tomb or his *pādukā,* or anything connected with his mortal remains, the divine power of the *pīr* is transferred to human beings.

The third section comprises papers which focus on the interpretation of the theme of death in textual traditions and on how death is portrayed in various cultural performances. In his paper, 'An Indian Myth of the Creation of Death and Life', Claus Peter Zoller presents twenty variants of a myth which describes the creation of death and life. In each variant it is the Primeval Goddess Ādi Śakti and the Triad (Brahmā, Viṣṇu and Śiva) who are of crucial importance. Since the variants of the myth, which come from different areas and times, are sometimes handed down 'incompletely', and since they are not part of an 'acknowledged' tradition, they have sometimes provoked derogatory comments. Whitehead (1921: 137) sees the south Indian version as full of 'absurdities and extravagance', Lorenzen (1987b: 289) speaks of an 'eccentric theology', and Meyer (1986: 47) finds her version 'confusing'. However, when the stories are taken as variants of one myth, one is able to see the structural logic and meaning behind the 'weird details in description' (Whitehead 1921: 127). The Triad is born through the Goddess, and Ādi Śakti, as her mother, subsequently wants to marry her sons. To escape her incestuous advances, Śiva burns Ādi Śakti to ashes, out of which the three goddesses (Pārvatī, Lakṣmī and Sarasvatī) are created. In other versions, where a 'father' of the Goddess is explicitly mentioned, a more or less overt incestuous act is frequently said to have taken place between the Goddess and her creator. In several versions the incestuous relations (whether carried out or not) are mediated by a trickster-like figure or demiurge. Zoller concludes that the prototype of the myth consists of two elements which are joined by the Goddess: Lord of the World—Demiurge (the Lord's 'son')—Goddess (the Lord's or the demiurge's 'daughter') and Brahma-Viṣṇu-Śiva ('sons' of the Goddess). The two triads are associated with two distinct modes of creation, an asexual parthogenesis and creation through a sexual (incestuous) act. The underlying structure, more or less clearly present in all variants of the myth, suggests, according to the author, a mirror-image concept of creation and destruction, where cremation ground and creation ground collapse into one.

Aditya Malik's paper, 'Stringing a Necklace of Heads: Sacrifice and Death in the Cult of Devnārāyaṇ', focuses on death as it occurs in the context of the oral epic and cult of Devnārāyaṇ in Rajasthan. Malik shows that death is not expressed as a singular event but as an event in a series of transmutations and transformations. In the epic, there are altogether four instances in which death occurs, each death being violent and premature. However, death is not only depicted as the end of someone's life, but each death results in a creative act, such as granting offspring, wealth, or fame, or even the creation of God. From the series of four narrated deaths, which are all extremely violent, it appears that it is the violence itself which is a precondition for the creation of new forms of life in a cycle of transformations. Thus, the twenty-four heroes of the epic, called the Bagaṛāvats, come into being after Śiva has eaten twenty-four Ṛṣis who are then reborn as the twenty-four sons of Bāgh Siṃh (who is born as a result of his father's killing a lion). The wealth which the twenty-four Bagaṛāvats are able to accumulate is due to the violent death of the ascetic Rūpnāth. Later, the twenty-four brothers are killed by the Goddess. The killing of the heroes by the Goddess bears parallels to the Goddess killing a demon. The Goddess deceives the heroes by exploiting their erotic feelings towards her. She demands that the heroes offer their heads to her and kills them one at a time on the battlefield. Thus, the heroes are not simply defeated by martial power but they themselves offer their lives to the Goddess. Their death may be interpreted as a gift to the Goddess, showing their devotion towards her. The heroic death, though violent and premature and therefore potentially 'bad', is transformed into a 'good' death by an act of voluntary self-sacrifice on the part of the hero. After the heroes have been defeated by the Goddess, Bhagvān fulfils his boon. In the form of Devnārāyaṇ he is born as the son of one of the heroes' wives.

Heidrun Brückner's article approaches the theme of death in the context of oral narrative and ritual drama of Tulu folk culture in Karnataka. Death plays a central part in the oral texts, about deified humans and princely deities, which are recited and performed during the annual festival rituals. Brückner focuses on how the event of death is described in the texts, how the hero determines 'his style of dying', how death, or rather the act of being killed, is staged in ritual drama, and how narratives and ritual correspond to each other. The texts on deified humans have certain motifs in common. There is the basic pattern of social conflict between an unusually talented member of a lower caste and a king who fears the hero's power. The hero decides to give up his human existence, since revenge or the restitution of justice is impossible in the human social setting of a hierarchic caste society. Only as deified being can the hero execute his revenge and demand the respect and honour refused to him as a human being. In comparing the narration of the hero's death with its ritual enactment, the author is able to show that ritual is not theatrical in the sense of staging what is scripted by the narrative. Only central notions of the narrative, such as the hero's readiness for self-sacrifice, are translated into ritual action. In the texts and rituals of the princely deities, social conflicts also play a central part. But here, death, in most cases, is not dramatized in the form of a self-injuring play with the sword, but as a stylized, playful mock-fight which eventually results in a dance. The author concludes that narrated and dramatized death appear as two sides of the same coin, the narrative stressing the suffering and tragedy of the victim whereas ritual drama focuses on the self-induced 'play with death' and restores the agency of formerly human victims.

Alf Hiltebeitel investigates the fluid and oscillating boundaries between life and death in his description of Kūttāṇṭavar, or Aravāṉ, a Tamil 'village deity' worshipped in the form of a red-painted head. Death is focused in this god in the form of the multiple deaths and revivals which he undergoes in the course of various rituals, and which indicate the god's mastery over death as a village deity. Behind the name Aravaṉ hides Irāvān, a minor actor in the Sanskrit *Mahābhārata*. His cult seems to have come from Draupadī cults, in which the fallen heroes are mourned at the end of the war. Portraying the god in connection with various festivals (especially a *Mahābhārata* festival in Kūvākkam), Hiltebeitel works out Kūttāṇṭavar's gradual embodiment (which resembles *sapiṇḍīkaraṇa*-ceremonies) and disembodiment, and describes how the god, who, as a head, watches the eighteen days of the *Mahābhārata* war, is identified at the end of the festival in Kūvākkam with Dharma/Yuddhishthira. Since Dharma is widely believed to rule over the dead, this fact too underlies the deity's close relation with the realm of death. Therefore, 'a *Mahābhārata* festival brings matters of life and death, as lived in a village, under divine regulation'.

NOTES

1. Haas discusses critically the various theological positions and the reductionist psychological theories of 'mystical' experiences.
2. In fact, the first position above and the third below are also 'conceptualizations'. They, too, cannot articulate themselves directly out of the midst of an 'afterdeath-state'. But, whereas the second position advocates a 'conceptualization of continuation', the first and the third stress a 'conceptualization of rupture'.
3. There exist also all sorts of complications to this dual imagery: as the body is commonly said to be formed of two components (frequently it is male seed and female menses), the soul may comprise two or even more components, and there may be two or more souls in the body, as there may also be two or more bodies in a person, etc.
4. It may be pointed out that these notions frequently characterize a symmetrical process: often the dead first remain in a liminal state before they are integrated into some other-worldly 'society'.

5. This is, in fact, not just a pessimistic Indian view, but one also maintained in Catholic theology. Thus, Karl Rahner points out that the soul does not have the power of absolute control over its body, as a result of which many people have to suffer Purgatory in an 'other-worldly body' (Rahner 1958: 24-5).
6. This 'family-tree' of creation is known not only in the classical texts, which describe the creation of both (a sphere of) life and (a sphere of) death (see Doniger 1982: 25-55), but also in a 'folk myth' found all over India (see the contribution of Zoller).
7. We are aware that the concepts of rebirth and redeath are not really 'explained' by the concept of *karma. Karma* itself had and has various meanings which do not fully coincide. Moreover, rebirth can also be explained as the result of other agencies (see Halbfass 1995). Nevertheless, it should be noted that those groups in India who do not believe in rebirth usually also have no concept of *karma.*
8. Although Parry seems to portray here the view of the Banaras Brahmins, it cannot be substantiated by their 'death manuals'. Müller has pointed out (1992: 30) that Parry's description of cremation as a sacrifice to Agni has no basis in the *Antyeṣṭipaddhati.* There, however, it is not the dead who are sacrificed, but the sacrifice is *for* the dead and for Agni and other deities. The sacrifice is then followed by the cremation. Since in the Banaras of the 1980s these two rites have collapsed into one, the meaning of 'sacrifice' came to be associated with cremation.
9. The idea of voluntary 'self-annihilation' is even at the core of *bhakti,* where the devotee has to give himself (emotionally and intellectually) totally to his God. The fact that there is again a great diversity both in the more ascetic and in the more devotional schools regarding the degree of becoming one with the non-created and how fast this aim can be achieved is of no further relevance here.
10. Müller sees the custom of collecting the bones, of burying them, and of unearthing them at a later date with subsequent immersion in a river, in connection with shamanistic practices (Müller 1992: 27, note 68). In fact, this custom also resembles the 'double disposal of the dead', a practice found in many cultures (see the contribution of Köpping). This 'double disposal of the dead' seems to be closely related to widespread ideas of a 'second death' in the other world (for instance Vitebsky 1993: 15 *et passim*).
11. See Atkinson 1973: 925.
12. The practice of sati (*sahamaraṇa, sahagamana* 'dying together, accompanying') probably also has to be understood in this sense of 'wilful dying at a proper moment' (see Michaels 1992).
13. This is certainly a very problematic notion, but it is thought to include here all those non-performed deaths—for instance, those caused by diseases—which are not believed to have a special influence on the post-death existence of the dead persons.
14. This latter cause refers to narratives found, for instance, in the central and western Himalaya, according to which someone who does not live up to his social status or role can be deified. There exist a number of narratives which describe, for instance, how kings who behave cruelly toward their subjects,

who decide to become ascetics, or who maintain illicit intercaste relationships, or how king's daughters who become warriors, first turn into malevolent spirits and later on become deities. Violent death is not a necessary element in these stories, although it can occur (Zoller, forthcoming).

REFERENCES

Atkinson, Edwin T. 1973 (1882). *Himalayan Gazetteer.* Vol. II, Part II. Delhi: Cosmo.

Blackburn, Stuart H. 1985. Death and Deification: Folk Cults in Hinduism. *History of Religions* 24: 255-74.

Das, Veena. 1976. The Uses of Liminality: Society and Cosmos in Hinduism. *Contributions to Indian Sociology* (n.s.) 10 (2): 245-63.

Doniger, Wendy. 1982. *Hindu Myths.* Harmondsworth: Penguin.

Haas, Alois Maria. 1989. *Gottleiden—Gottlieben. Zur volkssprachlichen Mystik im Mittelalter.* Frankfurt: Insel.

Halbfass, W. 1995. Zum Verhältnis von Karma und Tod im indischen Denken. In Gerhard Oberhammer (ed.), *Im Tod gewinnt der Mensch sein Selbst. Das Phänomen des Todes in asiatischer und abendländischer Religionstradition. Arbeitsdokumentation eines Symposions.* Wien: Verlag der Österreichischen Akademie der Wissenschaften.

Knipe, David M. 1977. *Sapiṇḍīkaraṇa*: The Hindu Rite of Entry into Heaven. In Frank E. Reynolds and Earle H. Waugh (eds.), *Religious Encounters with Death. Insights from the History and Anthropology of Religions.* University Park and London: The Pennsylvania State University Press.

König, Ditte. 1984. *Das Tor zur Unterwelt: Mythologie und Kult des Termitenhügels in der schriftlichen und mündlichen Tradition Indiens.* Wiesbaden: Steiner.

Lorenzen, David N. 1981. The Kabir Panth and Politics. *Political Science Review* 1: 263-81.

———. 1987a. Traditions of Non-caste Hinduism: The Kabir Panth. *Contributions to Indian Sociology* (n.s.) 21,2: 263-83.

———. 1987b. The Kabir-panth and Social Protest. In Karine Schomer and W.H. McLeod (eds.), *The Sants: Studies in a Devotional Tradition of India.* Delhi: Motilal Banarsidass.

Meyer, Eveline. 1986. *Aṅkālaparamēcuvari: a Goddess of Tamilnadu, Her Myths and Cult.* Stuttgart: Steiner.

Michaels, Axel. 1992. Recht auf Leben und Selbsttötung in Indien. In B. Mensen VD (ed.), *Recht auf Leben, Recht auf Töten. Ein Kulturvergleich* (Akademie Völker und Kulturen St. Augustin, Bd. 15), Nettetal: 95-124.)

Müller, Klaus-Werner. 1992. *Das Brahmanische Totenritual nach der Antyeṣṭipaddhati des Nārāyaṇabhaṭṭa.* Stuttgart: Steiner.

Oberhammer, Gerhard (ed.). 1995. *Im Tod gewinnt der Mensch sein Selbst. Das Phänomen des Todes in asiatischer und abendländischer Religionstradition. Arbeitsdokumentation eines Symposions.* Wien: Verlag der Österreichischen Akademie der Wissenschaften.

Palgi, Phyllis and Henry Abramovitch. 1984. Death: A Cross-Cultural Perspective. *Annual Review of Anthropology*. 13: 385-417.

Parry, Jonathan P. 1974. Egalitarian Values in a Hierarchical Society. *South Asian Review* 7(2): 95-121.

———. 1981. Death and Cosmogony in Kashi. *Contributions to Indian Sociology* (n.s.) 15: 337-65.

———. 1989. The End of the Body. In M. Feher with R. Naddaff and N. Tazi (eds.), *Fragments for a History of the Human Body*. Part II. Cambridge, Mass and London: MIT Press.

———. 1994. *Death in Banaras*. Cambridge: Cambridge University Press.

Rahner, Karl. 1958. *Zur Theologie des Todes*. Freiburg: Herder.

Rosaldo, Renato. 1984. Grief and a Head-hunter's Rage: On the Cultural Force of Emotions. In E. Bruner (ed.), *Play, Text and Story*. Proceedings of the American Ethnological Society. Washington.

Settar, S. 1986. *Inviting Death. Historical Experiments on Sepulchral Hill.* Dharwad: Institute of Indian Art History, Karnatak University.

———. 1990. *Pursuing Death. Philosophy and Practice of Voluntary Termination of Life.* Dharwad: Institute of Indian Art History, Karnatak University.

Stein, Edith. 1950. *Endliches und ewiges Sein. Versuch eines Aufstiegs zum Sinn des Seins*. Freiburg: Herder.

Turner, Victor. 1969. *The Ritual Process: Structure and Antistructure*. Chicago: Aldine Publishing Co.

Vitebsky, Pier S. 1993. *Dialogues with the Dead. The Discussion of Mortality among the Sora of Eastern India.* Cambridge: Cambridge University Press.

Weil, Simone. 1989. *Schwerkraft und Gnade*. München: Piper.

Whitehead, Henry. 1921. *The Village Gods of South India.* Calcutta: Association Press.

Zoller, Claus Peter. forthcoming. *Himalayan Heroes*.

Death as Experience and Institution in Anthropological Theory

KLAUS-PETER KÖPPING

The problem of the attitudes toward death and the disposal of the corpse, a problem of 'ultimate concern' (Dobzhansky 1969), has occupied the theoretical discussions of anthropologists for considerable time, as it does raise questions about the meaning of life. Death confronts all, researcher and researched, with an empirically observable irreversible but logically inexplicable rupture. Many nineteenth- and early twentieth-century scholars took refuge in the facile explanation, based on a number of strange customs reported from diverse cultures, that many non-European people were just not advanced enough on the scale of rationality to cope with this rupture and were therefore using diverse customary and apparently 'irrational' forms of behaviour to battle their 'fears' of the unknown: such views did not cease with Frazer but also permeated many functionalist systems such as those of Malinowski or Radcliffe-Brown (see Frazer 1933; Radcliffe-Brown 1933; Malinowski 1948). Yet one cannot but suspect that the very same fear permeated the minds of these scholars who did not or could not quite believe in the superiority of their own scientific and enlightened outlook on the meaning of life. It is to the lasting merit of the Durkheim school of social scientific enquiry, that they overcame simplistic notions of customs surrounding death. It was in particular Robert Hertz who, while not denying the pan-human dread of death, advanced a rather sophisticated scheme of explanations which took into account the 'rationality' of customs surrounding both the event and the perception of rupture and discontinuity. He pointed to the ambivalence surrounding these events and the socio-structural purpose of various beliefs in those transformations which—contrary to the often stated results of Hertz' survey of the extant literature of his time—affect not only the living but also the dead. In order to put Hertz' seminal contribution to the debate into a wider perspective in the light of recent ethnographic approaches and explanations, it may be worthwhile to delineate the general method which he as a member of a group of like-minded researchers around Durkheim pursued.

It may be as true today as it was more than thirty-five years ago when

Evans-Pritchard wrote his introduction to the English translation of Robert Hertz' *Death and the Right Hand* that, as he put it, 'the theoretical capital on which anthropologists today live is mainly the writings of people whose research was entirely literary, who brought to bear great ability, much learning, and rigorous methods of scholarship on what others had observed and recorded' (Evans-Pritchard 1960: 24). In admitting his own intellectual adherence to the precepts of the comparative method of the Année School, he is not saying that fieldwork is either useless or sterile or even unnecessary. Quite the opposite is implied. However, if the pursuit of data for its own sake, without a theoretical framework guiding the research process, were to become the aim of anthropology, then Evans-Pritchard's stricture would apply: 'we are in danger of falling into mere empiricism, one field-study after another adding to the number of known facts, but uninspired and uninspiring' (ibid.).

Over the years, not only anthropology but also classical studies and those in culture history have accumulated an immense array of data on indigenous perceptions of almost all facets of what since the seminal work of Arnold van Gennep's *Rites de passage* of 1909 is conveniently labelled as 'life-cycle' events. Rituals of birth, puberty, marriage and death have, particularly since the acceptance of the general canon of fieldwork of Malinowski in the second half of this century, taken a prominent place in descriptive ethnographic accounts. In contrast to the mere collection of various customs from around the globe in 'cabinets of curiosity'—a tendency which doubtlessly influenced the nineteenth-century evolutionist systems of classifying societies along a random selection of 'traits' on a scale from savage and primitive to modern and progressive—modern anthropology is organized around the notion that customs and habits have to be seen in the context of a particular time and place.

Modern ethnographic fieldwork is guided by two basic notions. First, the insistence on the importance of establishing the meaning which a custom has in a particular social group, 'in the eyes of the natives', as Malinowski would put it, the insisting on the precept of the indigenous collective perception as the basis for a comparative approach to 'social facts' (including their 'representations'), a precept ultimately derived from Johann Gottfried Herder in the German backlash against the facile systematization and abstractions of the French Enlightenment. Malinowski enshrined this in the canon of 'participant observation' in the 1920s, it had also influenced the rise of detailed and systematic ethnographic work through the figure of Boas since the 1890s in the United States. Second, anthropological data-collection became guided by the realization of the interconnectedness of various customs in a particular society which when put in the framework of a functionalist paradigm means that concepts, ideas and values guiding social actors in such diverse activities as economic pursuits, marriage practices and ritual are systematically related with each other, which when put into a structuralist framework means that diverse customary practices are governed by a structure the similarity of which permeates the whole gamut of events.

It is this insistence on the search for the connection between a cluster of closely related 'social facts' where the meaning of social actions would be shown to lie not in themselves, considered separately, but in their interrelation which Evans-Pritchard rightly identifies as the methodical rigour of the comparative method which the Durkheim School bequeathed to us as intellectual capital (Evans-Pritchard 1960: 14f.). To put it into a wider framework, summarizing and extending on Evans-Pritchard's unsurpassed lucid assessment of the contributions of the Année School, I would point to the major landmarks of this school with the publications on classifications (Durkheim and Mauss 1903), the notion of the person (Mauss 1938), on sacrifice (Hubert and Mauss 1899), on gift-exchange (Mauss 1925), and in particular, on death (Hertz 1909).

In the case of the treatment of the double disposal of the dead, which Hertz chose as focus for his essay which has inspired a number of recent approaches—and whether approving, generalizing, falsifying or just modifying Hertz, all acknowledged their debt of inspiration to that essay (see for instance Bloch 1971; Needham 1973; Traube 1977; Huntington and Metcalf 1979; Danforth 1982; Bloch and Parry 1982)—the methodical rigour consists in arranging into a cohesive framework such diverse habits as belief in ghosts, the nature of the soul, the treatment of the body, or the rules of mourning with their accompanying taboos for behaviour and attire, all from one specific ethnographically restricted area, in this case the Indonesian region, with special reference to the cultural groups of Borneo. Only then does Hertz embark on a comparison with such structural 'transitions' in other areas with the similar custom of double burial, or, by sticking within one societal framework, comparing this particular transition with the structural features of other transitional periods such as birth, puberty or marriage. Radcliffe-Brown hoped that such methodological carefulness could yield general laws of functional interdependence for social life on a universal basis, replacing the search for origins and the reconstruction of assumed stages of development of the nineteenth-century evolutionary approaches of Tylor, Spencer or Frazer. Evans-Pritchard showed a cautious and proper scepticism in this matter.

However, fruitful generalizations about the scope and meaning of a variety of ritual processes applicable to different social settings have come from the structural-functionalist approaches of scholars who see themselves as Neo-Durkheimians, as for instance Victor Turner and Mary Douglas. Turner, through a combination of the precepts of the Durkheimian search for those collective representations which ensure and create social cohesion and renew such, with the notion of the importance of the period of 'liminality' between stages of action or of personal status as derived from van Gennep (whose work on transition rites appeared only two years after the publication on second burial by Hertz) was able to show the universality of the structure of ritual processes through the stages of separation, liminality and re-integration (Turner 1969). Mary Douglas in turn focused very much on the notion of the individual and social body and the protection of it through ritual practices from the dangers of pollution which occur generally through the presence of things or persons who are considered ambiguous, ambivalent or not unambiguously classifiable (Douglas 1966 and 1970).

Many of these propositions, if not directly elaborated, can at least be discerned incipiently in the work of Robert Hertz whose two publications on the problem of death and second burial 'The collective representation of death' (1907) and the related paper on the 'Pre-eminence of the right hand' (1909)—which shows the influence of the treatise of Durkheim and Mauss on classificatory schemes of 1903—tread much the same ground as van Gennep does, who developed his ideas parallel and independently from the Année School—Hertz extends what Mauss would call a 'total social phenomenon' to the problem of the widespread classificatory scheme which equates death with the left side of the body. Such correlations were to become the inspiration of a whole generation of Dutch ethnographers of the so-called Leiden School about cosmological and numerological equivalences in Indonesian idea-systems and social arrangements (see for instance Kruyt 1941). The historical impact of the binary division of left and right only received extended treatment in Needham's collection of 1973 in which he points out that the impact of Hertz' work was negligible in the English-speaking world prior to his translation of the two treatises in 1960.

This latter work on the binary opposition of left and right points the way to the correlations of symbolic orders, where the physiological and anatomical correspond to the natural-geographical, the seasonal and the cosmological categories (the great similarity to Mauss' approach to the 'total social phenomenon' is quite apparent when considering the latter's treatise on the seasonal variations in Eskimo society; see Mauss 1904-5). While this piece is certainly indebted to the other members of the Année School who postulate that mental and symbolic categories and their correlations are grounded in social structural arrangements, it also paved the way for various forms of structural analysis of mythologies, such as those later undertaken by Marcel Granet on Chinese thought systems (1934-50), by Dumézil on the Mitra-Varuna complex in the Indo-European pantheon (Dumézil 1948), not to speak of the multi-stranded approaches of Lévi-Strauss which in turn influenced the approaches of a number of classicists such as those by Vernant and Detienne on the Greek origin myths (Vernant 1974; Detienne 1972; see Lévi-Strauss 1962).

Unresolved remain those fundamental questions of Durkheim and Mauss: can the social be proved to exist prior to mental or linguistic categories; can binary correspondences such as left is to right as is female to male be read in columns of equivalence and opposition, so that whole categories such as on the one hand moon, left, death, female can be seen as opposed in a systemic way to the column sun, right, life, male? The first point cannot be resolved without an elaborate philosophical excursion with evidence from socio- and psycho-linguistic data. Needham took a sound approach to the second in pointing out that the religious dignitary of the Meru of Kenya, the Mugwe, may be considered to possess his sacred power in the left hand but that this anomaly has to be put into specific context: though the Mugwe is superior in religious matters, he is subordinate to other chiefs in political matters (see Needham 1973: 111ff.). Yet, merit or demerit of Hertz does not rest on such intricate details but rather on the fact that he removed social classifications from a naïve naturalistic explanation, for they are social facts, the hands or the body becoming the symbols of polarities which exist in the ideational framework of a group.

As regards Hertz' approaches to second burial, it may suffice to point to the main elements which make his essay a master-piece of descriptive integration of various features connected with this form of the disposal of the dead. This linking of ideational with behavioural features pointed the way for many fieldworkers investigating this 'total social phenomenon' in a diversity of contexts. Hertz deals with the manifold ethnographic reports about the lengthy period which passes between death and first burial—taking his clue from an observation by Lafitau that in 'most primitive societies the dead bodies are only stored, so to speak, in the tomb where they are first placed. After a time they are given a new funeral and they receive the final funerary rites which are due to them' (Hertz 1960: 28, citing Lafitau 1724). He sees the meaning of this custom in the three transitions death creates. First, the body has to be given time to decompose, for only then, free from soft tissues, and thus unpolluting, can the essence of the corpse in the form of the bones be interred and disposed of. Second, in the in-between period the soul is attached to the body and, being volatile, can be extremely dangerous to the surviving kin and the whole community, so that all kind of restrictions are incurred by the living in dealing with the decomposing corpse (Hertz 1960: 37). Only then can it join the other ancestors. Third, the living or surviving kin as well as the wider community need time to adjust to the loss of one of its members, to renew structural arrangements and to renew communal ties, re-integrating all those who not only have incurred a loss but who have been seriously polluted and been in contact with dangerous forces, thereby liberating them from the restrictions of mourning obligations

(1960: 75). Hertz notices also that in a great number of societies a sacrifice must be performed to end the mourning period, thus pointing either to the unnaturalness of death itself or to the imputation that death is often seen as a result of the malice of other persons (1960: 40f.).

Only when all three transitional stages are passed, can society return to normal, or in his words: '... death as a social phenomenon consists in a dual and painful process of mental disintegration and synthesis. It is only when this process is completed that society, its peace recovered, can triumph over death' (1960: 86). In his concise depiction of death rituals in a variety of societies which practice a second burial, Hertz also notes the differentiation of treatment of different status-positions, so that the features of restrictive taboos, of secrecy of names, of transfer of life-force to a new incumbent in the position of a chief or king ('One must wait for the King to be entirely dead before one can cry: Long live the King!' Hertz 1960: 49), are commonly hedged in most cases with extremely restrictive taboos and obligations. This line of research has since been successfully continued, partly independently from Hertz' propositions, in such diverse fields as historical investigations on the funerary customs of European kingship since the Middle Ages (see Kantorowicz 1957), or the continuity of kingship among the Shilluk and in South Asia (see Schnepel 1995; for an early summary of Indian notions along the lines of Kantorowicz' argument, see Zimmer 1948).

Other lines of field-research suggested by Hertz' propositions have led to emphasis on other features, and I shall only refer to a small number of studies which have significantly modified or clarified some of his suggestive insights into the total phenomenon in other areas of the world. One of the outstanding results of Hertz' study seems to me to lie in his perceptive integration of contradictory features in death rituals: the corpse can be polluting, but has to be fed for a period after death; it is feared, but transformed into a benevolent ancestor; death leads to grief about the loss to the kin-group and the whole society transformed into joy for the soul which joins other ancestors in a happy state; and death has inherently disruptive features which in the end lead to a renewal of the social identity. Much of the criticism of Hertz, which centres on his Durkheimian features of putting society as a superagent and static entity over the acting individual, is mere quibbling over points of view. Hertz thus often speaks of society in a reified mode as in the following referring to the death of chiefs among the Confederation of Hurons: 'the final ceremony always has a pronounced collective character and entails a concentration of the society' (1960: 71), or more generally 'in establishing a society of the dead, the society of the living regularly recreates itself' (ibid.: 72). Bloch has pursued this problem in depth and holds that 'death as disruption, rather than being a problem for the social order... is in fact an opportunity for dramatically creating it' (Bloch in Bloch and Parry

1982: 218). It most likely depends here on the emphasis, whether the social actor is seen as agent who can modify existing 'norms', or whether norms are seen as overwhelmingly determining action. We should after all not forget that Durkheim, in spite of the preponderance of the notion of collective representations in his writings, has also pointed to the immoral or anarchic inclinations of all individuals who always try to manipulate rules.

Bloch, in an earlier publication, took up the notion of the ambiguity of death in his narration of the event of a second burial among the Merina of Madagascar. As he points out, the ritual of the taking out of the decomposed bones from the first temporary resting place and the placing it into the lineage tomb is 'breaking one of the basic precepts of society which is respect and avoidance of the dead' (Bloch 1971:155). In similar vein, he reports that the ceremony entails a dance, in particular by kinswomen of the deceased, which is 'both excited and tense', as the participants are elated as well as frightened at the same time (ibid.: 154f.). The other feature expressing the ambivalence toward the dead which Bloch mentions with explicit reference to Hertz is the rough handling of the bones of recently deceased as well as other ancestor skeletons at the occasion of the opening of the lineage tomb during the second burial. As Bloch explains it, 'close relatives who have the most intimate memories of the dead person are forced to handle the skeleton so that the realization of death is fully accepted' (ibid.: 168).

Here we come close to the experiential dimension of the ethnography of death which tries to convey, in addition to rejoicing for the departed spirit, some of the mental anguish about the loss to a particular kin-group which may lead to ambiguous and contradictory forms of behaviour. Danforth in his extensive study of funerary practices among Greek Orthodox villagers collected a number of dirges which show the pain of separation, whereby the exhumation before the second burial is seen as a period at once 'both desirable and undesirable', as it indicates the final and necessary separation of the dead from the living yet also the return of the dead from the tomb to the world, as is apparent from the custom of a mother kissing the exhumed skull of her daughter and greeting her as one greets a relative returning home. However, this temporary return of the exhumed body to the surface is seen by the participants also as an illusion. When villagers said to the mother that she had received the deceased daughter well when exhuming her, she replied: 'What did I receive?.... Look what I put in and look what I took out! I put in a partridge, and I took out bones' (Danforth 1982: 65). Danforth also reports the existence of the metaphor of the funeral as a wedding, which 'establishes an analogy between departure from the world of the living for the grave, on one hand, and a departure from one's home and family of origin for the home of one's affines, on the other' (Danforth, 1982: 89), thus corroborating a hunch which Hertz suggested explicitly (Hertz 1960: 80).

We find a most moving and convincing report about the ambiguity of death and its resolution through contradictory actions in Monica Wilson's account of the Nyakyusa and their 'ritual madness': despite the Nyakyusa's having strong taboos against unclean things, in particular faeces, and despite it being a sign of madness to eat dirt, they deliberately cover themselves with pollution during mourning ceremonies in order not to be driven mad by sorrow (Wilson 1957: 53ff.; 80f.).

There may be many faults discoverable in specific parts of the generalizations about death rituals as proposed by Hertz, and there is certainly much scope to extend by field-research venues he suggested. I have foregone a discussion of recent approaches by culture historians or classicists about the relation between myths of origin and the origin of death in the world or the analysis of the relation between death and sacrifice, of death in life and forms of renunciation, or of specific forms of metaphorical death in general initiation-rituals and the specific initiations of sacred personnel such as shamans. The whole field of ancestor-cults in their relation to notions of memory and history in oral societies has made great advances since Hertz' times, as researchers on such divergent areas as medieval Christian cult-practices of martyrs and saints and re-incarnation beliefs among Australian Aborigines have shown the complexity of cultural variations in dealing with the notion of mortality and the desire and ritual enactment of beliefs in immortality, and of realms of death as worlds-upside-down (on the cross-cultural notion of anamnesis, see Köpping in Eliade 1987).

Most of these topics were touched upon by Hertz, though his tendency to put diverse practices under the same category is open to debate, as is his reliance on the assumed strict separation of the Durkheimian sacred and profane, a reliance which his own awareness of contradictory attitudes and ambiguous practices in regard to the treatment of the dead in the same culture area should have avoided. But it is undeniable that in spite of all theoretical shifts the very same questions which spurred Hertz to undertake a structuring of the plethora of available field-data still inform modern fieldwork or analysis of texts dealing with the question of the meaning of death for specific societies. The specific contributions which ethnographers can make to this total social phenomenon lies in my opinion not so much in the theoretical advances which only decades of sifting the existing ethnographic reports would yield, but rather in the art of conveying the ambiguity on the mental and emotional level as they affect the participants in death and burial rituals as well as the coping strategies.

Field-reports as those of Monika Wilson, of Danforth and of Bloch, try to convey to distanced readers the strong emotive forces which are called forth in the experience of death among the surviving relatives, conveying something of the emotional intensity which Hertz notes for the cases of violent deaths, for the death of children, or for death in childbirth. He saw that the collective consciousness takes scarce notice of these forms of death, yet he opposes the notion that the shortened ceremonies for such occasions indicate a weakness of emotion:

> . . . on the contrary it is the extreme intensity and suddenness of this emotion . . . We have seen that birth, like death, frees dangerous forces which make mother and child taboo for a while. Usually these forces gradually disperse and the mother can be freed. But if the event occurs in an unusual fashion—for instance, if twins are born—then . . . "this birth is death", for it excludes from normal life those who seem fated to such a birth. It endows them with a sacred character of such strength that no rite will ever be able to efface it, and it throws the entire community into a state of terror and consternation. (Hertz 1960: 85f.)

It is at these points where the modern ethnographers, in describing the anger and despair of Greek villagers or the coping mechanism through contradictory behaviour, the acting as if they were 'mad', of the Nyakyusa, can show how close Hertz came to an understanding of the meaning of social experiences. A further example of the stark terror and emotions mixed between anger and despair comes from Elizabeth Hill's description of two funerals among the Kadazan of North Borneo, one for a baby and one for a little girl of five years of age, where the ceremonies (now Christian) are indeed short, but where the emotional gamut of fear, anger, thoughts of revenge, despair, frustration and terror about avenging spirits is played out in extreme concentration in the span of one night, when not only the life-story of the young children is recounted in detail, but affairs of omens and bad signs over the period of the last year are remembered as affairs of the whole village, while the men, but also the attending children, are plied with strong alcohol to fortify them against the appearance of the spirit of the dead child (Hill 1976: 143ff.).

However, such attempts at conveying the experiential dimension through recourse to the researcher's own discomfort have been undeservedly savaged by sarcastic criticism through the arch-advocate of the hermeneutic or 'thick description' procedure in American anthropology, Clifford Geertz. The attempt of Danforth to relate his field-experiences to his own family background: 'I thought of my own brother and cried', is dismissed by Geertz as the philosophical meditation model of 'Heidegger in Greece' or the anthropologist as humanist who is worried that he is insufficiently engaged (Geertz 1988: 15), while the report by Renato Rosaldo in his article 'Grief and a Headhunter's Rage: On the Cultural Force of Emotions' of 1984 where the researcher reports how through the experience of anger in grief over the accidental death of his wife during fieldwork he gained insight into the motive force behind the head-hunting ritual performed at the occurrence of a death among groups in the North Philippines, is equally trivialized by Geertz as a 'modern or post-modern complaint' (ibid.: fn 3).

Considering that we in the modern world are living in an environment which has less and less ritual space and time to accommodate the multiplicity of attitudes, feelings and values surrounding the event of a death, where ritual is replaced by what Jean Ziegler has called the culture of thanatopraxis, where bureaucratic and streamlined services take care of the 'disposal' of the dead (Ziegler 1975), and where community has almost no chance to re-create itself, the efforts by ethnographers to gain an understanding of—to use Hertz' terms—physical and mental dissolution and the realignment of human ties by ritual performances through the conveying of their personal anguish seems also quite in the spirit of the Année School, known for the social commitment of their scholars to urgent social problems of their own time. Through this procedure, anthropology could fulfil the promise that the specific methodological approach of this discipline would be able to 'hold up a mirror to mankind', as Kluckhohn once put it, or to gain insight into the humanity or inhumanity of our own, the researchers' cultures, as Malinowski and Boas expected.

REFERENCES

Bloch, M. 1971. *Placing the Dead.* London and New York: Seminar Press.

Bloch, M. and J. Parry (eds.) 1982. *Death and the Regeneration of Life.* Cambridge: Cambridge University Press.

Danforth, Loring. 1982. *The Death Rituals of Rural Greece.* Princeton: Princeton University Press.

Detienne, Marcel. 1972. *The Gardens of Adonis.* Hassocks: Harvester Press.

Dobshansky, Theodosius. 1969. *The Biology of Ultimate Concern.* London: Rapp and Whiting.

Douglas, Mary. 1966. *Purity and Danger.* Harmondsworth: Penguin.

———. 1970. *Natural Symbols.* London: The Cresset Press.

Dumézil, G. 1948. *Mitra-Varuna: essai sur deux représentations indo-européennes de la souveraineté.* Paris: Gallimard.

Durkheim, E. and Marcel Mauss. 1903. De quelques formes primitives de classification. *L'année Sociologique* 6: 1-72.

Evans-Pritchard, E.E. 1960. Introduction. In Robert Hertz, *Death and the Right Hand.* (translated by Rodney and Claudia Needham) London: Cohen and West.

Frazer, J. G. 1933. *The Fear of the Dead in Primitive Religion.* London: Macmillan.

Geertz, C. 1988. *Works and Lives.* Stanford: Stanford University Press.

Granet, M. 1953 (1933). La droite et la gauche en Chine. *Études sociologiques sur la Chine.* Paris: Presses Universitaires.

———. 1934. *La Pensée chinoise.* Paris: Albin Michel.

Hertz, Robert. 1907. Contribution à une étude sur la représentation collective de la mort. *L'Année Sociologique* 10: 48-137.

Hertz, Robert. 1909. La pré-éminance de la main droite: étude sur la polarité réligieuse. *Revue Philosophique* LXVIII: 553-80.

Hubert, H. and Marcel Mauss. 1899. Essai sur la nature et la fonction du sacrifice. *L'Année Sociologique* 2: 29-138.

Hill, Elizabeth (Köpping). 1976. Death and the Significance of Funeral Rites: an Animist-Christian Tandem in Borneo. *Occasional Papers in Anthropology.* Anthropology Museum, University of Queensland 6:143-58. Brisbane: Queensland University Press.

Huntington, R. and P. Metcalf. 1979. *Celebrations of Death: the Anthropology of Mortuary Ritual.* Cambridge: Cambridge University Press.

Kantorowicz, E.H. 1957. *The King's Two Bodies. A Study in Mediaeval Political Theology.* Princeton: Princeton University Press.

Koepping, K.P. 1987. Anamnesis. In M. Eliade (ed.), *Encyclopedia of Religion.* Vol. 1: 253-61. New York: Macmillan.

Kruyt, A.C. 1941. Rechts en Links bij de Bewoners van Midden-Celebes. In *Bijdragen tot de Taal-, Land- en Volkenkunde van Nederlandsch-Indie* 100: 339-56. (English in Needham 1973: 74ff.).

Lévi-Strauss, Claude. 1962. *La pensée sauvage.* Paris: Plon.

Malinowski, B. 1948. *Magic, Science and Religion.* Glencoe, Ill.: The Free Press.

Mauss, Marcel. 1904-5. Essai sur les variations saisonnieres des sociétés eskimo. *L'Année sociologique* 9: 39-132.

———. 1925. Essai sur le don, forme archaïque de l'échange. In M. *Mauss, Sociologie et Anthropologie.* Paris: Presses Universitaires de France.

———. 1938. Une catégorie de l'esprit humain: la notion de personne, celle de 'moi'. In M. Mauss, *Sociologie et Anthropologie.* Paris: Presses Universitaires de France.

Needham, Rodney. 1973. The Left Hand of the Mugwe: An Analytical Note on the Stucture of Meru Symbolism. In R. Needham (ed.), *Right and Left.* Chicago: Chicago University Press.

Radcliffe-Brown, A.R. 1933. *The Andaman Islanders.* Cambridge: Cambridge University Press.

Rosaldo, R. 1984. Grief and a Headhunter's Rage: On the Cultural Force of Emotions. In E. Bruner (ed.), *Text, Play and Story.* Proceedings of the American Ethnological Society. Washington.

Schnepel, B. 1995. Twinned Beings. Göteborg: The Institute for Advanced Studies in Social Anthropology.

Traube, Elizabeth. 1977. *Ritual Exchange among the Mambai of East Timor: Gifts of Life and Death.* Cambridge, Mass.: Harvard University Press.

Turner, Victor. 1969. *The Ritual Process.* Chicago: Chicago University Press.

Van Gennep, A. 1909. *Les rites de passage.* Translated by Monika B. Vizedom and Gabrielle L. Loiffer 1960. Chicago: Chicago University Press.

Vernant, Jean-Pierre. 1980. *Myth and Society in Ancient Greece.* Hassocks: Harvester Press.

Wilson, Monica. 1957. *Rituals of Kinship among the Nyakyusa.* Oxford: Oxford University Press.

Ziegler, Jean. 1975. *Les vivants et la mort.* Paris: Editions du Seuil.

Zimmer, Heinrich. 1948. *The King and the Corpse.* Washington: The Bollingen Foundation.

PART I

THE CREATION OF ANCESTORS

The Making of Good Ancestors

Separation, Transformation and Exchange in Mewahang Rai Funerary Rites

MARTIN GAENSZLE

Most rituals among the Mewahang Rai of East Nepal[1] ultimately aim at providing *saya* (M.), the all-important 'head-soul' which may also be regarded as a 'life-force'.[2] During the great ancestral rites, like *nāgi* (N.), or *Sarandew* (N.), the tribal priest (M. *ŋo:pa*) travels to the abode of these deified ancestors in order to 'buy head-soul' (M. *saya khe:^ma*), i.e. he presents offerings and brings back the valued soul-force for his clients. Thus it is in the power of ancestors to give *saya* or to withhold *saya*, to provide strength, health and prosperity, or to cause weakness, disease and disaster.

But not all ancestors are in an equal position to provide *saya*. On the one side there are those who met with some kind of 'bad death' and became evil spirits (M. *i:si^*): persons who died in accidents, murder, suicide (M. *hillasi*), women who died in childbed or during pregnancy (M. *ma:maksi*), or babies who died in their mothers' womb (M. *cha:nu*).[3] These spirits are regarded as highly dangerous and have to be driven out of the village in a special funeral rite (M. *samlo*). No ordinary burial takes place—thus no tomb remains as visible sign—and the soul of the victim never enters the household shrine (M. *khamaŋ*). Instead the spirit is taken to its mythic place of origin, which is located in the plains. This is a particularly difficult task which can only be fulfilled by a special category of shamans, the *selemi* (M.), as the spirit attempts to come back to haunt the living. So these may be called the bad ancestors, and the only thing one asks of them is that they stay away.

On the other side are the proper ancestors who resulted from ordinary death (M. *nu:si^* < M. *nu:ma* 'to be well' + M. *si:ma* 'to die', cf. fn. 23). These may occasionally become dissatisfied and roam around to trouble their descendants as ghosts (M. *ca:p*, N. *bāyu*), but their expected fate is to become and remain good ancestors, i.e. ancestors who reside in the household shrine (*khamaŋ*) and appear at regular intervals as ancestral spirits (M. *sùkla*) who partake of the harvest's first fruit offerings (N. *nuwāgi*). In principle all the ancestors who have resulted from 'good death' can provide *saya*, but whereas ancestral deities, being particularly powerful, always have a malicious side as well and can be called upon in times of affliction in order to appease them, the *sùkla* spirits represent the orderly and regular source of *saya* which generally can be 'tapped' only once a year during the harvest festival. The only exception to this is the time after death, when the *sùkla* are called in the context of the funerary rites (see later). Thus, in short, the *sùkla* can be regarded as the Mewahang ideal of a good ancestor who is in harmony with the living.

It seems quite plausible that beings which originated from an inauspicious death are not considered a source of life, but it is still difficult to explain precisely why ordinary ancestors are in a position to give *saya*. To explore possible answers to this question I want to pose it in a more limited form: Why can the good ancestors (*sùkla*) provide head-soul to the living? This paper will attempt to clarify this by taking a closer look at the funerary rites of the Mewahang, in order to see how, exactly, good ancestors are made.

That rituals of death often abound with symbols of 'fertility', or more generally, the regeneration of life, has been widely observed by anthropologists (cf. Parry and Bloch 1982). The forces of decay, mortality and impermanence are contrasted with those of productiveness, vitality and eternal stability, and by thus creating a transcendental sphere the funerary rituals can 'dramatise the victory of order over biology' (1982: 15). Seen in this perspective, the giving of *saya* by the dead can be taken as an expression of ancestral benevolence and authority: the image of the good ancestors who regularly provide *saya* for the living represents the ideal of a smoothly functioning social as well as natural order. This, of course, is a very general kind of interpretation, and we first have to consider the ethnographic details before we come back to it.

As Parry and Bloch have pointed out, the ideal order evoked in rituals of death is often characterized by the fiction of a bounded social group and the absence of exchange (1982: 27sq.). In the Himalayan context, however, one is struck by the pervasive theme of affinal exchanges in the funerary rites of Tibeto-Burmese peoples. Here it has been shown that the exchanges between wife-givers and wife-receivers following death directly relate to the interactions between these groups which create the marriage bond (e.g. Oppitz 1982, Toffin 1986). Moreover, it has been observed that in this cultural setting, death rituals are usually of greater importance than marriage rituals, which clearly contrasts with the Hindu setting.[4] Though among the Rai, who belong to the Tibeto-Burmese-speaking groups, this is not clearly the case, it can be shown that much of the marriage ritual today is the result of Hinduization and that formerly weddings were much simpler and mainly matters of gift exchanges (Allen 1987). So the following discussion of the Mewahang Rai way of making good ancestors also promises to throw some light on the specific place of funerals in the traditional world-view and their role in the foundation of the social order.

Another issue which I will discuss is the role of language. As among the Mewahang Rai the oral tradition, known as the *muddum* (M.), is fundamental to ritual life I will partly draw on the use of ritual speech in the course of my description. I would like to show that language usage in Rai ritual is a highly important means to create, perpetuate and manipulate social reality and is therefore a very illuminating object of study.

In the following I will first give a detailed description of the ritual sequence of an ordinary Mewahang funeral. Then I will focus on one particular ritual invocation which is crucial in the process of transforming the dead person into an ancestor, the *sùkla che:ˀma* (M. 'Calling the Good Ancestors'). This, in fact, is basically the same rite as is held annually as a first fruit offering (*nuwāgi*), but the wording here, reflecting the specific context of the funeral, clarifies some of the issues under discussion.

FUNERAL

As in many societies, the death rites among the Mewahang Rai form a process of separation of the deceased person from the society of the living followed by a process of transformation and integration (van Gennep 1981: chapter 8). After the burial there is an intermediate, liminal period (lasting several days or weeks) after which the soul of the dead is integrated into the world of the ancestors by being invoked into the ancestral shrine (*khamaŋ*). Section A describes the rites accompanying the burial, section B deals with the rites marking the end of the mourning period, and section C will give a short analysis.

A. BURIAL RITES

When a person in the village dies, the people are immediately informed through shouting. It is said that if the death occurs at night the dogs howl in a particular way because they can 'see' the ghost (*ca:p*). Also a certain bird called *malāmi cara* (N.) is said to announce death by its chirping.

Inside the house the dead person is laid out in the 'back' half, with the head below the *khamaŋ* shrine in the most 'sacred' quarter of the house, the feet facing 'downhill'. The body is covered in a white or yellow cloth, but the face remains uncovered. Beside the head is kept an oil lamp (N. *battī*) and a plate with rice. The mourning relatives keep vigil and take care that the corpse is not touched by animals (like chicken, dogs, etc.). This is explained through reference to the myth of tiger and bear in which bear looks for a place to bury the corpse of their mother Somnima, who had been killed by tiger, and eventually eats part of it because he cannot properly fit her into a hole in the ground (Gaenszle 1991: 266). Clearly, such a 'pre-cultural' act has to be avoided.

On the day of the burial, the dead person is moved to the lower part of the house, the feet facing the door, and in this position he or she is laid in state on a bamboo bier. Now the person is prepared for the voyage to the ancestral world. A coin (M. *chebewa*) is put on the forehead and two more into the hands: this money is to be used to 'buy food on the way'. Altogether six little parcels of cooked rice wrapped into a leaf of the *tukima:phu* (M.) shrub (most probably *Didymocarpus*, N. *tuṅma?*) are attached to the body: two are put into the armpits, two into the hands, and two are put on the feet between the toes. These parcels are called *lapo:kcam* (M. < *lam* 'path', *po:kma* 'to raise', *cam* 'rice')—'path raising rice', likewise provisions for the journey. A particular 'flower' called *miceremma* (M.)[5] is put into the ears. It is referred to as *nu:rùrùbuŋ* in ritual speech: this term may be translated as the 'flower of good souls' (M. *nu:ma* 'to be well' + *rùrù* 'life soul' + *buŋ* 'flower'), but—as will be shown below—the meaning of *nu:rùrù* has a more emotional quality as well.

Now the dead person is sent on the final journey in a rite called *lam ti:ma* (N. *bāṭo lāune*) 'guiding away', which is done by an elder in the role of *nakchoŋ* (M.).[6] The relatives and neighbours from the vicinity come to pay their last homage: each household is expected to bring one wooden container (N. *kaṭhuwā*) of millet beer, from which a few drops are 'fed' to the dead person. The *nakchoŋ* uses a frilled bamboo stick (N. *guṅgri*, M. *hibriŋma*) to sprinkle some beer on the dead person's lips and calls out the names of the bringers, e.g.: 'la hai, this is the one of Suntale, drink it and take it with you, . . . go and become a good soul (*nu:rùrù*)'.

After helpers have prepared the grave on a field below the house, the closer relatives of the deceased and all the other mourners (N. *malāmi*) assemble for the procession which takes the corpse down to its last resting place. The procession is headed by men who fall into the category of *makcha* (CM. 'DH, yZH') or—if none is available—a *bhānij* (N. 'ZS') in relation to the deceased. These 'sons-in-law',[7] who open the way to the beyond, carry leaf-plates (again made from *tukima:phu* leaves) with popped ricegrains (M. *capoŋwa*) which are strewn on the path, a frilled bamboo-stick with cloth stripes, and a bamboo container (M. *toŋba*) with beer. They are followed by the men carrying the corpse, feet in front, then the main mourners (sons, wife, etc.), the wailing women and others.

The grave is circled three times in anti-clockwise direction, and before the corpse is laid into the stone-coffin a fowl is killed by hitting its head on the stone plate. It is thrown away and may not be eaten: clearly this is not an ordinary sacrifice. The dead person is bedded in the coffin together with food and drink, some money, and personal belongings, such as the curved knife (N. *khukuri*) of a man, the sickle *khurpā* (N.) of a woman, the eating plate, etc. These belongings, to be used by the deceased, are partly damaged, thus signalling the non-ordinary state of their owner.

After closing the coffin but before filling up the grave a revealing ritual gesture takes place: the 'pulling out the soul' (M. *lawa la:ma*). Two straight branches of a thorny shrub (M. *tutum*, N. *aiselu*) into which slanting notches have been cut, are stuck through a cleft of the coffin. One has the notches facing upward, the other has them facing downward. Now the former is pulled out, and with it—it is said—the free-souls (M. *lawa*) of the living which may have stayed with the dead are drawn out.[8] The other branch, with the notches pointing downward, is let loose and falls into the coffin—and so does the soul of the deceased which tends to cling to those of the living. In short: the *lawa* of the dead person is separated from its surviving consorts. The act is accompanied by ritual requests. For example the son calls his deceased mother in the following manner:

> *la hai, aŋma:, kopabiko, anâ a lawa yakhetunaho* !
> La hai, mother, now, don't take the souls along!
>
> *ana ko masuŋmale, amlam tù:khetumaŋ khedaho* !
> You are a female elder, follow your path and go!
>
> *bāyu jāgidra mapùkmabù* !
> Don't become a ghost!

After this the main mourners and the elders light wicks and throw them onto the coffin (N. *dāgbatti* 'sign lights'): one onto the head end of the coffin, one in the middle, one onto the foot end. The dead relative is asked to use it for cooking food:

> *aŋmâ a mu: mùkumaŋ cam ŋica:ho*
> O mother, light a fire and cook yourself rice!

Eventually everybody throws some earth into the grave with the left hand and the helpers quickly fill it up, covering the mound with two bamboo mats (N. *bhakari*) and 'cleaning' it with a branch of the *semali* (M.) shrub (N. *sevāli*, Vitex negundo). The food offerings which had been carried by the 'sons-in-law' are placed at the head end of the tomb, and after once again calling on the dead person to go his or her proper path, everyone leaves the site to wash at the nearest watertap. Here the sons of the deceased get their heads shaved: this, again, is the task of the *makcha*, i.e. the 'sons-in-law'. Before entering the house everyone sprinkles water, burns a handful of *tite pāti* (mugwort) and moves each foot in a circle over a small fire.

After this purification a plate of cooked rice and vegetable as well as beer is presented below the *khamaŋ* shrine: it is an invitation to a meal at the place where the deceased should now go to reside. Finally a divinatory procedure called *yayem* (M.) is started which is to establish the cause of the death: small needles made of bamboo are stuck at regular intervals onto the core piece of a banana stalk, each interval representing a possible cause (written separately on a bamboo container). This is wrapped in a piece of cloth and kept below the *khamaŋ* for several days. When eventually a dark spot appears in one of the intervals, this indicates the cause which led to the death.

B. END OF MOURNING

But it takes time until the dead comes to rest. After the burial the soul (*lawa*) is said to be roaming around the village area as a *ca:p*, still not quite able to detach itself from the living. Now all the members of the local clan group are said to be 'polluted'—*juṭho* (N.)—and ideally all of them observe a taboo against eating salt and oil.[9] The *kirya putra* (N.), i.e. the main mourner (the eldest son in case of the father's death, the youngest son in case of the mother's death) even abstains from eating rice altogether and sits in the most sacred corner of the house, not being allowed to speak. This symbolism is obviously influenced by Hindu ideas,[10] but, as we will see, has still different layers of meaning.

The integration of the dead into the world of the ancestors is seen as a gradual process, and the lifting of restrictions on the living relatives during the concluding rites is directly linked to it: in the terms of van Gennep they mark their reintegration into society. These rites are ideally celebrated in two steps: first there is the removal of pollution (N. *cokhine*) which usually is celebrated three days after death (dependent on the *yayem* divination, see above), secondly there is the *barkhānta* (N.), the final rite, which lifts all remaining restrictions and marks the return to normal life. Only then the spirit is firmly established in the *khamaŋ* shrine and the feast is a rather happy occasion, with food, drink, singing and dancing. This can be celebrated three, five, or any uneven number of days after the *cokhine* (ideally thirty-five, or forty-five days or later). It is particularly auspicious if it can be made to coincide with the first fruit offering (*nuwāgi*), as in this case the new ancestral spirit may be called together with the others and be presented a lavish offering. In practice, however, there is a lot of variation. Both, *cokhine* and *barkhānta* can be done in one day (in fact, in order to save expenses, this option is often made use of), and both can even be celebrated right on the day of the burial.

a. Purification: cokhine

The rites of *cokhine* mark the end of death pollution, and for the majority of relatives all restrictions are lifted. The spirit of the deceased is sent on its proper path to become an ancestor. A focal symbol of this day is little white flags with chestnuts (M. *saŋgoŋ*, N. *dhajā* < Sk. *dhvajā*)[11] a pair of which is prepared by the elders in the name of each daughter of the deceased.[12] Again a procession of mourners, headed by the 'sons-in-law' who carry the flags, moves down to the grave. Elders scatter rice grains, little bits of meat (fish or pork) and millet beer on the way, and after the whole group has circled the grave the flags are stuck at the head end of it, together with the offerings. It is said that these flags 'provide shade', and some say they serve as 'cloth', while the chestnuts signify wealth: in any case the construction is meant to enable the spirit to feel comfortable on its journey.

As on the day of the burial the dead person is called upon by the participants of the procession to go and enter the *khamaŋ*; promises are made (e.g. to build a commemorative resting-place, N. *cautarā*), and the time of the *barkhānta* is announced. After returning to the house the mourners purify themselves by sprinkling some water and then enter the house to present offerings to the deceased below the *khamaŋ*: he or she is invited to join the world of the ancestors. Then all the clan members ritually touch salt and oil (N. *nun tel chunu*), which from then on can be eaten again.

Eventually, after the meal which marks the return to unrestricted eating habits, a ceremonial dialogue takes place which is an essential feature of this day: it is held between elders representing the household of the deceased on the one side, and the *malāmi*, the helping mourners, on the other. This exchange of ritual speeches is called *malāmi pharak* (N., literally 'helping mourners distinct'). A *kaṭhuwā* of beer and a bottle of *rakshi* are presented to the *malāmi* as a kind of compensation for their help and then they are requested to excuse all troubles which may have been caused—wounds from digging the grave and making the stone coffin or other inauspicious influences (N. *dasa graha*). After this compensation—in words and in kind—the *malāmi*, i.e. all the mourners from outside the deceased's household, are 'freed' from the adverse effects which come from the contact with death: these may be described as 'pollution', 'vulnerability to superhuman attacks', or simply 'mourning'.

b. End of Mourning, barkhānta

For the direct descendants of the deceased restrictions continue until the final rites of *barkhānta.* In the case of the father's death the sons have to refrain from eating game (in ritual language *dibuksa:*, e.g. N. *thār* = a kind of wild sheep, N. *jhāral,* N. *mṛga* 'deer'), in the case of the mother's death they are not allowed to eat fish (in ritual language *yaŋasa:*), milk, *ghiu* (N. 'clarified butter'), buttermilk or touch anything from a tree which releases a milky substance (e.g. *pipal* tree leaf plates). Moreover, the immediate relatives are not allowed to sing, dance, laugh, play drums or bow down in greeting (N. *dhog dinu*).

On the day of *barkhānta* a big feast is held. All relatives and neighbours come with rice and beer, and a pig has to be killed on the occasion. Again a procession to the grave, lead by the 'sons-in-law', is held, in a similar way as it was done during *cokhine*. For the last time the spirit of the deceased is exhorted to go and enter the house shrine. This time, however, the climax of the procession is the cutting off of the white *saŋgoŋ* flags with a *kukhuri*, which is the task of a man from the wife-receiving category of *makcha*. As symbolic compensation he receives four paisa. This dramatic act, it is said, marks the end of mourning. All the utensils containing food offerings are turned over and stuffed under the bamboo mat. From now on the grave is not visited any more.

Back in the house again an offering under the *khamaŋ* is presented and the deceased's spirit is now assumed to have become a *sùkla*, a good ancestor who has joined the world of the ordinary dead. The rite of calling the spirit is very much like that of calling the good ancestors at the first fruit offering (I will discuss this ritual invocation below in more detail). If the feast falls on a first fruit offering (*nuwāgī*), as ideally should be the case, it is called together with the other ancestors.[13] Then a *saya po:kma*, a 'raising of the head-soul' ceremony for the *nakchoŋ* (the ritual specialist who fed beer to the deceased) is celebrated to relieve him from the bad effects of his soul-guiding services. Finally a ceremonial dialogue is held between the host's side and that of the elders in general (N. *bāyu gaṅgā*). Now all the remaining restrictions are lifted: the inauspicious effects of death are removed, they are invoked to be taken away by the winds and the rivers (hence *bāyu gaṅgā*). After this the feast can take a happy turn, as singing, dancing and laughing is now allowed again.

C. ANALYSIS

Looking at the funerary rites as a whole, it becomes clear that they largely conform to the classical pattern of 'rites de passage' as defined by van Gennep: after being separated from the world of the living, the dead person is gradually transformed into an ancestral spirit who is then safely integrated into the world of ancestors.

Accordingly, the burial is characterized by a symbolism of separation. The metaphor of 'journey to the beyond' is dominant: the deceased is fed and 'guided away' before leaving the house, a procession leads the body to its last resting place, and there food, money and other provisions are given to make sure that he or she may travel comfortably. Symbolic inversions of the ordinary world signal that the deceased is no longer part of it: the anti-clockwise circlings, the non-ordinary sacrifice of a fowl, the symbolic destruction of the deceased's belongings. Most clearly the separation of the two worlds is performed in the 'pulling out the soul' rite (*lawa la:ma*). The free-souls of the living and the dead, which tend to mingle, are separated with the thorny branches. Here the major problem is brought out: Not only do the living continue to be emotionally attached to the dead, but also the soul of the deceased is still clinging to those of the living, it still behaves much like an ordinary person, trying to lure others to go with it.[14] And it is this luring which makes the following period particularly dangerous.

The liminal period is marked by a number of taboos, mainly food restrictions (ban on oil and salt, meats, milk, etc.). The symbolism here shows strong Hindu influence: head-shaving, white cloth, purification bath, etc. But it seems questionable whether the notion of pollution is really so central in the traditional system of ideas. The Rai word for this period is *sikdamdum* (< M. *si:ma* 'to die' + M. *dum* 'rite, tradition'?), which only points to the normative aspect of it. But as can be concluded from the rites removing the inauspicious influences, which more or less explicitly are rites for 'raising the head-soul' (see the *saya po:kma* for the *nakchoŋ*) the liminal state is not so much seen as a pollution of the body substance but as an emotional state, characterized by a 'fallen head-soul (*saya*)'.[15] In the light of this interpretation the liminal period is one of low vitality (e.g. lacking vital foods) which is equally a result of low *saya* as sadness and grief. It appears as if the mourners, by exhibiting a behaviour of low vitality and non-sociability (e.g. not speaking), attempt to give the wandering soul as little cause as possible to cling on to the living, in order to facilitate its emotional detachment.

The rites of aggregation, though they may be spaced as a gradual process, clearly express a return to ordinary life. The wandering soul is summoned to take its place in the ancestral shrine, where it is assimilated to the other ancestor spirits and where it is asked to accept the regular offerings. Thus the dangers of a potentially harmful spirit of the deceased have been controlled and all restrictions can be lifted. But there is more to it: the end of mourning marks not only a return to the previous state of normalcy, but also it achieves the positive reconstitution of the proper order of things. By becoming regular recipients of first fruit offerings 'the dead are incorporated into the predictable cycle of the year and are harnessed (however imperfectly) to the reproduction of social life' (Bloch and Parry 1982: 10, commenting on Harris' article). In other words: the dangerous power of the roaming soul is transformed into the life-giving power of a good ancestor.

Before returning to the initial question of why precisely the good ancestors are in a position to give *saya*, I will focus on the ritual speech used in summoning the soul to the shrine. It seems to me to be a major characteristic of the Rai way of dealing with the dead that—at all stages—they continue to speak to them in a specific way. So it is advisable to have a closer look at the wording involved.

CALLING THE DECEASED AT THE *khamaŋ*

The following invocations were recorded at a funeral feast which collapsed both *cokhine* and *barkhānta.* As the ritual speech is much the same in both settings it can be taken as typical for the final funerary rites. Like the calling of the *sùkla* during *nuwāgi* this invocation is done by a good dozen of relatives simultaneously, in a cacophony of voices, so the 'text' here cannot be regarded as complete. Rather it consists of the phrases which were most intelligible, and thus the text is the product of ethnographic textualization. But still it gives a good impression of this specific form of speaking, which may be described as formulaic in character, as certain idiomatic phrases are used in a standardized yet partly creative manner. This form of ritual speech does not require any special competence—as is the case with other rites—but can usually be done also by young adults, both male and female. The dead person addressed in this example is an old Kulunge woman whose ritual line is called *sakhamaŋ* and who was married to a Mewahang of the *sakchami* line.[16]

A. THE 'TEXT'[17]

1 A: *ana sakhaman sùkla,*
You are the Good Ancestor of the *sakhaman* line,
2 *sakchami-ci, sarima kô-kheda, sarima ke ne: kegami-pho*
(When) the illness got worse, the *sakchami* people have given all their help,
3 R: *he ni:no, apto-l pùkmam-bù?*
He, father's sister, what can we do?
4 M: *malāmi pharak ne: asi-ŋa-pho, am-barkhānta asi-ŋa-pho*
The ritual of Separating the Mourners will be today, your End of Mourning ritual will be today,
5 *sarima-ŋ kô-kheda, anâ a-ŋ le:-khetu-pho,*[18]
The illness got worse, you knew it from the start,
6 *ap-cha:châ a (...) chobasekha ne: musikka-pho*
Your children . . . we all have done the Pig Sacrifice
7 *chobasekha ne: musami*
They have done the Pig Sacrifice,
8 *chobaksa:-pi sanùk ta:ye, sanùk ta:ma-bù*[19]
Come upon the Pig's Meat with a pleasant mind!
9 *ana-n masuŋma:-nale, āyu pî da:ma-bù*[20]
You who is a Female Elder, give us life-force
10 *i:-ca:ma ma-yokma-bù, su:-ca:ma*[21] *ma-yokma-bù*
Don't try to keep talking, don't try to keep scorning!
11 B: *ap-cha:châ a kodalo-ŋ cil-lenci-bù*[22]
Your children have prepared everything now,

12 R: *chobasekha ne: musami*
They have done the Pig Sacrifice
13 B: *ap-cha: kānchā cahi (khù-pi hê na) . . .*
Your youngest son, he (is not in the house). . .
14 *ca:ri-kùŋwâ a am-hû-laŋ cho:ge, kopabiko*
Wash your hand and feet with the territory's water
15 M: *sicila macila ne: jamma-ŋ anâ a bû-khetu-ho*
And gather all the Bad Spirits and take them away!
16 *kupi am-namme-ci āyu rùrù pî-da:ma-bù-ne.*
Here (are) your daughters-in-law, give life-force and soul,
17 *rùrù pî-da:ma-ha:-ci, saya pî-da:ma-ha:-ci*
Give them life-soul, give them head-soul!
18 *sanùŋ ta:-loŋ, nùŋlu ta:-loŋ*
Coming with a pleasant mind, coming with a happy mind
19 B: *kupi ca:na holā du?ana holā*
And you might eat and you might drink
20 *phoba-lam moma-lam tù:-khê ma-bù-pho*
Follow the path of your father, the path of your mother!
21 *nu:-rùrù nu:-sakha*[23]
(Be) a happy soul, of a good kind!
22 *kupi narka kuṇḍamā nabhulnu*[24]
Don't lose your way in the Lakes of Hell
23 *vaikuṇṭha-tu*[25] *cu:kmi holā*
They are probably up in *vaikuṇṭha*
24 M: *chadi:ma-ci chadi:pa-ci yo(k)-khê ma-ha:-ci*
Go and look for the parents-in-law
25 *māhilā sasurā yo(k)-khê ma-bù*
Go and look for the father-in-law who is the second eldest brother
26 *semmak-pi ne: khaŋma ma-yokma-bù*
Also don't try to appear in our dreams
27 *am-cino-cautarā ne: kāncha ta:k-maŋ mu:-pî ci-ne:mo*
And when the youngest brother comes they (the two brothers) will also build a memorial resting-place for you
28 *modolo hone, am-cino-cautarā ne.*
At that time your memorial resting-place (will be built)
29 *ati bisantok pùkna-ho, soptu-ma-lu:ma-bù ne.*[26]
Don't be dissatisfied, and don't feel bad
30 *mayuma leŋnaye*[27]
Don't take the form of a mouse
31 *jeṭhā . . . dāju-bhāi khopkaera cino-cautarā ti:-pikāuncha*
The eldest brother . . . the elder and younger brother will get together and construct a memorial resting-place
32 *santok mu:ma-bù ne.*
So be satisfied!

33 *häkuru tumaru*[28] *ma-lenma-bù ne:*
Don't take the form of a Grave-Haunting Spirit
34 *wacho:k-khê ma-bù*[29] *ne:*
Wash and go away!
35 B: *sukha-deś ujyalo-deś vaikuṇṭhamā jānu, vaikuṇṭha khê ma-bù-ne:*
Go to the Sweet Land, the Light Land, to *vaikuṇṭha*, go to *vaikuṇṭha* then!
36 *kupiko kuyama mayama (ma-pùkyen?) ma-leŋye-ŋa*
Don't (become) take the form of an Evil Spirit here
37 *ana kupi ma-cu:ma-bù*
Do not stay here!
38 M: *rùrù pî-da:ma-ha:-ci saya pî-da:ma-ha:-ci*
Give them life-soul, give them head-soul!
39 *chārchimekmā cāla ne: ma-mu:ma-bù, ana-ŋ le:-khetu-bù-pho*
Don't beckon in the neighbourhood, you knew it from the start!
40 *anami-na cāl musa-lo "ùŋkhalo kô o ka:k-pù" isu-bù*
When you were beckoned, you said: 'What is this shouting?'
41 *ap-cha: am-namme-ci ne: lawa ma-yakhê ma-m-pho, ati!*
So do not take the soul of your son and your daughters-in-law, don't!

B. ANALYSIS

Looking at the formal aspect of the text it is striking how the spirit is spoken to in an almost colloquial fashion: though it is addressed as *sakhaman sùkla* (good ancestor of the *sakhama* line) it is not an abstract, generalized ancestor but still the unique individual whom one knows. The language is much as in ordinary speech, but certain expressions, the recurrent parallelisms, and the style of intonation clearly mark it as a form of ritual speech.

The contents of the invocations can roughly be grouped into three categories:

1. *Situating and presenting.* After addressing the spirit directly in the second person, the speakers refer to the present situation, e.g. clarifying the temporal context of the ritual sequence (line 4). It is indicated that the younger of her two sons is not able to be present (he was away in India as a migrant labourer), but that he will come later to pay his due respect (lines 13, 27). The speakers recall the difficulties and hardships which were suffered prior to death, the vain attempts to help (lines 2, 5). And they point to what has been done by them during the funeral, the ritual activities, especially the killing of a pig, of which meat is offered to the spirit (lines 6-8, 11,12). Later promises are made to build a memorial

resting-place to honour the dead mother (lines 27, 28, 31). All this gives the impression as if the deceased needs to be assured that everything has gone its proper course, that all that could be done was duly done, and that there is no reason for worry or misgivings.

2. *Positive requests.* The spirit is asked to come 'with a pleasant mind' (i.e. benevolently, satisfied, lines 8, 18) and even—as the semantic range of *nu:ma* suggests (fn 23)—to feel good and happy! It is requested to wash its hands with the water presented (line 14), and to eat (line 19). Like a respected guest the dead person is now invited and offered the best of foods, mainly rice, pork and beer. Of course, someone who has eaten well is less likely to have bad feelings and become dangerous. But more is requested than only benevolence: the spirit is asked to give head-soul (*saya*), and life-soul (M. *rùrù* or N. *āyu* 'long life') to those present (lines 9, 16, 17, 38). So the satisfied spirit does not only receive, it has something to give in return. Eventually it is asked to 'follow the path of the ancestors', to join the other good ancestors (lines 20, 24, 25). Having consumed the offering, it now should be satisfied (lines 29, 32), and is requested to wash its hands and go away to the world of the ancestors, *vaikuṇṭha* (lines 34, 35).

3. *Negative requests.* Just as one asks the spirit to be a good ancestor, one asks it not to become an evil spirit (*kuyama mayama*, line 36, or Grave-Haunting Spirit, line 33). It should not trouble the living and try to lure them 'by talking' (line 10, also 39). Nor should it come into their dreams—thus indicating imminent deceased (line 26) or be reborn in the form of an animal (line 30).[30] Here the reluctance of the deceased to accept her fate is clearly spelt out: there is always the danger that she will return or 'rise' again to become a *jāgidra* (N. <*jāgnu* 'to wake up') which takes away the free-soul (*lawa*) of her beloved relatives (line 41). Just as the dying old woman has been lured into the spirit world (line 40), she herself might do the same to others. Therefore the spirit is exhorted not to stay, but to leave for its proper place.

Thus the deceased is approached in a way which defines her new identity: after it is spelt out what the new situation is like, she is told what one expects from her, what she should do and what she should not do. But besides defining a new role there is something specific which one wants to receive. In short, the deceased is now made a partner in an exchange: she is presented with food (and drink) in order to please her. But having achieved this new status of a good ancestor, she is also expected to fulfil certain expectations to reciprocate: to be a benevolent giver of *saya.* Only in this exchange relationship the full separation of the living and the dead is accomplished.

CONCLUSION

I will now return to my initial questions. First of all: Why are the good ancestors in a position to give *saya*?

As we have seen a good ancestor is characterized by a complete detachment from the world of the living. Much of the funerary ritual is concerned with separation: because there is a tendency for the souls of the living and the dead to cling to each other, they first have to be clearly separated.[31] We have seen that the liminal period of 'pollution' is a period when the bereaved's vitality and sociality is diminished, and this condition, it seems, facilitates the deceased's detachment. Only after this is accomplished, and both sides have returned to their proper worlds, is happiness possible again.

But here—and now I come to my main point—one may go a step further and not only say that happiness is possible again, but it is even socially expected. It is precisely because the deceased, after finally having entered the house shrine, is a satisfied and happy ancestor, that he is now able to provide *saya* to the living. Having relinquished the world of mortals without misgivings, having accepted the food and drink offered, and having listened to the flattering words of the relatives, the dead person's 'spirit' is strengthened and 'high', and only then can it give *saya* in return. So likewise, on the final feast of *barkhānta*, the living have good reason to be happy: What had been a source of danger before has now become a source of strength and prosperity. During the feast which ends mourning, one looks ahead rather than back. Not infrequently it is the time when flirtatious approaches mark the beginning of a new marriage arrangement.

This brings me back to my second initial question: What is the role of funerals in the traditional foundation of the Rai social order?

From what has just been pointed out, it is clear that the making of good ancestors is a crucial task: as the overall well-being of the living, their health, their strength, but also their crops and hunting success depends on the *saya* provided by the ancestors, life simply couldn't go on properly without the good ancestors. And for this reason, it seems, the help and assistance of the 'whole society' is required: all the available relatives and neighbours, men and women, the helping mourners (*malāmi*), particularly the elders, one of whom fulfils the role of *nakchoŋ*, and most of all: the *makcha*. We have seen that the wife-receiving category of 'sons-in-law' plays a significant role at all the important stages of the funeral: they lead the procession to the grave, they serve their affines as ritual barbers when shaving the head of the deceased's sons, and they are the ones to cut the *saŋgoŋ* flags to end the mourning period. Of course these services can be explained, as they usually are, as a form of repaying the debt after having taken a woman (e.g. Toffin 1986: 42). But still, I think, this is not the whole truth. As I have argued in more detail elsewhere (Gaenszle 1991: 209sq.)

the categorical collapsing of DH, yZH, and ZS in the role of 'sons-in-law' points to a diachronic dimension of the affinal link: if the role of the 'ideal' DH may also be fulfilled by a ZS, is it not because this ZS could—if not should—*become* the deceased's son-in-law? Of course, this is no longer a possible form of marriage—except in a classificatory sense. But the role of the *makcha* can only be fully understood in the light of an older system of exchange.[32] As the ZS has not received a woman for whom he has to repay any debt, what else explains his obligation? Obviously the ZS merely replicates the role of his father (the ZH), whose 'debt' has devolved upon the son. But if the son has the same duties towards his affines as his father, he may also have the same chance to find a wife there. Though the case is not as clear as among the Kham Magar, the Tamang or the Gurung, the funerary services of the wife-receivers in this perspective appear not only as repaying former debts, but also as a token which allows future advances, thus giving the affinal relationship a diachronic dimension (cf. Dumont 1957).

In any case: the appearance of the theme of affinity, or marriage, in the funerary rites is no surprise if one is fully aware of their regenerative aspect. Apart from providing *saya*, strength and general prosperity, the ancestral forces are also regularly requested to 'arrange for good marriages' (e.g. in the *khamaŋ* ritual).[33] In this way the good ancestors are a general source for the proper functioning of the natural, social and moral order: it is their goodwill and also their happiness which keeps society going. This, I think, is a major difference to the Hindu view, where the ancestors are seen primarily as negative, dangerous forces. Among the high castes of Nepal there is the saying that 'the gods (N./Sk. *devatā*) give but the ancestors (N./ Sk. *pitṛ*) destroy'. Whereas the former live in heaven (N./ Sk. *svarga*) and are relatively free of human needs, the ancestors in their realm of *pitṛlok* are dependent on the regular food offerings provided by their living descendants, and therefore they are potentially dangerous (Bennett 1983: 93-4). Here the ancestors are clearly not a force to be tapped by the ordinary householder for the regeneration of life. Instead the ritual maintenance of the cosmic order is a task which is delegated to the Brahmins.

NOTES

1. For ethnographic details on this group see Gaenszle 1991. The transcription of Mewahang terms—marked by 'M.'—follows the conventions laid down in Appendix 1 of this monograph: i.e. 'ù' stands for the high, central vowel, ':' signifies 'long vowel' and '^' signifies a glottal stop; the velar nasal is here represented as 'ŋ'. Nepali terms are transliterated according to the system

of Turner 1980 and are marked by 'N'. Where Mewahang terms and Nepali terms are frequently used interchangeably both terms are given. 'M*' means 'Mewahang ritual language', 'Sk.' = 'Sanskrit'. I would like to thank Boyd Michailovsky for revising my English.

2. *Saya* is translated in Nepali as *sir sāto* (N. *sir* 'head', N. *sāto* 'soul') as its proper location is said to be in the head. Related concepts have been described by Allen 1976a: 135, 1976b: 547, Hardman 1981, n.d., Sagant 1985.
3. Cf. Gaenszle 1992: 201ff. For a detailed discussion of a ritual dealing with the *ma:maksi* see Gaenszle 1994. Similar concepts among the Limbu have been described by Michailovsky and Sagant (1992).
4. E.g. Holmberg describes the prominence of rituals surrounding death in creating and affirming the 'social totality' among the Tamang (1989: 190sq.).
5. This shrub with longish green leaves and white flowers blooming in April to June could so far not be identified with certainty. It is sometimes said to be *dhayaro* in Nepali, but it is definitely not *Woodfordia fruticosa*, also known under this name.
6. The priestly role of *nākchoŋ* can be taken by any knowledgeable elder not belonging to the lineage of the deceased. The term *nakchoŋ* however also is used among the Mewahang to denote the priest who is in charge of the territorial cult (Gaenszle n.d.). This perhaps is an indication of some older category which was linked with tasks related to the territory. Among the Kulunge the priestly category of *nokcho* (obviously a cognate term) is in charge of the ancestral, agricultural, territorial as well as funerary rites (McDougal 1979: 123sq.).
7. As I have tried to show elsewhere (Gaenszle 1991: 176sq.) the kinship terminology of the Mewahang reflects a former system of symmetrical alliance, still evident in the specifications of certain terms: thus *makcha* also covers SWB and may at some stage have been the general term for male 'cross'-relatives (or affines in Dumont's sense) in G-1. Nevertheless this symmetry is no longer felt and the term *makcha* primarily denotes the wife-receiving 'sons-in-law' (in Nepali called *juwāī*).
8. Whereas the vital soul, the *saya* is firmly located in the body, particularly in the head, of a living person and may either rise or fall, the *lawa*, often likened to a small flying insect like a butterfly, tends to roam and leave the body, as, for example, following sudden shock or surprise. When it is kidnapped by an ancestral deity illness is the result, and a tribal priest has to go on a ritual journey to retrieve it (cf. Gaenszle 1991: 131, Hardman 1981, n.d.).
9. The local clan group is that part of a named clan which has certain links with a locality and is characterized by exogamy (cf. Gaenszle 1991: 149sq.). The food taboo, though in practice not adhered to by all members with equal strictness, may be seen as a symbolic expression of this unit's social solidarity.
10. The elaborate high caste practices during the period of social isolation (N. *kirya basne*, 'sitting in mourning') following death pollution have been described by Bennett (1983: 98-107). As she points out, they may be

interpreted as a temporary asceticism aimed at reducing the impurity, but also have the effect of avoiding defiling contact.

11. A flag is made by attaching two small bamboo sticks (N. *nigālo,* Arundinaria) with frilled ends to a square piece of white cloth. The chestnuts are strung up like beads and fixed to the lower stick, whereas the upper stick is hung onto the end of a pole (usually made from a *semali* twig).
12. The prestational significance of these flags is not entirely clear. Among the Kulunge similar flags (called *sibalo*) are given by the out-married 'sisters' to their deceased sibling (McDougal 1979: 82sq., 125-7) and it is possible that this was the case among the Mewahang as well. McDougal sees them as an expression of the 'brother-sister' bond. Even after marriage women continue to have obligations towards their natal clan.
13. Always the person who has died last is called first. It is then asked to call upon and bring along the others.
14. Even if a person has not suffered a violent death, the deceased only slowly realizes that he is no longer alive (cf. Michailovsky and Sagant 1992: 25).
15. Similarly during the *nwāran* (N.) ceremony after the birth of a child the mother's period of 'pollution' is terminated with a 'raising the head-soul' ceremony.
16. Besides the ordinary clan names the Mewahang—and other Rai—possess certain ritual same names which are used in the ritual language to refer to individuals as well as kinship groups (cf. Gaenszle 1991: 129sq.)
17. In order to make the structure of the text more lucid, I have opted to use hyphens to mark the conjunction of verbs and nouns, non-flective suffixes as well as prefixes in the Mewahang words.
18. M. *le:ma* 'to know' + M. *(ya)khe^ma* 'to take'.
19. *Sanùk or sanùŋ (ta:ma)* is part of a standard ritual expression (M* *sanùŋ* [*ta:ma*] *nùŋlu* [*ta:ma*] see line 18) containing the root **nùŋ* from M. *nùŋwa* 'mind', i.e. the centre of thought and emotion. A specific meaning of the prefix and suffix could not be identified with certainty, but the expression was commonly translated into Nepali as '*rāmro man liera* (*āunu*)' (N. *rāmro* 'nice', N. *man* 'mind') or '*khusi bhāera* (*āunu*)' (N. *khusi* 'pleased', 'cheery', 'happy').
20. N. *āyu* 'age', 'life' is often used as a quasi-synonym for M. *rùrù*. M. *pi^ma* 'to give' + *-da:ma* (aspectivizer giving emphasis on relinquishing aspect: 'to leave').
21. M. *ca:ma* 'to eat' here is a continuative aspectivizer (with *i:ma* 'to speak' and M*? *su:ma* 'to scorn')
22. M. *cimma* 'to be ready' + M. *lemma* (inchoative, here in the dual form).
23. The notion of happiness is semantically closely linked to the notion of well-being/ pleasantness: both meanings are contained in the verbal form of M. *nu:ma* which is used here in the ritual expressions. In ordinary language the sentence 'I am happy', for example, is expressed as '*aŋ-nùŋwa ca:-nu:kpù*', literally 'my mind tastes good' (< M. *ca:ma* 'to eat' + *nu:ma*). Compare this to related forms like *yen-nu:kpù* ('sounds pleasant', < M. *yemma* 'to hear') or *khen-nu:kpù* ('looks good' < M. *khaŋma* 'to see'), the opposite of which would be *yen-i:kpù* or *khen-i:kpù* respectively. The categorical opposition of *nu:-* versus *i:-*, is also contained in the concepts of *nu:si^* ('good spirits of the

deceased') and *i:sî* ('bad spirits of the deceased') referred to in the beginning. The term *sakha* is not entirely clear. It contains the root **kha* 'place' and was explained by one informant to mean 'those who have died at good places' (i.e. not in accidents, etc.).

24. As this kind of ritual speech is not restricted to ritual experts, there is an occasional code switching into Nepali, in this case an entire line. N. *narka* 'hell', N. *kuṇḍa* 'basin', 'lake'.
25. The Hindu concept of *vaikuṇṭha* which refers to Vishnu's heaven is of course of fairly recent origin among the Rai.
26. N. *bisantok* < *visantoṣ* 'dissatisfaction'. M* *soptu* < M.? *som* 'mind' + M. *tukma* 'to hurt'.
27. M* *cuˆyuma mayuma* 'mouse'.
28. M* *hăkaru tumaru* 'grave', here taken metonymically.
29. The expression M* *wacho:kma* 'to wash (esp. hands)' occurs only during the Calling of the *sùkla* (< **wa* 'water' + M. *cho:kma* 'to wash').
30. I am not sure whether this can be taken as evidence for a 'tribal' theory of rebirth or whether this is the result of recent influence from 'outside'.
31. Similar observations have been made by Charlotte Hardman among the Lohorung Rai. There the dead are explicitly requested to give up their attachment not only to their relatives but also to their cattle, fields, cooking utensils, etc. (Hardman n.d.: 347).
32. In a system of cross-cousin marriage as seems to have existed among the Rai (cf. fn 7) one would expect an identity of DH=ZS (which might have existed in the term *makcha*). Today all nieces and nephews ('parallel' and 'cross') are called *yaŋcha.* That the Nepali term *bhānij* is used here indicates the need to single out the 'cross' nephews: the nephew who is a potential marriage partner.
33. The expression used repeatedly in this ritual offering for the household deity when asking for 'good marriages' is *khewasu wàkamma* (M*). The term *khewasu* alludes to the mythical sister of the culture hero Khakculukpa called Khewa, who 'married away'; the term *wakamma* is the ritual expression derived from M. *kamma* 'to arrange'. A 'good marriage' is characterized by a harmonious relationship, free of fights and quarrels, and, of course, by numerous offspring.

REFERENCES

Allen, Nicholas J. 1976a. Shamanism among the Thulung Rai. In John T. Hitchcock and Rex L. Jones (eds.), *Spirit Possession in the Nepal Himalayas.* Pp. 124-40. Warminster: Aris and Phillips Ltd.

———. 1976b. Approaches to Illness in the Nepalese Hills. In J.B. Loudon (ed.), *Social Anthropology and Medicine.* Pp. 500-52. London, New York, San Francisco: Academic Press.

———. 1978. Sewala Puja Bintila Puja: Notes on Thulung Ritual Language. *Kailash* 6 (4): 237-56.

Allen, Nicholas J. 1987. Thulung Weddings: The Hinduisation of a Ritual Cycle in East Nepal. *L'Ethnographie* 83(100-1): 15-33.

Bennett, Lynn. 1983. *Dangerous Wives and Sacred Sisters. Social and Symbolic Roles of High-Caste Women in Nepal.* New York: Columbia University Press.

Bloch, Maurice and Jonathan Parry (eds.). 1982. *Death and the Regeneration of Life.* Cambridge: Cambridge University Press.

Dumont, Louis. 1957. Hierarchy and Marriage Alliance in South Indian Kingship. *Occasional Papers of the Royal Anthropological Society of Great Britain and Ireland.*

Gaenszle, Martin. 1991. *Verwandtschaft und Mythologie bei den Mewahang Rai in Ostnepal. Eine ethnographische Studie zum Problem der 'ethnischen Identität'.* Beiträge zur Südasienforschung, Band 136. Stuttgart: Steiner Verlag Wiesbaden GmbH.

———. 1992. Ancestral Types: Mythology and the Classification of 'Deities' among the Mewahang Rai. In Véronique Bouillier and Gérard Toffin (eds.), *Classer les dieux? Des panthéons en Asie du Sud.* (*Puruṣārtha* 15) Paris: EHESS. Pp. 197-218.

———. n.d. Aspects of the Territorial Cult among the Mewahang Rai. *Contributions to Nepalese Studies* (in preparation).

Hardman, Charlotte E. 1981. The Psychology of Conformity and Self-expression among the Lohorung Rai of East Nepal. In Paul Heelas and Andrew Locke (eds.), *Indigenous Psychologies. The Anthropology of the Self.* Pp. 161-80. London: Academic Press.

———. n.d. *Conformity and Self-expression: A Study of the Lohorung Rai of East Nepal.* Ph.D. thesis, School of Oriental & African Studies, London (unpublished dissertation).

Holmberg, David H. 1989. *Order in Paradox. Myth, Ritual, and Exchange among Nepal's Tamang.* Ithaca and London: Cornell University Press.

Michailovsky, Boyd; Philippe Sagant. 1992. Le chamane et les fantomes de la malemort. Sur l'efficacité d'un rituel. *Diogène* 158 (Chamanes et chamanismes au seuil du nouveau millénaire): 20-36.

Oppitz, Michael. 1982. Death and Kin amongst the Northern Magar. *Kailash* 9 (4): 377-421.

Sagant, Philippe. 1985. With Head Held High: The House, Ritual and Politics in East Nepal. *Kailash* 12 (3-4): 161-222 (French original publ. 1981).

Toffin, Gérard. 1986. Unités de parenté, système d'alliance et de prestations chez les Tamang de l'Ouest (Népal). *Anthropos* 81: 21-45.

Turner, Ralph Lilley. 1980. *A Comparative and Etymological Dictionary of the Nepali Language.* New Delhi: Allied Publishers. Reprint (orig. 1931).

Van Gennep, Arnold. 1981. *Les rites de passage.* Paris: Editions A. et J. Picard (orig. 1909).

How to Make the Spirit of the Dead Happy

The Rhetoric of Words and Deeds in a Jēnu Kuṟumba Death Ritual

ULRICH DEMMER

> Words and deeds in that commonplace world of our daily lives constitute a context of mutual implication that is the background of our awareness and, when they fly apart in deception, dishonesty, and error, the object of it.
>
> (Tyler 1987: 63)

The present article is concerned with the meaning of death as made public in the death rituals of the Jēnu Kuṟumba, a community of gatherer/hunters in south India. To arrive at an appropriate vantage point to approach this question of meaning in ritual, I will first consider, from the Jēnu Kuṟumba point of view, some of the important consequences of death.[1]

Among the Jēnu Kuṟumba social life is throughout a life in sociality. In sociality persons live in mutual relatedness 'delicately attuned to one another, and to themselves in relation to others, in a taut web of interaction' (Carrithers 1992: 63). In case of the Jēnu Kuṟumba, moreover, the actors in this web are close relatives expected to behave according to a moral order stressing mutual care and support of kinspeople. And, finally, good sociality is based on trust. It is built on the commitment of people towards each other. It is built on 'people's ability to give words of promise' (Nietzsche 1957: 47) that they are willing to follow this moral order. Death, however, puts this commitment into question. It puts into doubt that people are willing to live according to their moral order—it makes 'words and deeds fly apart'. As we will see later, the spirits of the dead (*gāḷi*, lit.: wind) return to their living relatives during the course of death rituals. In these ritual settings they are able to speak (through a medium) with the living.[2] In fact, in the death rituals the spirits of the deceased are engaged in a series of interactions and dialogues with their living relatives.

Listening to the voices of the living and to the voices of the spirits of the dead in these discourses we can hear them speak of separation leading to sorrow, loneliness and confusion. Especially the spirits of the dead, who roam about in the forest after death, feel homeless and long to reach the place of their deities. But they are confused, weak and therefore unable to get there. They need the support of their living relatives and it is the explicit goal of the actors in the death rituals to help the spirits of the dead to reach their deities.

But in the death rituals we can hear that death has additional consequences. The spirits of the deceased make their living relatives responsible for their death and for the suffering that followed on their death. The dead reproach the living that they did not help them when they were sick and about to die. Furthermore, there is always the suspicion that a death was caused by relatives[3] (e.g. through black magic). At least, the spirits of the dead question whether the living did their best to protect them from such attempts. And they bemoan that even now, in the ritual, the living do not take care of them. They suspect that the living are unwilling to live according to the moral order of kinship. Death, then, is interpreted as a violation of the social order of the community. It is an event that leads to reproaches of misbehaviour and to mistrust. Accordingly, the spirits of the dead hesitate to cooperate with the living in the rituals.

But to achieve the goal of the rituals, namely to bring the spirits to their deities, the participants in the rituals have to overcome this crisis of trust. However, it is not the social order itself that is put into question by death, but the trust and the commitment of relatives towards each other. Accordingly, it is not a symbolic (re)-presentation of relationships and of a given social order that is at issue here, but rather a 'working out' of proper relatedness. To be sure, several studies concerned with the meaning of death in other cultures (e.g. Hertz 1960; Bloch and Parry 1982; Metcalf and Huntington 1979) suggest that there it is indeed a representation of social order that is at issue. In these cultures death is interpreted as a negation of society (understood as permanent, static and incontingent) and as 'a manifestation of the contingency of events' (Bloch and Parry 1982: 11). Death is the supreme symbol of arbitrariness and transitoriness. Actual events, and praxis in general, are thus to be placed in opposition to social order, the latter understood as enduring and eternal, situated prior to any concrete acts. What happens in death rituals, then, is that society, in order to emerge as 'triumphant over death' (Hertz 1960: 86), either represents itself as *the* eternal and outlasting institution, or it is created as such, namely as an eternal, static, 'external force' (Bloch and Parry 1982: 6) and an 'ideological representation' (ibid.:18).

Yet, as we saw above, the Jēnu Kuṟumba do not share the idea that death is a 'symbol of arbitrariness', nor would they share the other assumptions made in the above cited literature, i.e. the disqualification of social praxis as being (merely) contingent and separated from given structures and rules of relationships. Instead, the Jēnu Kuṟumba share with other gatherer/hunters, such as the Pintubi (Myers 1986, 1988), what F. Myers has termed a 'negotiated quality' (1988: 54) of social life.

This is patterned by a good deal of 'politicking and negotiation' (1986: 17):

> Relationships among people are not totally given in the rules of a defining structure relating, say, to land-ownership, kinship or residence. Instead, the relationships must be worked out in a variety of social processes. (1988: 54)

Among the Jēnu Kuṟumba one process of 'working out relationships' is the death ritual we are concerned with here.[4] Whenever we were sitting together to discuss the problems[5] I had with the logic of this ritual, it was made clear to me that my interlocutors thought of the ritual in terms of the work (*kelsa*)—in terms of the deeds constituting the process. Rather than stressing the meaning of artifacts employed in a referential sense, they pointed out to me what has to be done with these things. Instead of providing me (to my disappointment) with an elaborate semantic exegesis of, e.g. the water pots or the green leafy branches employed during the ritual, they pointed out to me what they are good for. The leafy branches are brought to build a hut for the spirit, the small clay pots are taken because one has to carry the deities and the spirit of the dead person and so forth. And all that work is done in order to make the spirit happy.

The meaning in ritual, then, is seen as emerging in a process where symbolic action is used as an instrument to achieve a result. Taking into account such a qualification of meaning and the negotiated quality of social life among the Jēnu Ḳuṟumba, I think it is appropriate to understand this ritual in a pragmatistic way too.[6] I will understand it as a strategy to overcome the crisis in actual relatedness and trust. In particular I will treat the ritual as a rhetorical strategy—defined as:

> the disciplined use of oral and gestural behaviour for the purpose of convincing or persuading others of the propriety or appropriateness of the speaker's values and actions. Rhetorical acts are confrontations of active beings in problem-solving situations, which rhetoricians call exigencies or urgencies . . . (and where) . . . confrontations of persons extort and define commitments. (Sarbin 1986: 89)

Yet it is crucial to realize, that this is not solely accomplished by verbal acts. To overcome the crisis it is most important to re-establish the sincere correspondence of words and deeds—that people do what they say and say what they do. Since death makes 'deeds and words fly apart' it is their genuine relatedness that is at issue here. To accomplish that, non-verbal actions are intended to speak too—indeed, even louder than words.

I will therefore follow J. Fernandez' (1986) lead and argue that the actors in this rhetorical project employ not only words but also symbolic actions or 'images' as arguments. In the present article I am thus less concerned with referential meanings than with intended and purposive meanings of utterances. What I want to ask is what the participants in the ritual want their verbal and non-verbal deeds, their 'speaking acts', to achieve when they confront death in ritual.

THE ETHNOGRAPHIC CONTEXT

Following the various accounts[7] of the Census of India publications, the Jēnu Kuṟumba are the numerically largest gatherer/hunter people (around 15.000 to 20.000 people) in south India. Their home range stretches along the western side of the ghat forests, forming today a part of Kerala, Tamil Nadu and Karnataka.

The Jēnu Kuṟumba I studied live in the forest regions of the northern Nilgiri area (including the hills north of the Moyar River in Karnataka). These forests constitute the traditional foraging areas of the Jēnu Kuṟumba in the region. But since the establishment of reserve and forest areas and the wildlife sanctuaries of Mudumalai and Bandipur (in the middle of this century), the Jēnu Kuṟumba have been deprived of their rights to forage in these forest regions. Today they are forced to live in settlements (comprising from one to twenty-five conjugal families each) at the periphery of the sanctuaries and reserve forest areas. In the latter they are, however, entitled to gather minor forest products (honey, tamarind, treemoss, soapnuts, etc.). Moving through the reserve forest areas in small, flexible camps, the Jēnu Kuṟumba gather these products throughout the year and they usually sell them to non-tribal (private or public) agents.

The Jēnu Kuṟumba I worked with constitute a small, quasi-endogamous network, similar to the micro-castes found by N. Yalman (cf. 1962), S. Barnett (1975) and G. Burkhart (1978). The network I studied embraces between 250 and 300 married persons, all related with each other through kinship ties of filiation and marriage. But, in contrast to the micro-castes, the networks of the Jēnu Kuṟumba are neither denoted by names nor situated in a hierarchical organization—therefore they do not exist as indigenous categories of the social order. This, in turn, is related to the fact that an explicit representation of their society as a totality (be it as a verbalized model or in mythology) does not exist. Likewise the Jēnu Kuṟumba do not conceptualize a clan- or moiety-system for the network or for the *jāti* as a whole.

Since there are no lineages, unilinear or agnatic descent groups, that act or define themselves as corporate units, the social order is not framed in a group model of society but rather in terms of interpersonal sociality. People in the network are situated in a chain of mutual obligations, in a moral order of kinship, that stresses, as we will see later, filiative and, most important in the context of this article, affinal bonds. Affines, *bā mayika,* i.e. all those who are bound through repeated marriage (genealogical and terminological cross-cousins: ZH-WB, MB-ZS, FZ-BD, WF-DH, HM-SW) should share among themselves, the Jēnu Kuṟumba say. They should support each other if one of them runs into difficulties (having no cloths, no money, no cigarettes, no food provisions, etc.). In the particular context of the death ritual this means that especially the husbands of the dead person's sisters and/or daughters (ZH, DH) are expected to contribute their share, as do the children or (if the person was unmarried), the parents of the dead person. But ultimately all kindred members (including the spirit of the dead person) present themselves as responsible for one another.

Within the network, there are three socio-religious offices—that of the *bandari*, that of the *yajman* and that of the *pūjari*. The *bandari* acts mainly as a mediator or messenger, calling together all concerned people for important rituals. The *yajman* on the other hand conducts, in our Western sense, the religious tasks proper. It is the *yajman* who makes offerings to the deities and to the spirits of the dead during certain public rituals, he has to take out the first handful of earth in order that a grave can be dug, etc. The *pūjari* is the mediator between the living people and their deities whenever their communication takes place in a rather private setting (i.e. in the deity's shrine). In such a setting (he has no duties in the death ritual) the *pūjari* presents offerings in a small ceremony (*pūje*) to the deity and the Jēnu Kuṟumba can speak to their deity, e.g. they can ask for the deity's support.

The deities (*deyiva*) of the Jēnu Kuṟumba are called upon and denoted as grandfather (*ettan*) or grandmother (*acci*) respectively. In principle, people are associated with at least two deities, namely, as they say, father's deity and mother's deity. Accordingly there is no unilinear prescription for all those who have a relationship with a specific deity. All people related in an active manner with a deity regard themselves as 'people of the deity' (*deyivagāru*), i.e. they consider themselves as belonging to or joining (*sēr*) this specific male or female deity.[8] In practice, however, the Jēnu Kuṟumba will, as they say, 'look after' one deity most intensively. That means that they will give offerings to it, speak with it and listen to its demands. The deity in turn looks upon the living as its children. The deity is expected to listen to its children's demands and to protect them. This is also the reason why, as we will see below, the deity wants the spirits of its dead children to live, in the form of *māya* (invisibility), in its company.

The Jēnu Kuṟumba, then, have an encompassing concept of sociality. Their sociality includes human beings, but also other social beings as deities or the spirits of the dead. And since the Jēnu Kuṟumba practice 'spirit mediumship' all these beings are able to communicate, i.e. to interact and speak with one another.

THE RITUAL (PART I)

As in many other cultures (cf. Hertz 1960; Huntington and Metcalf 1979; Bloch and Parry 1982) death rituals among the Jēnu Kuṟumba proceed in two separate phases. In the first phase no direct interaction between the living and the spirit, the main topic of the present article, takes place and I will give only a brief and generalizing summary of it here.

The first part of the rituals is, in comparison to the second part, of relatively short duration and is accomplished within a day's time. It is performed as soon as possible after a person has died and consists mainly in the burial of the dead body and public wailing. This is accomplished in several sequences of acts. First, people prepare the corpse for burial, construct and decorate a barrow and subsequently carry the corpse (which lies on the barrow) to the burial place. There they dig the grave, put the dead body in it and finally fill it with earth. All sequences involve as many of the dead person's kindred as possible. Here as in all parts of the whole ritual, not only the brothers, sisters and children of the deceased but also the affinal kinspeople play important roles. As it were, all those who regard each other as *bā-mayika* are expected to cooperate. Thus, in this first part the close male relatives (B, S, DH, ZH, WB, F, etc.) of the personal kindred help each other to carry the barrow, they dig the grave together and all (male and female) participants are expected to throw a handful of earth into the grave. Finally, when some of the male relatives have filled the grave up with earth, the one taking the position of *yajman* performs (at the head side of the grave) what the Jēnu Kuṟumba call a *pūje*. He offers a split coconut, three bananas, three incense sticks and parched rice (*puri*), together with some betelnut. After performing this small ceremony, the first phase of the ritual is accomplished.

Especially the first sequences of acts are interspersed with public mourning. Here the female relatives of the personal kindred (W, Z, D, M, FZ, M, SW, etc.) are predominantly active, but also male relatives (see aforesaid) of the deceased take part. Addressing the spirits of the dead persons directly, they bemoan that the dead persons are now alone and that they have no support any more. They articulate that the living miss the dead persons' contributions to communal life. They also memorize these contributions and tell a kind of life story of the dead persons—how good life was when the dead persons were alive and supported them. And again and again, especially the members of the dead's conjugal family express how sad they are that the dead persons are no longer with them (e.g. 'I can't eat since you left. My tears don't stop', etc.). However, in this stage of the ritual, the dead persons' spirits do not speak back. Immediately after persons have died the spirits of the dead persons (*gāḷi*) are thought to roam about in the forest. Until the second part of the death ritual is carried out the living and the spirits can't communicate with each other any more.

IN BETWEEN

The time between the two parts is, to use R. Hertz's term here (cf. 1960: 29-54), a time of intermediacy, characterized by separation and confusion. The death of a person causes a crisis, a break in social relations. Among the Jēnu Kuṟumba this concerns the social relationships among three categories of beings, namely among the living, the spirits and their deities. Kinsmen who could once claim each other's support are now separated from each other. The living can no longer expect the help and assistance of the ones who have died. The dead persons' spirits also have no one to support them and, as we will see later, they feel neglected by their kinspeople, they feel lonely and they are in a state of mind called *bějaru*, i.e. confusion, worry, being without orientation—a state of being deprived of any social life and community. Thus the spirits are roaming about without a home. In addition, the living as well as the spirits are separated from their deities and without their support.

The spirits in their miserable state of being, are homeless and separated from their deities, because they cannot reach the deities' company until their kinspeople help them and bring them to the deities through the performance of the ritual. In addition, the deities will neither speak nor listen to the living relatives of the dead persons, nor even let them into their little shrine, unless the living have made the spirits of their dead kinsmen 'to be in the company of the deity', as people say. This then, is one of the explicit intentions of the participants in the ritual—to make the spirits come together with their deities. This, however, is difficult, as we come to know when we listen to the particular ritual discourse on which the description in the present article is based.[9]

The (male) spirit, in his state of confusion, fear, and helplessness, and lacking his protecting social bonds, does not clearly know where he has to go and even whether he has strength enough to go anywhere. Moreover, he doubts that the living will do their best to relieve him of this state of suffering. And the spirit is also angry with his kindred, arguing that they did not help him before he died, that he feels neglected and not taken care of, thus suggesting that the living are somehow responsible for his death. In sum he does not trust in the support of his kindred—that they will really help him in reaching the company of the deity. He suspects that the living would rather fight with each other than take care of him (and of each other) and that they will not follow their moral obligations of kinship. In such a community the spirit does not want to leave his children behind either and he hesitates to go.

The only way to make the spirit literally go and sit with the deity is to convince him that all his worries and reproaches of improper behaviour are unfounded. In turn the participants want the spirit to tell them that he is not angry with them, that he acknowledges their doings, gives his contributions too and ultimately does not hold them responsible for his sufferings any more. And as often in times of crisis, people are not satisfied with verbal confessions but action has to be shown—that something is not only being said but also being done. Accordingly, the kinspeople demonstrate their contributions to the spirit. The participants not only claim their commitment to their moral order verbally but demonstrate and perform their social commitment. That way they convince the spirit and themselves that all (the living, the spirit and the deity) are 'one' (*ondeve*, as my informants formulated it), that all kinspeople (including the spirit of the dead) are concerned with each other's well-being, and that the moral order of kinship is being followed, i.e. that people are behaving as they should, supporting and helping each other.

For all this to happen, it is first necessary to construct what anthropologists have termed a discursive space (cf. M. Gaenszle 1992)—a space in which communication and interaction between the living and the spirit of the dead can take place. As we will see later, the *bandari* and the *yajman* play important roles in this. Yet, as it were, the Jēnu Kuṟumba think that not only the ritual specialists but everybody has to do, i.e. to contribute, something. This is the work to be done in the second part of the ritual.

THE RITUAL (PART II)

After the burial of the body, it may take weeks or months until the second part of the ritual can be carried out. In the meantime the *bandari* has to bring the people together. He visits all the members of the kindred, if necessary several times, informs them about the death, inquires about the contributions that especially the affines are willing to bring with them (food or money, so that food can be bought), and he tries to settle a convenient date for coming together. After he has accomplished this task and the kindred is gathered, the ritual starts with the first sequence of works, called 'the cutting and bringing of leaves'.

1. THE CUTTING AND BRINGING OF LEAVES (*SOPPU*)

In this first sequence all the male members of the kindred walk, guided by a special tune of music played by kin (and called the 'tune of the footpath', *dāri-koḷal*), in a line to a nearby river, to get branches with green leaves that are needed to build the small hut wherein the *gāḷi* should take his seat for a while. After reaching the river, the *yajman* selects a special tree (*oŋge-mara*) and first he performs a *pūje* at the root of this tree. This is understood as an offering to the spirit of the dead person. The offering is meant to invite the spirit to come and it initiates the ritual as a rhetorical event. Due to this offering, the spirit feels a desire (*āse*), as people say, to 'climb on someone's back' (*bennegu eragi*). That is, a person becomes a medium for the spirit.[10] Now the spirit is for the first time present among his kindred as an active participant in the ritual. And that is what his relatives expect him to do, namely, to act—to cooperate with them and support them.

In the meantime one of the younger members of the kindred has climbed the tree, has cut enough branches to build a small hut, and has thrown them down. These are now taken by the spirit and distributed among all males present. Thereafter, it is the living's turn to convince the spirit to come with them or, even better, to lead them on their way to the place in the forest where they will build a hut for him, because it cannot be taken for granted that he is able or willing to do so. He wants to be sure that all of his kinspeople have come and doubts that they will really help him. So he hesitates to come in their company and articulates his doubts through speech and a very peculiar style of body movement. He runs for some seconds, then suddenly stops, as if in pain. He looks around eventually as if searching of somebody, then he runs again, stops, and so forth. The living accompany him and walk as close as possible to him because along the way the first series of dialogues between the spirit and his kinspeople takes place.[11]

In the present case, this first dialogue is between the spirit and one of his close male relatives, the dead person's sister's son. First his sister's son asks the spirit to tell them who of his kinspeople he thinks did any wrong to him. Secondly he demands that the spirit recognize what the living are doing for him in this ritual. The spirit is asked to tell whether what they have done was good or bad and he is asked to be just with them. Furthermore, he expects the spirit to keep a friendly and supportive relationship with him after they part. He argues that they must be friends in the future, because he, the spirit, was a human being too (implying that he was the receiver of many good deeds, and that this somehow will continue to bind him). But he, the spirit, should not hesitate to go, because, of course, he has first to join the deity. And therefore the living interlocutor asks him repeatedly to go ahead and come with his people. This dialogue is clearly dominated by the living speaker. The spirit in turn most of the times gives in to the demands of his sister's son and gradually proceeds on his way. Yet—giving in to the demands he demonstrates his weakness, tiredness and confusion and thereby his need of help and support:[12]

SISTER'S SON: Make us hear one word (speech, *mātu*). One word, say one word. You stop and tell. Who, who put [black magic] in your stomach and walked [away]?[13]

SPIRIT: Oh oh, my stomach, . . . [the spirit's reply fades away].

SISTER'S SON: Hm, hm,—you, suffering confusion (*bējaru pāḍ-*), we all want to make it good. Who wants to be weak, (tired, *suḷi*) once one is coming [to be] in front of four invisibles (*māya*) [i.e. deities from both father's and mother's sides, here addressed as *māya*]?

SPIRIT: Yes, four invisibles (*māya*). . . ; [the spirit's reply fades away].

SISTER'S SON: After taking you with us, we want to be told whether it [what they did] was good or bad. *Māya*, you have been born as a social being (*mayisan*). Wherever you go, be happy (*santōsāgi*). After you have

left us, we must become friends (*oḍen*), everywhere! You give us justice (*nyāya*) [You be just].
Walk, walk, walk, otherwise you will not come over to the grandfather (*ettan*, i.e. the deity). And didn't you yourself say that you want to be made to sit with the grandfather (*ettan*) and grandmother (*acci*)? And didn't you say that you want us to make the death ritual? And what haven't we done for you yet. How many of your children have gathered?

Between these requests the spirit is not allowed to speak much about his weakness and confusion. Instead he is asked to go ahead. The spirit in turn gives in to the demands, but only to fall back into hesitation and doubt again and again. Thus he laments heavily that his stomach still hurts very much and that he cannot walk. He announces that he will tell his children what was wrong—but then he only hesitates to proceed further arguing that he can't trust his people:

SPIRIT: How can I leave my children and go to our grandfather [to the deity]?

But his sister's son simply pushes this argument aside:

SISTER'S SON: This is nothing. We will take care of them. There are huts for them [for your children] here. What is this? Walk. And don't be confused (*bējaru*).

But the spirit worries about his own future too.

SPIRIT: What, what is there [in the invisible realm]? What do you see [do you know]?
SISTER'S SON: Like with us there are huts. Where the invisibles are there are four huts. But—about this I have no knowledge (*buddi*). What it is? As it is among us. Is there not family (*kuḍumba*) and is there not strength (*bala*)? You think about us. What will happen to us if you don't go? Quick, you, in the company of our grandfather (*ettan*) we will drop you [with the grandparents in *māya*]—no?
SPIRIT: Okay, okay , if it is like this, if it is like this, I will leave you—But—I don't know, will you do it [the things that are necessary in this ritual now]?
SISTER'S SON: Don't you see how much has been done already here?
SPIRIT: Okay [the spirit gives in].
SISTER'S SON: In the company of our grandfather I will drop you. Wherever you go, be happy (*santōsāgi iru*).

This dialogue with its alternation of doubts and the refutations of these doubts, with its refusals and agreements, continues but finally the whole group reaches a wooden frame that some members of the kin group have built earlier. The whole group now circumambulates (anti-clockwise) this frame three times and puts the leafy branches on the frame. In this way the people have constructed a small hut together. Thereafter, the medium sinks to the ground. This is the sign that the spirit has left the person and returned back into the forest again.

After some hours of rest, the kindred continues with its project of building a hut and making the spirit sit there, with the second sequence:

2. THE BRINGING OF WATER AND THE CIRCUMAMBULATION OF THE PROTECTING-HUT (*UḌI-MANE*)

In this sequence the whole kindred, not only its male members, walks (as usual led by the 'tune of the footpath') again to the river. The women carry water vessels, while the *yajman* brings two small clay pots. After reaching the river bank, the *yajman* performs a *pūje* [as before an offering of bananas, coconut, incense, and parched rice] in front of the water vessels and one of the small clay pots. This is meant to ask the deity of the deceased to come. Then this small clay pot is filled with water and from now on the deity is said to reside in it.[14] Yet, someone is missing—the spirit himself. The spirit, it seems, has to be asked to come with more arguments, and this time it is done by way of a gesture expressing respect and fond memories. This gesture is performed as follows: Each of the close family members (here his wife and children) while standing in the river takes the second clay pot (called shadow pot, *neḷal-maḍake*) in both hands, turns around and bows to all four directions with the pot in both hands. Thereafter, the pot is put down on the water and as soon as water flows into the pot, this is taken as the sign that the *gāḷi* has come and dipped the pot down. In our particular case, however, he shows some hesitation to participate and refuses to come. The pot simply drifts around without water getting in, and the kinspeople start to employ other strategies to convince him to come. They weep publicly and display their grief in order to show the spirit (as some participants explained it to me) how much they miss him, how nice it was when he was among them (in his lifetime) and gave them food and clothes and how confused (*bējaru*) they feel without him. However, here as in all cases I witnessed or heard of, the spirit finally got persuaded and did come, thus indicating his willingness to be with his children and to help them.

And this is what he is expected to do, after climbing again on one kinsman's back and acting through a medium. It is the spirit himself who now has to fetch the water in the big water vessels and distribute it to the women. But nevertheless, he does not do it straight away. Again he hesitates and articulates his doubt and mistrust—and again the living are involved in a series of arguments to refute the reproaches of the spirit.

The main interlocutor with the spirit is now his wife's brother (*bā-mayidan*). His wife's brother tries to persuade the spirit that he, the spirit, should speak to them about their faults in the past. But he requests him also to recognize how seriously they all want to help him now in the ritual—he should not worry and hesitate but give them the water. The spirit however argues against that and complains that people did not share food with him in the past, that none of the children has come today to help him and that he will not go to the deity.

WIFE'S BROTHER: You who are the *māya* one, tell after you came.
SPIRIT: To distribute the water is okay for me. And you, today, you gave food to me. But before, people made bad (*mōsa*) [treated him badly].
WIFE'S BROTHER: What was wrong (*tappu*)?
SPIRIT: In ten huts, there is no mistake (*tappu*) [by his relatives], *appa*. But—why, why have people done it [sickness and death] to me? No, I cannot go.
WIFE'S BROTHER: Why?
SPIRIT: It happened to me, no?
WIFE'S BROTHER: But didn't you want us to make you sit in the protecting hut (*uḍi-mane*)? Can we leave you in the forest? Can we leave you [in your miserable state like this] after taking you with us [that far]?
SPIRIT: Okay, you do, you do, you do [the spirit gives in—only to take back]. But . . .

Here the wife's brother stops him immediately:

WIFE'S BROTHER: Don't you understand this? How can we leave you in the forest?
SPIRIT: But here is no food for me. And nobody of the children has come to help me. Not like this, *appa*, today there is no speech (*mātu*), this time there is no knowledge (*buddi*) for me, *appa*; tomorrow you catch it [the knowledge about the sickness].
WIFE'S BROTHER: Shall I tell you? You don't know. Let us be fine. You are saying all this, no? But we make you sit in the protecting hut (*uḍi-mane*). We like to do it.

Then the spirit gives in and starts to tell what his wife's brother has done wrong. For example, the spirit accuses him of not having shared food with him in the past. Against this, however, his wife's brother defends himself and denies all misbehaviour. Instead he insists that he did share with his sister's husband whenever he needed something. After a while the spirit indeed accepts, but nevertheless he refuses to forget about his other relatives' misbehaviour. Again he pretends that no people are here for his ritual, and asks:

SPIRIT: Where are the women to give the water to, where are the people?

But ultimately the spirit gives in, distributes the water and the people start to move. Nevertheless, the dialogue between the spirit and his people continues all the way to the already constructed leaf hut, towards which the whole group, led by the music, proceeds after the water vessels have been filled. These are carried by some women of the kindred, while two of the children carry the clay pots. At the same time other male members of the kindred set out to bring the foodstuff (contributed by the *ba-maiyka,* i.e. the sons of the dead person and their affinal relatives) to the small leaf hut.

When the group approaches the leaf hut the males with the food and some unmarried kinspeople (carrying pieces of burning firewood) join it. Now the whole sequence reaches a climax. Laden with the water vessels and foodstuff, and with the spirit in the middle the whole kin group circumambulates the hut three times, screaming loud and joyfully in one rhythmic voice: 'Hooo, hooo, hooo—Hooo, hooo, hooo'.

Immediately after the circumambulation, the small clay pots are put to rest in the leaf hut, the foodstuff is deposited there, and a fire is made with the burning firewood. Lastly, the spirit himself takes his place in the small clay pot after leaving the medium. Henceforth, until the next morning, the spirit and the deity are said to remain in their clay pots, in order that the people can make the spirit happy through their good deeds of eating, dancing and being happy with each other. Until the next morning, the spirit thus will be an observer and silent participant, but, to be sure, the living are fully aware of his presence. (My interlocutors were clear that the spirit was aware, indeed was the addressee, of their deeds even now.)

After the spirit has taken his place in the pot, the *yajman* erects a wooden pole (*ranga kamba,* festival- or dancing pole), adorned with leaves from the small hut, in the vicinity of the *uḍi-mane* and performs a *pūje* in front of it. Then, gradually, the living males start to dance in circles around the *ranga kamba,* accompanied by their musicians, who play the 'tune of the dance' (*āṭa-koḷalu*). A little later the women (married and unmarried) dance in a separate circle, at a distance from the males (The women have no instruments but clap their hands and sing). This dancing lasts the whole night, and the dancers will only make a break when the food is ready and has been distributed to everybody (by those who cooked it). The *gāḷi,* of course, gets his share first from the *yajman,* who offered a small portion of the cooked food.

This demonstration of being united in joyful common action lasts the whole night because it is a contribution in the ongoing discourse between the living and the spirit of the dead. It is a speaking act too, intended as my interlocutors explained to me, *to make the spirit happy.*

However, whether the doings of his children have really made him happy—i.e. convinced him that his people were taking care of him and had contributed their deeds in accordance with the moral order—this the spirit himself will say when the ritual proceeds further the next morning.

3. MAKING THE SPIRIT TO 'JOIN THE DEITY' (*DEYIVA*)

First his close family members (here wife and children) perform a rite in the course of which the spirit indicates symbolically, by non-verbal signs, whether or not he is willing to leave the living and join his deity. In that rite the small clay pot (where the deity is said to have taken its seat) is taken out of the leaf hut. The family members, one after the other, put two drops of oil in this pot which is still filled with water. If the drops come together, this is taken as a sign that the spirit is willing to join the deity. At the same time this means, as my informants explained, that his family members have done well.

As soon as the spirit indicates his willingness to be united with his deity, the unification is ceremoniously enacted. The spirit and the deity, both still in their clay pots, are now brought in a procession, again led by music, to a tree in the forest. At the bottom of the tree, the *yajman* erects a small stone (approx. 7 inches in height), performs a *pūje* (as usual with incense, bananas, coconut and parched rice) and then pours the water of both pots down on the stone. This is interpreted by the participants as their ultimate contribution to 'making the spirit to sit in the company of the deity'.

However, the ritual process proceeds beyond that point. The living want to make sure that the spirit is really satisfied with their deeds. And they want to know whether he is happy and has reached the deity. And the spirit too has the desire (*āse,* as the Jēnu Kuṟumba say), to speak with his people. As soon as he has climbed on the medium's back to speak through it, his people approach him impatiently:

PEOPLE: What, tell, tell. Whether it was good or bad, you tell. All that is here, tell!

In reply the spirit first addresses one of his sons:

SPIRIT: Okay, okay, I looked at the back side, looked in front, looked on the left side, for you I give words. My son. . . .

And then he reports, that his deity, grandfather Uncigal (*uncigal-ettan*), was standing in front of him:

SPIRIT: Grandfather Uncigal was standing, grandfather Uncigal himself. My son, what has been done [was good], that way for you is justice (*nyāya*).

Then he addresses his second son—but again displays weakness, confusion and helplessness, thus leaving the second son doubtful about this son's deeds and thus doubtful about whether he, the spirit, has really taken his place in the company of the deity.

SPIRIT: I am here. *Appa,* I am here. I don't know. I stand here with empty hands. I must remain here like this.

But then, suddenly, he changes his mind and says that indeed he was in the company of his deities:

SPIRIT: Aah, it was my grandfather, it was my grandmother, it is my friends. My grandfather, grandmother, today I have been taken by my people, and didn't they [all participants] give immediately? What has been done, what has been given [is good].

But now he turns to the assembly and puts the deeds of his relatives and accordingly his own well-being into question again:

SPIRIT: Okay, my son gave, but what deeds (*karma*) did he give [what are the consequences of his deeds]?

However, now the *yajman* himself intervenes and tries to bring this no doubt serious play to an end:

YAJMAN: You must say it.

But the spirit is still doubtful:

SPIRIT: What deeds did he give?
YAJMAN: You must say. If you say it, we will know, if you don't say it, how can we know [whether this son also did well]? No, you show it (*tōrsnu*)—(Now you tell!

And now, suddenly, the spirit puts an end to all doubts and tells everybody:

Spirit: This being said—concerning me, for you justice is there. Now there is grandfather Uncigal. Deity Uncigal.
YAJMAN: Is it?
SPIRIT: Now there is grandmother! [i.e. the deity].

With this remark the spirit leaves his people and the medium sinks to the ground. Thereafter, the spirit's immediate family members (wife, children) offer some food on the grave for the dead person. Now the ritual is really over. The spirit, as the participants told me, is happy (*santōsa*) and has taken his place in the company of the deities.

CONCLUSION

In the ritual process I have decribed here, death appeared as a metaphor for what happens if social relations break down. Death led to separation and as voiced and demonstrated by the spirit, it led to confusion, weakness and loneliness. But it was also interpreted as a violation of the moral order of the community. The spirit reproached his relatives for wrong behaviour towards him, suggesting their responsibility for his suffering. Death led him to suspect the living that these are unwilling to live according to the moral order of kinship and led to suspicion and mistrust. But to accomplish the goal of the ritual—the unification of the spirit with his deity—the participants had to overcome this crisis in relatedness.

To accomplish that, the living had to bring forth convincing arguments. Recognizing this discursive and rhetorical aspect, we could understand the ritual, with J. Fernandez (cf. 1986 and 1991), as a 'colloquial process' where words and symbolic actions (or better, deeds) are employed as arguments. All males contributed the leafy branches. The women the water. The sons, daughters and their affines carried the food. Other, unmarried, members of the kindred contributed the firewood. Affines cooked the food, male members played the music, female members carried the water pots, children the deity. They all together contributed to the construction of the 'protecting hut' for the spirit to sit in. These deeds were employed as arguments to convince the spirit that his mistrust and his suspicion of the asociality of his relatives were unfounded.

The verbal rhetoric underlined and enforced these 'speaking acts'. The people asked the spirit to come with them, to go forward, to take his place in the protecting hut and to reach the deities. They assured him that they had come together to help him. But the living actors asked the spirit also to talk about their deeds. The living wanted the spirit to acknowledge their deeds and to do them justice, instead of holding them—the living—responsible for his sufferings. Instead of reproaches and mistrust they wanted justice and reconciliation. In fact, the spirit's reproaches of wrong behaviour were used by the living simply as opportunities to convince the spirit that his reproaches were unfounded. The reproaches were always denied with verbal arguments that pointed out the contributions that the people had made. To be sure, the spirit created a dramatic atmosphere through his continued refusals to go forward and his demands that action be carried out for him. But he could not ignore the good deeds of his relatives and gave appropriate answers. He trusted his relatives, he joined them, he distributed leafy branches, he gave water to the women, etc. Finally he confirmed that his people had acted well and that his mistrust was unfounded.

For the time being, the actors were successful with their arguments. Death was an event that made words and deeds 'fly apart'. But the people argued against that. The spirit was gradually convinced that his kinspeople are committed to him and to the moral order of kinship. Social life was reconstructed as a household where relatives take care of and help each other. In the ritual they gradually realized an image of social life as protection, support and mutual care. They performed the ritual as a process where, as J. Fernandez (1986: 42) has argued, metaphors can be taken literally. Here people really did what they said. This sincere nexus of words and deeds allowed the participants to, quite literally, move the spirit. They thus transformed loneliness into communion and doubt and suspicion into trust. That made the spirit happy. The spirit could leave the living happily and reach the deities.

Henceforth social life, based on trust again, can proceed. The dead kinsman will certainly help and support the living in the future—though from a new, invisible, social position. Accordingly, the communication between the living and the dead does not end with the death-ritual. Their conversation will continue in other discourses (as, e.g. in healing rituals). The people will continue to live in a nexus of words and deeds—provided, of course, that the living and the spirit of the dead are ready for a further exchange of arguments.[15]

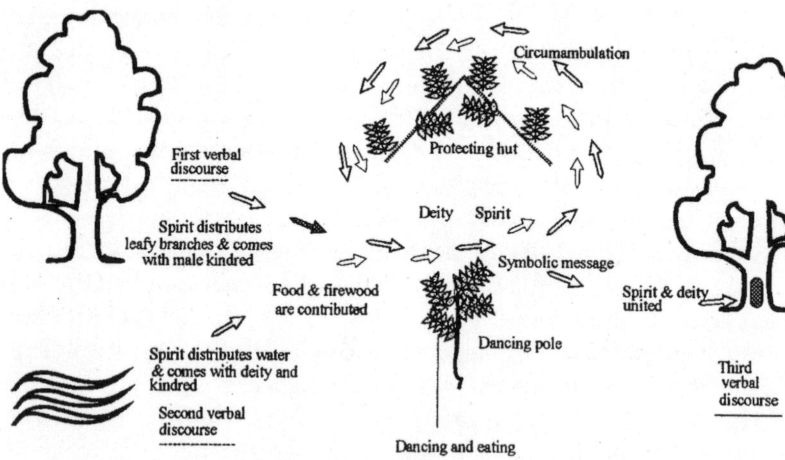

Fig.1. Synopsis of the death ritual.

NOTES

1. Not all consequences of a death are taken up in ritual. For example, death, because it is in general thought of as a caused and intended event, often leads relatives of the dead to strive for retaliation. This is done through a series of acts of black magic, in order to harm or kill the person (s) regarded responsible for the death of the relative. Yet these retaliatory acts are not

accomplished in the death ritual itself but in the post-history of the ritual proper. Keeping this in mind, the present article will address only those consequences of death, that are in fact met with and taken up by the participants in this ritual event.

2. The living and the dead communicate with each other (through 'spirit mediumship'. Cf. E. Schoembucher 1993 for this type of possession) also in other settings, e.g. in healing rituals. Dialogues between living and dead people are also described for other cultures in India (cf. E. Schoembucher this volume and P. Vitebsky 1993).
3. In all cases I know, the death of a member of the community was understood as an intended result of other people's actions. The Jēnu Kuṟumba assumed that the death was caused by another Jēnu Kuṟumba, who employed black magic. For example, a snake bite resulting in death was interpreted as the result of black magic that had caused the snake to bite this very person.
4. For another context, cf. U. Demmer, forthcoming.
5. I worked with the Jēnu Kuṟumba of the northern Nilgiris for three years (in stints of 23, 3, 6, 2 and 4 months) between October 1987 and December 1994. I wish to acknowledge the support of the Deutsche Forschungsgemeinschaft, the DAAD and the Friedrich Naumann-Foundation, whose scholarships made my work possible. I also wish to thank Martin Fuchs for his helpful critique of an earlier version of this article. Last but not the least I wish to thank my wife and colleague Miriam Gossel for her help in all stages of my work. Of course, responsibility for the remaining shortcomings rests exclusively with me.
6. This does not mean that I wish to deny a semantic level of symbols and exegesis. Cf. Tambiah (1979) for the interdependence of the two levels.
7. Cf. Bibliography.
8. All those joining one deity (between 20 and 50 adults) have in common their relationship vis-à-vis that deity. But, as far as I can see now, they do not share any obligations or rights in land or property, so that these people neither act nor regard themselves as corporate groups.
9. The following description is based on a ritual that was performed for a male elder. I visited him for some days because he complained about severe stomach pain. I tried to convince him to come with me to a hospital but he refused continually, arguing that black magic caused his problems and he died after four days. His spirit is addressed either in the third person singular, masculine or sometimes as *māya.*
10. As we will see, he will 'climb on someone's back' more than once in the course of this ritual and indeed on several other persons' backs too. Among the people I work with, there are several elderly males who become media for the spirits of the dead or for the deities. For them to act that way is not dependent on anything but their experience and their being males. Women never become media.
11. The texts that follow below are by no means exhaustive. The actual dialogues are, in this case and in general, much longer and may last up to one hour each. Within the framework of this article it is impossible to cite them more extensively.

12. The translation is as *verbatim* as possible. But utterances like panting, groaning, etc., and bodily expressions like shivering, weakness, reeling, etc., are left out, even though they are very important messages. My own explanations of utterances are put in square brackets.
13. This refers to the conviction that his death was caused by somebody putting something into his stomach by black magic.
14. However, some of my interlocutors said that not only one but several deities—three or four—enter into it. Indeed in the following dicourses the spirit and the living too speak of more than one deity. This makes sense because every person indeed has relations with at least two deities (cf. ethnography above) but very close relations with only one.
15. Such an exchange takes place for example in healing rituals where the living, the dead and the deities work out the moral responsibilities for the illness of the patients.

REFERENCES

Barnett, S. 1975. Coconuts and Gold: Relational Identity in a South Indian Caste. *Contributions to Indian Sociology*. (NS) 10 (1): 133-56.

Bloch, M. and J. Parry (eds.). 1982. *Death and the Regeneration of Life*. Cambridge, London: Cambridge University Press.

Census of India Publications. 1961. Vol. IX, Part V-B(1), Preface. Vol. XI, Part V-A. Vol. VII, Part V-A, p.125.

———. 1971. Series 19, Part IX, p. 227; Series 9, Part II-C(I), p. 215.

Burkhart, G. 1978. Marriage Alliance and the Local Circle among some Udayars of South India. In S. Vatuk (ed.), *American Studies in the Anthropology of India*. pp. 171-211. New Delhi: Manohar.

Carrithers, M. 1992. *Why Humans Have Cultures. Explaining Anthropology and Social Diversity*. Oxford, New York: Oxford University Press.

Demmer, U. forthcoming. Voices in the Forest: The Configuration of the Field of Gathering among the Jēnu Kuṟumba (South India). In: P. Hockings (ed.), *Blue Mountains Revisited: Cultural Studies on the Nilgiri Hills*. New Delhi: Oxford University Press.

Fernandez, J. 1986. *Persuasions and Performances. The Play of Tropes in Culture*. Bloomington: Indiana University Press.

———. (ed.) 1991. *Beyond Metaphor: The Theory of Tropes in Anthropology*. Stanford: Stanford University Press.

Gaenzle, M. 1992. The Text Within: Studies of Oral Ritual Texts in Nepal in the Last Decade (Review Article). *European Bulletin of Himalayan Research*. 3: 5-16.

Hertz, R. 1960. *Death and the Right Hand* (1st publ. in French: 1907). Aberdeen: Cohen & West.

Huntington, R. and P. Metcalf (eds.). 1979. *Celebrations of Death: The Anthropology of Mortuary Rituals*. Cambridge, London: Cambridge University Press.

Myers, F. 1986. *Pintupi Country, Pintupi Self: Sentiment, Place and Politics among*

Western Desert Aborigines. Washington, D.C.: Smithsonian Institution Press.

———. 1988. Burning the Truck and Holding the Country: Property, Time and the Negotiation of Identity among Pintubi Aborigines. In T. Ingold, D. Riches, J. Woodburn (eds.), *Hunters and Gatherers*. 2: 52-75. London: Berg.

Nietzsche, F. 1975. *Zur Genealogie der Moral. Eine Streitschrift* (1st ed. 1887). Berlin: Goldmann.

Sarbin, Th. R. 1986. Emotion and Act: Roles and Rhetoric. In Rom Harre (ed.), *The Social Construction of Emotions*. Oxford: Basil Blackwell.

Schömbucher, E. 1993. Gods, Ghosts, and Demons: Possession in South Asia. In H. Brückner, L. Lutze and A. Malik (eds.), *Flags of Fame: Studies in South Asian Folk Culture*. New Delhi. Manohar.

———. This volume. Death as the Beginning of a New Life: Hero-Worship among a South Indian Fishing Caste.

Tambiah, S. 1979. A Performative Approach to ritual. In *Proceedings of the British Academy* 65: 113-69. Oxford: Oxford University Press.

Tyler, S. 1987. *The Unspeakable. Discourse, Dialogue, and Rhetoric in the Postmodern World*. Madison: University of Wisconsin Press.

Vitebsky, P. 1993. *Dialogues with the Dead. The discussion of mortality among the Sora of eastern India*. Cambridge: Cambridge University Press (Cambridge Studies in Social and Cultural Anthropology 88).

Yalman, N. 1962. The Structure of the Sinhalese Kindred: a Reexamination of the Dravidian Terminology. In *American Anthropologist* 64: 548-73.

Mourning, Mortuary Exchange and Memorialization

The Creation of Local Communities among Dalits in Gujarat

SHALINI RANDERIA

Death is a highly visible occurrence and a frequent and familiar experience in the villages of Gujarat. This does not mean that it fails to generate intense emotions or that it is ungrudgingly accepted. Mortuary rites are the most complex, protracted and elaborate of all life-cycle rituals among the Dalits, as I prefer to call the 'untouchable castes', using the relatively recent term of collective self-reference coined by them.[1] These rites are of greater social and ritual significance than those of birth, pregnancy or marriage. This is not only because death is the most potent source of impurity, necessitating a series of rituals to phase out mourning (*śok*) and gradually reduce pollution (*sūtak*). Mortuary rites, and especially memorial feasts which constitute their climax, are the very occasions on which the caste is created as a locally defined is *nāt*, the very word for caste in Gujarati.[2]

This paper is based on data generated during sixteen months of fieldwork among the Dalits in several villages of Sabarkantha and Mehsana districts (north Gujarat) in 1983-4, 1987 and 1990. The discrete set of the lowest castes grouped together under the label 'Dalit' is not a monolithic bloc, but internally differentiated into many endogamous groups traditionally following different occupations.[3] The castes whose mortuary rituals are considered here are the Garo (priests), Vankar (weavers), Chamar (tanners), Tidgar (bow-and-arrow-makers), Turi (musicians-cum-genealogists), Shenava (basket-makers) and the Bhangi (scavengers and cremation ground attendants).[4] Regional differences and minor variations in the mortuary practices of different castes are ignored so as to focus on a number of common themes. I have been present at the rituals described here between three to five times in different castes and villages.

Apart from ending liminality and bringing about a reintegration of the social world with the cosmic world (Das 1977), mortuary rituals serve to present as a whole the social fabric which has been torn through the death of a member. Not surprisingly, therefore, these rituals are the occasions on which 'the society of the living regularly recreates itself' (Hertz 1960: 72). Following Hertz, they have been interpreted as rites of transition which equally affect the body and soul of the deceased and the mourners (e.g. Huntington and Metcalf 1979).

Hertz has shown that implicitly, if not explicitly, funerals everywhere have a dual aspect—the separation of the individual from society, followed by the reaffirmation of society's victory over death. Among the Dalits in Gujarat the category of mortuary ritual action includes three types of performance—rites of burial; post-burial rites, which correspond to Hertz's first stage, the phasing out of mourning and death pollution; and a spectacular climactic mortuary feast, which fulfils the functions he attributes to secondary burials. Contrary to Hertz's idea of a reified 'society' reasserting itself in the face of the disintegration caused by death, I follow Bloch and Parry (1982) in arguing that mortuary rituals are occasions for the production of social order. As Bloch puts it, 'Death as disruption, rather than being a problem for the social order, as anthropologists have tended to think of it, is in fact an opportunity for dramatically creating it' (Bloch and Parry 1982: 218-19).

However, the mortuary rituals of the Dalits do not reaffirm an abstract idea of a moral order but instead generate verbal and visual images of locally situated communities of kin, affines and neighbours at various levels within the caste. These rituals are occasions for the production of the social group but also for the creation of locality. In this context the ritual life of every Dalit caste unfolds at four levels—agnatically related households (*bhāionā ghar, kākā kutumb*), the co-residential community in the village (*vās, vastī*), the territorially defined sub-unit of the caste (*paragṇū*) and its smaller sub-divisions (*vibhāg, bhaipāna gām*). The performance of a prolonged sequence of death rites periodically achieves group unity, reproducing and strengthening social relationships at various levels of local communities from the *vās* to the *paragṇū*. Various mortuary rituals also produce the hierarchy of these local communities within the caste, in which each lower level is encompassed by the level above it.

The memorial feasts for those who have lived a long and fulfilled life, in which these rites culminate, create the hierarchy of local levels and the wholeness and sacredness of the caste (*nāt*), or more specifically of the local sub-caste (*paragṇū*), and the caste assembly and its leaders (*panch*). These feasts are occasions for joyful celebrations, the competitive exchange of intercaste and intracaste prestations, the lavish consumption of food, the enhancement of prestige, the exercise of oratorial skills, the ostentatious display of wealth and the affirmation of authority in the face of challenges. Their organization is the prerogative of the community's elders, who give permission to host such feasts, supervise the cooking and oversee the exchange of gifts. And they are the only context in which the caste leaders are brought into the *vastī* in a colourful procession, accompanied by music and drums, and honoured individually and collectively through gifts of money.

Narrative presentations at these events emphasize the sacredness of the *panch* (caste assembly and caste elders) and the *paragṇū*, both of which are referred to metaphorically as God (*Parmeshwar*) or the river Ganges (*Gangā*). It is the legitimate authority of the *panch* and the moral order of the *paragṇū* which are reasserted at these events. To speak in this context of the *paragṇū* is to affirm the idea of a whole produced from its parts (villages, or rather *vās*) and of the unity and permanence of this locally situated community. Members of a caste scattered in different exogamous villages belonging to the *paragṇū* reconvene at mortuary rituals to enact dramatically their ideal unity, to locate themselves in a spatially defined community of kin and affines, and to maintain its boundaries vis-à-vis other such local communities within their own caste. The celebration symbolizes the integration of the *paragṇū* or the caste—both referred to by the Dalits as '(our) society' [(*amāro*) *samāj*]—in the face of disruption and reasserts order in the face of the chaos caused by death.

In this respect, my data on the Dalits in Gujarat is much closer to the non-Indian cases considered in the Bloch and Parry volume (1982) than it is to Parry's Hindu material from Banaras (Bloch and Parry 1982: 74-86, Parry 1994). Remarking on the difference between the Hindu case and the Merina or the Lugbara, for example, Parry formulates this contrast: 'But while elsewhere the mortuary rituals guarantee the continuation of specific groups, in Benares they re-enact the creation of the whole universe and regenerate the cosmic order. The real difference between this case and the others is the difference between a system in which the mortuary rituals dissolve the fundamental units of society into an *undifferentiated* universe, and those systems where they shore up these units and give them a permanent and transcendental value' (Bloch and Parry 1982: 38; italics in original).

In talking about death rituals, Dalits foreground the sociology of performance rather than the cosmology of the rites, which rather few ritual specialists are able to explicate. In my analysis, I follow the Dalit discourse in privileging social, political and strategic interests over symbolic meanings, theology and cosmological aspects of mortuary practices.

POST-BURIAL RITES: THE PHASING OUT OF MOURNING AND POLLUTION

Most Dalit castes in rural Gujarat bury their dead. They are not allowed to use the Muslim burial ground, if any, on the outskirts of a village. Each Dalit caste buries its own dead separately in an undemarcated area outside the boundary, close to its own settlement on the edge of the village. The burial, in an unmarked grave, is a simple affair carried out by male kin and affines. The body is placed facing south, the direction associated with death in Hinduism. The chief mourner (the deceased's son or brother's son) touches the toe of the dead body (the right toe of a male corpse, the left toe of a female corpse) with fire brought from the domestic hearth. Relatives then fill in the grave and place stones on it to prevent animals from digging it up. The Bhangi families who take turns to collect gifts from the cremation and burial grounds of the village, take away the wooden bier, the clothes of the deceased and the utensils used for pouring water at the burial (Randeria 1989).

Some informants told me that burial was preferred as a cheaper substitute for cremation, while others emphatically stated that the body should not be burnt: 'dust it is, it should be returned to dust' (*māṭī che, māṭīmā samāvavun joyīe*). The practice often varies according to the village or caste and sometimes even within the same caste, a few lineages (*kuḷ*) cremating their dead while most bury them. Thus the few instances of cremation among the Dalits reflect neither individual preference nor a recent change in practice.

Death pollution affects different degrees of kin and affines, men and women, for varying lengths of time. It is gradually and successively phased out over a long period of mourning lasting several months, a process in which the *kunvāsī* (married sisters and daughters) are responsible for reintegrating their natal kin into the community. Mourning is considered to render both grief and pollution publicly visible. Both are associated primarily with women, though men too outwardly manifest their sorrow and impurity, for example, by not shaving, or by covering their heads with a rough piece of cloth (*fāḍīyun*) instead of the usual cap or turban. I was often closely questioned by my Dalit hosts on mourning practices in Germany, my conversation partners invariably concluding from the lack of visible signs and protracted rituals of mourning that grief and affection for the deceased were absent. Despite the presence of ritual specialists among the Dalits (Garo priests, Shenava barbers and Bhangi burial-and-cremation-ground attendants), who perform various death-related duties, women play a pivotal part in the lessening of mourning during the first twelve days after a death.

Ritualized wailing, both individual and collective, is the work of women, as is the giving and receiving of condolences. As conduits of gifts between their natal and conjugal families, women are also responsible for phasing out and ending the grief and mourning of their natal kin. Close women relatives (e.g. W, Z, D, SW, BW) of the deceased keep their faces entirely covered during this period, do not oil or comb their hair, and take off their nose-rings, which symbolize their married status. All male relatives, agnates and affines, who have attended the burial, as well as other 'close relatives' (*aḍīne sagū*) to whom death pollution (*sūtak*) 'attaches', have their heads and moustaches shaved (*vāḷ ane mūch utrāve*) in a rite known as *sunvāḷā kāḍhvān.*

There was considerable disagreement among my informants as to the exact categories of kin and affines affected by pollution. Many men pointed out that those working in schools and offices, young men at college, etc., no longer adhere strictly to these conventions. But most stressed the importance of affection (*lāgṇi*) or grief (*dukh*) and emotional attachment to the deceased, as determining their actions rather than closeness of genealogical connection. Similarly, when I enquired about the gift-giving obligations of various categories of relatives at mortuary rituals, my informants emphasized that 'kinship is a matter of care/caring' (*sāchavaye eṭlun sagpaṇ*) and that the exchange of prestations expresses affection and nurtures relationships rather than simply reflecting the degree of kinship ties. Relationships are inseparable from gift-giving obligations, or rather, the ritual obligation of exchange constitutes relationships.

The Garo, as domestic priests to all the Dalit castes except the Bhangi (considered to be beyond the pale for their ritual association with the cremation ground), perform mortuary rites only for their Weaver and Tanner 'customers' (*gharāk*). In the absence of an untouchable caste of Barbers, the Garo act in this capacity for the Weavers and Tanners in Sabarkantha district, a role which is performed by the much lower caste of Shenava in the adjoining district of Mehsana. As barbers to the Weavers and Tanners, they not only regularly shave their clients and trim their hair (*vatun karvun*), but are also responsible for shaving the heads of male mourners affected by death pollution (*sunvāḷā kāḍhvān*). The former is no longer so important, as hair-cutting facilities in cities and larger towns are available to men of all castes, but the latter, the more polluting of the two duties, which the Garo are increasingly seeking to give up, is a bone of contention between them and their 'customers' (Randeria 1989: 179).

The first, severe phase of pollution ends on the third, fifth or seventh day following a death, the day on which *lokāhī* is performed. Until then, no food is cooked in the household of the dead person or his 'close agnates' (*aḍīne sagū* or *bhāīyonā ghar*), all of whom receive food and tea from their more 'distant agnates' (*cheṭīnū sagū*) or fellow caste-mates in the *vās.* On the day of *lokāhī,* relatives from all the villages in which the dead person has kin and affines arrive at his house 'to rinse their mouths' (*kogaḷo karvā*). This acceptance of water from the household of the deceased marks the resumption of commensality as a first step towards the lessening of mourning and pollution.

The number of relatives who 'come to weep' at *lokāhī* is seen as an index of the status of the dead person and his or her family. Each of his or her female relatives (e.g. MBW, MBD, MZ, WeZ), especially the *kunvāsī*

(FZ, Z, ZD, D, DD, FBD), mobilizes a large number of women from her caste in her own conjugal village to accompany her on the mourning visit. How many women she can gather together depends on the size and influence of her husband's family, her own personal networks of friendship, the number of women to whom she can trace connections through her natal kin, the number of women from her natal village who are married into her conjugal village, etc. Her prestige depends on the number of women mourners (known as *sāth*) she can marshal.

During my stay in Mau in 1987, old Punjima, a Tanner woman more feared for her sharp tongue than respected, was trying to persuade several women to join her the next day in mourning for her eldest sister. Many of the women pleaded that they could not afford to forego a day's wage as agricultural labourers, an argument she accepted with bad grace. She then went to the house of her HBSW, a school teacher, but Laduben pointed to her inability to go to *lokāhī* on a working day. Punjima left the house shouting furiously that these days, one was forced to die keeping holidays in mind.

The groups of women mourners not only provide an intricate social map of the relationships of the dead person but also map the caste as a local community. The men who come to offer their condolences enter the village of the dead person individually as and when they arrive, while the women mourners sit waiting outside the village boundary in order to regroup themselves according to their conjugal villages. The groups, each led by a close kinswoman or affine of the dead man, enter the *vās* at intervals. Each is announced by naming the woman leading it and the name of her husband's village (e.g. 'Maniben has brought the *sāth* from Hathrol'). The women enter the village wailing loudly, their saris completely covering their faces. They stop at the edge of the *vās* lamenting in a circle before entering it in file. They then proceed directly to the house of the deceased and enter it, past the men who are silently sitting outside or talking in hushed voices.

The visiting women weep and lament together with the women of the deceased's household. After a while, each of the visitors seats herself opposite one of the grieving women of the household, swaying to and fro with her while she laments, consoles her, strokes her head and urges her to stop crying. Each visitor gives a 'mourning gift' of ten paisa but receives no prestation in return. The women then leave the house, rinsing their mouths with water from a pot kept outside, before going off to visit other relatives in the *vās*. After a few minutes, the next group of women mourners enters the house. In talking about *lokāhī*, women foreground their attachment (*lāgṇī*) for their dead relative, their expression of grief through weeping and lamenting, and their need to express solidarity with the kinswomen of the deceased and the women of their *vās* by accompanying them in the *sāth.* The men represent these occasions as the women getting a day off with the opportunity to visit their kinswomen in order to exchange news and gossip.

Prior to the streamlining and economy drive in every Dalit caste during the last three decades to 'reform' (*sudhār*) mortuary practices, which limited the *lokāhī* ceremony to a single day, mourners were free to go for *lokāhī* on the third, fifth, seventh and ninth day after a death. They used to be served a plain meal of boiled rice and lentils (*khichaḍī*) and vegetables, a practice known as *kān sāchavavī.* The acceptance by kin and affines in the *paragṇū* of food cooked in the deceased's household marked a further lifting of pollution and the gradual reintegration of the dead person's household into the local community at a level higher than that of the *vās.*

Over the past 30 years most Dalit castes in north Gujarat have given up the practice of *kāṇ,* though it continues to be a matter of some controversy. Several 'caste constitutions' explicitly forbid it and have fixed a fine to be levied on the host (a lump sum or sum per person fed) for a violation of the new rule. Punjima, the elderly Tanner woman whom I accompanied on *lokāhī,* brought up the matter when we went to mourn her elder sister. Calling aside her sister's sons, she reminded them of their duty towards their mother. She felt that their mother, widowed at a young age, had had to suffer great hardship in order to educate them and was, therefore, entitled to this honour. To the arguments of her nephews that *kāṇ* had been discontinued ever since they could remember and that the *panch* would levy a fine, she replied, 'What has been abolished can always be revived. You pay for the meal, I will take care of the fine.'

Whereas *kāṇ* reestablishes commensality with the kin and affines of the deceased at the level of the *paragṇū,* the practice of *kāndhiyun* which precedes it by a few days marks the recommencement of food exchange at the level of the village. The family of the dead person distributes 350 gram of uncooked rice and lentils as also 50 gram of *ghee* per adult person to each household in the *vās,* which cooks the *khichaḍī* for itself. Being intensely affected by death pollution, the dead men's household can only distribute uncooked food (*kāchū sidhā*) to its own caste members, using the purest medium of food exchange usually reserved for transactions with the higher caste of Garo priests. *Kāndhiyun,* which produces a local community of kin and neighbours at the level of the *vās,* constitutes the minimal requirement for a resumption of commensality with fellow caste members. Poor or tight-fisted men who have performed only *kāndhiyun* and failed to host other higher level mortuary feasts thereafter are subjected to the lifelong taunt *kāndhiyo.* A less derogatory term, *bāramiyo,* is used for men who resort to the somewhat more expensive option of combining a meal for the relatives with the twelfth-day ritual of *bārmun,* instead of holding a higher order mortuary feast (*kānotrun, nāt*).

Whereas women predominate at the *lokāhī,* the ritual of *sarāmaṇū* on the eleventh or twelfth day (also called *bārmun,* 'the twelfth') is a mainly male affair. Male affines, close and distant, as well as *kunvāsī,* married sisters and daughters, return to the village of the deceased person 'to give water' (*paṇī dēva*). Seated outside the house with the Garo priest, the chief mourner forms balls of rice (*pinḍ*) mixed with *ghee* (clarified butter). Each relative sprinkles water on these balls, saying, 'eat this last meal and drink this last water'. The Garo priest collects the five or ten paisa coins left there by each mourner. In addition, he receives a fee (*dakṣiṇā*), a few kilograms of wheat and a few grams of ghee, the copper utensil used to mix the *pinḍ* and the new loincloth worn by the chief mourner. From her natal kin, the widow receives a sari and also a heavy silver bangle to replace her glass bangles, which were smashed after the burial. Similarly the natal kin of each of the women married into the dead person's household is responsible for 'changing the mourning sari' (*shokno sadlo badlāvavo*) of its own *kuṇvāsī.* Each wife-giver comes with a sari for his daughter or sister, who is married to the deceased's sons, brothers or brother's sons. Similarly, all the married Z, D, ZD, DD of the deceased receive saris from their own natal families in order to 'break/chase away the mourning' (*shok bhāngva/ bhagāvava*) of the latter. These *kunvāsī* bring wheat, ghee and *gol* (jaggery) or sugar from their conjugal homes to cook the first sweet after a death in their natal family, symbolizing an end to their mourning.[5]

The stage is now set for the central ceremony of 'mourning exchange' (*shokno vahevār*) between wife-givers and wife-takers. Male agnates of the dead man (referred to as 'owners of mourning' or *shoknā dhaṇī*) form a circle inside the house to receive gifts of money from their male affines. The Garo who officiates at this ritual is not the family priest but the one holding the hereditary office of *pradhān* (chief) to the *paragṇū.* He calls out village by village, the name of the male affine who is asked to 'offer mourning' (*shok āpvo*) in the form of a specified sum of money. At the *sarāmaṇū* for Dhanabhai, a prominent Weaver leader, at which I was present in 1983 there were 68 transactions with affines from 22 villages. These were divided into three categories according to the closeness of the affinal tie. For example, his DH, ZH, ZDH and WyZH were asked to give a rupee each, his DDH, WZDH, MBDH and SWeZH fifty paisa each and his FZDDH and SWMZDH twenty-five paisa each. All these gifts were noted down village by village in a list which also contained the names of absent affines along with the amount outstanding, to be recovered at a later date. Next morning, each affine received in return (*vaḷtar*) double the amount he had been asked to give the previous evening. All those who had been asked to give a rupee also received a sari.

PARAGṆŪ AND *PANCH*: CASTE AND LOCALITY

Spatially defined communities provide the framework for mortuary exchanges. At the same time, these rituals are the context in which local communities are produced, so that mortuary feasts and territoriality are in turn ground and figure. Although represented as memorial feasts for the deceased, the latter's body is not the object of the ritual and there is no reference to his person, biography or achievements in the ritual oratory, which valorizes the moral order of the local community.

Although locality is marked at other life-course rituals as well, mortuary rites are the only occasions at which the entire *paragṇū* is represented as a whole. For example, towards the end of the *sīmant* ritual in the seventh month of pregnancy, the names of each of the villages from which invitees are present is called out. The host honours each village, in turn by making a small gift of money (ten or twenty-five paisa) to one male guest who embodies his village. However, the only life-cycle rituals at which representatives of all the villages of a *paragṇū* must participate are mortuary rituals. And the presence of at least one representative from each village of the *paragṇū* is the *sine qua non* for the successful hosting of a mortuary feast.

Although joyous occasions celebrated like a 'second wedding', mortuary feasts are nevertheless tense affairs as they are inextricably entangled in the politics of affinal alliances. Considerable uncertainty accompanies the preparations in the weeks between the *sarāmaṇū* and the feast. Smouldering subliminal tensions in the host lineage, *vās* or *paragṇū* can erupt into the open, and 'private' grievances turn into 'public' issues. Unresolved affinal conflicts (a broken engagement, the estrangement from a husband for ill-treatment, a separation without divorce before the *panch*, the custody of children following a divorce or remarriage) must either be resolved or suppressed for the time being.

The pervasive feeling among the Dalits is that *vās* and *paragṇū* are constantly threatened by division, that social relationships are fragile in nature, and the composition of the local community is inherently unstable. A *paragṇū* is not a rigid bounded structure with fixed boundaries and unchanging constituent villages but one whose boundaries must be carefully maintained. Mortuary feasts are markers of space and time in the shared history of a *paragṇū*, which is a fluid conglomeration with a tendency towards fission, realignment and fusion. Strenuous work is necessary periodically to create a spatially defined community bound through mutual exchange and to produce a sense of continuity over time.

In his ethnography on the Pramalai Kallar of Tamil Nadu, Dumont (1986) separates kinship as a process of social formation from politics and territoriality. For him, society is limited to the domain of caste, with kinship as the fundamental principle of organization. As Dirks (1987: 257-8) has rightly pointed out, although for Dumont territory can create political units, it has no social value, being irrelevant for descent or alliance relations. Contrary to Dumont, Dirks is right in emphasizing that territoriality does not merely mediate the social and political spheres but is so inextricably interwoven with them that both territory and kinship must be recognized as autonomous principles. However, as Dalit death rituals show, locality is a fluid and fragile social construction possessing none of the stable taken-for-grantedness which Dirks attributes to it.

Each Dalit caste in northern Gujarat is subdivided into several named local units constituted by a set of villages spread over a particular area. These units or *paragṇū* often do not encompass contiguous villages.[6] Following Weber, Klass (1980) treats such a subdivision of a caste as an autocephalous *Verband*, a corporate group with its own leadership and internal control, admitting no other or higher level of authority. Rather than emphasize their corporate character, I have chosen to stress the territorial and political nature of these units, whose borders are often congruent with those of the many small chiefdoms which dotted the region up to 1947 (Randeria 1992b). In the anthropological literature on Gujarat, such sub-divisions of middle-ranking castes have been termed *goḷ* or 'marriage-circles' (Pocock 1972), since they have been seen as the unit within which intermarriage in a caste actually takes place.[7] Although these unions of villages may in some cases function as units of endogamy among the Dalit castes, they are basically territorial sub-divisions of a caste which administer all local caste affairs, including, of course, the rules of connubium and commensality. All Dalit castes in Sabarkantha district allow marriage alliances outside the *paragṇū* into certain other neighbouring *paragṇā* as well.

In northern Gujarat, *paragṇā* are often designated by numbers instead of names.[8] The Chamar caste in the Bhiloda and Idar Talukas of Sabarkantha District, for example, is divided into a union of fourteen villages (*chaudonū paragṇū*, literally the *paragṇū* of the fourteen), a union of eighteen, (*adhāronun paragṇū*) one of twelve (called *bārīsī*, from *bār* twelve), and two unions of thirty-five (known as *moṭī pāntrīsī* 'the large thirty-five' and *nanī pāntrīsī* 'the small thirty-five'). These five *paragṇā* form a *gol* (circle) which owns property, including a *dharmaśāḷā* at the nearby pilgrimage centre of Shyamlaji.

Each *paragṇū* has its own written and printed 'caste constitution' (*nātnū bandhārān* or *dhārādhoro*), drafted and periodically revised by its adult male members, which contains the rules of exchange to be followed at various life-cycle rituals.[9] Autonomous caste assemblies [(*nāt-*)*panch*] which legislate, administer and adjudicate the internal affairs of each *paragṇū*, are responsible for enforcing the rules and punishing their violation. All constitutions contain, for example, the exact number of persons to be invited to life-course ceremonies, the number of days the guests have to be fed, the details of the food to be provided, the amount of the fine to be paid by the host for contravening these rules, the details of the gifts to be given to the Garo priest and the Turi musicians officiating at these rituals, the details of the gifts to be given by the wife-givers of the host family and the counter-prestations to be received by them in return, etc. The constitutions also list the mortuary practices which have been discontinued or truncated by the caste assembly often in order to cut costs.

The constituent unit of a *paragṇū* is the *vās* or *vastī* comprising all the households (*ghar*) of a particular caste in a village. For example, when the village of Mau is said to belong to the 'Chamar *paragṇū* of 12' or be present at a mortuary feast, the reference is not to the entire village but only to the Chamar households in it. The terms *vās* (dwelling space) and *vastī* (population) are used interchangeably to refer to the area inhabited by the members of a caste in a village and to the social group living in that area. The image of living together in one place symbolizes the ties that bind these persons irrespective of genealogical ties. This representation of co-residential unity, produced at all major festivals (Holi, Diwali, Dashera) and at mortuary rituals, ignores the divisions of a *vās* on the basis of lineages (*shākh* 'branch'), each of which traces descent from a common ancestor, a common place of origin and a shared history of migration into the village. Unlike the upper castes in the area, all Dalit castes practice strict village or rather *vās* exogamy. Large towns like Idar or Patan, with several hundred households of Weavers and Tanners dispersed into separate localities or *vās*, prohibit marriage only within the natal *vās*.

At a higher level of organization, the *vās* or *vastī* is incorporated into the *paragṇū*, with 'villages of brotherhood' (*bhaīpānā gām*) (also known as *vibhāg* 'section' or *goḷ* 'circle' in some castes) forming the intermediate level. The latter is a group of neighbouring villages within it which use the idiom of agnation to symbolize the closeness of emotional and social ties based on geographical proximity. Marital alliances among these villages are common. The Weaver '27 *paragṇū*' in Sabarkantha district, for example, is divided into three such units, consisting of 14, 10 and 8 villages each.

HIERARCHY OF MORTUARY FEASTS

Mortuary feasts can be hierarchically graded on a scale of prestige depending on the scale of participation which corresponds to the three levels of locality: whether in addition to kin and affines within and outside the *paragṇū*, only fellow caste members of one's own village (*vās*) are invited; whether caste members from all 'villages of brotherhood' are invited as well; or whether invitations are extended to each village of the *paragṇū*. The greater the social span represented by the participants, the greater the expenditure incurred by the host. The higher one goes up the scale of mortuary feasts, the larger the group of invitees, the greater the number of meals served, and the more elaborate the menu for each meal. The greater the social value represented by the event, the greater is the prestige to the sponsor. Of course, the higher the feast is in the prestige scale, the more expensive are the gifts that the host family gives to its *kunvāsī* and wife-takers and those it receives from its wife-givers.

Families of lesser means usually settle for holding a lower level feast for the 'villages of brotherhood', a less expensive if also less prestigious alternative. Rich families may hold a feast on this scale (known as *kānotrun* in the Weaver '27 *paragṇũ*') after the death of one parent and sponsor a higher order feast (*nāt*) inviting all the villages of the *paragṇũ* in honour of the other parent. Alternatively they may choose to host *paragṇũ*-level feasts in memory of both parents, or prefer the most prestigious option of hosting both *kānotrun* and *nāt*, in addition to *kāṇ* and *kāndhiyun*, for each of the parents. The scale of the feast is an important determinant of prestige (*varpat*) in the *paragṇũ*. The families of many of the caste leaders have long histories of having hosted such lavish feasts (*varo*), a record of which is kept by the genealogist of the *paragṇũ* and recited on similar subsequent occasions.

Over time, the prestige accruing to a village from the holding of feasts by its member households gives it the status of a 'big village' (*moṭũ gām*) within the *paragṇũ*. In the past, within each Dalit caste such differences of status were reflected by the order in which representatives of high-status villages entered and were received at a feast and by the different 'welcome gifts' they received. Within the broader egalitarian ethos prevailing in the *paragṇũ* such a public marking of status differences in the context of mortuary feasts has come to be given up, as the conflicts arising out of it were perceived to disrupt further the unity of the caste, which is increasingly frayed due to growing economic differentiation.

Mortuary feasts are collective endeavours requiring the cooperation of several categories of participants—the agnates of the dead person and the *vastī* as feast-holders, the wife-givers and wife-takers of the deceased's family, representatives of each village belonging to the *paragṇũ*, the caste elders or *panch*, and the leaders of the neighbouring *paragṇā*. Religious preceptors (Sādhu, Bāwā, Guru) of the host lineage and of the *paragṇũ* as a whole must also be invited and honoured on the occasion. The Garo domestic priest of the family and the Garo *pradhān* of the *paragṇũ* officiate at the ritual, the Turi genealogist recites verses praising the hosts, and the Bhangi remove the left-overs.

Many months may elapse between the initial deliberations on hosting a feast and the final celebration. The charged period between the burial and the feast provides ample opportunity to air grievances, settle disputes, renew the sense of mutual obligation and work on social relationships. Agnates who decide to sponsor a mortuary feast must confer with all their castefellows in the *vastī* which is represented as sponsoring the event. Before requesting the *panch*'s permission to invite the entire *paragṇũ*, the agnates and *vastī* leaders together must consult the 'village of brotherhood'.

The agnates are the hosts only in the narrow sense of the term, for it is they who bear the chief financial burden. But a couple of hundred guests cannot be invited for some two to three days without the goodwill and organizational support of all the families in the *vās*, each of whom has the responsibility of accommodating and looking after those visitors who are assigned to them. Conflicts at the level of the *vastī* or *paragṇũ* which may mar the festivities or even lead to their failure are a continuing source of anxiety for the host family.

The extreme vulnerability of the host on these occasions is evident from an incident narrated to me in 1987 in Sabarkantha district. After the failure of the third consecutive monsoon the state government was forced to declare parts of Gujarat 'drought affected areas'. This involved the initiation of relief measures for the rural poor, and also the enforcement of the Guest Control Order, banning the hosting of a party for more than 50 invitees, which poses a serious problem for those sponsoring a mortuary feast. Longstanding hostility between two Tanner lineages in Dungari village led to one filing a police complaint against its rival lineage, which was entertaining some two hundred guests. The police arrived, interrupted the proceedings, ordered the guests to disperse and confiscated the sweet (*lāpsī*) which had been cooked. The policemen, who belonged to the middle and upper castes, would not eat food cooked in an 'untouchable' household, so they auctioned it. The village Weavers bought it at a giveaway price and consumed the sweet!

MORTUARY CELEBRATIONS, INTER-CASTE AND INTRA-CASTE PRESTATIONS

It is difficult to give a brief summary of a mortuary feast, which is a complex performance, lasting three to five days, with some two to three hundred participants. It includes a joyous welcome procession, extravagant feasting and food distribution, the singing of songs by the women of the host family, ostentatious affinal prestations, and gifts to members of service castes, the *gharāk* (customers) of the feast-holders. This tense drama, with a variety of plots and sub-plots, does not unfold smoothly but is punctuated by protracted and acrimonious public disputes and negotiations over rules of procedure, the presence or absence of particular villages, the cooking of the food, the quality and quantity of prestations and the entitlements of the service castes. For reasons of space, only ritual sequences concerned with the creation of locality will be considered here.

On the morning after the *sarāmaṇũ* ritual, the *panch* assembles outside the house of the dead person. The names of the villages of the *paragṇū* are called out to ascertain that at least one representative from each village is present. The *pradhān* honours the leaders by applying a dot of vermilion to their foreheads, receiving ten paisa per person in return. The *panch* then invites a couple of elders of the *vās* to join their circle. In a tone and posture of utmost humility, using the conventional understatement expected in this context, the eldest son of the deceased requests that he and his brothers be allowed to serve the caste *pāsher ghensh* (a very small quantity of rice cooked in buttermilk). The caste leaders dismiss the idea to begin with. The son must persist, saying that they hardly have the means 'to do a big work' (*moṭun kām karvun*) and would require support (*ṭeko*) from the *panch.* The *panch* elders, at first seemingly reluctant to place such a heavy strain on the family of the deceased, finally agree. The *pradhān* is then asked to consult his almanac to decide on an auspicious date in consultation with the *panch.*

A village, if powerful enough, can hold up the proceedings or ruin the feast (*nāt bagaḍvī*) by staying away, and no prestige accrues to the host if the food cooked is not consumed (*dhān verāvvā*) by the entire *paragṇū.* If the completeness of the spatially constructed community cannot be evoked, the mortuary feast is deemed to have been spoiled or even not to have been held at all. Locality produced through the ritual simultaneously validates the latter.

Mortuary feasts are particularly sensitive barometers of unresolved social conflicts and are classic settings for a dramatic highlighting of disunity, at all levels of the caste. The absence of a village may indicate a trial of strength or be a tactic to force the solution of unresolved conflicts (e.g. marital disputes, violations of caste rules and *panch* decisions). More seriously, it may be the first formal sign of exit, of an impending fission (*tad*). Messengers may be sent out to these villages to discuss matters and hold out the promise of a solution. Or the absent village(s) may then be 'put out of caste' (*nāt bār mūkvū*), leading to a gradual cessation of all relations of exchange with it/them and over time with all the villages of the *paragṇū* which continue to maintain relations of exchange with it/them. The *paragṇū* is then said to have 'broken' (*bhāngyū*). My male informants stressed that the most grave consequence of such a split was the inability to visit and give gifts to their married sisters and daughters in those villages, and especially to mourn a death in their conjugal families.

On the day prior to the feast, the host village sends a man to each of the invited villages to ensure that at least a few leading representatives attend. The guests arrive and are accommodated by the house to which they have been allotted. Male relatives begin to seat themselves in a circle on the floor under the baldachin in front of the sponsor's home. Its centre is formed by elderly relatives of the sponsors especially those whose families have a high status because of their hosting such feasts in the past.

Younger men, who merely listen but do not speak in the *panch*, sit at the outer edge. The women of the family are keen commentators from inside the house, and the anthropologist is seated on the threshold.

To begin with, a *vastī* elder is in charge of the proceedings. Representatives from each household in the *vastī* are seated together with the sponsoring family and its relatives. After a spokesman of the host family has welcomed all the guests, a few men from the *vastī* are dispatched to lead the *paragṇū*, embodied in its important leaders, to the sponsor's house. The *paragṇū* elders, leaders from neighbouring *paragṇā*, along with the religious preceptors of the family and *paragṇū* are led into the *vās* from outside in a joyous, noisy procession (*sāmaiyun*). The religious preceptors are garlanded by an elder on behalf of the *vastī* and are honoured with a *chāndalo* (a dot of vermilion on the forehead) by the Garo *pradhān* of the *paragṇū* after being offered seats on chairs. The caste elders who represent the *paragṇū* form a circle on the floor at their feet. Each of them is also respectfully greeted by the *pradhān* with a *chāndalo.*

The name of every village in the *paragṇū* is then called out to ascertain that it is represented. Who represents a village is a tricky matter, as no delegates are elected and any adult male may be said to represent it.[10] It is, however, important for the host to ensure the presence of influential elders from each village, so as to nip in the bud any conflicts about non-attendance, inadequate representation, authorization to commit oneself on behalf of the village, participation in the deliberations of the caste assembly, etc. One member of the *vastī* and of the sponsoring family are then invited to join the circle of the *paragṇū*, symbolizing their inclusion in the larger local community.

Men from each of the Garo households in the village come with utensils of their own to collect both the sweet cooked in *ghee* and grain (*kāchū sīdhun*). Leaders of the *paragṇū* are served first, followed by other invitees, then the men of the *vastī* and finally the hosts. Regardless of the size of the household, each house in the *vastī* is sent the same quantity of food for the women who eat in their respective homes. Inside the house of the host family additional food is cooked and served separately to the religious preceptors (and the anthropologist). It is now the turn of the women to eat. The women affines (BW-HZ, DHM-SWM) sit facing each other in a row inside the house, each eating the first mouthful out of the plate of the other. Among the Weaver '27 *paragṇū*' this practice of food exchange between women affines is known as 'putting a hand into the food' (*bhāṇāman hāth nākhavo*). Once all the men of the caste have eaten, the Turi musicians are served food in their own utensils, which they themselves clean. They also have the right to take away food for distribution to their families in their own villages. At the end of the ceremony men from the Bhangi *vās* are called to collect the leftovers.

Mortuary feasts are the only life-course rituals at which the caste elders supervise the cooking of the sweet. Most Dalit castes in the area only allow a sweet cooked in 'pure *ghee*' (clarified butter made from cow's milk) rather than in 'vegetable *ghee*' (a cheaper substitute made out of margerine) to be served at mortuary feasts. Every night of the feast it is the responsibility of caste elders to weigh the ingredients for the sweet and to inspect the quality of ghee before giving permission for the sweet to be cooked. They also depute men from the *panch* and the *vastī* to oversee its cooking, which is done late into the night by the men outside the house. All other food is cooked inside the house by the women of the family.

Male guests eat their food seated in rows facing each other in the narrow lane outside the house of the dead person. Young boys of the host family serve *khichaḍī* and vegetables, and the sweet is served by a senior relative, but additional ghee is poured on the sweet (*lāpsi*) or *khichaḍī* by a *vastī* elder. This marks the *vastī* as co-sponsors of the feast and also asserts the authority of the *vastī* and *paragṇū* to exercise control over the cooking, consumption and distribution of the food.

The next morning, after the same caste has reassembled, the leader of the *vastī* requests the permission of the *panch* to begin the day's proceedings. This is given after a renewed count of the villages at which the names of the 'villages of brotherhood' are singled out for special mention. Members of the *vastī* and the *paragṇū* form separate circles, the hosts sit with the *vastī* on the fringes of the circle, and the Garo *pradhān* of the *paragṇū* mediates between the two local communities thus represented. As on the previous day, he escorts a few men of the *vastī* across to the circle of the *panch.*

A senior member of the host family welcomes the guests, begs forgiveness for any mistakes (*bhūlo*) which may occur due to ignorance (*ajāṇ*) and in a speech emphasizing the sacredness of the caste ['(You) are the *panch*, (you) are God. The beholding of the caste is holy' (*Panch cho, Parmeshwar cho. Nātnā darshan pavitra che*); 'the advent of the caste increases lustre, Ganga comes to (our) house' (*nāt aye vadhe nūr, gher āve gangā*)], asks its permission to display the *sajjā dān* (gift of a bed) and to begin the exchanging of affinal prestations (*vahevār*).

A cot covered with a mattress is brought out of the house and all the objects to be gifted to the Garo priest are arranged on top of it—a pillow, a quilt, a bedsheet, a set of clothes (a loincloth if the deceased is a man, a sari in case of a woman) and a coconut, on which are placed eleven rupees. There are also a few tiny gifts made of silver—a cow, a fan, a ladder, a boat, a flag and a snuff box, everything that is required by the deceased on his or her onward journey. Twelve water pots are placed under the bed, and one on top of it, along with thirteen *thāḷi*, each containing several objects of daily use—a comb, a mirror, biscuits (as the favourite food of the deceased), things the deceased played with as a child, etc.

This was the most elaborate *sajjā dān* that I saw during my entire fieldwork. It was given in Kaipur village (Mehsana district) in 1987 by a large joint household of the Garo caste, whose members no longer followed their occupation as domestic priests. Some of them had migrated several decades ago to work in the textile factories of Ahmedabad, while others were school teachers or state employees. One of them had political ambitions in the local Congress Party and was keen to invest in strengthening his family's local ties.

Wealthy Garo families, of course, have a much greater interest in a lavish *sajjā dān*, which are distributed among their own *kunvāsī* and their husbands. In the absence of a caste or sub-caste higher than themselves in the untouchable hierarchy, Garo wife-takers act as domestic priests to their wife-givers on ritual occasions. Weaver and Tanner families give much more modest *sajjā dān* (clothes and money) since the recipients in their case are their Garo domestic priests rather than their own married sisters and daughters. These prestations are not regarded as inauspicious nor do the Dalit see them as symbolizing the transfer of evil or inauspiciousness. They are given on the occasion of the mortuary feast which is considered to be as auspicious and joyful an event as a wedding.

As the *sajjā* is arranged, presided over by two caste elders from the circle of the *paragṇū*, the Garo priest, using white and red powder, draws a pattern on the ground near the cot for the ritual of Nine Planets (*nav grah pujā*) and places in it a copper pot filled with water with a coconut on top of it. The chief mourner makes the last offerings of food and water to the deceased. At the close of this ritual, the *Garuḍa Purāṇa* is recited by men of the caste among the Garo.

The most elaborate sequence of mortuary feasts, however, is the exchange of affinal prestations known as *maraṇ māmerū* (death *māmerū*), which constitutes their climax. Prestations from the natal kin to their married sisters and daughters in life-course rituals are termed *māmerū* (from *māmā* mother's brother). The structure of gifts constituting the *maraṇ māmerū*, given at a mortuary feast held by the *kunvāsī*'s conjugal family, is the same as that of the *māmerū* given at a wedding or pregnancy ritual.

Each *māmerū*, whether given at a wedding, a pregnancy ritual or a mortuary ritual, consists of between ten and fifty separate transactions, in which wife-givers give gifts of clothes or money to their wife-takers. The core of the *māmerū* is constituted by the gifts of jewellery, money and clothes brought by the father and brothers of a *kunvāsī*. Mortuary feasts are the only occasions on which several *māmerā* are exchanged—the *māmerū* from the dead woman's or widow's natal kin is followed by those from each of the wife-givers of her sons in order of seniority. And the status of women in their conjugal families depends in no small measure on the value of the gifts they receive from their natal families who compete with one another at mortuary feasts.

The money, clothes and jewellery which are given are sacred in character and are accepted after sprinkling raw rice and vermilion on them. Widows do not give or even touch these gifts. Every gift is passed round among the men constituting the circle of givers, and each man touches it to his forehead as a matter of respect. The gift is then given to the Garo officiating as priest or *pradhān* for the occasion, who announces it (*ṭahūko pāḍavo*) and hands it over to one of the men in the circle of the wife-takers, where it is also handed from person to person, touched to the forehead and critically examined. Once announced, the gift is written down by a male member of the host family for the record and for future reference. The sacredness of the brother-sister tie and the gifts which symbolize it, the 'merit' (*puṇ*) they generate and the moral obligation to give to one's *kunvāsī* are emphasized in everyday conversations as well as in the speeches of the religious preceptors, the Garo *pradhān* and the host during the mortuary feast. The unity of the *paragṇū* enables this flow of gifts, as fission (*taḍ*, literally 'crack') results in a woman's natal kin being unable to give gifts to those of their sisters and daughters whose conjugal villages belong to the opposite faction.

Contrary to the apparent rigidity of norms and obligations of gift-giving, there is ample room for the expression of sentiments, as well as the possibility of manipulating the rules to serve strategic ends. The exact amount of a cash gift, the quality of a sari, the value of an item of jewellery, the timing of the gift, whether an obligation is merely fulfilled by giving to one's immediate *kunvāsī* alone or generosity is shown by giving to more distant affines as well, who is sent with the gifts as a representative of the family, the relationship of the gift to the entire history of exchange between the families all are matters of affinal politics. But these preferences are articulated by the giver in terms of his inability rather than his unwillingness. The receiver interprets the inadequacies, of course, as tight-fistedness and as an insult.

At mortuary rituals, this exchange of prestations takes place between the men seated in two circles, one representing the wife-takers (feast-holders and *vastī* elders), the other representing the *paragṇū* which also supervises the transactions. Within the latter circle each group of wife-givers forms an inner circle when its turn comes to give the *māmerū*, so that the composition of the *paragṇū* circle changes constantly during the affinal exchanges. The caste elders are consulted by the wife-givers in their midst and by the Garo *pradhān* on behalf of the wife-takers regarding rules and procedures, changes in constitutional provisions and the exact amount of money to be exchanged, all of which are subjects of acrimonious public disputes and negotiations. The *panch* also has the authority to intervene in order to press for an upward revision of the gifts of money in both intra-caste and inter-caste exchanges.

Both wife-givers and wife-takers contribute to the sum of money which is collected and given to the religious preceptors, whereas all other inter-caste prestations are given by the feast-holders. For example, at the memorial feast of the Garo caste in Kaipur which I attended in 1987, the Garo of the *paragṇū* was honoured with a *dān* of Rs. 101, the *paragṇū* genealogist (*ghaḍvī*) received Rs. 31, the various Turi musicians got Rs. 11 each, and a representative of the Bhangi *vās* was asked to distribute Rs. 5 among the households of his caste in the village. There was considerable controversy between recipient and the head of the host household and the caste elders about these amounts and about which representative of the caste should receive them. The former often prevailed over the latter not to set false precedents with regard to the claims of the various service castes (*māngaṇ*, literally 'askers'). Mortuary feasts are occasions on which rival lineages of *māngaṇ* stake their respective claims to serve the sponsors. Rather than allow embarrassing disputes to develop, many a host gives gifts to both, thus establishing future claims and obligations not only for his own family but for the *paragṇū* as a whole.

'PUBLIC' EXCHANGE AND THE CONTROVERSY OVER MORTUARY FEASTS

That sociality within each untouchable caste is constituted through relationships of exchange is evident from a remark that members of these castes often make in a variety of ritual and everyday contexts: 'we are in the world in order to exchange (women and gifts)' (*samsārman beṭhān chhīe to vehvār karvā*). The Gujarati word *vehvār*, which I have translated as exchange (of women and gifts), also means relationship, behaviour, social interaction and even a loan of money.[11] *Vehvār* in the strict sense of the term refers to prestations within the caste, so that at this level the Dalits make a semantic distinction between inter-caste and intra-caste prestations, which they often see as equivalent in other contexts. Gifts of women, food and money are reflective and constitutive of social relationships in a world in which movement and transformation through social exchange and consumption are the nature, if not the very meaning, of life. Reciprocal exchange constitutes castes as endogamous and commensal units, even as they mark the boundaries between and within them. Death rituals and mortuary feasts are socially approved contexts *par excellence* for elaborate affinal exchange or *vehvār*.

To insult a man who refuses to host a mortuary feast for his father or mother by saying that he 'eats (his wealth), but does not feed (it to others)' (*khāy chhe, paṇ khavaḍāvto nathī*) is to accuse him not only of stinginess but of sheer immorality. The purpose of acquiring wealth is not individual private consumption but public redistribution. My usage of modernist categories of 'public' and 'private' is not a literal translation of equivalent Gujarati terms. 'Public' here does not refer to 'civic life' or 'citizen culture' but to the world of the caste, one word for which is *samāj*, meaning society. Thus the 'public' domain in the context of consumption and exchange is the socially sanctioned realm of transactions among kin and affines. Similarly, 'private' in this context is not the sphere of the individual but refers to secret transactions between two partners inside the house or outside the caste settlement. Caste elders are, for example, honoured in public by gifts of money at a mortuary feast but they receive in private many times that amount to ensure that no problems arise about the representation of a village, the food to be served, gifts to service castes, etc. The contrast made by my informants is in terms of secret (*khāngī*), or 'inside' or 'in between' (*andar-andar*) versus 'in the caste' (*samājman*), 'exchange' (*vehvār*) or 'give and take' (*levaḍ-devaḍ*). At life-course rituals the latter category of prestations has to be announced by the priest and noted down by the receiver. Taking his lead from Veblen, Douglas and Isherwood, Appadurai (1986: 37) has argued that consumption is eminently social, relational and active rather than merely private, atomic and passive. I would suggest, however, that consumption *per se* is not social. Whether or not it is constitutive of sociality depends on its context.

To consume one's own money, food and resources would be to live in a world without social relations. Gift-exchange and public consumption engender social relationships, whereas individual personal consumption is barren. The mere hosting of a mortuary feast to honour one's parents is no virtue, but a *sine qua non* of belonging to the community. Prestige is acquired through the scale of the feast, generosity in exchange, the number of guests fed, the lavishness of the food served and the value of the gifts exchanged. Private consumption in the interests of the immediate family alone is considered unproductive, motivated by greed and selfishness. Lavish spending on a socially valued event in which the entire community participates and its leaders control the preparation of the food and supervise the exchange of gifts, is considered productive and moral.

This tension between 'public' and 'private' transactions is part of the tension between two different transactional orders, which Parry and Bloch (1989) have contrasted as the cycle of short-term exchanges within the legitimate domain of the individual and a cycle of transactions concerned with the reproduction of the social and cosmic order. Acrimonious debates over the last thirty to forty years between men of the older and younger generations of all Dalit castes over whether to continue or abolish mortuary feasts reflect the competing demands of these two value systems, the one valorizing social consumption, public exchange, the sacredness of the caste and obligations to the collectivity, the other emphasizing private consumption, personal accumulation and one's duty to one's children.

What is at issue in the discussions on the abolition of mortuary feasts is not merely a private saving and investment drive through the reduction of expenditure at rituals. Most Dalits, irrespective of age and educational status, have few qualms about discontinuing gifts to Garo and Turi, reducing expenditure at marriages by restricting the number of guests, or trimming down the number and quality of the meals that are provided. What is at issue in the demand of some educated men of the younger generation that mortuary feasts be abolished is the relationship between the transient individual and the enduring social order which transcends him or her. Bloch and Parry (1982) have argued that mortuary rites mediate this contradiction by giving those who wield political authority, the symbolic means to claim that they are responsible for the reproduction of life.

Whereas elders and caste leaders argue that the *paragṇũ* should be fed in memory of one who has eaten well in his or her lifetime, the younger generation counters by arguing that the real purpose of the feasts is to fatten the caste leaders, who eat and argue at the expense of others and exercise power over their lives through the caste-council deliberations which accompany the event. Whereas the younger men see in the abolition of mortuary feasts the demise of power of the caste elders, the latter argue that such a step would be the death-knell of the community as a whole. In view of the significance of these feasts for the social, political and moral life of the caste, moderate reformers often steer a course between the conservative and radical options. They suggest continuing the practice but on a more modest scale, reducing the amount of resources spent on mortuary feasts. Changes introduced in several caste constitutions in the last few years bear witness to the attractiveness of this compromise.

Memorial feasts are both contested celebrations and arenas for the contestation of status and political authority within the caste. The struggles over them in every Dalit caste are conflicts over control of the community, but also, and more importantly, struggles about the meaning and function of caste as an institution. For it is in this context that the caste is symbolically produced as a locally situated community constituted through exchange. Represented as memorial feasts for the deceased, in these celebrations it is the local community of kin and affines which unites to commemorate the ties which bind it.

NOTES

This article is a substantially revised version of the chapter 'Death and the celebration of life: Mortuary Feasts among the untouchable castes of north Gujarat' contributed in 1993 to the Festschrift for Professor Klaus Bruhn, edited by Joachim Bautze and Nalini Balbir (in press). The initial fieldwork was funded by a doctoral scholarship from the Friedrich Naumann Stiftung. I am deeply indebted to my parents as well as to the late Bhanubhai Adhvaryu and Achyutbhai Yagnik for their generosity and support during field research in Gujarat. From among those who warmly welcomed an intruding stranger in their midst and shared their lives with her, I would especially like to single out Karsanbhai Parmar and Ashok Shrimali.

1. Out of the State's total population of 34 million, about 8 per cent has been classified as belonging to these castes, grouped together under the official category of 'Scheduled Castes'. Considered to be ritually highly impure, these groups at the bottom of the local caste hierarchy are among the poorest in rural Gujarat. They continue to face considerable social discrimination despite attempts to improve their position through a policy of 'affirmative action'. Reservations in legislative bodies, institutions of higher education and the state bureaucracy have given rise to a small upwardly mobile urban section in many of these castes.
2. The hosting of a mortuary feast is known as *nāt karvī* (to do caste), or *nāt teḍāvavī* (to invite the caste). The terms designating these feasts (*bārmun, sajjā, kānotrun*) vary from caste to caste, the same word denoting mortuary feasts of different scales for different castes. I have, therefore, used the term mortuary feasts in preference to one of the indigenous terms.
3. The term Dalit, meaning 'broken' or 'oppressed', is defiantly used as a term of self-reference by educated urban sections of the so-called 'untouchable castes'. In the absence of a composite neutral term to designate these groups set apart by their polluted status at the bottom of the caste hierarchy, I use it in preference to 'scheduled castes', which is an artificial administrative category of little social significance. In Gujarat, none of these castes use the euphemism *Harijan* (people of God), coined by Gandhi for them, as a term of self-reference. The highly political question of individual and collective caste names among the Dalits is dealt with at length in my dissertation (Randeria 1992b).
4. Randeria (1989) explores the different discourses on the nature of untouchability in Gujarat in order to delineate the relationship between the collective, permanent pollution of these castes and their occupational specialization, involving the disposal of dead animals and human corpses.
5. In contrast to Raheja's (1988) material from north India, the *kunvāsī* in Gujarat are concerned with the lessening of mourning rather than the lifting of pollution and removal of inauspiciousness.
6. According to Sankalia (1949: 20), the Encyclopedia of Islam notes that the term *paragṇā* is 'an Indian name' for an aggregate of villages 'based on more ancient divisions in existence before the Muslim conquest'. However, he states that the word is not found in pre-Muslim sources and there is considerable dispute as to whether it is a Persianized Sanskrit word or a Persian one.
7. Elsewhere in India, they have been referred to as a 'network of neighbouring villages' (Dube) or a 'larger system of villages' (Karve); both quoted in Singh (1968).

8. Sankalia (1949: 27) notes that it is in the reign of the Rashtrakuta dynasty (AD 770-970) that records mentioning units formed by a numbered group of villages in the area of present-day Gujarat first appear. Altekar traces the practice back to the *Mahābhārata, Manusmṛti* and *Viṣṇu Purāṇa.*
9. These constitutions have been described and analysed in detail in Randeria (1992b) with a translation of one such document in Appendix II. The contents of caste constitutions and the mode of functioning of caste councils is often at variance with the laws and legal institutions of the nation-state. Caste councils refuse to recognize the jurisdiction of modern law courts, for example, though the latter accept the decisions of the former on matters of divorce or remarriage but not in cases of 'excommunication' of individuals from their castes (Randeria 1989).
10. A man represents his natal village regardless of his present residence, the only exception being an uxorilocal son-in-law (*ghar-jamāi*), who represents the village of his father-in-law.
11. The Sanskrit noun *vyavahāra* (from which Gujarati *vehvār* is derived) means 'action, practice, conduct, doing, performing, behaviour, commerce' or 'intercourse, usage, custom, ordinary life, mercantile transaction'. The verb *vyavh* means 'to exchange, transpose, to have intercourse with, to meet (as foes), fight with, behave towards or deal with, to carry on commerce' (M. Monier-Williams, *Sanskrit-English Dictionary:* 1043). Derrett (1976: 599) interprets *vyavahāra* as 'order' or 'world-plan' in its widest sense of cosmic order come down to earth.

REFERENCES

Appadurai, Arjun. 1986. *The Social Life of Things.* Cambridge, N.Y.: Cambridge University Press.

Bloch, Maurice and Jonathan Parry. 1982. *Death and the Regeneration of Life.* Cambridge, N.Y.: Cambridge University Press.

Das, Veena. 1977. *Structure and Cognition. Aspects of Hindu Caste and Ritual.* Delhi: Oxford University Press.

Derrett, J.D.M. 1976. *Essays in Classical and Modern Hindu Law. Dharmaśastra and Related Texts,* Vol. I. Leiden: E.J. Brill.

Dirks, Nicholas. 1987. *The Hollow Crown. Ethnohistory of an Indian Kingdom.* Cambridge, N.Y.: Cambridge University Press.

Dumont, Louis. 1986. *A South Indian Subcaste. Social Organization and Religion of the Pramalai Kallar.* Delhi: Oxford University Press.

Hertz, Robert. 1960. *Death and the Right Hand* (translated by R. Needham and C. Needham). New York: Free Press.

Huntington, Richard and Peter Metcalf (eds.). 1979. *Celebrations of Death. The Anthropology of Mortuary Ritual.* Cambridge, N.Y.: Cambridge University Press.

Klass, Morton. 1980. *Caste, the Emergence of the South Asian Social System.* Philadelphia: Institute for the Study of Human Issues.

Mines, Diane P. 1989. Hindu Periods of Death 'Impurity'. *Contributions to Indian Sociology* (N.S.) 23(1): 103-30.

Parry, Jonathan. 1980. Ghosts, Greed and Sin: The Occupational Identity of the Banaras Funeral Priests. *Man* (N.S.) 15: 88-111.

———. 1985. Death and Digestion: The Symbolism of Food and Eating in North Indian Mortuary Rites. *Man* (N.S.) 20: 612-30.

———. 1994. *Death in Banaras.* Cambridge: Cambridge University Press.

Parry, Jonathan and Maurice Bloch (eds.). 1989. *Money and the Morality of Exchange.* Cambridge: Cambridge University Press.

Pocock, David. 1972. *Kanbi and Patidar: A Study of the Patidar Community of Gujarat.* Oxford: Oxford University Press.

Raheja, Gloria Goodwin. 1988. *The Poison in the Gift: Ritual, Prestation and the Dominant Caste in a North Indian Village.* Chicago: Chicago University Press.

Randeria, Shalini. 1989. Carrion and Corpses: Conflict in Categorizing Untouchability in Gujarat. *European Journal of Sociology* 30: 171-91.

———. 1990. Ehe, Scheidung und Witwenstand. Lebensläufe Unberührbarer Frauen im Westlichen Indien. In G. Elwert, M. Kohli, H.K. Miller (eds.), *Im Laufe der Zeit. Ethnographische Studien zur Gesellschaftlichen Konstruktion von Lebensalter.* Saarbrücken: Breitenbach.

———. 1992a. Brahmans, Kings and Pariahs: Castes, Exchange and Untouchability in Western India Today. *Wissenschaftskolleg Jahrbuch 1991-92*: 294-312. Berlin: Nicolaische Verlagsbuchhandlung.

———. 1992b. The Politics of Representation and Exchange among Untouchable Castes in Western India (Gujarat). Unpublished Ph.D. Thesis (Freie Universität Berlin).

Sankalia, H.D. 1949. *Studies in the Historical and Cultural Geography of Gujarat.* Poona: Deccan College.

Singh, K.N. 1968. Medieval Town Settlement. *Annals of American Geographers,* LVIII: 208-20.

Ancestors, Demons and the Ritual Impossibility of Death in Brahmanical Hinduism

Bālā's Fourteenth in Deopatan (Nepal)

AXEL MICHAELS

Nicht die Unsterblichkeit, sondern die Sterblichkeit ist dasjenige, was "bewiesen" (. . .) werden muss.
E. Cassirer, Phil. d. symbol. Formen, vol. II, p. 50

1. INTRODUCTION

If men die, they become ancestors, ghosts, demons or heroes. In this paper I shall discuss the relationship between ancestors and demons or ghosts based on fieldwork on Bālācaturdaśī ('Bālā's Fourteenth'), a festival observed on the fourteenth day (*caturdaśī*) of the dark half of the moon in the month of Maṅgśīr (November/December) and celebrated in Deopatan, a small Newar city about three kilometres north-west of Kathmandu, and the site of the famous Paśupatinātha Temple. In the ceremonies and rituals of this festival, two aspects are dominant which concern the relationship between ancestor worship and demonism in Hinduism: the rituals focus on the remembrance of more or less recently deceased family members and the actions to be performed for their welfare, while the myths have to do with pacifying the demon Bālā, who is generally regarded as a fallen man from a low caste. Connected with the latter aspect is the so-called *bālāguṭhīpūjā*, an act of worship of the demon Bālā by a special religious group (*guṭhī*), performed one night after Bālācaturdaśī in the Mṛgasthalī grove.

In this paper I shall first give a short description of the rituals (2.),[1] and then draw preliminary conclusions on the type of ritual in question (3.). In the second part, I shall discuss the myths regarding Bālā (4.) and the little-known *bālāguṭhīpūjā* (5.),[2] before finally raising more general questions regarding the relationship between ancestor-worship and demon-worship in Hinduism (6.).[3]

2. A FESTIVAL IN REMEMBRANCE OF ANCESTORS

In terms of the people celebrating it, Bālācaturdaśī is the second largest festival of Deopatan,[4] ranking only after Śivarātri. It has the usual character of an Indian or Nepalese festival (*melā*), with stalls where *pūjā* supplies, ritual paraphernalia or pictures and small icons of deities are sold, and *samosā* and tea offered, almost everywhere.[5] The festival is generally celebrated in the following manner: the worship of Paśupati in his temple (*2.1*); a night vigil with the lighting of lamps and a *homa* ritual (*2.2*); at dawn a bath in the Bāgmatī and the launching of lamps onto the river, again followed by a *homa* (*2.3*); the worship of Paśupati and a temple with sixty-four *liṅgas* (Caũsāththīliṅgeśvara); a ritual pilgrimage through Mṛgasthalī, with the strewing of a mixture of seven seeds (*2.4*).

2.1 During the whole day before the night of Bālācaturdaśī, thousands of people gather at the Paśupatinātha Temple and in the Paśupatikṣetra, the holy area of Paśupati surrounding the temple. By sunset the nearby Mṛgasthalī forest and Kailāsa hill are full of pilgrims, many of whom come from the hilly regions. Most of them appear in their best clothes, which are packed with a number of items they need for the night to be spent in Deopatan. They usually come in family groups numbering up to fifteen or twenty members, and in some cases are accompanied by their family priest. The majority of the pilgrims belong to the Indo-Nepalese Bāhun/ Chetri community, but there are a considerable number of ethnic minority groups (Rai, Tamang, Magar, Gurung), who generally gather on Kailāsa hill.

2.2 After the usual obligatory worship of Paśupati, the pilgrims look for a suitable place to keep the night vigil (Plate 1). The family groups sit together. Some sing, and some even dance. They have brought straw on which to sit, and many are wrapped in shawls as protection against the chilly air. At nightfall hundreds of lights are lit. These are of two types:

(a) wicks in small, oil-filled clay bowls, generally called *battī*; these small lamps are often placed on dishes of hand-sewn leaves of the *bel* tree, which are filled with a mixture of supposedly seven seeds (e.g. rice, barley, wheat, lentils, corn, maize, sesame), and also bits of radish and sugar cane, as well as fruits, sweets (*naivedya*), bread (*roṭī*), vermilion (*sindūra*), flowers, *paisā* coins (*dakṣiṇā*) and incense (*dhūpa*).

(b) two-foot bamboo torches, generally called *mahādīpa*, which are stuck in bottles or in the ground (in small mounds of mud and cow-dung) (Plate 2).

The lights are lit either in remembrance of deceased family members or for Śiva/Mahādeva. Some members from Bāhun/Chetri communities say that the small lights are for Mahādeva and the torches are for the dead, while others claim that in the first year after death only a small light should be lit, and in the second year a torch.

Both kinds of light indicate that the festival is celebrated for at least two purposes: remembrance and pacification of the dead, and the accumulation of religious merit on the part of mourners or pilgrims (*dharma-ko lāgi*, as some said, meaning their own *dharma*). The lights, which are common in funeral ceremonies (compare the use in Christian death ceremonies of candles that burn throughout the night), show the departed soul the way to the afterworld, or else are burnt in order to avoid the return of the dead, since such spirits fear illuminated places.[6]

Both, the positive aspect (escorting the dead) and the negative aspect (warding off the dead), are related to each other: the dead person has not yet reached his final destination and is thus a potential source of danger. Faced with the fate of the dead person, mourners are compelled to help him; faced with their own fate, they are compelled to keep him away.

Similar structures can be observed in rituals performed during the night. Usually a *homa* is performed—a sacrificial fire in which several offerings (e.g. sesame seeds, barley, rice) are burnt after the name of the deceased person has been pronounced and his lineage (*gotra*) or the names of Mahādeva are proclaimed, and while Vedic hymns (e.g. Rudrīpāṭha) and *mantras* are being recited (Plate 3). The mourners in this case are clearly remembering a recently deceased person.

However, people also celebrate Bālācaturdaśī even when nobody has died in their family. Some say that 'as much *dān* as we offer during Bālācaturdaśī we'll get in return as gold'. The celebration of Bālācaturdaśī as a festival not necessarily connected with ancestor worship is mentioned in the seventeenth-century(?) *Himavatkhaṇḍa*:

mārgakṛṣṇacaturdaśyāṃ śivātmā bhaktito budhaḥ/
snātvārohati vāgmātyām ārambhya śaṅkarasthalīm //
mṛgasthalīgiriṃ bhrāmya brīhiṃ vikṣepya yatkṛtam /
suvarṇarattikātulyaṃ vrīhim [sic] *ekaṃ ca yat phalam //*

The wise man whose self is (concentrated on) Śiva will, out of devotion, take a bath in the Bāgmatī on the fourteenth day of the dark half of Mārga and climb up (to Mṛgasthalī). His reward will be as much paddy as he then scatters while wandering over the Mṛgasthalī hill, beginning at Śaṅkara's (Śiva's) place (i.e. Paśupati Temple): one grain of rice will be equivalent to one grain[7] of gold.

(*Himavatkhaṇḍa* 152.60-1)

Unfortunately, the text does not mention for what purpose the grains are scattered, but the reward (*phala*) of such an act benefits the ritual performer rather than the deceased.

Ethnic groups such as the Magars or Gurungs sometimes engage a

Bāhun (Brahmin) priest, but Tamang groups celebrate Bālācaturdaśī in their own way. The latter are usually accompanied by one or more Lāmā priests, who perform a rather grandiose ritual involving the recitation of texts and the worship of various Buddhist deities and a sacred water pot (*kalaśapūjā*). Small shrines are erected that contain a thangka painting (Nep. *pauvā*) depicting Buddhist motifs, such as the Buddha Śākyamuni or clan deities. In front of the painting are often many oil lamps in small copper bowls.[8]

2.3 Early in the morning, even before dawn, many pilgrims bathe in the chilly Bāgmatī River in order to purify themselves (Plate 4). Then they set leaf-plates containing a burning oil lamp afloat in the river or throw consumed torches into the holy waters. Some perform another *homa* at this time.

2.4 What follows is to a certain extent the climax of events. People first worship Paśupati again and, very often, the Temple of Sixty-four *Liṅgas* within the premises of Paśupati Temple. Then they go on a two-and-a-half-mile pilgrimage leading clockwise around Paśupati Temple. The following route is standard but not obligatory: Paśupati Temple—Āryaghāṭ—Pāñcadevala—Rāmamandira—Mṛgasthalī—the Gorakhnāth precinct—Guhyeśvarī—Gaurīghāṭ—Kailāsa hill—Paśupati Temple. Pilgrims do, though, generally stick to a certain portion of the route leading through the Mṛgasthalī woods to the Kirāteśvara and Dharmeśvara *liṅgas* (see *infra*). However, this processional route through Mṛgasthalī and up Kailāsa hill is not even partially identical with the path of the dead, i.e. the way corpses are required to be carried to the cremation ground (see Michaels 1994: 180f.).

All along the way *sadbhī*, a mixture of seeds—all grains are permitted except millet and buckwheat—is scattered on countless deities or temples, and also on the path itself. It is commonly believed that this is to strengthen the ancestors (*pitaraḥ*) or the deceased (*preta*), and to make sure that those who have died within the past year will safely reach the (Śaiva) Kailāsa or (Vaiṣṇava) Vaikuṇṭha regions.

By local tradition, the *mohī naike* (Nev. *mhya nāyaḥ*), an officer of the Paśupati Bhaṇḍāra Tahabil responsible for collecting the harvest from land belonging to Paśupati Temple, is the first to strew *sadbhī* on Bālācaturdaśī. The previous custom was for the seeds to be collected by him and his helpers after the festival and then auctioned off. The Triśūljātrā was financed from the proceeds of the auction (see Michaels 1987)—a point I shall come back to below. Nowadays the Poḍe and Kusle have the right to collect the considerable amount of grain after cleaning the Paśupati area (Plate 5).

3. A FESTIVAL OF SPIRITS AND ANCESTORS

As mentioned before, in Brahmanically influenced Hindu contexts the status or place of a departed person is not well defined unless certain rituals have been performed and the customary period of mourning (generally one year) has passed. The departed is regarded as a restless, wandering soul who is still in a semi-demonic state (*preta*), without a gross body (*śarīra*), and as yet not ritually transformed into a benevolent ancestor (collectively, *pitaraḥ*). It is a being whose *sapiṇḍīkaraṇa* (see Knipe 1977, Müller 1992: 173) has not yet been performed,[9] and who thus has—in Turner's words[10]—a liminal status. The departed person ranks somewhere between mortal men still physically remembered (*preta*), ancestors the memory of whose former individuality is weak (*pitaraḥ*), ghosts (*bhūta*, also *preta*) or, by a process of deification, semi-divine beings (*viśvedevāḥ*). Only after a natural death, after the passing of a set time and the performance of all death rituals, do the departed reach their fixed destination, a region of their own, the *pitṛloka*, which is neither the world of mortals (*bhūloka*) nor the world of gods (*antarikṣa* or *svarga*).

The rituals performed on Bālācaturdaśī reflect this ambivalent attitude towards the dead. The worship of Paśupati and/or other deities, *homa* rites, the night vigil with lights or lamps, bathing and processions are common elements of Hindu ritual, which may be either for the benefit of the mourner or the dead. Pilgrims wish to please the gods and to expunge the evil (*pāpa*) of death and, more importantly, to accumulate religious merit (*puṇya*). However, the above acts also appear in other rituals; they are so unspecific that one could—and Frits Staal (1979) indeed does—regard them almost as meaningless.

What is specific to and unique for Bālācaturdaśī is the fact that the bereaved family members strew seeds (*sadbhī*). *Sadbhī* (variants are *sat(a)biū* or *sat(a)byū*) is etymologically related to Skt. *śatabīja* ('hundreds of seeds') or *saptabīja* ('seven seeds'), but certainly not, as some people in Deopatan would prefer, with Skt. *satyabīja* ('seed/origin of truth'). The earliest historical source I have found for this ritual is in a copper-plate of King Girvāṇayuddhaśāha (regnal years AD 1799-1816). In this plate, dated VS 1870 Caitra vadi 30 (= AD 1814), a *satavirahi* [*sic*] *charnyā guṭhī* is mentioned,[11] a religious endowment (*guṭhī*) concerned with strewing (*charnyā*, modern Nepālī: *charnu*) *satavirahi*, which in this context must be read as either *śatabīja*, in view of the fact that the vast majority of pilgrims scatter numerous varieties and countless numbers of seeds, or as *saptabīja* (cf. Skt. *saptadhānya*), given the strong belief among pilgrims that exactly seven (types of) seeds should be strewn.[12]

The number seven is often mentioned in ancestor worship as a key genealogical figure. To mention just a few references: In *Ṛgveda* IV.42.8 the ancestors (*pitaraḥ*) are identified with the seven *ṛṣis*, i.e. the forebearers of mankind and the *gotras*; the *Brahmāṇḍa Purāṇa* III.10.1 speaks of seven classes of *pitaraḥ* that dwell in heaven, four that have form (*mūrtimat*) and three without form (*amūrta*); see Kane 1973: 348. More widely known is the concept of seven relatives closely knit together, the *avibhaktadāya sapiṇḍas*, viz., great-grandfather, grandfather, father, ego, full brothers, the son from a wife of the same caste, grandson and great-grandson (see, for example, *Baudhāyanadharmasūtra* I.5.113-15). In marriage alliances, the concept of seven generations building one exogamic unit is still influential, as reflected in the seven steps (*saptapadī*) during a wedding (and also common during initiation ceremonies of Rājopādhyāyas: see Michaels 1986a: 217). Moreover, in the Nepalese death ritual the pyre is often piled in seven layers.

In addition to this genealogical explanation, one could mention the seven kinds of domestic (*grāmya*) corn and seven kinds of wild (*āraṇya*) corn (*Mārkaṇḍeya Purāṇa*: see Kane 1973: 413). Also there is the myth of Indra drinking the *soma*, a few drops of which fell to earth and turned into the seven kinds of corn. Even more common are the notions of seven skies, worlds and holy places (*purī*). However, the most direct interpretation possible is based of the Pretakalpa (or Uttarakhaṇḍa[13]) of the *Garuḍa Purāṇa*, where seven kinds of grain are mentioned as means for purification:

tilaṃ lauhaṃ hiraṇyañ ca kārpāsaṃ lavaṇaṃ tathā /
saptadhānyaṃ kṣitir gāva ekaikaṃ pāvanaṃ smṛtam //
Sesame, iron, gold, cotton and salt, seven kinds of grain, land, cows—each is known as a means for purification.\

(*Garuḍa Purāṇa*, Uttarakhaṇḍa IV.39 = Pretakalpa VIII.33)

And in the same text (Pretakalpa VIII.48) the seven kinds [rice, barley, wheat, *mudga*- and *māṣa*-beans (*Phaseolus mungo* and *Phaseolus radiatus*), fennel and chickpeas] are mentioned: The scattered seeds are purifying since they ward off evil spirits and demons. The fact that the grains are scattered during the night supports such an interpretation, for what is eaten after sunset becomes the food of demons (*rākṣas bhojan*, see also Parry 1985: 618). This is especially true for black sesame (Skt. *tila*),[14] which is regarded as having a protective power due to its origin from Viṣṇu's perspiration;

śrīkṛṣṇa uvāca
mama svedasam udbhūtās tilās tārkṣya pavitrakāḥ/
asurā dānavā daityā vidravanti tilais tathā //
Kṛṣṇa said: '*tilas* (sesame seeds or plants) have sprung up from the perspiration on my body and are thus purifying. Therefore *asuras*, *dānavas* and *daityas* run away because of *tilas*.'

(*Garuḍa Purāṇa*, Pretakhaṇḍa IX.11[15])

Similar ideas are found expressed in many Dharmaśāstra and Purāṇa texts. Thus the *Jaiminīyaghṛyasūtra* (II.1) 'states that [in the case of death] the whole house should have sesamum grains scattered about in it' (Kane 1973: 418). According to the *Nārada Purāṇa*, 'the performer of *śrāddha* should scatter *tilas* in the midst of brāhmaṇas invited and at the doors with the mantra [Vājasaneyisaṃhitā II.29] "apahatā" (may the asuras and evil spirits that sit on the altar be struck and run away). [...] The Kūrmapurāṇa (II.22.18) states that sesame should be scattered all around and a goat should be tied near the spot, since *śrāddha* polluted by *asura* become purified by sesame and a goat. The Viṣṇupurāṇa (III.16.14) prescribes that by *tilas* scattered on the ground one should ward off evil spirits.' (Kane 1973: 419).[16] In Nepal, sesame is also thrown on the burning platform by the chief mourner, who then says *agati nahos, narakamā jāna naparos* (Do not be damned,[17] may you not go to hell).[18] Moreover, paddy (Nep. *dhān*) is strewn on the path taken by the dead body (the rice is then called Nep. *burkī*) in order to purify the path.

Grains are thus also used to strengthen and protect the dead on their way in the afterworld. This is again explicitly stated in the *Garuḍa Purāṇa*:

saptadhānyasya dānena prīto dharmadhvajo bhavet /
tatra gatvā pratīhāro brūte tasya śubhāśubham //
Dharmadhvaja is pleased at the giving of seven kinds of grains, and the others who watch over the three gates [of Yama's city] are also satisfied.
(*Garuḍa Purāṇa*, Uttarakhaṇḍa IX.6 = Pretakalpa VIII.47)

The custom of feeding the dead by scattering seeds seems to be old. Thus, the *Atharvaveda* (XVIII.4.32-4) states that grains scattered for a deceased person will become milch-cows in the afterworld, and sesame their calves (see also Oldenberg 1917: 535 n. 1). Moreover, it is a popular (totemistic?) folk belief that the souls of the dead provisionally continue to live in plants (for trees, see Hodson 1921, cf. also Schmithausen 1995: 51 with further references) or as birds, which usually live on grains. To scatter grains would then mean to feed the departed, though the offering of *piṇḍas* (*sapiṇḍīkaraṇa*) seems to be more important in this regard (see Parry 1985: 615-24).

In Nepal, it is believed that the dead will be reborn as worms if no care is taken for them. If they are fed with *sadbhī*, though, they will not be hungry, and thus not need to destroy plants. Death is linked to the (re)creation of life, and many such beliefs are bound up with the farmer's world. It is, for example, said that all seeds planted or sown earlier than Bālācaturdaśī will not grow. Moreover, the relationship with the above-mentioned Triśūljātrā, which is partially financed through the auctioning of the grains left over from the Bālācaturdaśī festival, is significant, since the Triśūljātrā takes place on a day (*bhalabhalāṣṭamī*, i.e. *āṣāḍhakṛṣṇāṣṭamī*) when the first heavy rainfall—essential for rice planting—is expected. Bālācaturdaśī itself marks the beginning of the cold period and winter season: it is from Bālācaturdaśī until Ghoḍejātrā (Caitra kṛṣṇa 15 =

March/April) that any water used for the ritual washing (*abhiṣeka*) of Paśupati is first warmed. And it is believed that the abode of Yama, the god of death, is closed from Bālācaturdaśī until Gāijātrā, a procession of beautifully decorated cows, which are supposed to help the spirits on their long journey to Yama by allowing them to cling to their tails (see Anderson 1971: 99-104), so that the dead need the special care which is given during Bālācaturdaśī.

Both acknowledged purposes for scattering grains—strengthening the departed soul (for the sake of its welfare and eventual rebirth) and warding off the evil spirits (of the departed soul)—are, again, interrelated due to the liminal state of both the dead and mourners. Both classes of beings are in a transitional state fraught with ambivalence, pollution, weakness and low vitality. Both have lost their 'normal' place in society. Post-death rites and festivals are to a large extent meant to re-establish the solidarity of the family groups associated with the dead. However, the dead do not 'live' forever. They are totally at the mercy of damnatio memoriae (Gladigow 1985: 121), the social memory of the family, which fades away after a certain period of mourning. Once this time has come, the deceased really is dead.[19] This is often the time when the dead lose their 'personality' and are classified as more anonymous ancestors. Then rites of aggregation—to use Arnold van Gennep's term—become more and more common. Joint funeral meals, prayers, sacrifices and processions for the dead are common elements of such rites, which often signify the reintegration of the members of the bereaved family into society.

In other words, the closer the date of death and the closer the relationship between the dead and mourners, the more restrictive the death rituals are; and the more remote the date of death and the more distant the relationship between the dead and mourners, the more communal death rituals can be. Following Lynn Bennett (1983: 92ff.), death rituals of the Bāhun/Chetri or Indo-Nepalese communities can be classified into four levels, with a decreasing degree of personal relationship between the dead and the mourners, and a decreasing hold of the date of death on the latter. These forms of worship conform broadly to prescriptions for the funeral rites (*antyeṣṭi*) and ancestor worship (*śrāddha*) of the Dharmaśāstra.[20]

(*a*) *Kriyā* (or *kiriyā*) *basne*: death rituals which follow the death of an individual and which include the rituals for the immediate family (especially the eldest son) during the first thirteen days after death. These rituals are personally polluting (making *jūṭho*) and thus require a large number of observances (shaving, fasting, monodiet, special clothes, etc.) on the part of close family members. They involve disposing the corpse, feeding the *preta* and reconstituting its provisional body by transforming the *preta* into a *pitṛ* through rice-balls (the *piṇḍa* ceremonies), thus purifying the family and the chief mourners.

(*b*) Monthly *śrāddha* (Nep. *kājkriyā*): regular monthly mourning rituals during the first year after death.

(*c*) *ekoddiṣṭhaśrāddha*: observed for three generations on the lunar anniversary of a person's death by his or her male descendants.

(*d*) Collective honouring of all ancestors on certain days, such as Pitṛpakṣa or Sora Śrāddha, the fortnight preceding the fall festival of Dasaĩ, when it is believed that the spirits of ancestors come back to the world of their descendants to occupy their homes and to seek worship.

Bālācaturdaśī belongs to the fourth category. It is a collective ceremony with food offerings to several ancestors at the same time, open in regard to participation, with a rather weak obligation to perform the rituals and the freedom to include a wide range of collaterally and affinally or even fictively related persons or ancestors. Also common is the subservient role of the worshipper, who offers food to the spirits and treats them like a guest—another step in the transformation of potentially dangerous spirits of the dead (*preta*) into more benevolent ancestors (*pitaraḥ*). After the *pretas* have reached their abode, the *pitṛloka*, they can participate in the regular worship of ancestors which is a preliminary part of almost any family ritual.

Bālācaturdaśī thus belongs to the type of communal celebration for which Brahmanical Hinduism, with its ritual focus on lineage and the privacy of the house, has little place. However, it is more than a collective honouring of ancestors in the way that annual Sora Śrāddha ceremonies are. It is a festival of the demon Bālā, from whom it has taken its name, and it is intimately connected with a special ritual, the Bālāguṭhīpūjā (see later).

4. FESTIVAL OF THE DEMON BĀLĀ

Bālā is a demon who used to terrorize not only the inhabitants of Deopatan but also all people carrying corpses to the burning *ghāṭs* located east of Paśupati Temple. Several myths concerning the fate of Bālāsura, a demon who consumes human flesh, are told in Nepal (to my knowledge, all these myths have been orally transmitted). I first summarize the myths collected by Mary Anderson, which are basically the same as what I was often told in Deopatan, and then translate a printed version of Bālāsura's beheading published by L. Munaṃkarmī, supplementing it with a variant told to me by a Karmācārya priest from Deopatan.

4.1 THE MYTHS OF BĀLĀSURA CONSUMING HUMAN FLESH (CF. ANDERSON 1971: 201-7)

A sweeper or caretaker at the burning *ghāṭs* named Bālā or Bālānanda[21] once consumed unknowingly a piece of a corpse and became addicted either to eating human flesh or to breaking skulls in order to eat the brains of corpses brought for cremation. He thus became a demon, called Bālāsura or Bālādaitya, who could not resist snatching corpses for his own monstrous purpose.[22] People came up with several methods to defeat this terrifying ogre: The king (or a member of the Mānandhar caste, or else a barber friend) first made a solemn oath of friendship. Gaining Bālāsura's confidence, he gave a feast for him, and as soon as the latter became drunk, the king (or the Mānandhar or the barber) led him to a well and pushed him into it, or killed him by some other means. In another variant, a witch hypnotized the demon and induced him to lay his head in her lap—and then knifed him to death.

4.2 THE MYTHS OF BĀLĀSURA'S BEHEADING

The following is a slightly abbreviated translation of Munaṃkarmī (1987: 72-4), who does not mention his source.

A long time ago, during the time of King Bhuvanakeśarī,[23] there was a Vaiśya named Bālānanda. One day the duty of carrying the corpse of a member of his funeral group (*guṭhī*) to the burning *ghāṭ* fell on Bālānanda.[24] At that time there was the obligatory tradition of eating something while the corpse was burning. By accident a piece of the brain fell out of the corpse into the food of Bālānanda, who ate it unknowingly. As soon as the brain entered Bālānanda's mouth, his head took on a resplendently vigorous silver form. And having thus become a demon (*rākṣasa*), he cultivated the habit of eating corpses and destroying everything. That is why Bālānanda's name became Bālāsura. From that time onwards Bālāsura, who took up residence near the cremation ground (*śmaśāna*) in the Śleṣmāntaka forest, violently snatched corpses brought for burning and ate them in the middle of the forest.

Because the people could no longer burn the dead according to their caste (customs), they approached King Bhuvanakeśarī: 'Mahārāja, we subjects living in your kingdom cannot burn any more our dead according to our caste customs.' The king decided to have the demon killed and sent for a friend (*mīta*) of Bālānanda, a Vaiśya called Vṛṣasiṃha. Having told him what had happened, he said to him, 'If you can kill your friend after putting him to sleep, I promise to grant you much land and wealth.' Thus emboldened (to kill the demon), Vṛṣasiṃha left the palace.

However, Bālāsura being too strong, Vṛṣasiṃha did not dare to fight with his friend. He therefore started to practise asceticism like Śiva (*Mahādeva-ko tapasyā garna thālyo*). One day Śiva came with Pārvatī and saw him sitting there. 'Who are you? Why are you meditating on me (*mero dhyāna garī*)?' he asked Vṛṣasiṃha. Vṛṣasiṃha told him the story and then asked Śiva for the boon of getting the strength to kill (the demon). Mahādeva granted Vṛṣasiṃha the required power, but he asked for the head of Bālāsura, to be offered to him after the demon's death.

Vṛṣasiṃha went to town and bought a large jar of liquor (*ghyāmpo raksī*) and so much meat, flattened rice (*ciurā*), etc., that ten or twelve young men had to carry it. He took everything on the path of death. When Bālāsura saw that a corpse was being brought, he came out. Vṛṣasiṃha said to him, 'Oh friend, hello! We haven't met for many days. So I've brought something for you.' He had all the food placed in front of Bālāsura, who was pleased and greedily consumed it all. Bālāsura soon fell senseless from the liquor. Grabbing their chance, the crowd took a rope, tied him up, dropped him into a well and killed him by throwing stones, etc. Afterwards Vṛṣasiṃha climbed down and cut off the silver head of Bālāsura. He brought it to King Bhuvanakeśarī and requested him to make an ornament from the head and to let him present it to Paśupati (i.e. Śiva). The king was delighted and granted Vṛṣasiṃha the promised land and wealth.

The man went to Paśupati Temple and, since Paśupati was pleased, asked for another boon (*varadāna*): 'Lord, Bālāsura was my friend. Since I killed him I am tainted by the sin of killing a friend (*mitrahatyā-ko pāpa*). Nevertheless, please grant me liberation (*mocana*).' Mahādeva said: 'Those who come to worship me every year on the day Bālāsura was killed and I was adorned with his silver head are freed from the sin of killing a friend. Moreover, the relatives of he who scatters on that same day (seven?) seeds (*satabīja*) in the Śleṣmāntaka forest and comes to walk on foot through the Paśupati area will obtain liberation (*mokṣa*) up to the seventh generation (*pustā*) and may rest in my world (Śivaloka).'

Mary Anderson also quotes a version in which the head of Bālāsura somehow survives as a demon in the form of a solid ball of silver, from which a precious ornament was fashioned after his defeat and presented to Paśupati. Moreover, she mentions that his 'head' is believed to have taken refuge in a forest den or cave.

The following is the version a Karmācārya priest from Deopatan told me in Nepālī:

Once a demon called Bālāsura terrorized Deopatan by eating children. The inhabitants of the city went to the king and complained. The ruler put a price on Bālāsura's head. Hearing this, a Mānandhar (a member from the caste of oil-pressers) made friendship with Bālāsura, but this ogre suspected that the Mānandhar only did so to kill him. He asked him, 'Did you become my friend because you want to kill me?' The Mānandhar said 'No!' and offered him a great quantity of alcohol (*raksī* and *jād*). Again Bālāsura asked, 'Do you offer this just because you want to kill me?' The Mānandhar said 'No!' Bālāsura became tired after much drinking and finally laid his head into the Mānandhar's lap, asking a third time, 'Do you want to kill me?' This the Mānandhar again denied. Then Bālāsura said, 'You lied three times; there is no truth any more in this world.' When he said this, the Mānandhar cut off his head and threw it away. Bālāsura became a *mūkaṭṭa*, a headless demon, and the head was hidden in a special area of the Mṛgasthalī forest called Bhāgalbugal (see *infra*). That is why Mānandhars still go on Bālācaturdaśī to that place, namely to secretly worship Bālāsura's head.

Common to all these myths is the fact that somebody eats human flesh and that another person breaks an oath. Destroying the bonds of blood (snatching the corpse) or the bonds of an oath (breaking a ritual friendship) endangers the established order. The connection with the aforementioned forms of ancestor worship is not very clear, particularly since most pilgrims do not know about the myths in the first place. The structural link seems to me to be the fear of ritual fault during death rites. The future of the dead and the mourners are endangered if these rites are not properly performed—if death is not pacified.

5. THE BĀLĀGUṬHĪPŪJĀ

Only a few people, even in Deopatan, know that a ritual exists which to a certain extent reenacts the myths of Bālācaturdaśī. The ritual is a worship of the demon Bālādaitya performed by a religious group called Bālādaityaguṭhī or Bālāguṭhī, of which only Mānandhars from Pāṭan are members (*guṭhiyār*). The *pūjā* takes place in the middle of the night following the festival of Bālācaturdaśī, at a location called Bhāgalbugal, which is located in exactly the same area of the Mṛgasthalī forest mentioned by the Karmācārya priest in his story of Bālāsura (see earlier).

The place is also known for a hidden 'entrance' into Kailāsa hill, symbolized by some stairs leading into the hill, to a door which is always closed. Some say that it is a subterranean path or tunnel which connects Deopatan with Kathmandu, or Nepal with India, or Kailāsa with Muktinātha, etc. Also one hears stories that this is the place where the five Pāṇḍavas from the *Mahābhārata* epos arrived when they had to escape from Kurukṣetra, and that the *liṅga* nearby is thus called Pañcapāṇḍavapraveśadvāra (Entrance Door of the Five Pāṇḍavas) or Kurukṣetreśvara (Lord of Kurukṣetra), or else simply Dharmeśvara (Lord of Dharma) (Plate 6).

Around midnight five *guṭhī* members together with two Gubhajyū priests and four musicians proceed from Pāṭan (via Śaṅkhāmūl, New and Old Baneshvar) to Bhāgalbugal. Then a very elaborate ritual commences—basically a *homa* mixed with Tantric elements (e.g. alcohol, fish; see later)—comprising the following main features:

The main priest gives *dīkṣā* to the participants. Both priests purify the ritual ground (Plate 7) with cow-dung and then draw with rice powder a *vajra* pattern and an octagonal pattern (two *catuṣkoṇas*) on the ground, sticking one-foot sticks at the corners and connecting them with cotton threads. This is the place where later a *homa* fire is lit. Before the *homa* starts several other items are prepared and purified: a vessel (*kalaśa*), a bell, a conch, a *vajra*, bottles with alcohol (Nev. *tvā*). The main items are two copper fishes, called Nev. *kāy-nyā* (Plate 8), which are later needed for the *pūjā*. Unhusked rice (*dhāna*) is lit and burnt, becoming the incense (*dhūpa*) required for the ritual. A bell is rung and two musicians blow long trumpets (Nev. *kahaḥ*) for two minutes. Barley and flowers are thrown on the sacrificial ground and sacrificial items; the latter are purified by connecting them with threads and pouring water on them. The priests prepare themselves by executing Tantric gestures (*mudrā*). One *guṭhīyār* places four leaf-plates filled with fruits, cooked rice, onions, spinach, fish and minced meat on the *liṅga*. The *homa* is lit. A text (*Dinahomavidhi*) is recited. Grains are strewn, and special spoons are used to pour purified butter (*ghiũ*) over the fire, during which music is played (one *kahaḥ*, drums and cymbals [*jhālī*]). Flowers and incense are thrown on the fishes, and barley and flowers on the *liṅga*. Four *guṭhīyārs* jointly take in hand the *kalaśa*, a fifth takes the two fishes filled with water; they pour the water on the fire while music is played. All circumambulate the fire three times. The wooden sticks are burnt. All grains, flowers, spoons and other items are burnt. The priests give a *ṭīkā* to the participants. With farewell rituals the Bālāguṭhīpūjā ends.

Most unusual is the pair of fish used during the ritual. The mythological 'reason' for their presence is given by a Karmācārya informant, clearly a variant of the Śivarātri myth (see Michaels 1988 and 1994: Chap. 13):

Once a local thief killed somebody. In fear of the people who tried to catch him, he fled to Paśupati and climbed a tree where he exclaimed, 'Śiva! Śiva!' However, he fell from the tree and died, but he was reborn in the form of a fish, as Matsyabhairava. His family learned of this and took care of him. When the fish died he went to Śivaloka. To celebrate this event, his relatives still come to Deopatan on Bālācaturdaśī.

Fishes as oblations in *śrāddha* ceremonies are mentioned in the Dharmaśāstra (see Kane 1973: 422f. and 425). Their function in the Bālāguṭhīpūjā, however, is different and has little to do with ancestor worship. Generally a pair of fish (*matsyayugma*) is a symbol of auspiciousness and fertility. In Hinduism, Buddhism and Jainism, they are listed among the Eight Auspicious Items (*aṣṭamaṅgala*, sometimes also called *mīnamithuna*). Fish (*matsya*) are also one of the five Tantric M's (*pañcamakāra*). In Nepal, however, the use of fish has added implications, due to the influential cult of Matsyendranātha. This deity (see Locke 1973, Slusser 1982: 367-80) is connected with rain and fertility. Regardless of his esoteric meaning, in popular understanding Matsyendranātha is a god with rain-making powers.[25] Moreover, the festival of Bālācaturdaśī is, as we have seen, linked with the Triśūljātrā, also 'a rain-making festival' (Michaels 1987: 169, 191). And finally, one does well to consider that the festival takes place in the Śleṣmāntaka forest, a mythological residence of the rain-producing snakes (Nāga) and one of the main seats of Gorakhnāth, the pupil of Matsyendranātha. Given all this, the Bālāguṭhīpūjā seems to be more a ritual of fertility than ancestor worship.

It would seem, then, that Bālācaturdaśī has a twin mythological and ritual structure connected with the regeneration of life. On the one hand, it is the worship of a demon who destroys the circle of rebirth by snatching corpses before the funeral rites can be performed, and thereby rendering redeath (and rebirth) impossible. By mythologically killing and ritually pacifying him, one ensures that the chain of being is not interrupted; life can be regained, and the dead can become ancestors. On the other hand, Bālā is a demon who has nothing to do with ancestors. He eats up seeds (a symbol of food or new life) planted at the time of the Matsyendranātha festival. He is pacified by the scattering of seeds during Bālācaturdaśī and through the Bālāguṭhīpūjā, so that fertility is not endangered.

Both types of ritual, the festival of Bālācaturdaśī and the Bālāguṭhīpūjā, may originally have been unconnected, but since ancestor worship and demon worship enjoy a complementary relationship, they became joined. In the next section I shall go so far as to argue that festivals like Bālācaturdaśī are complements necessary for solving certain problems in the ritual conception of death in the high (Brahmanical) tradition of Hinduism.

6. ANCESTORS, DEMONS AND THE RITUAL IMPOSSIBILITY OF DEATH

Most scholars who have written on death in Hinduism (see Blackburn 1985: fn. 2 and 3) make a distinction between the worship of malevolent demons, spirits, ghosts, devils, etc., and rather benevolent, almost godlike ancestors. Both categories concern post-death life, but their sources are different. Stuart Blackburn (1985) has aptly shown that the deification process in folk cults and the funeral ceremonies of high castes, as reflected in the rituals for the dead, have developed in different directions. Whereas in folk cults the dead are worshipped as 'small gods' only when they die a premature, violent death, in Brahmanical Hinduism the dead are venerated only after their transformation into ancestors. However, during a limited period the dead are, as we have seen, more demons than ancestors, and it is this intermediary period[26] which is the most impure and dangerous. Motivated by the common 'fear of the dead' (Frazer), post-death worship in Hinduism is, in its primary phase, engaged in avoiding the return of the potentially demanding spirit of the dead,[27] to make sure that the deceased person (*preta*) does not become a malevolent demon, and to help him to reach the semidivine region of the ancestors (*pitaraḥ*), where he will not trouble his kin (see Sprockhoff 1985: 268) and envy those who are still living. Only then is 'true' ancestor worship possible. The vague category of *pitaraḥ* fades into even further oblivion after three generations, when the great-grandfather is promoted to the category of the almost imperceptible *viśvedevāḥ* (lit. 'all gods'), who are, however, not necessarily immortal. Most Indians are rather vague about the identity of the *viśvedevāḥ* (see Parry 1985: 622).

Brahmanical ancestor worship should thus be differentiated into primary rites, when a certain deceased individual is worshipped (e.g. *nitya-* and *naimittika-śrāddha*), and secondary rites, when generalized ancestors are (often collectively) worshipped. This differentiation is justified by the fact that two separate groups of priests are generally involved in mortuary rites (see Parry 1980 and 1985: 614-5): the impure funeral priest, called often euphemistically *mahābrāhmaṇa*, presides over rites addressed to the disembodied marginal ghost (*preta*), while a priestly Brahmin 'with a rather less equivocal status' (Parry 1985: 615) is responsible for the *śrāddha* rites, i.e. after the *preta* has safely reached the world of the ancestors (*pitṛloka*).

During Bālāçaturdaśī, a festival named after a demon, both types of rituals are performed: individual *śrāddhas* and worship with a reference to collective or generalized ancestral spirits. In the second case, the dead are usually not personally addressed and the main offerings are *scattered* grains, an element often found in rituals of repelling ghosts, while in the first case *cooked* rice-balls (*piṇḍa*) are dominant, signifying a close family relationship between the dead and the mourners (see Parry 1985).

One should also keep in mind that Death (Yama) itself is often considered a demon in Hindu mythology,[28] one who has to be overcome in order to gain immortality. However, despite the affinities between funeral rites and demon worship, one does not find a festival like Bālācaturdaśī mentioned in the various lists of permitted *śrāddhas* or catalogues of death ceremonies of the Dharmaśāstra texts,[29] presumably because 'those castes (generally Brahmins) who follow the *śrāddha* ceremonies in detail are usually not involved in cults to local gods and goddesses' (Blackburn 1985: 265). Demon worship and Brahmanical ancestor worship seem to be incompatible, for

> folk cults and the *śrāddha* ceremonies have developed their rituals for the dead in different direct-ions. . . . This folk tradition, in other words, has developed the funerary base into that complex of gods and temples usually referred to as village or popular Hinduism. The *śrāddha* ceremonies, on the other hand, have developed the base in the other direction, into a system of ancestor worship. (Blackburn 1985: 265-6)

Ancestor worship is, it seems, different from demon worship because of the lack of individuality in Brahmanical conceptions of the after-life: as long as deceased persons retain their (recollected) individuality—that is, within the first year(s) after death—they are regarded as potentially demonic. Once this period is over, they become more or less anonymous. Why, then, does the Brahmanical conception of the after-life not mesh with that of individuality?

One reason seems to be that Brahmanism accepts the idea of a singular, irrevocable death—one basic for a certain type of demon cult in folk religion—only in asceticism (see later). If a natural death has taken place and the death rituals are carried out correctly, Brahmanism considers the result primarily as a change of status: the dead become, either immediately or after sometime, first an ethereal body and then a gross body prior to reincarnation. In both cases, the soul or self (*ātman*) remains immortal but has no individuality. In other words, what changes and is reborn is not the *ātman*. Mortality is *ātman*-lessness.[30] Along with E. Cassirer, in words originally addressed to Lévy-Bruhl, one could say: It is not immortality that has to be proven but mortality (see epigraph). Death leads to redeath but not the end of life; it is more a transformative process than an event:[31]

tathā śarīrāṇi vihāya jīrṇāny anyāni saṃyāti navāni dehī //
As a man puts off worn-out raiment and takes on new, so does the embodied soul put off its worn-out bodies and enter other new ones. (BhG 2.22; cf. BĀU IV.4.4 and Kane 1973: 335)

Hindu death rituals are full of instances of consumption and digestion (see Parry 1985): the fire that burns and eats the gross body (*sthūlaśarīra*) of the deceased person, so that the soul can become a partly disembodied being with an airy body (*sūkṣmaśarīra*); and the impure funeral priest and the pure Brahmin who consume the sins, and sometimes even body parts, of the dead, thus bringing them into a state of purity. 'By "digesting" the deceased his pure essence is distilled, and translated by the digestive fire of the stomach to the other world, while his impure sins are eliminated. This distilled ancestral essence then becomes the source of progeny—as is the sexual fluid distilled out of the good part of food' (Parry 1985: 614).

However, there is an 'essence' of the individual—not its 'ancestral essence', but its *ātman*—that is beyond change and death (or time: *kāla* means both time and death!). A personal identity after death is more or less impossible. The individualized soul, which still has an airy body (*sūkṣmaśarīra*), cannot find an eternal place of no return (heaven or hell) where it could be deified. What it can find is a temporary abode until it is reborn, while one who is not reborn cannot form an object of veneration, being without individuality. Individuality causes rebirth (and redeath). Natural life and rebirth, presupposing change and alteration, growing and dying, death and birth, is by definition not eternal and thus impure. In other words (those of Dumont): Impurity and rebirth and redeath arise when the biological breaks into the ritual concept of life. After all, death *and* birth are polluting and create a state of impurity (*aśauca*).

Thus a deified death finds no place in the Brahmanical conception of the after-life, either in the negative form as demon worship or in the positive form as hero worship. This does not leave much scope for personal cults and the worship of any deceased individual. Votive items for naturally deceased persons (photos, death masks, memorial stones, etc.) are comparatively rare in India. No graves, no memorials, no memorial services and no minute of silence are resorted to to commemorate the dead. Each *nitya-* and *naimittika-śrāddha* is the same; only the names and genealogical clans (*gotra*) of the deceased person and the date of his or her death mentioned in the rituals change.

However, the case is different when a person has died a violent or a heroic death, including self-sacrifice or ritual suicide (Michaels 1992a). Then votive *liṅgas* and memorial stones are quite common,[32] and opportunities for mourning ceremonies commemorating the deceased and 'cults of the deified dead' (Blackburn) arise; and then the other, non-Brahmanical concept of post-death life becomes dominant.

The same structure can be seen for ascetics, who, in certain sects (e.g. Daśanāmīs), die a ritual death before their biological death, and for whom a positive, personal worship through relics and other commemorative items (e.g. graves) is possible after their biological death, whereas—and wherefore—ancestor worship for and by them is not possible. And *vice versa*: for twice-born who first die a biological death and then a ritual death (i.e. *antyeṣṭi*), ancestor worship is possible and necessary, but no positive, personal memorial and worship. Ancestors are reborn; ascetics, demons and heroes are not.

Like asceticism, such a conception creates problems for 'reality'. For whereas ascetics do not 'really' die when they ritually die, men 'really' do, even if their essence cannot die. The solution to this problem in Hinduism is not different from the well-known paths of liberation: it is either by correct knowledge or by correct ritual action that the victory over death and redeath is gained. Only if the intellectual or ritual substitution (or identification) is performed without mistakes can one be identified with eternity or that which never dies, i.e. immortality. Only then will there be no death, or even change. Change presupposes something lost, which therefore cannot be eternal (unless the change itself is, as in early Buddhism, considered eternal). Thus, in Brahmanical Hinduism, one finds the strongly ingrained concept of a permanent substitution of father and son (the wife is genealogically identified with her husband at marriage) which avoids, in a ritual sense, death (see Michaels 1986: 106ff.). Both are identified with the fire (*agni*), which itself only dies if it is not tended. In other words, death only occurs when this ritual identification is not possible any more—when somebody dies, for instance, a premature, unnatural death, before he marries or before a son is born to him (who continues to tend the fire), or when he himself decides to destroy the identification (asceticism). Death, then, is ritual inaccuracy, not fate.

All this is based on ideas which go back to the Brāhmaṇa period. As evidence, I quote a passage from the *Śatapatha Brāhmaṇa*, which shows how early in India death was thought of as something which could be overcome by mortals through knowledge or sacrifice, even if at the expense of their individuality and thus post-death worship:

> Even the gods did not attain immortality before they came to know about the proper (ritual) identification of Death and the Year or Prajāpati who said to them: 'You are not laying down my forms; either you overdo it or you leave something out. That is why you do not become immortal.' After they had been told how to lay down the bricks of the altar they became immortal. But then Death said to the gods, 'All men will become immortal in precisely this way and then what share will be mine?' They [i.e. the gods] said, 'From now on, no one else will become immortal together with the body. But as soon as you have taken (the body as) your share, then, after separating from his body, he will become immortal—if he is someone who has achieved immortality through knowledge or through action (*karma*).' Now, when they said, 'through knowledge or through action,' they meant by 'knowledge' the knowledge of the fire (-altar), and by 'action' the ritual of the fire (-altar). And those who have this knowledge, or who do this ritual, they come to life again when they have died, and as soon as they come to life again they come to immortal life. But those who do not have this knowledge or who do not do this ritual, when they die they come to life again, but they become the food of this (Death) again and again. (*ŚBr* 10.4.3.1-10, transl. O'Flaherty 1988: 12-13)[33]

To sum up, the Brahmanical conception of death does not satisfy the need of an individualized, commemorative worship of the deceased person, either in a positive way (hero worship and deification) or in a negative way (demon worship). Festivals like Bālācaturdaśī fulfil this need and are thus not an additional but rather complementary element of Hinduism.

NOTES

1. I have witnessed the festival two times, in 1983 and 1989. In the descriptive material on the festivals of Nepal with which I am familiar, only a few authors mention Bālācaturdaśī (Nev. Bālācaḥre): Anderson (1971: 301-7), Goodman (1981: 112-13), Majapuria and Gupta (1981: 123-5), Munaṃkarmī (1987: 71-5), Levy (1990: 421).
2. To my knowledge, this *pūjā* has not yet been noticed by the literature on Nepalese festivals and rituals.

3. I would like to express my gratitude to Noutan Sharma for his assistance in the field-work, to Mrityunjaya Karmacarya for his kind answers to my many questions, and to Philip Pierce for correcting my English. My thanks are also due to the Deutsche Forschungsgemeinschaft for financially supporting the fieldwork.
4. For a further description and analysis of festivals in Deopatan, see Michaels 1984, 1987, 1988, 1992, 1993 and 1994 (chs. 12-14).
5. In 1989, for these stalls a fee of 5-25 rupees had to be paid to the Paśupati Bhaṇḍāra Tahabil (account office of Paśupati Temple).
6. When in Christian milieux a mirror is covered after death, windows are opened or the chair of the deceased person is turned upside down, the purpose of such traditions is also to ensure that the dead do not return. Even the wake over the corpse must partly be understood in this way.
7. *Rattikā* is a corrupt Sanskrit form related to Nep. *ratti,* the smallest unit of weight, measured in corns or seeds; compare Skt. *raktikā,* 'Abrus precatorius and its seed used as a weight' (Turner 1931: s.v. *ratti*).
8. Since I am not familiar with the Tamang culture and language, I have neglected this aspect of Bālācaturdaśī.
9. See Sprockhoff (1985) for a luminous distinction between pacified and pacifying death.
10. See Turner (1969) and, in an application of Turner's methods to an analysis of Brahmanical death ritual, Das (1976).
11. Ed. G. Ṭaṇḍan vs 2046: pt. 2, no. 257, and Michaels (1994: App. A 6, line 10).
12. In the *Nepālī Bṛhat Śabdakośa,* s.v. *sadbhī,* the notion of seven seeds is not mentioned. However, Anderson (1971: 202) or Majapuria and Gupta (1981: 124) refer to it.
13. Abegg's translation of the Pretakalpa is based on Naunidhirāma's *Garuḍa-purāṇa Sārodhāra* in the Nirṇayasāgara Press (Bombay 1903) and on Jīvānanda Vidyasāgara's edition of the *Uttarakhaṇḍa* (Calcutta 1890). The former edition was not available to me.
14. In regard to the role of sesame seeds in Nepal see Slusser (1982: 247).
15. See also VIII.35 and Kane (1973: 418).
16. During the construction of a cremation ground (*śmaśāna*) the Taitirīyaśākhās and Śaunakins also scatter seeds to strengthen the dead; see Caland (1896: 151).
17. *Agati,* lit. 'state of not having gone', i.e. not dead.
18. For descriptions of funeral rites in Nepal, see Toffin (1979) and (1983: 144-52), and Quigley (1985) and Ishii (forthcoming).
19. Perhaps the idea of redeath (Skt. *punarmṛtyu*) originates from *damnatio memoriae.*
20. See, for example, Caland (1893), Kane (1973), Müller (1992).
21. Bālānanda, lit. 'a person whose delight is [consuming] children'? 'Bālāsura' or 'Bāladaitya' could also refer to the untimely death of a child (*bāla*), who could thus easily become and remain a threatening demon (*asura, daitya*).
22. In certain cremation rituals, a small portion of the flesh from the corpse is buried in the sand near the river; this portion is for the demons who eat corpses. Another piece is thrown into the river and thus carried to heaven (see Bennett 1983: 99). It is also a fact that during the cremation of

Nepalese kings a piece of the king's skull or brain is eaten by a Bhaṭṭa priest (see Toffin 1987: 229).

23. A king who ruled in the independent kingdom of Bhaktapur from AD 1505 to 1519.
24. Among Newars, there is the tradition of helping each other in funeral organizations. For references see fn. 18.
25. See Slusser (1982: 376) for further evidence.
26. See Kane (1973: 335-6) for a discussion of this point.
27. See also Schmithausen (1995: 49), who here refers to the pre-Hindu origin of such ideas.
28. I ignore this aspect in the following; it has been treated in extenso by O'Flaherty (1976: 212-47).
29. See, for instance, *Smṛticandrikā*, Śrāddhakāṇḍa, II.1ff.: regular or optional *śrāddhas* (*nityaśrāddha, naimittikaśrāddha, kāmyaśrāddha*), *vṛddhiśrāddha* (on an auspicious occasion), *sapiṇḍaśrāddha* (with *piṇḍas*), *pārvaṇaśrāddha* (on new and full moons), *goṣṭhiśrāddha* (in the cow barn), *ekoddiṣṭhaśrāddha* (subsequent lunar death anniversaries), *śuddhyarthaśrāddha* (feeding of Brahmins for purposes of purification), etc.
30. See Heesterman (1995: 39-42) for a discussion of this point.
31. Thus the conclusion of Hertz' famous essay 'Contribution à une étude sur la representation de la mort' (1907). Cf. Cassirer (1924: 49): 'Es gibt für das mythische Denken keinen bestimmten, klar abgegrenzten Moment, bei dem das Leben in den Tod oder der Tod in das Leben übergeht. Wie es die Geburt als Wiederkehr denkt, so denkt es den Tod als Fortdauer. . . . Das in sich ungeschiedene und unreflektierte Bewusstsein weigert sich, eine Trennung zu vollziehen, die in der Tat nicht unmittelbar und zwingend im Erlebnisgehalt als solchem liegt, sondern die letzten Endes nur durch die Besinnung auf die empirischen Bedingungen des Lebens—also durch eine bestimmte Form der kausalen Analyse—gefordert wird.'
32. See Blackburn (1985: fn. 10) for references.
33. The myth has been translated and discussed by various authors: see O'Flaherty (1988: 11-13), with further references, as well as Long (1977: 75) and Mooren (1995: 66) (the latter, unfortunately, with several mistakes).

REFERENCES

Abegg, Emil. 1956. *Der Pretakalpa des Garuḍa-Purāṇa. Eine Darstellung des hinduistischen Totenkultes und Jenseitsglaubens.* Aus dem Sanskrit übersetzt und erklärt. 2nd. ed. Berlin: de Gruyter.

Anderson, Mary M. 1971. *The Festivals of Nepal.* London: Allen & Unwin.

Bennett, Lynn. 1983. *Dangerous Wives and Sacred Sisters.* New York: Columbia University Press.

Blackburn, Stuart. 1985. Death and Deification: Folk Cults in Hinduism. *History of Religions* 24: 253-73.

Caland, W. 1893. *Altindischer Ahnenkult.* Leiden: E.J. Brill.

———. 1896 (1967). *Die Altindischen Todten- und Bestattungsgebräuche.* Reprint. Wiesbaden: Sändig.

Cassirer, Ernst. 1924 (1973). *Philosophie der symbolischen Formen.* Vol. 2: *Das mythische Denken.* Reprint. Darmstadt: Wiss. Buchgesellschaft.

Cederroth, S., C. Corlin, and J. Lindström (eds.). 1988. *On the Meaning of Death: Essays on Mortuary Rituals and Eschatological Beliefs.* Stockholm: Almqvist and Wiksell International.

Das, Veena. 1976. The Uses of Liminality: Society and Cosmos in Hinduism. *Contributions to Indian Sociology* (N.S.) 10: 245-63.

Dumont, Louis. 1966 (1970). *Homo Hierarchicus: The Caste System and Its Implications.* Reprint. London: Weidenfeld & Nicolson.

Durkheim, Émile. 1912 (1981). *Die elementaren Formen des religiösen Lebens.* Reprint. Frankfurt am Main: Suhrkamp.

Garuḍa Purāṇa. 1890. Uttarakhaṇḍa: ed. Jīvānanda Vidyāsāgara. Calcutta: Sarasvatīyantra. See also Abegg 1956 and fn. 13.

Gladigow, Burkhard. 1985. Naturae deus humanae mortalis: Zur sozialen Konstruktion des Todes in römischer Zeit. In G. Stephenson (ed.), *Leben und Tod in den Religionen.* 2nd ed. Darmstadt: Wissenschaftliche Buchgesellschaft.

Goodman, Jim. 1981. *Guide to Enjoying Nepalese Festivals.* Kathmandu: Kali Press.

Hanchett, Suzanne. 1988. *Coloured Rice: Symbolic Structure in Hindu Family Festivals.* Delhi: Hindustan Publ. Corp.

Heesterman, Jan C. 1995. Feuer, Seele und Unsterblichkeit. In Gerhard Oberhammer (ed.), *Im Tod gewinnt der Mensch sein Selbst: Das Phänomen des Todes in asiatischer und abendländischer Religionstradition.* Vienna: Verlag der Österreichischen Akademie der Wissenschaften.

Hertz, Robert. 1907. Contribution à une étude sur la representation de la mort. *L'année sociologique* 10: 48-137.

Himavatkhaṇḍa of the Skandapurāṇa. 1956. [with Pariśiṣṭa]. Gorakṣagranthamālā 69. Kāśī: Gorakṣaṭillākāśī, vs 2013.

Hodson, T.C. 1921. The Doctrine of Rebirth in Various Areas in India. *Man in India* 1 (2): 1-17.

Ishii, Hiroshi. 1988. Change of *sanā guṭhī* in a Newar Village. In S. Lienhard (ed.), *Change and Continuity: Studies in the Nepalese Culture of the Kathmandu Valley.* Torino: Centre Piemontese di Studi sul Medio ed Estremo Oriente.

Kane, P.V. 1973. *History of Dharmaśāstra.* Vol. 4. Poona: Bhandarkar Oriental Research Institute.

Knipe, David M. 1976. *Sapiṇḍīkaraṇa:* The Hindu Rite of Entry into Heaven. In F.E. Reynolds and E.H. Waugh (eds.), *Religious Encounters with Death: Insights from the History and Anthropology of Religions.* London, University Park: Pennsylvania State University Press.

Levy, Robert I. 1990. *Mesocosm: Hinduism and the Organization of a Traditional Newar City in Nepal.* Berkeley: University of California Press.

Locke, John R. 1973. *Rato Matsyendranath of Patan and Bungamati.* Kirtipur: Tribhuvan University.

Long, J.B. 1977. Death as a Necessity and a Gift in Hindu Mythology. In F.E. Reynolds and E.H. Waugh (eds.), *Religious Encounters with Death: Insights from the History and Anthropology of Religions*. London, University Park: Pennsylvania State University Press.

Majapuria, T. Ch., and S.P. Gupta. 1981. *Nepal: The Land of Festivals*. New Delhi: S. Chand.

Metcalf, P., and R. Huntington. 1991. *Celebrations of Death: The Anthropology of Mortuary Ritual*. 2nd. ed. Cambridge: Cambridge University Press.

Michaels, Axel. 1984. Śiva's Wild and Wayward Calf: The Goddess Vatsalā, Her Temple and Yātrā. *Kailash* 9 (3-4): 105-47.

———. 1986. *Ritual und Gesellschaft in Indien*. Frankfurt am Main: Verlag Neue Kritik.

———. 1986a. Der verstoβene Sohn: Nepalesische *bālyogis* und der *deśāntara*-Ritus während der Initiation. In B. Kölver (ed.), *Formen kulturellen Wandels und andere Beiträge zur Erforschung des Himālaya*. Nepalica 2/6. St. Augustin: VGH Wissenschaftsverlag.

———. 1987. The Triśūlyātrā in Deopatan and its Legends. In N. Gutschow and A. Michaels (eds.), *Heritage of the Kathmandu Valley: Proceedings of an International Conference in Lübeck, June 1986*. Nepalica 4/10. St. Augustin: VGH Wissenschaftsverlag.

———. 1988. Śivarātri at Deopatan. In S. Lienhard (ed.), *Change and Continuity: Studies in the Nepalese Culture of the Kathmandu Valley*. Torino: Centre Piemontese di Studi sul Medio ed Estremo Oriente.

———. 1992. Lukumahādyaḥ—The Hiding Śiva: A Nepalese Stone Deity and Its Cult. In B. Kölver (ed.), *Aspects of Nepalese Traditions: Proceedings of a Seminar under the Auspices of Tribhuvan University Research Division and the German Research Council, March 1990* (with comments by Govinda Tandon). Nepal Research Centre Publications 19. Stuttgart: Franz Steiner Verlag.

———. 1992a. Recht auf Leben, Tötung und Selbsttötung in Indien. In B. Mensen (ed.), *Recht auf Leben—Recht auf Töten: ein Kulturvergleich*. Nettetal: Steyler Verlag.

———. 1993. Śiva under Refuse: The Hidden Mahādeva (Lukumahādyaḥ) and Protective Stones in Nepal. In H. Brückner, L. Lutze, and Aditya Malik (eds.), *Flags of Flame: Studies in South Asian Folk Culture*. New Delhi: Manohar.

———. 1994. *Reisen der Götter: Der nepalische Paśupatinātha-Tempel und sein rituelles Umfeld*. 2 vols. Bonn: VGH Wissenschaftsverlag, Bonn.

Mooren, Thomas. 1995. *Die vertauschten Schädel: Tod und Sterben in Naturreligionen, Hinduismus und Christentum*. Düsseldorf: Patmos Verlag.

Müller, Klaus-Werner. 1992. *Das brahmanische Totenritual nach der Antyeṣṭipaddhati des Nārāyaṇabhaṭṭa*. Stuttgart: Franz Steiner.

Munaṃkarmī, Līlābhakta. 1987. *Hāmro Sāṃskṛtika Parva ra Jātrāharū* [Our traditional festivals and processions]. Kathmandu: Dayāratna Śākya, vs 2043.

Nepālī Bṛhat Śabdakośa. 1983. Kathmandu: Nepāla Rājakīya Prajñā-Pratiṣṭhāna, vs 2040.

O'Flaherty, Wendy Doniger. 1976. *The Origins of Evil in Hindu Mythology*. Delhi: Motilal Banarsidass.

———. 1988. (ed. and transl.) *Textual Sources for the Study of Hinduism*. Manchester: Manchester University Press.

Parry, Jonathan. 1980. Ghost, Greed, and Sin: The Occupational Identity of the Benares Funeral Priests. *Man* (N.S.) 15: 88-111.

———. 1985. Death and Digestion: The Symbolism of Food and Eating in North Indian Mortuary Rites. *Man* (N.S.) 20: 612-30.

Schmithausen, Lambert. 1995. Mensch, Tier und Pflanze und der Tod in den älteren Upaniṣaden. In Gerhard Oberhammer (ed.), *Im Tod gewinnt der Mensch sein Selbst: Das Phänomen des Todes in asiatischer und abendländischer Religionstradition.* Vienna: Verlag der Österreichischen Akademie der Wissenschaften.

Slusser, Mary Sh. 1982. *Nepal Mandala: A Cultural Study of the Kathmandu Valley.* Princeton: Princeton University Press.

Sprockhoff, Joachim Friedrich. 1985. Die feindlichen Toten und der befriedende Tote: Die Überwindung von Leben und Tod in der Entsagung. In G. Stephenson (ed.), *Leben und Tod in den Religionen.* 2nd ed. Darmstadt: Wissenschaftliche Buchgesellschaft.

Staal, Frits. 1979. The Meaninglessness of Ritual. *Numen* 26: 2-22.

Toffin, Gérard. 1979. Les rites funéraires des hautes castes hindouistes néwar (Népal). In J. Guiart (ed.), *Les hommes et la mort: rituels funéraires à travers le monde.* Paris: Le Sycomore-Objets et Mondes.

———. 1984. *Société et religion chez les Néwar du Népal.* Paris: Éditions du Centre National de la Recherche Scientifique.

———. 1987. Funeral Priests and Caste System in the Kathmandu Valley. In N. Gutschow and A. Michaels (eds.), *Heritage of the Kathmandu Valley: Proceedings of an International Conference in Lübeck, June 1986.* Nepalica 4/12. St. Augustin: VGH Wissenschaftsverlag.

Turner, Victor. 1969. *The Ritual Process.* Chicago: Aldine.

Le sacrifice des os

CHARLES MALAMOUD

Dans le rituel védique[1] et brahmanique, une distinction très nette, et de grande conséquence, est faite entre le sacrifiant d'une part, les officiants de l'autre. Le sacrifiant (*yajamāna*) est celui qui prend l'initiative d'offrir un sacrifice: il assume toutes les dépenses et il doit recueillir les bienfaits, les "fruits" (*phala*) qui résulteront de ses offrandes. Il est véritablement le "maître du sacrifice": tel est le sens du terme *yajñapati* parfois employé comme synonyme de *yajamāna*. Son action, parce qu'elle engage constamment sa propre personne, est rendue par le verbe *yaj*, "offrir un sacrifice", à la voix moyenne (*yajate*). En revanche, les officiants (*ṛtvij*) sont des techniciens, des spécialistes des opérations rituelles, des "prêtres", si l'on veut, qui mettent leurs savoirs et leurs compétences au service du sacrifiant, qui est tenu de les rémunérer: les honoraires rituels (*dakṣiṇā*) qu'ils reçoivent du sacrifiant sont les avantages qu'ils vissent;[2] les gestes qu'ils sont amenés à exécuter sur le terrain du seul sacrifice, les textes qu'ils récitent ou chantent, toutes ces prestations se font pour le compte du sacrifiant. Aussi bien, comme ils agissent pour autrui, leur action est exprimée par le verbe *yaj* également, mais à la voix active (*yajati*), et, plus fréquemment, au causatif (*yājayati*): les officiants, par leurs services, rendent possible le rite entrepris par le sacrifiant, ils font en sorte que le sacrifiant sacrifie.

Deux formules permettent de rendre compte de la relation entre le sacrifiant et les officiants: tous sont animés par le désir (*kāma*) mais le *kāma* du sacrifiant, ce sont les fruits de l'acte sacrificiel, en premier lieu le ciel (*svarga*), c'est-à-dire une place dans le monde céleste après la mort; tandis que le *kāma* des officiants est en premier lieu d'obtenir de riches *dakṣiṇā* (Mais, bien entendu, ces richesses peuvent être pour le *ṛtvij*, le symbole ou l'origine de biens beaucoup plus précieux, l'immortalité, la joie, la force, exaltés avec ferveur par example en Śatapatha-brāhmaṇa IV 3, 4, 28-31). Ces deux *kāma* convergent, se garantissent l'un l'autre et leur rencontre permet la réalisation du sacrifice.[3] D'autre part, le sacrifiant, pour pouvoir commencer le sacrifice, doit se soumettre à une série d'observances de caractère ascétique qui aboutit à une sorte de consécration ou d'initiation, *dīkṣā*.[4] Or cette *dīkṣā* lui est conférée par un des officiants; mais les officiants, eux n'ont pas à recevoir cette *dīkṣā*.

Ainsi le sacrifiant devient-il un "consacré", un *dīkṣita*, par l'action d'officiants qui ne sont pas des *dīkṣita*, et n'ont pas à l'être, puisqu'ils ne sont impliqués dans le sacrifice que par le travail qu'ils fournissent. Mais il faut noter que le sacrifiant n'est pas seulement le commanditaire et le bénéficiaire du sacrifice; il a, lui aussi, sa "partie" à tenir dans le déroulement même du rite: il y a des formules de prière à prononcer, des gestes rituels à exécuter qui sont des éléments indispensables du sacrifice et que seul le sacrifiant peut prononcer et exécuter.

Quelles conditions faut-il remplir pour être le sacrifiant d'un sacrifice solennel? (Nous ne considérons ici que les règles du culte solennel, *śrauta*, les rites prescrits par la *śruti*, c'est-à-dire le Veda en tant qu' "audition", texte à apprendre et transmettre oralement à qui est digne de l'entendre).

Voici comment le traité de Kātyāyana sur les sacrifices solennels (Kātyāyana-śrautasūtra) énonce ces conditions:[5]

(1) il faut appartenir à l'espèce humaine. Est donc rejetée l'idée selon laquelle des dieux, des démons ou des animaux pourraient eux aussi assumer le rôle de *yajamāna*. Cette idée pourtant n'est pas absurde: les commentateurs observent qu'aucun texte du Veda lui-même ne réserve aux hommes, tous les autres êtres étant exclus, l'action sacrificielle. Nous pouvons même ajouter que le Veda mentionne fréquemment des sacrifices offerts par les dieux, des Asura démoniaques ou même vaches; mais il est vrai qu'il s'agit d'événements qui relèvent de la mythologie et dont it est toujours dit qu'ils se sont produits dans les temps originaires; or les Śrautasūtra, qui font partie des "members" (*aṅga*) du Veda, non du corpus védique lui-même, ont pour objet de décrire et de classer les rites védiques et de montrer comment concrètement il faut les exécuter, et les récits mythologiques qui, dans les textes védiques proprement dits, traitent de l'origine, de la raison d'être ou du "symbolisme" des rites ne sont pas de leur domaine.

(2) Parmi les hommes, seuls sont admis à entreprendre un sacrifice solennel et donc à se soumettre à la consécration préalable, *dīkṣā*, ceux qui sont dépourvus de toute infirmité corporelle grave.

(3) Il faut être instruit du Veda, à tout le moins connaître les textes védiques qu'il incombe au sacrifiant de réciter pendant la cérémonie.

(4) Il faut donc appartenir à l'une des rois premières "classes" (un des trois premiers *varṇa*) de la société brahmanique. Seuls, en effet, les brahmanes, les kṣatriya et les vaiśya ont reçu l'*upanayana*, initation qui équivaut à une deuxième naissance et qui donne accès à l'apprentissage du Veda.

(5) Enfin, mais c'est l'objet d'une discussion serrée, il faut être du sexe masculin. La femme est elle aussi une sacrifiante et elle est elle aussi apte à recevoir la *dīkṣā* si elle satisfait aux conditions qu'on vient d'énumérer, mais comme les filles n'ont pas droit à l'initiation au Veda, c'est en tant qu'épouse (*patnī*) du sacrifiant que la femme joue son rôle dans le sacrifice. Réciproquement, un homme ne peut être *yajamāna* que s'il a son épouse auprès de lui. Le véritable sacrifiant, c'est en fait le couple que le *yajamāna* forme avec sa *patnī*.

A ces conditions que nous fait connaître Kātyāyana, il convient d'en ajouter quelques autres, tirées d'autres textes de même nature:

(1) pour être *yajamāna*, il faut être rituellement pur, ne pas être souillé par ces événements polluants que sont une mort récente mais aussi une naissance dans la famille proche.

(2) Il faut respecter la gradation des sacrifices: on ne peut entreprendre un sacrifice complexe que si on a accompli toute la série des sacrifices plus simples.

Mais si détaillées que soient ces listes de conditions, on est frappé par l'absence de mention explicite d'une donnée pourtant primordiale: pour entreprendre un sacrifice, il faut être vivant. On peut supposer que cette règle, qui n'est pas un truisme, est en quelque sorte incluse dans celle qui interdit aux infirmes le rôle de sacrifiant.

Il est toutefois une circonstance rituelle pour le moins où cette évidence est mise en question et où nous voyons qu'un mort peut avoir le statut ou exercer la fonction de sacrifiant; c'est en tout cas ce que donnent à entendre de façon elliptique, il est vrai, certains texts védiques à propos de l'*asthiyajña,* "sacrifice des os", rite qui prend place dans ce type particulier de sacrifice qu'on appelle *sattra,* littéralement, "session".[6]

La session sacrificielle se distingue du sacrifice "normal" par sa durée d'abord: une "session" s'étend sur douze jours au moins et peut occuper tout une année, ou douze ans, et les textes nous font connaître des sessions mythiques de cent ans et de mille ans.[7] D'autre part, plusieurs opérations qui, dans le sacrifice ordinaire, se font debout exigent dans le *sattra* la posture assise; le fait d'être assis est même si caractéristique du *sattra* que pour dire "mettre fin au *sattra*" on emploie le verbe "se lever" (*utthā*). Mais surtout, tandis que le sacrifice ordinaire est le fait d'un sacrifiant unique (ou plutôt du couple qu'il forme avec son épouse), sacrifiant qui, comme nous l'avons rappelé, loue les services de toute une équipe d'officiants spécialisés, dans la "session" il y a plusieurs sacrifiants, généralement dix-sept, au maximum vingt-quatre: ces sacrifiants multiples agissent ensemble comme une sorte de sacrifiant collectif, et ils assument les uns à l'égard des autres le rôle de prêtres officiants.[8] Que tous les officiants doivent être en mesure d'être aussi des officiants, des *ṛtvij*, implique qu'il ne suffit pas qu'ils appartiennent à l'un ou l'autre des *varṇa* de "deux fois nés", il faut encore qu'ils soient tous brahmanes, puisque seuls les brahmanes ont qualité pour être *ṛtvij*. Chacun de ces sacrifiants-officiants reçoit d'un de ses confrères la *dīkṣā*, la "consécration" qui le mettra en état d'offrir son sacrifice. (La règle qui veut que ce soit par l'action d'un *ṛtvij* non consacré que le *yajamāna* devienne lui-même consacré est respectée ici: un sacrifiant ne peut conférer la *dīkṣā* à un de ses compagnons que tant que lui-même ne l'a pas reçue.)[9] Et les procédures qui, dans le sacrifice normal, règlent les rapports entre le sacrifiant et les officiants qu'il emploie n'ont pas lieu d'être dans la "session": dans le *sattra*, nous ne trouvons ni le "choix des officiants" par le sacrifiant, ni le versement des honoraires, ni la célébration du *tānūnaptra*, rite par lequel, dès le début de la cérémonie, le sacrifiant et les officiants s'engagent à collaborer loyalement et à ne pas chercher à se nuire.[10] La solidarité entre les sacrifiants multiples d'un même *sattra* est donc d'une tout autre nature que celle qui lie dans le sacrifice normal le sacrifiant unique et l'équipe des *ṛtvij*: dans ce dernier cas, cette relation est foncièrement contractuelle, elle unit des hommes dont elle montre, en même temps, qu'ils occupent dans le dispositif sacrificiel des fonctions et des statuts différents; et nous avons vu que le sacrifiant et les officiants ne sont pas animés du même désir. Au contraire, dans le *sattra*, les sacrifiants-officiants forment un groupe d'êtres semblables. (Ce n'est que secondairement, une fois bien établie l'identité de ce sacrifiant collectif, que se dégagera de cet ensemble un individu qui, sur le plan des opérations rituelles seulement, tiendra la "partie" du *yajamāna*: c'est, en l'occurrence, le *gṛhapati*, "maître de maison".)

Il faut avoir présents à l'esprit ces principes du sacrifice védique pour comprendre le rite que nous allons examiner maintenant et qui a nom *asthiyajña*, "sacrifice des os".

Dans les textes qui forment le Veda proprement dit, dans les manuels qui exposent les règles à suivre pour exécuter correctement les rites prescrits par le Veda et enfin dans les raisonnements et discussions des philosophes *mīmāṃsaka* qui fondent leur doctrine sur l'exégèse des injonctions védiques, on rencontre le problème qui se pose quand un des sacrifiants-officiants engagés dans un *sattra* vient à mourir avant que la cérémonie ne soit achevée. Dans le sacrifice ordinaire, la mort du sacrifiant entraîne en quelque sorte automatiquement l'arrêt de la cérémonie. La situation dans le *sattra* est différente, puisque la mort d'un des participants lèse, amoindrit le corps collectif des sacrifiants-officiants, mais n'entraîne pas sa disparition: il y a une oeuvre commune à effectuer, et les résultats bénéfiques de cette oeuvre doivent revenir à tous ceux qui s'y sont engagés. 'Les hommes qui reçoivent la consécration pour célébrer un *sattra* agissent en vue d'un sacrifice commun, pour un mérite dont ils bénéficieront en commun' (Jaiminīya-brāhmaṇa I 345).[11] Il ne faut pas que la mort d'un élément du groupe soit un obstacle à l'obtention de ce résultat, ni pour les survivants, ni pour le défunt. On le verra: le mort a besoin des survivants, mais les survivants ont besoin du mort. C'est-à-dire que le mort, en tant que participant au sacrifice, aura lui-même, jusqu'à ce que le sacrifice soit achevé, une sorte de survie sur le terrain du sacrifice qu'il ne faut évidemment pas confondre avec quelque forme de survie dans l'au-delà.

Voici donc quelle est, d'après Kātyāyana-śrautasūtra XXV 13, 28-46, la marche à suivre. Si un des participants au *sattra* vient à mourir, ses compagnons doivent sans tarder incinérer son cadavre soit dans un feu nouveau produit par friction (un feu *manthya*) tout exprès pour cela, soit dans un feu prélevé sur le feu dit *śāmitra*. (Le feu *śāmitra* est le feu du "bourreau", *śamitṛ*, installé à l'extérieur du terrain sacrificiel mais tout près du coin nord-est, il sert, normalement, dans les sacrifices comportant mise à mort d'animaux, à la cuisson des parties comestibles de la victime, une fois qu'elle a été dépecée. Que ce feu *śāmitra* puisse servir, même de façon médiate, à la crémation d'un sacrifiant est une illustration inattendue mais frapante de l'idée maintes fois affirmée dans les textes védiques que le cadavre qu'on fait brûler est une offrande sacrificielle au dieu Agni.)[12] Cette crémation n'est pas totale: elle laisse entiers les os, que l'on recueille et que l'on coud dans un sac fait de la peau d'antilope noire, symbole du sacrifice, que le défunt devait avoir constamment près de lui depuis le moment où il a été "consacré". Ce sac est alors posé près du feu *mārjālīya*, feu installé dans la partie sud du terrain du sacrifice. (Ce feu sert à "purifier" les récipients et ustensiles divers dont on a besoin dans le rite.) Il apparaît donc, bien que les textes ne le disent pas explicitement, que les rites funéraires qui normalement accompagnent la crémation ne sont pas exécutés et que le mort, par conséquent, n'est pas encore engagé dans les transformations qui doivent faire de lui un ancêtre, *pitṛ*, ses restes, on le voit, ne polluent pas le site sacrificiel, l'événement de sa mort n'est pas cause de deuil pour sa famille et n'empêche pas ses proches de célébrer des rites.

Ses compagnons, en effet, désignent un de ses plus proches parents pour le remplacer. Il le font passer par tous les rites de consécration qui font de lui un *dīkṣita*. (Les textes ne donnent pas de détails et ne disent pas comment, dans cette équipe de sacrifiants, on a pu à ce stade, trouver un non *dīkṣita* qui soit en mesure de lui conférer la *dīkṣā*). Et c'est avec ce substitut, *pratinidhi*, inclus dans leur groupe que les survivants mèneront le sacrifice jusqu'à son terme. Mais on notera que l'épouse du mort continue à exercer sa fonction de *patnī*: elle n'a pas été remplacée par l'épouse du substitut.

Le mort est donc non seulement représenté mais encore rendu

effectivement présent, par ses ossements d'une part, par son épouse de l'autre qui est comme une partie de lui-même.

La cérémonie dès lors suit son cours normal, avec les modifications que voici. Le *sattra* dont il est question ici est, comme c'est en général le cas, une forme élargie d'offrande de soma. Pour l'essentiel, le rite consiste à écraser les tiges de la plante soma pour en extraire le jus (ce sont les opérations de pressurage—*savana*—qui ont lieu trois fois par jour), et à prendre dans le liquide ainsi obtenu des "puisées" (*graha*) dont on fera des libations après les avoir filtrées. Dans le cas que nous examinons, il faut faire les pressurages prévus au programme de ce jour, mais avant de procéder aux "puisées" et aux libations, ceux qui parmi les sacrifiants-officiants ont pour spécialité d'être des chantres (*udgātṛ*) se rendent à l'angle sud-est du terrain sacrificiel, ou bien viennent s'asseoir au nord du foyer *mārjālīya* et exécutent une cantate en trio (*stotra*): la mélodie (*sāman*) est caractéristique du dieu de la mort Yama, car le but est d'aider le mort à parvenir au royaume de Yama; quant aux paroles ce sont les trois premières strophes de l'hymne Ṛk-saṃhitā X 189. Ce poème, traditionnellement attribué à la Reine des serpents est pour l'essentiel une invocation au soleil et n'a pas de rapport bien net avec la situation. Mais on lit en Pañcaviṃśa-brāhmaṇa IX 8, 8 que le serpent mythique Arbuda s'est débarrassé de sa peau morte grâce à ces strophes et le texte ajoute qu'en récitant ces strophes, les sacrifiants-officiants se débarrassent eux aussi de leur peau morte.[13] Nous avons donc affaire ici à un des nombreux rites apotropaïques inclus dans les funérailles: les vivants s'emploient à faciliter le départ du mort et se défont de ce qui, en eux, est signe de la présence de la mort. Qu'il s'agisse bien d'un élément de rite funéraire est prouvé encore par le fait que les chantres doivent alors porter le cordon sacrificiel sur l'épaule droite (comme c'est la règle quand on a affaire aux morts et aux ancêtres, tandis que le cordon sur l'épaule gauche est ce qui convient lorsqu'on s'adresse aux dieux ou aux hommes vivants), et qu'ils ont le visage tourné vers le sud, point cardinal des morts. Pendant qu'ils récitent, ou tout de suite après, il font trois fois le tour du foyer *mārjālīya*, en se frappant la cuisse gauche et en ayant à leur gauche l'objet autour duquel ils tournent, mouvement *apasalaiḥ* qui est encore un trait propre au rituel funéraire. (Quand on veut honorer un objet qui appartient au monde des dieux ou des hommes vivants, on tourne autour de lui en le tenant à sa droite, sens *pradakṣiṇa*.)

Le substitut n'élimine donc pas complètement le personnage qu'il vient remplacer. Cependant, bien que le mort reste présent sur le terrain du sacrifice, les rites autour du *mārjālīya* montrent que l' on est conscient que cet homme, dont on veut pourtant qu'il garde une place dans le dispositif sacrificiel, est bien mort et qu'il est destiné à se joindre, dans le royaume de Yama, à la troupe des ancêtres. Les textes (Pañcaviṃśa-brāhmaṇa IX 8, 11, Jaiminīya-brāhmaṇa I, 345) rappellent qu' "ils s'écartent du chemin, ceux qui officient (littéralement: "agissent", *kurvanti*) pour un mort" ou qu' "ils meurent, ceux qui servent d'officiants à un mort". Les cérémonies autour du sac d'ossements protègent de ces risques les participants et constituent un rite de réparation pour le sacrifice lésé par la défaillance de l'un d'entre eux, et mis en danger par la présence d'un cadavre sur le terrain. Telle est aussi la fonction assignée à la récitation du tercet Ṛk-saṃhitā IX 66, 19-21, qui a lieu quand on reprend la séquence normale des pressurages et des libations: ces invocations à Agni purificateur et donneur de longue vie sont destinées à détourner des survivants la souillure et le malheur. Mais ces rites sont aussi le moyen d'apaiser (*niravaday-*) le mort en l'assurant qu'il obtiendra la part à laquelle il a droit (*apibhū*) depuis le moment ou il est devenu *dīkṣita.*

Au bout d'un an (un an après le début du *sattra* ou après la mort du sacrifiant ou encore après la fin du *sattra*? Les textes sont imprécis, sauf Kātyāyana XXV 13, 36 qui affirment nettement: un an après la fin du *sattra*) a lieu l'*asthiyajña* proprement dit. Il est défini comme une offrande de soma (du type *jyotiṣṭoma*) dans lequel le rôle du sacrifiant est tenu par les os cependant que les autres participants servent d'officiants à ce squelette. Nous lisons chez Kātyāyana toujours que les tâches rituelles qui incombent au *yajamāna* et que les os ne peuvent remplir doivent être éxécutées par le *pratinidhi,* le substitut qui, nous l'avons vu, a été désigné sans tarder pour remplacer, dans le *sattra,* le sacrifiant mort. Cela donne à penser, sans que nous puissions en être sûrs, que cette deuxième étape est un prolongement ou une sorte de reprise du *sattra* lui-même, que ce sont les mêmes personnes qui se retrouvent, et que la structure du *sattra* se reproduit, c'est-à-dire que les hommes qui entourent les os du mort et leur attribuent le statut de sacrifiant sont pour lui non pas de simples officiants mais des compagnons de *sattra,* des sacrifiants-officiants.

Concrètement, si on comprend bien, le fait que dans ce rite le squelette est considéré comme un sacrifiant signifie que chaque fois que l'ordre de la cérémonie exige l'éxécution de cantates en trio (*stotra*), l'homme qui est chargé des fonctions d'officiant *adhvaryu* va chercher le sac d'ossements et le pose à coté de lui, tandis que le reste du temps ce sac reste près du foyer *mārjālīya.* D'autre part, quand vient le moment pour tous les participants du sacrifice de boire (en se les offrant mutuellement) les restes de soma, une fois que les libations aux dieux ont été faites, ce qui, normalement, aurait dû être absorbé par celui qui est mort est versé dans le feu *mārjālīya.* Puis, nous apprend toujours Kātyāyana, quand cet *asthiyajña* est terminé, on dépose les os, de même que les récipients appartenant au mort, quelque part dans la forêt. Ou bien on procède à une deuxième crémation des os, et commence ensuite toute la série des rites qui constituent les funérailles proprement dites.

Ces manières de faire relatives au sacrificant mort en cours de *sattra* ont été, pour les philosophes de l'école Mīmāṃsā, l'occasion de discussions d'allure juridique mais qui portent en fait sur quelques concepts fondamentaux du rituel.

Il y d'abord la question du substitut. Dans son commentaire à Taittirīya-brāhamaṇa I 4, 6, Sāyaṇa reproduit l'argumentation de Śabara *ad* Jaimini-sūtra VI 3: c'est une règle bien établie que dans le sacrifice védique il ne peut y avoir de substitut ni pour la divinité à laquelle l'offrande est destinée ni pour le feu où il est prescrit de verser l'offrande, ni pour les mantra qu'il convient de réciter en de telles circonstances, ni pour l'action proprement dite (VI 3, 18). Et il ne saurait plus être question de remplacer le sacrifiant par un autre homme (VI 3, 21). Mais dans cette forme spéciale de sacrifice qu'est la *sattra*, il faut prendre garde que le sacrifiant a une double fonction (*kāryadvayam*): il est le *phalin*, le *phalabhoktṛ*, celui qui est destiné à consommer le résultat, le "fruit" (*phala*) que doit produire le rite s'il a été correctement éxécuté; et d'autre part, il est aussi un agent (*kartṛ*) dans le déroulement des opérations sacrificielles, il a par conséquent un certain rôle sacerdotal à tenir. En tant que bénéficiaire, consommateur des fruits du sacrifice, le sacrifiant mort ne peut pas avoir de substitut. Le bénéfice de l'acte sacrificiel est réservé au sacrifiant initial, quelle que soit la manière dont il lui sera possible d'en jouir. En revanche, la mort peut avoir un substitut qui le remplacera dans ses fonctions de *kartṛ*, d' "opérateur" ou officiant. Les *mīmāṃsaka* précisent l'argument: l'ensemble des fonctions sacerdotales, dans un sacrifice solennel, doit être rempli par un groupe de dix-sept officiants. Or dans les sacrifices de type *sattra*, rappelons-le une fois de plus, tout sacrifiant est aussi un officiant. Si donc un sacrifiant fait défaut, "seize seulement des tâches sacerdotales seront remplies, il en manquera une". C'est pourquoi, bien qu'il ne puisse y avoir de substitut au sacrifiant, mais parce qu'il est possible de remplacer un officiant défaillant, il est prescrit de chercher parmi les proches du mort un homme qui puisse tenir son rôle. Ce substitut, qui ne jouira pas du fruit du sacrifice, est tenu cependant à toutes les obligations de celui qu'il remplace et, tout comme lui, il doit recevoir la *dīkṣā*, "consécration" à laquelle sont soumis les seuls sacrifiants. Pourquoi, ayant reçu la *dīkṣā*, le substitut n'est-il pas pleinement l'équivalent de celui auquel en somme il succède? Pourquoi n'est-il pas, comme ses compagnons les autres *dīkṣita*, un "maître" (*svāmin*) du sacrifice, mais un simple "faiseur d'actes", un "travailleur" (*karmakara*)? C'est qu'il a été convoqué sur la scène sacrificielle par les "maîtres", et nourri, "porté" (*bhṛta*) par eux et qu'il est en quelque manière à leur service. Śabara va jusqu'à dire que ce substitut qui est "loué", qu' on "achète ses services", bien qu'il soit expressément affirmé dans les Śrauta-sūtra (et dans les textes de la Mīmāṃsā) que dans un *sattra*, où les sacrifiants sont en même temps des officiants, il ne peut y avoir de *dakṣiṇā*. En fait, continue Śabara, pour être véritablement un "maître" dans un sacrifice, il faut l'avoir entrepris et s'être dès le début engagé à le mener à son terme. Cet engagement implique que le sacrifiant ait par avance le désir d'obtenir les fruits qui en résulteront. Or le substitut n'a pas ce désir, du moins ce désir n'est-il pas à l'origine de sa présence dans le sacrifice. Le sacrifice était déjà commencé quand le substitut y est entré. Sur cette question du substitut les *mīmāṃsaka* parviennent à tirer des textes une doctrine cohérente.

En revanche, le statut et la fonction des ossements dans l'*asthiyajña* fait l'objet de débats plus complexes et plus incertains. Comment rendre compatibles les injonctions du Veda avec le sens commun? Les ossements sont un reste inerte. Quelle capacité d'action peut-on leur imputer pour pouvoir les considérer comme la personne même du sacrifiant et quelle est au juste la relation entre les os et les hommes vivants qui les manipulent? Comment comprendre l'expression *asthiyajña*, "sacrifice des os"? (Pour les os? Par les os? Avec les os?) et plus précisément l'expression *asthīni yājayeyuḥ* "on doit faire en sorte que les os sacrifient"? Qui sacrifie (*yajate*), les os ou les vivants? Tels sont les problèmes qu'examinent les *mīmāṃsaka*, prenant pour base les sūtra X 2, 47 à 50 de Jaimini.

Śabara expose d'abord en détail la thèse de l'adversaire qu'il s'attachera ensuite à réfuter. Selon cette thèse, la phrase *asthīni yājayeyuḥ* implique que ce sont bien les os qui sacrifient, puisqu'ils sont amenés à sacrifier: c'est la structure même de la phrase et la valeur du verbe causatif qui exigent cette interprétation. Dira-t-on que les os, étant inanimés, sont incapables de "faire" quoi que ce soit, à plus forte raison d'exécuter un des actes du sacrifice? La réponse à cette objection est qu'en vertu de cette injonction directe, qui a toute l'autorité du texte védique, les os du mort, quand ils sont mis en mouvement par les hommes vivants, peuvent bien réaliser certaines des tâches qui incombent au sacrifiant: par exemple le pilier en bois d'*udumbara* qui est érigé au centre du *sadas* (sorte de hangar mis en place dans la partie occidentale du terrain du sacrifice) doit avoir la même hauteur que le sacrifiant. Le sacrifiant sert donc à mesurer ce pilier, et cet office, qui ne demande pas d'action de la part de celui qui le remplit, peut fort bien être exécuté par le sacrifiant inerte, réduit à l'état d'ossements. L'action accomplie par les personnes vivantes par le moyen de ces os est interprétée comme une action accomplie par les os par le moyen de ces personnes vivantes. Les vivants qui font agir les os, qui mettent les os en action sont comparables aux officiants qui (contre rémunération) fournissent au sacrifiant les services dont il a besoin pour pouvoir offrir son sacrifice. Le raisonnement, ou l'analyse grammaticale, se ramène à ceci: il y a des personnes qui font agir les os, c'est donc que les os agissent. Si faibles et limitées que soient les actions que l'on fait faire aux os, elles suffisent à qualifier les os comme sacrifiants, à leur donner le statut (*dharma*) de sacrifiant. Entre la situation normale, où les officiants vivants font en sorte que le sacrifiant vivant sacrifie et cette situation particulière où des vivants font agir le squelette et le mettent en mesure de jouer son rôle de sacrifiant, il n'y a qu'une différence de degré, non de nature (et l' observateur extérieur remarque, ce que ne font pas explicitement les ritualistes dont on résume ici la thèse, qu'il y a une continuité entre l'homme vivant qui, au début du *sattra*, avait fait le voeu d'être un des sacrifiants, un des *svāmin* du sacrifice qui allait commencer, et le tas d'ossements à quoi il est réduit maintenant. Cette continuité ne s'est pas rompue dans l'intervalle pendant lequel le sacrifiant, empêché par la mort, a été remplacé par un substitut vivant). Conclusion réaffirmée par l'opposant: il faut prendre l'injonction védique au pied de la lettre: dans le "sacrifice des os", le sacrifiant, acteur principal et bénéficiaire de la cérémonie est bien le squelette, c'est-à-dire la personne, dont le squelette est le reste.

Cette thèse est rejetée par le *siddhāntin*, le tenant de la conclusion juste. Il considère que dans le sacrifice des os ce ne sont pas les os qui sacrifient, mais les personnes vivantes présentes sur le terrain. Voici ses arguments:

(1) Si on dit que les os sont le sacrifiant, cela implique que les personnes vivantes qui les font agir ou qui les mettent en situation d'agir sont des officiants et que ces officiants sont payés. Or le Veda ne dit nulle part que les os les payent ni que ces officiants reçoivent des richesses du défunt. (Remarque: le *siddhāntin* fait comme si le "sacrifice des os" n'était pas sous le régime du *sattra*).

(2) Si les os sacrifient, il faut prendre le verbe "sacrifier" dans un sens particulier, différent de son sens ordinaire (Remarque: les *mīmāṃsaka* parlent de sens *gauṇa*, "métaphorique". En fait l'action sacrificielle attribuée aux os est partielle plutôt que figurée). Or dans les injonctions védiques, il est impossible—c'est une règle herméneutique—de prendre un verbe dans un sens "metaphorique". Par conséquent, c'est le substantif *asthi*, "os", qui doit être pris figurément (*lakṣaṇayā*). Ce mot ne se réfère pas aux ossements du sacrifiant mort, mais a le sens de *asthimant*, "pourvu d'os" et désigne les personnes vivantes qui, en compagnie de celui qui maintenant est mort, ont entrepris ce sacrifice. Et le *siddhāntin* réitère sa thèse: "le sacrifice des os est le fait de personnes vivantes".

Dans sa volonté de concilier le bon sens et l'injonction védique, le *siddhāntin* fait une construction arbitraire que rien n'autorise sur le plan linguistique (*asthi* pour *asthimant*) et qui repose sur l'idée extravagante que les "os" dont il est question à propos de l'*asthiyajña* peuvent être autre chose que les os du sacrifiant mort, os, qui, d'après les instructions concernant l'étape précédente, availent été cousus dans le sac fait de la peau d'antilope noire appartenant à ce même sacrifiant. Le *siddhāntin* est du reste si peu sûr d'avoir raison qu'il envisage un peu plus loin, "à titre d'hypothèse" (*kṛtvācintā*), ce que serait la situation si c'était l'adversaire qui avait la position juste: il énumère alors les observances auxquelles est tenu un sacrifiant normalement consacré et qu'il serait évidemment impossible d'exiger d'un squelette (se raser la tête par exemple!) mais il n'affirme plus que ces limitations sont rédhibitoires et doivent entraîner le rejet de l'interprétation littérale de l'injonction védique.

Ce rite de l'*asthiyajña* est riche d'enseignements quant à la notion de personne dans l'Inde védique. Le sacrifiant se définit par son voeu et son engagement. Sa personne, en tant que sacrifiant, n'est affectée que partiellement et, peut-on dire, empiriquement, par la mort. Pour l'essentiel, le devoir (le *dharma*, le devoir constitutif d'un statut) a toute la force d'une obligation à persévérer dans l'existence. Il crée les conditions d'une sorte de survie, de partage avec la mort: la mort est passée, mais on conserve assez de vie pour faire ce qu'on a à faire dans ce monde d'actes stylisés qu'est le monde sacrificiel. Tout comme son être physique, réduit à son squelette, est cousu dans la peau d'antilope, symbole du sacrifice, de même la personne de ce mort, enfermée mais aussi sublimée dans sa définition sacrificielle, est effectivement présente sur le terrain du sacrifice, non sous forme d'effigie, ni dans un monument funéraire, ni comme fantôme ou comme souvenir, mais comme support de promesses, tâches à accomplir, biens à espérer. Mais cela n'est pas vrai pour tous les sacrifices. Le devoir, le *dharma*, n'a cette efficacité créatrice de vie, ou, si l'on préfère, ne peut produire cette fiction que lorsque la promesse de sacrifier se double de l'engagement à sacrifier avec et pour les autres membres d'une communauté sacrifiante. Dans le *sattra*, chacun des sacrifiants fait en sorte de demeurer avec ses compagnons jusqu'à ce que le projet commun soit réalisé, aussi longtemps que le groupe a besoin de la présence de chacun pour que le nombre qui caractérise cette totalité soit maintenu. Cette survie sacrificielle, le temps d'un sacrifice, le suspens savamment ménagé entre le moment de la mort et celui où on aura à quitter complètement le monde des vivants, sont à la fois exigés et rendus possibles par la communauté.

Insistons-y: nous traitons ici d'une forme de sacrifice, le *sattra*, qui est archaïque, ou mythique, en tout cas exceptionnelle. Cette forme contraste avec la forme normale du sacrifice solennel, sacrifice où le sacrifiant, unique, est avant tout un individu dont la préoccupation essentielle est de construire son *ātman*, son être propre, dans un jeu complexe d'identification et de différence avec la victime ou l'offrande du sacrifice. Et jamais, dans le sacrifice ordinaire, le sacrifiant n'agit au nom d'un groupe familial, ethnique, local ou "politique". On l'a remarqué depuis longtemps: il n'existe pas dans l'Inde védique de rite solennel qui puisse être interprété comme un sacrifice "civique".[14] Cependant même dans le sacrifice normal, l'individu sacrifiant n'est pas totalement isolé; en quelques rares circonstances on voit surgir dans le sacrifice le groupe de ceux que le sacrifiant pourrait désigner comme "les siens".[15] Et surtout, comme nous l'avons vu, se met en place, pour le temps du sacrifice, la communauté contractuelle, mais aussi affective, du sacrifiant, de son épouse et de l'équipe des officiants.[16] Mais il est bien vrai que cette question de la relation du sacrifiant avec autrui prend toute son ampleur dans le *sattra*, précisément parce que les autres y sont des semblables et parce que la répartition des tâches et des statuts ne se fait pas entre les individus mais dans la personne de chacun d'entre eux.

La doctrine de l'*asthiyajña* fait penser, au moins par association d'idées, à la devise de la Hanse: *navigare necesse est, vivere non necesse.* Il n'est pas nécessaire que l'individu vive, ce qui importe c'est que les navires de la Hanse continuent à naviguer. Et même: L'individu doit prendre le risque de mourir pour que les navires naviguent. La formule brahmanique serait: il n'est pas néccessaire que l'individu soit vivant; ce qui importe, c'est que vivant ou mort, il puisse demeurer à bord, afin que le bateau du sacrifice aille jusqu'au bout de son itinéraire.[17]

ENGLISH SUMMARY

When a Vedic text gives intructions as to the performing of a rite, the first question that it almost invariably gives rise to, whether explicitly stated or not, is: who is the person qualified to perform the rite, who is the *adhikārin*? One of the conditions to be fulfilled in order to become a sacrificer and perform a solemn rite, is to be alive. This seems obvious, and it is probably for this reason that the demand has never really been explicitly put into words. There does happen to exist however at least one context which casts a doubt on this fact: in the joint sacrifice, the *sattra,* if one of the sacrificers happens to die before the ceremony is over, it does not stop him from being present at the sacrificial site and from carrying out his role as a sacrificer.

Provision is made for a twofold procedure to take place:

1. The deceased is cremated immediately and his bones are sown into the black antelope skin bag with which he has never been parted from since the time of his consecration as a sacrificer. The bag is then placed next to one of the fires on the sacrificial site. It is around this bag of bones that the survivors perform the rites intended to prevent the dead from remaining in a state of *preta,* without at the same time going as far as to being changed into *pitṛ,* and thus, being completely turned away from the world of the living. A man is however chosen, from amongst the closest members of the family of the deceased, to take his place and is in turn given the consecration

to become a sacrificer—the ritual is thus carried out without any real major break in the ceremony.

2. One year after the beginning (or the end) of the *sattra*, the survivors organize a follow up ceremony, in the form of a soma sacrifice, during which the bones of the dead are called upon to perform the duties of the main sacrificer: this is the actual *asthiyajña*, 'the sacrifice of the bones'. The bones are handled in such a way as to be able to carry out a certain number of the tasks that lay with the sacrificer, and it is for his sake that a part of the remains of the *soma*, which he would have drunk if he had been alive, is poured into the fire. The entire ritual of funeral rites can be fulfilled only upon completion of the 'sacrifice of the bones', and it is then only that the dead can finally leave the world of the living and join the crowd of ancestors in the kingdom of Yama.

We propose to investigate in this study, the instructions of the vedic texts and the *Śrautasūtra* dealing with the 'sacrifice of the bones', as well as the debate that they gave rise to amongst the philosophers of the Mīmāṃsā school of thought (the concept of a substitute, the respective roles and statutes of the sacrificers and the officiants in the normal sacrifice and in the *sattra*). This study furthermore examines, in the light of these rites, the concept of 'person' in vedism. We endeavour to show how 'duty' (*dharma*) and in this case the promise made to partners to carry out the sacrifice together with them, the joint responsibility contracted by and called upon for by the group, in short, the very structure of the rite itself, is powerful enough to fracture death and create the fictional set up or required 'mise en scène', in order to enable the deceased to carry out, until the very end, his task as a sacrificer.

NOTES

1. Sur le rituel védique, voir notamment P.V. Kane, *History of Dharmaśāstra,* Il 2,Poona 1941, pp. 976-1255 et L. Renou, *Vocabulaire du rituel védique,* Paris: Klincksieck 1954.
2. Sur la *dakṣiṇā,* voir Ch. Malamoud, "Terminer le sacrifice, remarques sur les limoraires rituels dans le brahmanisme", in M. Biardeau, Ch. Malamoud, *Le sacrifice dans l'Inde ancienne,* Paris: P.U.F. 1976, pp. 156-204.
3. Sur la façon dont le *kāma* du sacrifiant prépond au *kāma* de l'officiant, voir J. Gonda. *The Savayajñas,* Amsterdam 1965, p. 23 (à propos de Atharva-saṃhitā III 29, 7).
4. La *dīkṣā* fait l'objet d'une monographie très détaillée dans l'ouvrage de J. Gonda, *Change and Continuity in Indian Religion,* La Haye: Mouton 1965, pp. 315-462.

   La *dīkṣā* védique n'est pas une consécration permanente, elle est la phase liminaire de tout sacrifice solennel (quand la matière oblatoire est le soma). Il faut donc se soumettre à la *dīkṣā* à chaque fois que l'on offre un sacrifice de ce type. En revanche, l'*upanayana*, "initiation" (à l'étude du Veda) est un rite du cycle de vie: cette "deuxième naissance" est acquise une fois pour toutes.

L'étroite association de la *dīkṣā* du sacrifiant et de la *dakṣiṇā* des officiants, et le rôle primordial que ces procédures jouent dans la structure du sacrifice sont bien rendues, chez les philosophes *mīmāṃsaka*, dans la règle dite *dīkṣādakṣiṇanyāya* (Jaimini-sūtra III 7, 11 sq.) et dans la définition de Śabara ad Jaimini-sūtra X 2, 26: *dīkṣitam adīkṣitā dakṣiṇāparikrītā ṛtvijo yājayanti*, "les officiants, qui ne sont pas consacrés et qui sont rémunérés par les *dakṣiṇā*, font que le sacrifiant qui, lui, est consacré, sacrifie".

5. Nous nous référons à Kātyāyana-śrautasūtra I 1, 3-7, (avec le commentaire-moderne- dit Saralavṛtti), dans l'édition de Kāśī, Acyuta-granthamālā-kāryālaya, saṃvat 1987.
6. Sur les *sattra* voir Kane, op. cit., pp. 1239-46 et A.B. Keith, *Religion and Philosophy of the Veda and Upanishads*, Cambridge, Mass. 1925, pp. 349-52.
7. Cf., par exemple, Pañcaviṃśa-brāhmaṇa XXV 8 et 9.
8. Règles concernant les *sattra* dans Āpastamba-śrautasūtra, livre XXIII, Kātyāyana-śrautasūtra, livre XIII.
9. Il faut donc que le dernier à être consacré le soit par un homme destiné à ne pas être consacré lui-même et donc à rester en dehors de ce sacrifice. Cf. Śatapatha-brāhmaṇa XII 1, 1, 10: "car il est dit: celui qui est pur ne doit pas purifier" (*na pūtaḥ pāvayed ity āhuḥ*).
10. Sur le *tānūnaptra*, cf. Ch. Malamoud, *Cuire le monde, rite et pensée dans L'Inde ancienne*, Paris: La Découverte 1989, pp. 229-40.
11. Exemple de *sattra* (mythique) qui s'achève dans la confusion parce que les participants ont en vue des biens différents dans Jaiminīya-brāhmaṇa III 234. Cf. W. Caland, *Das Jaiminīya-Brāhmaṇa in Auswahl*, Amsterdam 1919, reimpr. Wiesbaden 1970, p. 278.
12. Cf. Ṛk-saṃhitā X 16, 5 et les textes des sūtra rituels cités par W. Caland, *Die Altindischen Todten-und Bestattungsgebräuche*, Amsterdam 1896, p. 175 et 178.
13. Même instruction en Taittirīya-brāhmaṇa I 4, 6, 5 sqq., avec une interprétation un peu différente: la Reine des serpents, c'est la terre. En récitant les strophes de la Reine des serpents tandis qu'on accomplit ce rite on confie le mort à la terre (c' est-à-dire à ce monde où nous sommes). Ce même texte montre comment, en combinant les strophes à Yama aux strophes à la Reine des serpents, on confie le mort aux deux mondes, le monde d'ici-bas et celui de l'au-delà; puis, parce qu'on fait trois fois le tour du foyer on évoque au sujet de ce mort le triple monde (terre, espace intermédiaire, ciel); enfin, dans cette version, il est prescrit de faire la triple circumambulation deux fois: ce total de six correspond aux six saisons de l'année. Par ces rites, et par cette interprétation des textes qu'ils récitent et des gestes qu'ils font, les survivants se débarrassent du péché que serait pour eux la présence parmi eux d'un mort qui n'aurait pas été correctement traité; ils gagnent ainsi pour eux-même la longue durée de vie. Comme le dit bien le commentateur Bhaṭṭa Bhāskaramiśra *ad* Taittirīya-brāhmaṇa I 4, 6, 11, il ne s'agit pas ici d'un *pretopacara*, d'un hommage au trépassé, mais

d'un rite de réparation destiné à protéger les survivants d'une mort prematurée.

14. Cf. H. Oldenberg, *Die Religion* des *Veda,* 2ème édition, Stuttgart-Berlin 1917, réimpr. Darmstadt 1977, p. 369 sq.

15. Par exemple, lors du transport du soma de la partie occidentale à la partie orientale du terrain du sacrifice (rite appelé *vaisarjana*) un cortège se forme, composé de l'officiant *adhvaryu,* du sacrifiant, de son épouse, mais aussi des *apivrata,* "ayants droit", fils, petits-fils et parents éloignés du couple, qui n'apparaissent qu'à cette occasion sur la scène sacrificielle. Tous les membres de ce cortège sont recouverts, le temps d'une libation, d'une même pièce de tissu dont une extrémité est tenue en main par l'*adhvaryu* Cf. W. Caland, V. Henry, *L'Agniṣṭoma, Description complète de la forme normale du sacrifice de soma dans le culte védique,* I, Paris 1906, p. 110.

16. Dans le rite *uparavamarśana,* l' *adhvaryu* et le sacrifiant enfoncent leur bras droit dans les "trous de résonnance" creusés dans le sol sous le chariot à soma. Par le boyau qui fait se communiquer ces trous, chacun cherche à atteindre la main de l'autre et lorsqu'ils y sont parvenus, ils ont entre eux ce dialogue: "qu'y a-t-il là? Ce qui est bon—Que cela nous soit commun". (Śatapatha-brāhmaṇa IV 5, 4, 16).

17. Métaphore du bateau pour decrire le sacrifice, notamment Ṛk-saṃhitā X 44, 6; Śatapatha-brāhmaṇa II 3, 3, 15.

PART II

THE EXTRAORDINARY DEATH

Rivers and the Death of Children

ANNE FELDHAUS

The connections between rivers and death in India are many and quite strong. The bank of a river is a preferred place for cremating the dead and for offering *piṇḍas* and other food to the ancestors. A river is also the best place to dispose of the ashes[1] of the dead, as it is to perform the *visarjan* of the clay festival image of a god. The Purāṇas and the *Mahābhārata* refer to a river of the dead, the Vaitaraṇī, and in at least one case that I know of a reason given for calling a river in the Deccan the 'southern Gaṅgā' is that it flows south, toward the realm of Yama. In addition, people in Maharashtra often connect deities who live in or near rivers or other bodies of water with death, by holding that such deities endanger people's lives.

In the present paper I will discuss one of the dangerous aspects of river (and water) deities, the danger of their killing children. This power is the obverse of that of rivers and water deities to give children and to preserve their lives. I will cite three stories, taken from three widely different kinds of sources, about the complex negotiations parents must go through to get children and to prevent a river or water deity from taking the children's lives. The three stories are among the materials I have collected during the past several years in the course of a study of the religious meanings of rivers in Maharashtra.[2] The first story is found in the Māhātmya of one of the rivers of Maharashtra, the second is a traditional oral story told in connection with the cult of a river goddess, and the third is the case history of a woman—or, rather, the reproductive autobiography of a couple—afflicted by a type of disease goddess associated with water and rivers. All three of these narratives regard death in our normal, common sense understanding of it—as something extremely undesirable that we should use all available means to prevent.

One of the most poignant and complex Purāṇic stories about the love of sons and the fragility of their lives is that of King Hariścandra. Hariścandra's story appears in several Sanskrit texts, but the version I am most familiar with is found in the *Gautamī Māhātmya,* a Sanskrit text praising the Godāvarī river.[3] In this version, King Hariścandra, who was childless, was advised to worship Varuṇa on the bank of the Godāvarī in order to get a son. Hariścandra did so. Varuṇa agreed to give Hariścandra a son, on condition that the king would promise to sacrifice the son. Hariścandra accepted the condition, left the Godāvarī, made an oblation to Varuṇa, and had intercourse with his wife. She gave birth to a son, Rohita.

As soon as Rohita was born, Varuṇa came to remind Hariścandra of his promise. But Hariścandra put Varuṇa off. 'When he is ten days old, he will be fit to be sacrificed,' said Hariścandra, and Varuṇa went away. Ten days later, when Varuṇa returned, Hariścandra put him off again. 'A sacrificial beast (*paśuḥ*) without teeth is not effective,' said Hariścandra. 'Come back when he has teeth.' Again Varuṇa went away. Seven years later, after Rohita's teeth had grown in, Varuṇa returned again. And again Hariścandra found a reason for delay. 'These teeth will fall out,' he said to Varuṇa. 'When other teeth have grown in, I will sacrifice him.' By the time the new teeth had grown in, Hariścandra had found yet another excuse. As a Kṣatriya, he said, the boy would make a much better sacrificial victim if he knew archery.

In this way, Rohita grew to be sixteen years old. After he had learned archery and other appropriate skills, Hariścandra finally declared him ready to be sacrificed. But when Rohita learned what had happened and that he was to be sacrificed to Varuṇa, he refused to cooperate. Before he would allow himself to be sacrificed to Varuṇa, he announced, he would first sacrifice Varuṇa to Viṣṇu. Varuṇa, enraged at the son, caused the father, Hariścandra, to contract dropsy.

Meanwhile, Rohita left for the forest, where he spent five years at the place on the Godāvarī where his father's prayers for a son had been answered. In the sixth year, when he had begun to feel remorse for what his father had to suffer on his account, the *ṛṣi* (Brāhmaṇ) Ajīgarta came along, looking 'destitute, emaciated, and sort of sad'.[4] With him were his wife and three sons. Because he had so many dependents and no other means of supporting them, Ajīgarta offered to sell his wife or one of the sons in exchange for food. Rohita bought Ajīgarta's middle son, Śunaḥśepa, for 1000 cows, 1000 measures of grain, 1000 gold coins, and 1000 garments.

Hariścandra, however, refused to sacrifice Ajīgarta's son. Brāhmaṇs are extremely holy, argued Hariścandra; it is the duty of kings to protect them. Finally a voice from the sky intervened, telling Hariścandra to perform the sacrifice, but without killing the victim. Only then did Hariścandra agree. The *ṛṣi* Viśvāmitra performed the sacrifice, bloodlessly, at the Godāvarī, and adopted Śunaḥśepa as his own.

Thus, in the end, Hariścandra's son's life was spared, Ajīgarta's son, the substitute victim, was spared, the debt to Varuṇa was paid, and king Hariścandra's morality remained intact. Only Ajīgarta lost, for he did not get back the son he had sold to be sacrificed. The episode of the poor Brāhmaṇ selling his son to be sacrificed adds to the pathos of the story.

If Hariścandra's story shows how parents must ever and again snatch their son from the clutches of death, Ajīgarta's tells us how they must sometimes place him in those very clutches.

Besides the fact that Hariścandra obtains his son by worshipping at the Godāvarī and the fact that Ajīgarta's son is 'sacrificed' there, the story has another important connection with water. Varuṇa, the god by whose power Hariścandra gets his son, is a god of water, although not usually one of rivers; at least once, the *Gautamī Māhātmya* (34.18) calls Varuṇa by his Vedic epithet, *Apām patiḥ*, 'Lord of Waters'. The god Varuṇa is not, in Maharashtra at least, actively worshipped today. But this story about him points to an important pattern that is still found in the worship of folk river goddesses and the Sātī Āsarā. These are the kinds of water deities who are nowadays the most widely held to care for, and also to threaten, the birth and survival of children.

At the same time as he enables Hariścandra to obtain a son, Varuṇa himself also becomes the chief threat to the son's life. Hariścandra initially must bribe Varuṇa in order to get a son, and then must placate him in order to keep the child alive. It is in this ambivalence of Varuṇa's role and of Hariścandra's relationship to him that his resemblance to folk river goddesses and to the Sātī Āsarā is most striking.

One of the most important reasons that people give for praying to folk goddesses of rivers is that these goddesses respond positively to promises of future acts of worship. In Marathi such a promise, or 'vow', is called a *navas.* A *navas* usually involves binding oneself to make a particular offering or to perform a particular ritual, if some specific desired object or goal is achieved. A *navas* can be made for any one of a number of practical, this-worldly goals, but most typically people make them for the birth and welfare of children.

In the cults of folk goddesses of rivers, a *navas* that people typically make is to allow the child they are asking for to be floated on a raft in front of the goddess's temple. A frequent motif in the lore about floating babies and children this way is that the child's parents must not become frightened. For example, in the cult of the folk goddess Bhivāī, whose home is a water hole in the Nīrā river, the story of a mother who became frightened when her child was floated on the goddess's raft is widely known and often repeated. The following version was narrated by a devotee of Bhivāī in Pune:

In the past, what did a woman do once? A woman had a small child like this one. And she placed it on the raft (*paraḍī*) and it was taken off to be circled around. And as it was being circled around, what thought came to her mind? 'Now, my baby is small. What if it falls into the water hole (*ḍoh*)?' [At this point, the narrator's mother-in-law interjected:] It's a big water hole, you see. There's no bottom to it. [The narrator resumed:] So she was worried that it might fall in. And, indeed, the baby did fall off [the raft]. Then, some time later, after she had had another child, what thought came to her mind? 'If this god is true (*kharaṃ jar yā devācaṃ sattva aslaṃ*), my child will be given back to me.' This is what she said as she let the raft go. And when the raft had circled around the water hole and come back, then in it was the other baby, the first one—I mean, the one that had died the last time. With the very same clothes on, in good shape. So she got both babies back at once.

The story of the frightened mother highlights in narrative fashion, then, something that the floating of children seems to express ritually: that the children who are floated on the raft are thereby being entrusted to the goddess, being put under her protection and care, but also into her power. The children could die; and if they do not die, that is only because the goddess gives them back. As in the case of Varuṇa, the same power that gives one the child can also take it away; and the power that takes it away can also restore it.

The third narrative I will relate here is the 'case history' of a woman who was afflicted by the Sātī Āsarā. The Sātī Āsarā are invisible beings who live in or near water and who afflict women by making them infertile or by causing them to have miscarriages, or by causing their children to die young. Rather than praying to the Sātī Āsarā or offering *navas*, vows to get them to provide children, people more commonly placate the Sātī Āsarā to prevent them from taking their children away. The woman whose story I will tell is named Kalāvatī. Kalāvatī was in her early forties when my friend Sudhir Waghmare and I interviewed her and her husband, Tulśīdās, at their home in a new suburb to the south-east of Pune in August of 1988. They are Buruḍs, members of a low caste whose traditional occupation is basket weaving. Kalāvatī and her husband have both lived in or near Pune their entire lives. They had moved from the old city to their new suburb only a few years before I talked to them.

When they got married, in 1962, Kalāvatī was fourteen years old. She believes that she was caught by the Sātī Āsarā during the first month and a quarter after her wedding. During this period, she explained, after the bride and groom have had turmeric applied to them at the wedding, the custom is that the bride should not go out of the house. However, the Navarātra festival fell during this period. For this festival the whole house and everything in it has to be cleaned, and the house has to be freshly whitewashed. Kalāvatī's mother-in-law sent her to the river to wash the household bedding. She left the house at 7 in the morning and did not return until 2 or 3 in the afternoon. 'That's when I think they got me,' she said. 'I mean, they have their rounds then, in the afternoon. Around 12 or 1 o'clock, they have their rounds. That's the time when they got me.'

The Āsarā who 'got' Kalāvatī are located under the New Bridge (Nevā Pūl), near Sanvār Vāḍā, on the south bank of the Muṭhā river in Pune. This is close to where Tulśīdās and Kalāvatī used to live. Kalāvatī did the washing at a spot on the river bank about 20 metres away from the Āsarās' place. She was not menstruating at the time.[5] She had no symptoms of having been 'gotten' by the Āsarā—'I didn't get sick, I didn't have chills, or fever, or anything. Nothing at all at that time.' As a result, for a long time she didn't realize what had happened. Her troubles began only when she started to bear children.

Three years later, exactly seven months into Kalāvatī's first pregnancy, she gave birth to a baby girl. The baby was kept ten days in the hospital (Sassoon Hospital, the largest public hospital in Pune), then died twelve days later, at home.

A year later Kalāvatī was again pregnant. Her second child, another girl, was born in the eighth month, in a different hospital, and died within fifteen or twenty minutes of birth. After that Kalāvatī began to suspect that some god was interfering with her pregnancies. Her husband didn't believe in gods, or at least he didn't believe that they would do a thing like that. In her words, 'He used to say, "I don't believe in that." He used to say, "I don't believe in god." That's how he used to talk. He used to say, "Does god do anybody harm?" '

The next time she became pregnant, Kalāvatī consulted a woman near the city market (*maṇḍāī*) who gets possessed by gods and performs divination. This woman diagnosed Kalāvatī as having the Sātī Āsarā. At the woman's instructions, Kalāvatī and her husband (assisted, it seems, by his parents) bought one each of several kinds of fruit—bananas, apples, sweet limes, and chikkus were named—and a lamp, small *pāpaḍs,* and the other things the woman told them to get. The offerings were placed in a large, shallow basket and waved around Kalāvatī's body; then her father-in-law took the basket full of offerings and placed them on the river. The basket tipped over and sank in the water. In retrospect, at least, Kalāvatī and her husband see this as a sign that the Āsarā had not accepted the offerings, that there had been some mistake in making them. The mistake, Kalāvatī and her husband later learned, was that they had offered only one each, and not seven, of the different kinds of fruit.

Soon afterwards Kalāvatī gave birth to a son. The boy was born at 4 o'clock in the morning. Premature like the other children, he was born in the eighth month of his mother's pregnancy. He seemed all right at birth, so much so that Tulśīdās went off to work, leaving his own father, laughing and joking, to take care of anything that was needed. But as soon as Tulśīdās reached his office, he received a phone call informing him that the baby had died. As Tulśīdās explained, 'By the laws of nature (*naisargikānī*) an eight-month baby generally cannot survive. . . . It's medical science that sometimes a seven-month baby survives, but if it takes even one or two days of the eighth month, a [premature] baby never survives. Sometimes a baby girl will survive, but an eight-month baby boy will never survive.'

After that Tulśīdās consulted a neighbourhood doctor who was his friend. The doctor recommended a specialist in gynaecology. The specialist examined Kalāvatī and said, 'Her womb is not right(?). It's big, and as the embryo grows, it gets out of control.' The next time Kalāvatī conceived a child, in the sixth month of her pregnancy the gynaecologist sutured her womb closed with a strong thread.

At the same time as Tulśīdās was consulting the doctors, Kalāvatī's maternal aunt took action of a different sort. She consulted religious specialists called Ārādhyās in her village. The Ārādhyās said, 'This woman has the Māvalayā—the Sātī Āsarā—of such-and-such a place; they have gotten her. That's why her children don't survive.' At the Ārādhyās' instructions, in the seventh month of Kalāvatī's pregnancy, her aunt sacrificed a goat to the Ārādhyās' goddess, offered the goddess a sari, and made a basketful of offerings for the Sātī Āsarā at the river. The aunt did all this at her own expense, without so much as telling Tulśīdās about what she had done. Kalāvatī's pregnancy went full term. A healthy baby girl was born. The girl is still alive; she has grown up and is herself married.

After this daughter was born, a dispute arose within the family about why the birth had been successful. As Tulśīdās put it, 'They [the aunt and her allies] would say, "The girl was born this way because we did what we did," and I would say, "No, first I went to the doctor, and that's why the girl was born." ' At the time of Kalāvatī's next pregnancy, her uterus was sutured shut again in the sixth month, but Tulśīdās refused to allow any offerings to be made to gods (*dev bīvkarāyacem nāhī*).

This time, too, the child who was born, another daughter, survived, but she was born in the eighth month of her mother's pregnancy. Kalāvatī attributes the premature birth to her husband's forbidding offerings to gods. The child weighed two pounds at birth and had to be hospitalized when she was two months old. At age two, the daughter developed epilepsy. (She had a bad fever that went to her brain and caused her to have 'fits'.) The girl had to be hospitalized again and nearly died; she was still taking medicine for the condition several years later, at the time I talked with Kalāvatī and her husband.

Kalāvatī's next two pregnancies, also helped by the suturing procedure, nevertheless resulted in premature births—a girl, born after six months of pregnancy, and a boy, born in the eighth month. Both babies died. The boy lived for ten days in an incubator, but he died before receiving an injection that was to be brought from Bombay in a thermos. After the boy died, said Kalāvatī, 'I began to feel very sad. We just had the two girls. So I used to be engrossed in that all the time. I couldn't pay attention to anything. Nothing. I was depressed (*nārāj*). Why? Because we had no son. So what? (*mag*) We had two girls. But we didn't have a boy.'

According to Tulśīdās, the doctor said, 'This will happen every time. The mouth of this womb is completely ruined. You must have a hysterectomy; don't try for a boy any more. . . . Even if she gets pregnant, the baby is sure to be born in the eighth month.'

But Kalāvatī and Tulśīdās were not willing to give up. A Marāṭhā woman neighbour of theirs took Kalāvatī to yet another religious specialist, a woman who became possessed. In her possession, this woman said that Kalāvatī was afflicted 'by the Sātī Āsarā under such-and-such a bridge', and that was why her children did not survive. Still in a possessed state, the woman promised that Kalāvatī would get pregnant again (and that the pregnancy would go full term). Kalāvatī did become pregnant, this time with a boy. As she explained, 'After I got pregnant with him, no matter how sick I got, whatever happened, whatever chills and fever I got, I wasn't ever supposed to take medicine, I wasn't supposed to be given any pills, I wasn't supposed to take even a simple pill. I wasn't even supposed to take a pill that cost four annas. . . . "I'll give up this profession," [that woman] said. She said to me, "If your cradle doesn't get filled, I'll give up this profession of sitting beside the goddess." ' In the seventh month, the woman herself made the Sātī Āsarā offerings, the cooked food being prepared in Kalāvatī and Tulśīdās's home. After full term—nine months and nine days—a son was born, a baby boy who is still, several years later, in good health.

Tulśīdās, himself converted to the religious method of assuring an uncomplicated birth, was particularly gratified by the doctor's reaction. Tulsīdās described this as follows:

> He had said to me, 'You should have a hysterectomy done. Even if I suture [the womb], she'll never be able to have a [nother] child.' But when a nine-month, nine-day child was delivered, when a boy had been born, he said, 'What god did you do a *navas* to?' That is, in the end even they come down to god.

Reflecting on the wonder, Tulśīdās remarked:

> This doctor gives a challenge—I mean, he says—that nothing will be of any use. A doctor is almost God (Parameśvar). If he says that nothing will be of any use, then we have to put our faith in him a hundred per cent. But there's a woman who gets possessed [by a goddess], and she says, 'Don't you do anything. This will turn out completely right.' And what that woman said came true.

Having finally produced a healthy son, the couple was ready to stop having children. They asked the doctor to perform an 'operation'. Usually this English word is used in Marathi to mean a vasectomy, but here it means a tubal ligation. The doctor refused, however, urging the couple to wait until the child had reached five years of age. 'Unless the boy gets to be five years old, there's no guarantee', the doctor said. But when Kalāvatī became pregnant yet another time, and when she had given birth, using the Sātī Āsarā method, to a full-term, healthy baby girl, the doctor did perform the tubal ligation. Three years later, five years before my conversation with Kalāvatī and her husband, she had a hysterectomy.

The three stories I have narrated here—the story of Varuṇa and King Hariścandra, the story of the frightened mother, and the story of Kalāvatī and Tulsīdās' childbearing years—all have to do with the death of children. In all of these narratives, the death of children is something dreadful, a source of suffering that is not mitigated by any belief in the survival of the child either in some other world or in some other form in this world. All three of the stories have more or less happy endings—some child or other does survive, or is brought back to life—but the endings do not suffice to eradicate the distress evoked by the narratives themselves. Nor do I have any happy ending to bring to this paper, anyway to mitigate our sadness as we contemplate the death of children anywhere—much less in a culture like India's where having children is so important an aspect of the enjoyment of life.

Perhaps even more disappointing in an academic context, none of the stories I have narrated seems to me adequately to indicate what connection the death of children has with rivers or even just water. Yet the fact that all three of the stories make this connection, and that the stories come from such vastly different contexts—a Māhātmya text, an oral folk narrative and the reproductive history of a particular living couple—makes me think that the connection must be quite generally important.

In a book I have written on some religious meanings of rivers in Maharashtra, I stress the connections Maharashtrians make between rivers and such human values as wealth, beauty, long life, good health, love, the birth of children, and especially food. The stories I have narrated here seem to me to present the obverse, or shadow side, of this auspicious image. They remind us of the instability of human happiness, and of the fact that the intensity of that happiness depends at least in part on a realization of its brevity.

The only specific connection anyone in Maharashtra has made for me between water and sadness is expressed in one of the very few traditional stories I have heard about the origin of the Sātī Āsarā. The narrator of this story was a man in his nineties who was a member of a caste of betel-leaf rollers. I met him in a remote village in Amrāvatī District, in north-eastern Maharashtra. He said:

These are the Āsarā of tears (*aśrūcyā āsarā*). They're Indra's tears. There was a meeting at Indra's house, of the thirty-three crores of gods. And a sacrificial fire (*hom*) was lit here, during Navarātra. The smoke went into [Indra's] eyes. Tears (*āsū*) fell from them, one at a time. In this way, the Āsarā (*āsumāy*) were born in it, in that sacrificial fire.

This man's story is remarkable for relating the earthly Āsarā to the heavenly *apsarases* of Indra's court, for its use of Vedic gods and sacrifices in a folk-tradition setting, and for the brilliant folk etymology that derives the name '*āsarā*' from the word '*aśrū/u*', 'tears'. Moreover, through the motif of tears, the story relates the watery nature of the Āsarā to the sorrowful aspects of their cult. The Āsarā are the tears of the king of the gods. Like the story of Varuṇa and Hariścandra and the stories of the mothers who get frightened when their sons are floated on river goddesses' rafts, the Āsarā represent the fragility of the joy our children bring us.

NOTES

1. Or bones, asthi.
2. All three of the stories are also found in Chap. 5 of my book *Water and Womanhood: Religious Meanings of Rivers in Maharashtra* (New York: Oxford University Press, 1995).
3. Chap. 34 of the *Gautamī Māhātmya*. Printed separately at the end of *Śrī Brahmapurāṇa* (Bombay: Venkatesvara Press, 1906; Reprint, Delhi: Nag Publishers, 1985).
4. *Gautamī Māhātmya* 34.47: *kṣīṇavṛttiḥ kṛśaḥ . . . durmanāiva.*
5. Menstruation is the condition that is most often cited as arousing the ire of the Āsarā.

Death as the Beginning of a New Life

Hero-Worship among a South Indian Fishing Caste

ELISABETH SCHOMBUCHER

You have an angel now.
It is good to have an angel in heaven.

(The author's great-aunt to her nephew on the occasion of the postnatal death of his fourth child.)

INTRODUCTION

Death as transition, death as entrance to a higher form of existence, early death as a precondition for deification, deification as victory over death: these and other conceptions of death may be of little comfort to the bereaved immediately after a member of their family dies at an early age. The sorrow caused by a sudden and unexpected death may appear to be too great ever to be overcome. In the course of time, however, a deceased child or young adult living in the realm of the deities may turn out to be helpful for the rest of the family, and eventually 'an angel in heaven' may prove to be in fact beneficial for the bereaved.

This paper deals with a specific form of hero-worship among a Telugu-speaking caste of fishermen on the coast of Andhra Pradesh. The worship of the dead as heroes on the basis of memorial stones as well as the deification of human beings and their further existence as 'little' gods and goddesses is well documented in the literature on Indian religion (Blackburn 1985; Knipe 1989; Thapar 1981). It is said that, if a person dies a violent or premature death, he or she is unable to become an ancestor. In these cases, the person becomes another kind of supernatural entity, ranging from malevolent spirits to different sorts of heroes and deified beings.[1] Like ancestors, these entities also have to be appeased and worshipped, but in different ways. Whereas ancestors are remembered after the second or third generation as a collective body (Knipe 1977), persons who die a violent death are remembered individually. The personal story of a hero or deified human being will be remembered in the form of a text, which can be either a hero stone (Thapar 1981) or an epic text which is recited and performed during states of possession (Blackburn 1985).

Among the Vāḍabalija, small children and young adults who die a premature death may become *vīrulu* (Telugu, heroes)[2] after their death. As deified entities they live in the realm of the regional goddesses, and, with their permission, they are able to come back to the living for a short time. Through a medium who is in a state of trance the heroes can communicate with their relatives.

Unlike heroes at other times and in other parts of India, the *vīrulu* of the Vāḍabalija do not get hero stones through which they can be remembered and worshipped, and, unlike other deified human beings who reside in their own or somebody else's shrines, the heroes of the Vāḍabalija are not represented iconographically. Rather their deified life seems to be limited, just like their human life span. A *vīruḍu* will communicate with his or her relatives as long as the communication is required. Mostly mothers but also sisters and grandmothers are interested in asking assistance of their deceased children, brothers and sisters, or grandchildren. A deceased child who became a *vīruḍu* is worshipped and needed usually for one (or sometimes two) generations. After that, there may be a new *vīruḍu* in the family whose help and consolation is sought by its relatives. There is no case known to me of a *vīruḍu* whose power became well known to people outside the family and across several generations and who then was worshipped by a larger group of people.

How then can the *vīrulu* of the Vāḍabalija be related to other deified beings in Indian religion, such as human and divine heroes or local and regional deities? And what are the concepts of deification on which the origin of the heroes of the Vāḍabalija is based? In this paper I will try to relate the status and role of the heroes to those of the other deities of the Vāḍabalija in order to find out what meaning a *vīruḍu* has for the Vāḍabalija.

THE PANTHEON OF THE VĀḌABALIJA

The Vāḍabalija are a Telugu-speaking caste of low social status. Their villages are located in the coastal areas of Visakhapatnam District in Andhra Pradesh. Vāḍabalija men fish in the Bay of Bengal with sail boats and gill nets (now also with motor boats), whereas Vāḍabalija women process and sell the fish. Since Orissa has no autochthonous maritime fishermen, the British government encouraged Vāḍabalija and Jālari (from Ganjam District in south Orissa) to settle in Puri in 1866. Again in 1956 large numbers of fishermen came to fish in Orissa. The Vāḍabalija who came from 1956 onwards are so-called migrating fishermen with their home villages still in Visakhapatnam District in Andhra Pradesh. They regard their stay in Orissa as temporary, although many of them have been living in Orissa for almost forty years. Their settlements are located on the outskirts of Puri and Konarak and near Chilka Lake.[3]

The pantheon of the Vāḍabalija is organized hierarchically according to kinship relations. Most powerful are the Vaiṣṇava gods of the region, such as Siṃhādri in Siṃhācalam (who is the eldest brother), Jagannātha in Puri (who is considered 'ruler of the place' by the Vāḍabalija who settled in Puri), and, somewhat lower in rank, Gōvinda in Tirupati and Veṅkaṭeśwara on Tirumala hill. Next to these four brothers come the female regional and village deities. These are the younger sisters of the Vaiṣṇava gods. Since they are much more numerous, they cannot be put into a hierarchy as easily as their elder brothers. The *vīrulu* are at the bottom of this hierarchy. Like other deified beings (such as heroes who died on the battlefield or 'little' gods and goddesses), the *vīrulu* of the Vāḍabalija have a text which narrates their personal story, although this text might not be as elaborate as others. The text of a *vīruḍu* spoken by the medium refers to the act of dying, the process of deification and the support a *vīruḍu* can give to the living.

Although many Vāḍabalija have been living in Puri more or less permanently for the past forty years, the village deities still have their temples in Andhra Pradesh where the yearly festivals take place. People try to go to their villages and attend the festivals. In Puri, the village deities are represented by bamboo poles (*janḍa*) which are erected by the individual lineages or families near the water line. The deities are worshipped in front of the bamboo poles; here animal sacrifices and other offerings are made by the priest (*dāsuḍu*). Besides this form of worship, there exists another form of communication with the deities on a regular weekly basis with the help of female media (*bhakturālu*), women who get possessed by various deities in a ritual context. I will concentrate here on this form of worship and on the texts spoken by the *bhakturālu*. The Vāḍabalija distinguish three types of *bhakturālu* according to the type of deity that possesses them: the *dēvuḍu bhakturālu* (a medium possessed by Vaiṣṇava gods), the *ammavāru bhakturālu* (a medium possessed by local and regional goddesses), and the *vīrulu bhakturālu* (a medium possessed by the deified dead, lit. 'heroes').[4] There are special days when the various divine beings can possess a *bhakturālu*. *Vīrulu* can possess a medium only on Monday, the Vaiṣṇava gods can come only on Saturday, and goddesses can come on Thursday, Tuesday or Sunday. There is no fundamental difference between séances in which *vīrulu* possess a medium or those in which deities possess a medium. The procedure is the same in both cases. The possession takes place in the house of the medium. The medium cleans her house, takes a ritual bath and lights a lamp in worship of her personal deity. Meanwhile, the persons who are going to ask questions gather in her house, bring their offerings (bananas, coconuts, a small amount of money, etc.), and worship the deity. After the *bhakturālu* has taken her seat, the priest (*dāsuḍu*) can begin with the invocation. The invocation reflects the divine hierarchy (see Schömbucher 1994). The Vaiṣṇava gods have to be asked first to give some of their time to the human beings and to allow their younger sisters to come for some minutes to help the human beings. If *vīrulu* are to be invoked, both the Vaiṣṇava gods and their younger sisters have to be asked to permit the *vīrulu* to come. *Vīrulu* cannot decide on their own.

A séance lasts for one to two hours, depending on the number of persons who ask the deity or their deceased relatives to come (one such section comprises approximately five to ten minutes). Although there is no difference in principle between possession by *vīrulu* and possession by deities, the medium experiences the various entities rather differently. A very experienced *vīrulu bhakturālu* who is now in her forties and who has been getting possessed for about twenty-five years, says that being possessed by *vīrulu* is still a somewhat frightening experience for her:

> The *vīrulu* come on my back and shoulders, they come all at once, 'like a whirlwind', they are heavy and they quarrel among themselves. Each says: 'I will speak to my relatives first. . . .' They are like air (*gāli*) just around me, and they will come one after the other onto my body. They will appear for only a few minutes.

In contrast to this, the goddess comes onto the *bhakturālu's* head, she feels light and she stays, there is no coming and going.

THE DEIFIED DEAD

I will now concentrate on the origin of one *vīruḍu* and on the question of who exactly becomes a *vīruḍu.* According to the Vāḍabalija, there is something like an ideal procedure. It is said that only a small child can become a *vīruḍu.* The body of the dead child is buried by a male relative 'in the forest'. It is covered with salt so that foxes will not dig it up. In almost every family known to me, there is at least one child who died at an early age. But not all these children have become *vīrulu.* Only some children appear after their death in the dreams of a relative and ask for an icon (*bomma,* lit.: 'doll'). In a special ritual, a *bomma* is prepared out of sand and mud and the relatives assure that the *vīruḍu* will be worshipped adequately. The appearance of the child in a dream indicates that it has become a *vīruḍu.* After that, the *vīruḍu* can come into the body of the medium and talk to his or her own relatives. But besides this ideal procedure there are other ways of becoming a *vīruḍu.* For example, if a deceased relative does not appear in a dream, it is still possible for a family member to go directly to a medium, make offerings and hope that the deceased person may appear as a *vīruḍu* and speak to his or her relatives. Although the ideal *vīruḍu* is a small child, there are exceptions to this rule. Two *vīrulu* on my tape were young men who were married and already had children of their own. One died in a fishing accident and the other man also died unexpectedly sometime after an operation. Thus, both died a premature death, but they were not small children.

Although *vīrulu* are at the bottom of the divine hierarchy, and although even for an experienced *bhakturālu* possession by *vīrulu* is a somewhat frightening experience, the Vāḍabalija prefer to ask a *vīruḍu* for help when they have problems such as illness, problems in the family or poor yields from their fishing expeditions. A family who has a *vīruḍu* for help and protection is in one way unlucky because it has lost a child, a sister or brother, or a husband. On the other hand, having a *vīruḍu* for protection and help eventually will have beneficial effects for the bereaved. However, knowing that one's relative is still there, although in the realm of a deity, is not always a matter of consolation. During *vīrulu* possessions I have seen several women being overcome with grief while talking to their deceased children or husbands or brothers.

Nevertheless, having a *vīruḍu* in one's family has some advantages. If a *vīruḍu* is worshipped in the proper way, he or she provides prosperity (which means a good catch for the fishermen), protection, good health, etc. Whereas a deity can speak to everybody, a *vīruḍu* speaks only to persons belonging to his or her immediate family. A deity is very inquisitive, asking for all the details and listing all the mistakes a person has committed. On top of that, a deity is very demanding. As one woman said:

> *dēvatālu* demand a lot of things. How many thousands of Rupees we have to spend! How many sheep, how many chicken we have to sacrifice! How many saris we have to offer!

Compared to that, *vīrulu* are rather modest. They want to be fed daily with a small amount of food and they want to be worshipped daily. Once a year they may demand a piece of cloth. Since *vīrulu* are members of the family (even after death they include themselves in the family and talk of 'my' family, 'my' brother, 'we'), they are good-natured and cannot be strict about the mistakes or 'sins' of their family members. Some persons even say that they believe more in *vīrulu* than in deities because *vīrulu* can protect them even better during typhoons for instance, and they provide much more fish than deities.

Vīrulu do not mention their deification process every time they speak to their relatives. If they are asked frequently, all the details are well-known and need not be recounted every time. However, Kokila, a girl who died in 1985 at the age of five, narrated the process of her death and subsequent deification when speaking to her mother in 1991. According to medical diagnosis she died of hepatitis; according to the *vīrulu bhakturālu* on whose body she comes, she was taken away by the goddess. This is clearly indicated by the fact that her death was accompanied by vomiting and diarrhoea. According to the *bhakturālu*, Kokila's life was not completed, therefore she is still there. Kokila herself, after greeting the other gods and goddesses, narrates the conditions of her death:[5]

> my mother, you
> you have not forgotten
> I have not forgotten
> I, on that day, you, mother
> I would have lived [been saved]
> I was eaten by the goddess, mother
> I was eaten by the goddess, mother
> uncountable answers
> what kind of pain came to me
> what kind of pain came to me
> in those seven minutes [at that short time], mother
> in my stomach, mother
> so much pain came to me
> you do not know, mother
> I, in that hospital
> when I was given medicines
> the goddess became angry
> the goddess took me away
> oh, my mother (*amma*), you
> oh, my mother (*talli*), you
> I, under the guidance of (the goddess) Bhūśatti [Bhūśakti]
> I became a goddess (*thakurani*)
> I became a respectable (noble) woman
> I became a *yogini* (female ascetic)

The narration of Kokila's death starts with the lines 'my mother, you', 'you have not forgotten', 'I have not forgotten' and then takes up the tragic circumstances of her death. She mentions her suffering, which was unbearably painful not only for her but also for her mother. She recounts the traumatic experience which neither of them can forget. She ascribes her death to the wrath of the goddess and even states that she might have survived, if only the angry goddess could have been appeased. Nobody gets accused directly of omitting important steps or doing the wrong things, but the tragedy of her death, which might have been averted, becomes apparent once again. After narrating her illness and how the goddess took her away, Kokila says that she lives in the realm of one specific goddess, Bhūśakti, and that with her help, she herself became a goddess, or at least a *yogini* or a noble woman. As a divine being, she may support her relatives, but she may also make demands on them. Kokila in a sense is a perfect *vīrudu*. She herself announced after her death that she had become a *vīrudu*. Nobody requested her. The *bhakturālu* recounts:

She told her mother: 'I will stand as a *vīrudu*, you worship me daily, then I will protect you.' Like that, a *vīruḍu* should come. It should be intentionally, but not all will come like that. When it is not meant for them to come then they won't come.

THE DIVINE WORDS

To show the similarities and the difference between a *vīruḍu* and a deity, I shall now compare two texts, one spoken by a *vīruḍu*, the other by a deity. Dēvuḍamma's elder brother, who was married and had two children, died in 1985 in Andhra Pradesh just shortly after their boat went into the sea. The boat turned over in a big wave and her elder brother was hit in such a way that he died. Since he was a very pious person (he used to sing *bhajans* all night long, as his younger sister explained), he soon became a *vīruḍu* (three months after his death). Dēvuḍamma, who is also married and mother of four children, told me before the séance (in March 1993) that her husband had been ill for the past three weeks. She had gone to different doctors and bought expensive medicines, but her husband's health had not improved. For more than three weeks he had been unable to go fishing. Dēvuḍamma was worried about him and wanted to ask her elder brother.

When her elder brother finally managed to come onto the shoulders of the *bhakturālu*, he began by speaking two lines:

amma, ēmamma, my companion
ole, my younger sister, you

After the second line, in which a younger sister is addressed, everybody in the room knew that now Dēvuḍamma's elder brother had arrived; Dēvuḍamma asked the following question:

DĒVUḌAMMA: why have you made me a bird without a nest, me here?

what kind of bird without a nest?
why would you become like that, *amma*?

DĒVUḌAMMA: you are not visible, nowhere!

my mother, my companion
ole, my elder sister,[6] *amma*
ole, the goddess [mother] on our side
ole, members in my native house
amma, you take them, my mother, you
to your goddess
amma, by offering so much
amma, it is not my lap, *amma*
amma, it is the lap of the goddess
the offerings in the goddess's lap
amma, five eyes, *amma*

amma, presented the offerings, *anno*
amma, five eyes, *ayyo*
amma, gave the offerings, *anno*
amma, he is of our house, *amma*
amma, my companion, you
amma, you tell that you have hundred eyes
amma, thousand crores of offerings
amma, to my thorny Gaṅga
amma, how many boons you ask
amma, so many boons she gives
amma, make *namaskar*, my younger sister
amma, otherwise you won't have the way, *amma*, you
amma, you won't have ways, my mother, you
amma, in the days of the past

The *vīruḍu* recommended that his sister take care of the goddess and worship her properly. She should convince the members of her household to worship the goddess. He says that the offerings she made just now should not be meant for him, but for the goddess instead. Because, as he says explicitly, if she and her family do not worship the goddess, she won't help them solving their problems. Thus, the *vīruḍu* constrains his own power and refers instead to the more powerful goddess, whose superior status he acknowledges. He also acts as a mediator, suggesting that Dēvuḍamma should have confidence in the power of the goddess. Just after the *vīruḍu* has started recounting events of the past, he gets interrupted by Dēvuḍamma.

DĒVUḌAMMA: In what kind of troubles are you, what kind of problem? I don't know anything. Don't hide anything about the goddess (*ammavāru*).

amma, in the days of the past, my mother, you
amma, in the days of the past, my companion, you
amma, they offered so many offerings, *ole, amma*
amma, the offerings of the five eyes went away
amma, the offerings of two eyes did remain
amma, the offerings of two eyes went away
amma, the offerings of a single eye remained
amma, if you offered one crore offerings, it is your will
amma, your goddess Errapilli Nûkamma
ole, sinful Masēnu, my mother, you
she is giving such big boons
so much *ganji* (rice) she poured
amma, the questions about you, companion

The *vīruḍu* is getting more precise now and refers to the time when all the members of the family lived together and worshipped the goddess jointly (five eyes). This is usually also a time of great prosperity, since all adult brothers work together and pool the income from their fishing expeditions. In the course of time, then, the brothers split into nuclear families; they live in different places and do not worship their goddess as a group any more. Again, the *vīruḍu* acts as an intermediary between the goddess and Dēvuḍamma. He points out that the goddess might be angry if not worshipped properly and he emphasizes that it was the goddess who gave all the wealth. But he does this in careful and gentle words. He does not abuse Dēvuḍamma for neglecting the deity (as the goddess would).

DĒVUḌAMMA: let this be, one has to lay blame on the goddess. Are we praying to the goddess, or what are we doing?

Obviously, Dēvuḍamma does not feel guilty concerning the worship of the deity and she interrupts the *vīruḍu* again. In her eyes the goddess gets worshipped sufficiently. With her interference she also indicates that her elder brother should drop the subject of the goddess since she is not convinced by this explanation. The *vīruḍu* finally presents an interpretation of the illness of Dēvuḍamma's husband which convinces Dēvuḍamma. The two different attempts at interpretation may also be seen as a careful way of negotiating various versions of Dēvuḍamma's problems.

amma, a thread of seven fathoms you take, *amma*
amma, a thread of seven fathoms you take, *amma*
amma, māyamma you, three *cīpuru* stalks
amma, you give, my companion, you
amma, three animals you give, my companion, you
amma, don't cover me with one crore sins
amma, don't throw one crore of false blames
amma, I will take away the difficulties
amma, I will take away the difficulties
amma, I will give such *nidānamu*[7] (stability, protection)

Dēvuḍamma knew that her brother was speaking of witchcraft now, because he was already telling her what kind of counter-witchcraft to provide (a thread of seven fathoms length, three *cīpuru* stalks, three animals). This interpretation seems to make sense to her and she approves of it with her next question.

DĒVUḌAMMA asks: *amma,* who did it? You have to tell everything!

amma, people[8] did it, *amma,* people did it
amma, the people who made offerings, *amma*
amma, the sinful people who made offerings
amma, the sinful people who made offerings
amma, ole, māyamma, you
ole, my mother, you

amma, people did it, *amma*
amma, people who make traps (snares)
amma, such people made it
amma, three people, *amma*
amma, who make offerings, *amma*
amma, in the city of Jagannāth
amma, people who are
amma, coming into the body
amma, somebody [who is] near to us
amma, one such man (person) was here
amma, a man (person) belonging to you
amma, three people, *māyamma,* you
amma, three people, *māyamma,* you
amma, here in the city of Jagannāth, *amma*
amma, people did it unexpectedly, *amma*
amma, he went up the road, *amma*
amma, on the road, *māyamma,* you
amma, by putting three items ['spells']
amma, [he] was made to walk forward
amma, then [he] was made to walk backward
amma, the deception he didn't know
amma, he was unable to know the deception
amma, emamma, you, *māyamma,* you
amma, for three months, both of us, *māyamma*
ole, māyamma, you
ole, for three months they put
amma, for three weeks this condition has lasted
amma, this gives pain, that gives pain, he is saying, *amma*
amma, this is aching that is aching, he is thinking
amma, he [the sorcerer] wanted to take his heart
amma, you are giving crores of medicines
amma, you asked the people of this town, *amma*
amma, you asked the people of this town, *amma*
amma, this was made on the road, *amma*
amma, they took him by accompanying him
amma, making him walk in front, *ole, amma*
amma, oh *amma,* you, you
amma, you are asking to show, companion
amma, people living in our huts, *amma*
they took him out to the road
on that day, on *amāvāsya*
on the *amāvāsya* day they took him
amma, they made him walk forward and backward
amma, they made him walk forward and backward
ole, māyamma, my companion, my younger sister, my companion
amma, within minutes three *cīpuru* stalks
amma, three bundles of *cīpuru* stalks, *amma,* you
amma, a thread of seven fathoms, *māyamma,* you

amma, a thread of seven fathoms you have to take, *amma*
amma, a thread of seven fathoms you have to take, *amma*
amma, four small knives you have to take, *amma*
amma, take eleven nails
amma, I will show you the happy way (*sukhadāramu*), companion
amma, I am showing the happy ways
nāyamma, you
amma, on the *amāvāsya* day at three o'clock
amma, three people went out on the road together
amma, three went together, *amma*
amma, who made [him] walk forward and backward
amma, you ask my brother-in-law [younger sister's husband, i.e. Dēvuḍamma's husband]
amma, it will come to his memory (he will remember), *ole amma*, you
amma, *māyamma*, you, my younger companion, you
ole, I will give such *nidānamu* (stability), I will give, I will give *nidānamu*
ole, such *nidānamu*, I will give
ole, such *nidānamu*, I will give
amma, such *nidānamu*, I will give
amma, I am going, *amma*, my younger companion
amma, I will give a happy share
amma, a happy share I will give
amma, do not worry about *ganji*. I am going.

Dēvuḍamma's question is followed by a rather long and detailed account of where and how the witchcraft was performed. The *vīruḍu* explains that three persons are to be made responsible for the witchcraft. Since all three of them reside in the city of Jagannāth (i.e. Puri), are pious persons making offerings to the deities, and are 'near to us', they can be blamed for being hypocritical. Instead of witchcraft, one should expect help and support from such persons, but, on the other hand, closeness is also a precondition for rivalry, ill-wishing and eventually witchcraft. The term 'witchcraft' is never used here, but the details of it are recounted. The three persons cast a spell on Dēvuḍamma's husband by leaving some items on the road and making him pass by. The spell was meant to last three months (now only three weeks have gone by). This causes pain all over the body and therefore medicines won't work. In the end of this account, the last new moon day (*amāvāsya*) is specified, a kind of day which is generally favourable for carrying out witchcraft. And the *vīruḍu* is sure that Dēvuḍamma's husband (his brother-in-law) would remember the circumstances, now that it was pointed out to him. After that details are given of the counter-witchcraft Dēvuḍamma has to arrange for. She has to provide stalks of the *cīpuru* grass from which brooms are made, a thread of seven fathoms' length,[9] four small knives, and eleven nails. In the end, the *vīruḍu* assures his younger sister that he will solve her problems (*sukhadāramu*) and provide her with happiness and stability (*nidānamu*), and says that she should not worry about *ganji*.[10] From this text, it is obvious that the *vīruḍu* first of all acts as an intermediary between the more powerful goddess and human beings. He speaks carefully, there is nothing threatening in his voice, he does not reproach his younger sister. He starts by focusing on the goddess who is not worshipped properly, but since Dēvuḍamma does not approve of this interpretation, the *vīruḍu* states man-made causes of the illness of Dēvuḍamma's husband and promises to help her.

In contrast to the words of a *vīruḍu*, in another example the goddess speaks to a woman, Kondamma, who has fallen ill with chickenpox (in March 1993) and who has had to ask Nūkalamma for help. Nūkalamma is a goddess of regional importance in Andhra Pradesh. She is the goddess of smallpox. Her younger sister, Peddamma, is the goddess who may manifest herself in the form of chickenpox. A couple of years ago Kondamma went to Revupolavaram, her home village, where Nūkalamma is also worshipped. She made a vow that if her children experienced no troubles she would attend Nūkalamma's festival in Bangaripalem, another fishing village. But she forgot to go there and to take her children to the festival. So, Nūkalamma sent her younger sister Peddamma (in the form of chickenpox) to her son. He was affected very badly and got many boils on his skin 'which were full of worms'. This happened three or four years ago. He was finally healed, but has still not fully recovered. Even after this mnemotechnical device of the goddess, the mother didn't fulfil her vow. She didn't take her son to Bangaripalem. So the goddess again sent Peddamma (chickenpox), this time to the mother. After Kondamma and her relatives asked the goddess for advice in the following séance, the family members agree that the patient should go to Nūkalamma's temple on *gantham amāvāsya* (which was three or four months in the future). This synopsis of the patient's story was told to me by the *bhakturālu* after the séance. She completed her account by saying, 'now this woman will remember'.

Nūkalamma is incorporated by a different *bhakturālu* and her recitations differ from the recitations of the *vīrulu bhakturālu*. This is partly due to the fact that every medium has her own personal style concerning lexical choice, length of lines, and lexical markers at the beginning and end of each line. For instance, whereas the *vīrulu bhakturālu* can be characterized as a gentle and modest woman in general, Nūkalamma's medium is rather boisterous and uses vulgar language in ordinary situations as well. But the different discourses are also based on the nature of the divine and deified entities. Nūkalamma is supposed to be a fierce and powerful goddess whose wrath human beings fear.

After greeting all the other gods and goddesses, Nūkalamma starts talking about the patient:

ole, sinful human beings
ole, they are going for sin
abba, crossing the border [of the village]
abba, the people showed their penis
abba, the goddess tied their hands [punished them]
abba, the golden garland has to be given
abba, the daughter's memory has to be there
abba, from the times of my grandfathers, Nūkalamma
abba, you have gone to the streets of my grandfathers
amma, even you, *amma*, Nūkalamma
abba, with my maternal uncles, *anna*
abba, since the time of my grandfathers
you [have been] there at the seventy thresholds
you, famous Nūkalamma, you
will you take the golden garland?
will you build this golden house?
goddess of my father's sister and my mother's brother, can you give?
ole, the promises (vows), where did you keep them, daughter?
I, Nūkalamma, who commit sins
I [was the goddess] who tied you
if Gaṅga is worshipped by your father's sister and your mother's brother
then you go to my place, to see the light
you [plural] will become the creepers, daughter
ole, for my light to come
you [sing.] will become support
since the time of your grandfathers, [I am] Nūkalamma
ole, you have kept [the promise] to yourself
to this day twenty-five, fourteen
four years, days are over
ole, to the seventy thresholds of Pentakota
ole, earning fame, *anna*
you, if it is Nūkalamma of the past
when you remember
ole, the day when you peel off your skin
the Gaṅga of your grandfather's time will be there
ole, if you don't peel off your skin
there will be no Gaṅga of your grandfather's time
there will be no Gaṅga of your grandfather's grandmother's time

Nūkalamma starts in a different tone than the *vīruḍu's*. Her recitation uses a completely different rhetoric from his. The language is abusive and threatening. She talks about the sinfulness of human beings, the anger and the punishment of the goddess. Such general accusations can apply to most of the persons who attend a possession séance. Once the deity begins this way, the direction of the further discourse is established: all the problems are caused by the faults of the human beings; they have to be blamed (and punished) for committing sins, such as offending the goddess or not remembering their vows. The statements of sin and punishment are similar to the discourses of other goddesses, but the vulgar language (showing the penis) is unique to this goddess (or rather to this medium). The general interpretation of the situation is followed by a demand to the woman who is addressed as 'daughter'. It is demanded that she fulfil her vow and that she worship the goddess (giving the golden garland). However, worshipping the goddess after all these failures is not an easy task. The goddess might not be willing to accept the offerings any more. Therefore, the goddess has to be convinced to do so. The following section, starting with the line '*abba*, from the times of my grandfathers, Nūkalamma'—at least according to the 'inner' logic of the text—is not spoken by the goddess and addressed to the audience, but by the medium and addressed to the goddess. The medium acts as a mediator, praising the power of the goddess and emphasizing the fact that she has been taking care of their lineage (the seventy thresholds) for many generations (since the time of the grandfathers). After that, the fame of the goddess is stated, and finally the medium pleads with the goddess to accept the offerings which will eventually be made, and to make the family prosperous and healthy again ('goddess of my father's sister and my mother's brother, can you give?').

After this intervention by the medium (which is not marked by a change of melody or rhythm), the goddess starts speaking again with an '*ole*, where did you keep the promises, daughter?'. This is followed by the statement that Nūkalamma herself punished the woman for not keeping her vow. Kondamma is urged to worship Nūkalamma. Only then will she get protection and support in return. She (and her family) will become creepers which eventually bear fruit. The goddess again states the faults of Kondamma. She has not kept her promise, although a long time has already passed (lit.: twenty-five, fourteen, five years, days). After inserting again the standard line ('Nūkalamma from the time of the grandfathers'), the goddess makes her most important statement. Only when Kondamma remembers (her promise) and fulfils her vow can she expect support and protection. But she has to be really faithful, just like Hanumān, who peels off his skin to show that Rāma, Sītā, and Lakṣmaṇa are in his heart. If Kondamma is not faithful, then not only will Nūkalamma not protect her, but she will even prevent Gaṅga from protecting Kondamma's family. This threat is not unusual, being uttered by other deities as well. On the one hand, it is an ultimate threat, while on the other hand, it exhibits the deity's power: human beings cannot solve problems just by worshipping another deity. In this case, Kondamma must worship Nūkalamma as well as Gaṅga and others, for only then will she get protection, prosperity and health in return. If she does not worship Nūkalamma, the wrath of this powerful goddess will cause the worship of other deities to be in vain.

Here, the medium stopped and the people immediately discussed the words of the goddess. Kondamma had come to the séance in a group of relatives, which is rather uncommon but which indicates the seriousness of her case. The priest (*dāsuḍu*) who invoked the goddess addressed her directly by confirming: 'But she is going [to your temple]. She is going.' A long discussion among Kondamma's relatives followed about which time would be best for going to Andhra Pradesh and they finally agreed upon *gandham amāvāsya*. While the people were still discussing this, the medium started reciting again. This time, she addressed the priest with the term *koḍuku* (son). He tried to pacify the goddess and to persuade her not to be too strict with Kondamma. While the medium was reciting again, the people in the audience became very excited and continued discussing the case among themselves and with the goddess. A brief summary of the following interaction between the goddess and her audience is given here.

Just as if to reconfirm her endangered power, Nūkalamma repeats the following lines again and again: 'I am the goddess since the times of your grandfathers', 'how many answers I have given', 'tell me, is there Nūkalamma of your grandfather's time or not?', 'tell me, haven't I always answered the three questions (solved all problems)?'. The *dāsuḍu* tries to mediate between the goddess and Kondamma. According to him, it is not the fault of the daughter (Kondamma) and he promises that she will definitely go (to Revupolavaram). Nūkalamma insists: 'The daughter has no shame (*siggu*)', and the *dāsuḍu* replies: 'It is not a matter of shame. We will definitely go. She will go. Her son will go.' The dispute, or rather the negotiation, between the *dāsuḍu* and the goddess continues for sometime while several other persons comment on the words of the goddess. The séance ends officially when the medium commands: 'bring me some sweet water!'[11]

CONCLUSION

A perfect *vīruḍu* among the Vāḍabalija is a child who, after its death, makes itself known in the dreams of a family member and is then worshipped by the family. However, anybody who dies an early death may become a *vīruḍu*. An 'untimely death' need not necessarily be a 'bad death', but can be interpreted as a 'good death'—even in Brahmanical conceptions about death, as shown by Parry (1994:166). Kokila's narration of the circumstances of her death averts any fear of the bereaved that her death, although 'untimely' and thus 'bad', might have been caused by her evil character and that subsequently she would have to exist as a malevolent ghost. Although the angry goddess somehow could not be satisfied (due to whose fault is not mentioned), nobody is made responsible for this omission directly. Instead, her 'bad death' is the precondition for her deification. But even five years after her death, her existence in the divine realm is only of little consolation for her mother, although life could be worse without the protection of a *vīruḍu.*

A *vīruḍu* lives in the realm of regional goddesses, and, due to their protection and support, the hero is able to develop into a divine being. But a *vīruḍu* among the Vāḍabalija cannot develop further into a deity. During the existence as a *vīruḍu* the entity retains its identity as a human person. A *vīruḍu* does not become an independent divine entity, but always depends on a 'higher' goddess. She decides whether the *vīruḍu* may stay in her realm, whether it is allowed to talk to human beings and even when it is reborn. (Since a *vīruḍu* doesn't develop into a deity, there is no reason for the Vāḍabalija why it should not be reborn—in contrast to other deified beings, who are never reborn).

The range of influence of a *vīruḍu* is not as great as that of a deity. A *vīruḍu* cannot refer to anyone's problems. He or she can only speak to members of the immediate family. Because of its dependent status, a *vīruḍu* acts as a mediator between deities and human beings. In the case of Kokila as well as in the case of Dēvuḍamma's brother, the greater power of the goddess is acknowledged and Dēvuḍamma's brother explicitly refers Dēvuḍamma to the goddess for help. A *vīruḍu* points out the faults of human beings, but neither threatens nor punishes them. Still a family member him- or herself, a *vīruḍu* fully understands the shortcomings of his or her relatives. In all cases which I have translated, *vīrulu* promised to help their relatives, and made only modest demands. Besides dying too early, a *vīruḍu* does no other heroic act. But this is a sufficient precondition for some of them to gain power as deified beings and to use it for the benefit of the living. Only if their divine status is continuously ignored by the living, they may harm them, but they cannot be categorized as basically malevolent or even ambivalent beings. The Vāḍabalija regard them as basically benevolent. One reason for their benevolence might be the fact that *vīrulu* are lesser beings and are less powerful than deities. Hence their behaviour cannot be as harsh as that of the deities. However, at least some of the Vāḍabalija say that in fact *vīrulu* protect them better during their fishing expeditions than deities and that they prefer to ask a *vīruḍu* for help, because *vīrulu* are much more lenient with their family members than deities are. Even if it is only for one generation, such low-status deified beings as the *vīrulu* of the Vāḍabalija have an immense power to protect human beings.

NOTES

1. For malevolent spirits see, for example, Obeyesekere 1977 and Kapferer 1983.
2. From Sanskrit *vīra,* hero. The plural form of Tel. *vīruḍu* is *vīrulu.* It shall be maintained here instead of speaking of '*vīruḍus*'.

3. Fieldwork for this study was carried out mostly in Puri and to some extent in the villages in Andhra Pradesh in the years 1990, 1991 and 1993.
4. A medium who may be possessed by *vīrulu* has to have a personal deity in addition. The *vīrulu bhakturālu* who is portrayed here also gets possessed by Kotta Rājulu, a regional goddess in Andhra Pradesh.
5. The text is composed in lines of approximately equal length. The symmetrical character of the lines is enhanced by using the same lexical beginnings and endings in several successive lines. See Schömbucher 1994.
6. It should be 'my younger sister'. Similar inconsistencies happen rather frequently and may be attributed to the improvised character of the recitation.
7. Telugu *nidānamu* can also be translated as 'diagnosis, first and primary cause'. The Vāḍabalija use it here in the sense of 'stability, calmness, steadiness'.
8. Telugu *naruḍu* 'man' in the general sense of human being.
9. One fathom = 1.828 m. In colloquial usage 'length of a man'.
10. *Ganji* 'rice cooked and soaked in salted water overnight'. It is used here in the general sense of 'food'.
11. Water mixed with sugar and sometimes limes is usually drunk by the medium to cool her down after the deity has left her body. Sometimes it has to be drunk to cause the deity to leave the medium.

REFERENCES

Blackburn, Stuart. 1985. Death and Deification: Folk Cults in Hinduism. *History of Religions* 24: 255-74.

Kapferer, Bruce. 1983. *A Celebration of Demons: Exorcism and the Aesthetics of Healing in Sri Lanka.* Bloomington: Indiana University Press.

Knipe, David. 1977. *Sapiṇḍīkaraṇa*: The Hindu Rite of Entry into Heaven. In Frank E. Reynolds and Earle H. Waugh (eds.), *Religious Encounters with Death: Insights from the History and Anthropology of Religions.* University Park: Pennsylvania State University Press.

———. 1989. Night of the Growing Dead: A Cult of Vīrabhadra on Coastal Andhra. In A. Hiltebeitel (ed.), *Criminal Gods and Demon Devotees. Essays on the Guardians of Popular Hinduism.* Delhi: Manohar.

Obeyesekere, Gananath. 1977. Psychocultural Exegesis of a Case of Spirit Possession in Sri Lanka. In V. Crapanzano and V. Garrison (eds.), *Case Studies in Spirit Possession.* New York: Wiley.

Parry, Jonathan. 1994. *Death in Banaras.* Cambridge: Cambridge University Press.

Schömbucher, Elisabeth. 1994. The Consequences of not Keeping a Promise: Possession Mediumship among a South Indian Fishing Caste. *Cahiers de Littérature Orale* 35: 41-63.

Thapar, Romila. 1981. Death and the Hero. In S.C. Humphreys and Helen King (eds.), *Mortality and Immortality: The Anthropology and Archaeology of Death.* New York: Academic Press.

No Heroes in Kaliṅga?

On Death in Kaliṅga Inscriptions

GEORG BERKEMER

INTRODUCTION

If one compares Western epigraphs, especially Roman ones, with the South Asian epigraphic tradition,[1] a striking difference becomes apparent. While most types of Roman inscription have their functional equivalents in India, the large number of Roman commemorative epigraphs have no analogues in certain regions of India before *c.* AD 1000. Considering the importance of inscriptional sources for the history of India, this imbalance is significant. In Roman inscriptions, the memory of the deceased individual and the cult of the ancestors (*manes*) make up a functional whole, expressed in both textual and architectural details, and those who have lost their lives for the city are remembered by their families as well as by the community.

In India, we only hear of heroic warriors of old in the epic and purāṇic literatures, where these characters are superhuman figures, although they lack godlike attributes,[2] while the heroic deeds of contemporaries do not enter the written tradition. In classical times, inscriptions form part of the high religion, for which the cult of the dead is a private or family affair. This means that our knowledge of the heroes and of the deified dead is almost exclusively from the perspective of the popular religions (Blackburn 1984). Apart from this, we find some faint traces of 'folk'-style treatment of the dead in the inscriptions in hero-stones of western India and the Deccan, in which folk cults and epigraphic traditions meet (Banerjee 1921; Mirashi 1978; Settar and Sontheimer 1982). Otherwise early Indian inscriptions in Prakrit or Sanskrit are conspicuously silent about individual heroism and violent death within one's own family.[3]

Later records, dated after AD 1000 from southern and western India (e.g. Karnataka, Rayalasima and Andhra) where there is a heroic tradition in folk religion, frequently mention the theme of violent death. These inscriptions are generally written in the vernacular. Hero-stones are not known in the epigraphy of Bengal and Orissa. This observation coincides with the absence of hero-worship in popular religion in many parts of these areas. In the border regions between Andhra Pradesh and Orissa, the region known in the middle ages as Kaliṅga,[4] a cult involving hero-worship is practised today among members of the Telugu-speaking landowning castes of the Reḍḍis and Kammas in the districts East Godavari, Visakhapatnam and Vizianagaram.[5] Another cult of the *vīrulu* (heroes) is known to be widespread among the Telugu fishing caste of the Vāḍabalija.[6] On the other hand, hero-worship seems to have no significance among landowning Oriyas, such as the Paiks of Parlakimedi and the Kāḷiṅgas of Srikakulam district.

In the present paper, I would like to show how the heroic theme was introduced into the regional culture of Kaliṅga. Since early historical records were based exclusively on the religion of the élites, only influences from neighbouring areas can explain the present situation. My hypothesis is that at the time when the politically sanctioned hero cults arose in Andhra (*c.* thirteenth century), Kaliṅga had already been a subsidiary part of the cultural region of Orissa for several centuries, where hero cults were not a popular form of worship. Kaliṅga remained culturally and politically a part of Orissa until the collapse of the Orissan empire in the sixteenth century. Only later, when new, politically dominant groups immigrated from Andhra, were hero cults introduced into Kaliṅga.

DEATH IN THE EARLY INSCRIPTIONAL RECORDS OF KALIṄGA

The earliest inscriptions from Kaliṅga are copper-plates issued by the rulers of the so-called Māṭhara 'dynasty', a group of kings who ruled from about AD 350 until AD 500.[7] We do not know much about the dynastic history of the Māṭharas or their contemporaries, such as the Pitṛbhaktas of Pithapuram, and their successors, the Early Gaṅgas of Kaliṅganagara and the Gaṅgas of Śvetaka (both of whom reigned in the second half of the first millennium AD). The reason for this lies in the fact that their inscriptions are silent about the deceased members of their families. In the oldest type of inscriptional records extant from Kaliṅga,[8] death is only referred to in the formula at the beginning of a text intended to characterize the king as a pious leader of his family and kingdom. In these inscriptions, the parents, sometimes just the father, of the ruler are mentioned following the deity to whom the king adheres. The king is very often described as one who shows proper respect to his—probably deceased—parents by calling himself he who meditates upon the feet of his parents.[9] It is worth mentioning that this epithet is placed between the statement of the king's sectarian denomination and his own royal titles. In this way, the issuer of the grant implies the successively decreasing sacredness of the god, the king's parents and the king himself. But this seems more likely to be a result of the king's image as the perfect representative of a prototypical *dharmic* ruler like Rāma or King Pṛthu of the Purāṇas than an actual allusion to the godlike status of his parents or of the king himself.

The introductory part of the inscriptions retains the same form as at the time of the Early Gaṅgas of Kaliṅganagara (sixth to tenth century AD). In the earliest complete Gaṅga inscription, the king has 'won many battles of four-tusked [elephants]',[10] but death is not explicitly mentioned, nor is the king characterized as a warrior or hero of any kind.[11]

Even when all the preconditions for the deification of an ancestor are fulfilled, inscriptional records try to avoid any allusion to a premature and violent death. This was the case at the end of the rule of the Early Gaṅgas. There had been a severe political crisis lasting a century, from approximately 940 to 1035. The Early Gaṅgas had been subdued by the Rāṣṭrakūṭas under Kṛṣṇa III (939-68). Later, after his death, they had to fight wars against the Cālukyas and Cōḷas. At least one Gaṅga king met a violent death in these wars in battle against the Cōḷas.[12] We do not know how the Gaṅgas overcame these difficulties, but there must have been considerable changes in the administration of the state and in the proceedings at court, judging from the new administrative titles and new chancellory style of the eleventh-century inscriptions. The most important innovation in the long run was the introduction of an elaborate eulogy (*praśasti*) into the copper-plate grants of the Gaṅgas. This *praśasti*, henceforward in verse and including a long genealogy, was the traditional place for the king and his royal ancestors to be praised.[13]

In the inscriptions of the Gaṅga king Vajrahasta III,[14] we have for the first time all the prerequisites necessary for the long awaited cult of the dead. First, there is the hero who had died a premature death on the battlefield as a ruling king just two decades earlier. Secondly, there are technical means of propagating the hero's death in a state cult via temple inscriptions a new and more public channel for the legitimization of power and the already known copper-plates. In addition, the son of the deceased had a motive to exploit his father's death. Vajrahasta III's attempts to reform the apparatus of his empire were probably directed against the interests of an older elite, since he himself was not a member of the main line of the Early Gaṅgas who had ruled before the crisis of the tenth and early eleventh centuries.[15] However, the inscriptions do not take this opportunity to introduce the newly available topic of individual heroism. The discourse remains the same as before, only the common stereotypes concerning the virtues of any Hindu ruler, such as his role as protector of the earth, as the giver of riches, as a treasury of all virtues, being mentioned. Even Kāmārṇava, a king who only ruled for a few months,[16] is said to have 'protected the earth, prosperous and resplendent'. Despite all the features taken over from the Cālukyas and Rāṣṭrakūṭas, there is no trace of a newly founded heroic tradition in Kaliṅga, for instance a local adaptation of the hero cult under the Rāṣṭrakūṭas of western India (Rajashekhara 1982).

DEATH IN THE INSCRIPTIONS OF THE IMPERIAL GANGAS AND THEIR SUCCESSORS

The manner in which a king's ancestors are described in the *praśasti* does not greatly change under the Imperial Gaṅgas of Orissa,[17] but which heroism plays at least some part in epigraphs of persons who were in high offices under the Gaṅga kings. Members of this social group do not issue copper-plates in Sanskrit, but donate gifts to temples and write temple inscriptions in Telugu or Oriya. The donors bear titles which praise their heroic deeds and they attribute to their kings titles such as 'hero of heroes' (*vīrādhivīra*). A good example is a Telugu inscription from Srikurmam, dated AD 1321 (*SII* 5, 1183). Here, an officer named Rāma Sēnāpatulu donates a lamp (*akhaṃḍa dīpamu*) for the merit (*puṇyamu*) of his father. The officer bears the titles *kaḷiṅggarakṣapālaku mēḷi bhaṃjana* (he who crushes the insurrections for the protector of Kaliṅga), *kaṃḍavāla* [=*khaṇḍapāla*] *śiraścēdana* (he who spits the skulls of the sword-bearers), *koṃddumarddana* (killer of the Khonds), *gaṃḍra dāmu* [tel. *gaṃḍla* or skt. *gaṇḍīra -dā*?] (deliverer of heroes?), *kodamasiṃhyamu* (lion of the mountains). Metaphors denoting heroism have thus reached the historical records. Still, they do not occur in the records of the imperial rulers, but can be found only in the inscriptions of their noble officers and little kings.[18] In contrast to the hero-stones of contemporary Andhra, these inscriptions do not commemorate a deceased hero but praise the accomplishments of he who issued it while he is still alive. From this is clear his enemies are to be killed and that he is the ever-victorious ally of his lord.

It is probably more than mere coincidence that these new trends in the inscriptions occur from the thirteenth century onward.[19] This is the time when the Gaṅga Empire was almost continually at war, first against the Kākaṭīyas of Warangal, later against the Reḍḍi families of Kondavidu and Rajamandri, and finally against the Vijayanagara kings. All of them are well-known for their patronage of regional hero-cults.[20] For instance Anavēma Reḍḍi (1374-83), who conquered the whole of southern Kaliṅga up to Siṃhācalam, is also known for his building a *vīraśiromaṇḍapa* (hall of the heads of the heroes) at Śrīśailam as a place for ritual suicide.[21] But apart from a few heroic statements in inscriptions, in which it is the host of enemies who perish on the battlefield, there is no evidence for this kind of religious practice in Kaliṅga.

There are several reasons for this. The first is the fact that the adherents of the hero cults were low-caste enemies of the Gaṅgas, who never supported this kind of religious practice officially. It was, moreover, exclusively the practice of the enemies of the Orissan empire and the popular cult of the state deity, Jagannāth of Puri. This deity was regarded as the real king of the Gaṅga empire, the human on the throne being merely his deputy (*rāutta*). The strong emotional ties of a large number of Oriya- as well as Telugu-speaking subjects of the Gaṅgas to their state deity may explain for the virtual absence of the hero-cult from the heartland of the Gaṅga empire. There, temples to Vīrabhadra, Śarabha and other violent hero-deities are unknown.[22] Only after 1568, when due to the collapse of the political authorities at Cuttack, the cult of Jagannāth became the sole focus of the regional tradition of Orissa and the Oriya-speaking population of the former empire, could the hero-cult gradually spread among both landowning and low-caste Telugu-speaking groups of Kaliṅga.[23]

A second explanation for the importance of the hero-cult in Andhra and its absence in Kaliṅga lies in the different ways the two regions fared in their relation with the Islamic dynasties of the Deccan. After the conquest of the Kākaṭīya empire by the Delhi Sultanate in 1323, the rulers of Andhra were almost constantly at war against the Bāhmani Sultanate and its successor states, and the whole society became militarized to a degree unknown before. This may have been one of the reasons for the importance of the *vīrulu* (heroes) not only on the battlefield, but also in popular religion. On the other hand, the Gaṅgas and their successors after 1434, the Sūryavaṃśa Gajapatis, saw as their 'arch enemies' not the Sultanates, but the Telugu warlords of Andhra and the Vijayanagara kings.[24]

THE HEROES OF KALINGA

While hero-cults are still not very popular in contemporary Orissa, the situation changes in Kaliṅga after the fall of the Orissan empire in 1568. From that time onwards, the southern part of the empire gradually came under the influence of the powers of the Deccan, especially the Golkonda Sultanate. Orissa, which became part of the Mughal empire in 1582, remained the region of Jagannāth. The Golkonda armies reached Madhyama Kaliṅga, the area around Srikakulam, in 1571 and established a provincial headquarter. Many officers of the Golkonda army were Hindu *sardārs* (officers) from Andhra who settled in the area and brought their own cultural and religious customs with them. In 1652, the families of two *sardārs*, a Velama called Pedda Rāyuḍu and a Kṣatriya named Pāsapāṭi Raghunātha Rāju, were allowed to settle in Bobbili and Bhogapuram. The Bhogapuram *sardārs* later became known as the Rājās of Vizianagaram. Within a hundred years, the heads of the two families gradually assumed the roles of the leading political figures in the province. As their power increased, so did the rivalry between them. Both families claimed to be of noble descent, and stressed their background. In the case of Bobbili, descent from the Velama kings of Venkatagiri leads directly into the centre of the heroic ideology of the time of the Reḍḍi kingdoms. The Velamas claimed divine origin as descendants of Vīrabhadra's hosts. They were traditional enemies of the Reḍḍis and fought as allies of Kapilendra against the pontiff of Śrīśailam (Subrahmanyam 1986: xvii).

The Pūsapāṭis, whose traditional place of origin is Pūsapāḍu near Vijayavada, claim to be descendants of the last Viṣṇukuṇḍin king, Mādhavavarman II (*c.* AD 556-615). This monarch, who lost his kingdom and maybe even his life in a war against the Cālukya King Pulakeśin II, 'became the centre of many popular legends in later times' (Nilakanta Sastri 1975: 107). This origin, which the Pūsapāṭis began to propagate in the eighteenth century, is represented in one of these legends, providing a convenient claim for a Kṣatriya origin, with a hero as forefather.

These traditions, however, do not figure in inscriptions at all. They can be found in the *Telugu Local Tracts* of the Mackenzie Collection and in popular *kathās*. Here, traditional heroic deeds like the beheading of an enemy in a duel between two heroes[25] or heroic deaths in action, with the subsequent self-immolation of the widows, are frequent topics. One such story is the tale of the *Bobbili yuddhamu*, the war between Rājā Raṅga Rao of Bobbili and the joint forces of Pūsapāṭi Vijayarāma Rāju I and the French General de Bussy in 1758.[26] In the *Bobbili yuddhamu*, the self-sacrifice of heroes on the battlefield became a sad reality. In the final siege of the fort of Bobbili, when the defenders realized that the only choice remaining was death or unconditional surrender followed by exile, the Bobbili Velamas made their last sortie and were all killed on the battlefield, their wives and children jumping into a fire-pit in the ruins of the fort. But the victorious Vijayarāma Rāju I was also to die at this same spot: an officer named Tāṃḍra Pāpayya, who had arrived at Bobbili after the fight was already over, sneaked into his tent and killed him in a suicide attack. Even today, the story of the *Bobbili vīrulu* is a popular topic and holds a prominent place in the history books of Andhra Pradesh.

The Rājā of Vizianagaram, Vijayarāma Rāju II, died in a similar way in an incident at Padmanabham in 1794. He had been ordered by the British East India Company to surrender his army and to proceed to Madras where he was to live in exile. Instead, he and his little kings encamped at Padmanabham and provoked the superior British forces to attack. The description of his death in a popular modern book in Telugu goes as follows: 'Thereafter, on the 10th of July 1794, there was a battle which lasted only 45 minutes between the forces of the Company, under the command of Colonel Prendergast, and the troops commanded by Cina Vijayarāma Rāju. Around the mortal remains of Cina Vijayarāma Rāju, who had bent down to the ground in a heroic death, the heroes built a wall with their bodies' (Dattatreya Sarma 1983: 48).

Thus the heroic tradition had finally reached Kaliṅga.

NOTES

1. The terms 'South Asia' and 'India' will be used indiscriminately for the geographical region south of the Himalayas.
2. For example, *Mahābhārata, Vana Parvan, Nalopākhyāna Parvan* 57.24f, where the hero Nala can be distinguished from the gods by certain characteristics typical of heavenly creatures. Gods do not perspire and never blink their eyes, their garlands of flowers do not wither and their shadows never fall on the earth. In other contexts, kings are addressed as '*deva*' (heavenly creature, divine being), even though the theme of the text is political (*nīti*) rather than religious (e.g. Pañcatantra, Kathāmukha, where Viṣṇuśarman begins his reply to king Amaraśakti with the vocative '*deva*').
3. The earliest known 'hero-stone' inscribed with commemorative lines is dated Śaka 6 (AD 84). This text has been published by Mirashi (1978). But while the stone itself has the typical liṅga-shaped form of a hero-stone, the religious background of the inscription is 'high religion': the epigraph erected in order to gain religious merit.
4. In the present context, 'Kaliṅga' refers to the medieval region of Kaliṅga, the coastal belt of north-eastern Andhra Pradesh between Rajamandri in the south and the Mahendragiri in the north. The Aśokan Kaliṅga is identical with the present-day Utkal which comprises the Mahanadi-Delta in Orissa.
5. Knipe (1989) and personal observations in Rajamandri, Ellesvaram and Vizianagaram.
6. See the contribution of E. Schömbucher in the present volume.
7. I hesitate to speak of a dynasty for two reasons. First there are in fact two sets of inscriptions, one from the north and one from the south, which leads to the conclusion that there were two groups of kings. One with its capital in central Kaliṅga, the other ruling from present-day Pithapuram near Rajamandri. Secondly, except for two inscriptions, both of which mention the father and grandfather of the king, no information is given about how the Māṭhara kings were related to one another (Berkemer 1993: 103-12). For the wider implications, see Hening (1975).
8. This type came into existence immediately after Samudragupta's southern campaign (Kulke and Rothermund 1986: 86; Majumdar 1967: 144). It is characterized by its unpretentious style of Sanskrit prose. The texts are engraved on sets of small copper-plates which rarely contain more than four lines of text. Regnal years, genealogies of dynastic names are not mentioned. The administration of the kingdom seems to have been very rudimentary, since it is often the minister in charge of the grants who writes the charter. Later, inscriptions from about AD 500 begin with an increasingly elaborate and poetic eulogy. This new introductory part centers around the person of the ruler himself and around the tutelary deity of the king.
9. *Mātāpitṛ-pādānudhyāta.* Examples of early formulas of the Māṭhara family are: *paramadaivata-bappabhaṭāraka pādabhaktaḥ śrī mahārājā-Viśākhavarmmā* (Koroshondā Plates of Viśākhavarman: IO 1/ii, No. 1), *pitṛpādānudhyātaḥ śrī mahārāja-Umavarmmā* (Tekkali Plates of Umavarman; IO 1/ii. No. 2).

10. There are now more developed formulas which use *alaṅkāras* instead of the simple epithets quoted above. Here again, the *dharma* aspect of kingship is explicitly stated, while nothing is said about war or heroism. The following example is the eulogy from the Jirjingi Plates of Indravarman, the first ruler of the Gaṅga-Dynasty of Kaliṅganagara (IO 2. No. 2), lines 1-12: '. . . he whose sins are removed without remainder by the greatness of the store of virtue, [which was accumulated] by his extended bowing before the highest Lord, who is the glorious cause of creation, existence, and dissolution of all the world, who is the sun at the firmament of the spotless family of the Gaṇgas, he whose pair of feet are held to be red from the touch of the emission of light caused by the radiant rubies inlaid into the crowns of all bearers of stainless drawn swords of the Sāmanta-king and provincial lords, who were defeated in many battles of four-tusked ones, who is the person who, for the sake of the destitute, friends, straightforward people and kinsmen, is the shade of the creeper-hut of large riches, obtained in unequalled battles, who mediates upon the feet of his mother and father, the overlord of Trikaliṅga and Mahārājā Indravarman.'
11. In Sanskrit copper-plate inscriptions death is explicitly mentioned only in passages which use the ornamental *kāvya* style, and only in connection with the death of enemies. It seems that there was the convention of not talking about death except metaphorically in *alaṅkāras.* Concerning the issuer's own family, the copper-plates reflect Brahmanical norms in which the popular cult of the dead would be out of place.
12. Cōla sources mention a king of 'Oṭṭa' and his younger brother who were both killed in the war (Berkemer 1993: 138; Venkatakrishna Rao 1973: 331). The king was either Vajrahasta II (980-1015) or one of his successors, Kāmārṇava II and Guṇḍama, who ruled in succession until 1018. It may have been Kāmārṇava II, who is known to have ruled for only half a year, who was slain by the Cōlas.
13. This form of *praśasti* as part of an inscriptional record is much older in the west of India (e.g. the *Aihole Inscription of Pulakesin II,* dated AD 634. [Kielhorn 1990]) than in Orissa and Kaliṅga, where it was not introduced before the Rāṣṭrakūṭa and Cōla invasions of the tenth and eleventh centuries.
14. Vajrahasta III was one of the greatest reformers of Kaliṅga. The first long genealogy in a Gaṅga copper-plate inscription, the first temple inscriptions of the Gaṅgas, the first inscriptions in the vernaculars in Kaliṅga (Oriya and Telugu), the first mention of officers called '*nāyakas*' in the service of the Gaṅgas, and the first record dated in the śaka-era (Berkemer 1993: 128f, 145-51). The new elaborate genealogy is found for the first time in the *praśasti* of the *Narsipatnam Plates of Vajrahasta* III. (Konow 1911).
15. The names of Vajrahasta's genealogy do not agree with the names of the early Gaṅga rulers as known from their own inscriptions. It seems that Vajrahasta III, who in successfully reestablishing the rule of his family made possible the rise of Gaṅgas to imperial status under Coḍagaṅga Anantavarman (1078-1147), was either a descendant in a collateral line or completely unrelated to the old Gaṅga family.
16. Cf. fn. 12.

17. The following features are new: (*a*) in referring to the name of the Gaṅga dynasty or the king's aspirations for imperial rule the name of the king becomes a dynastic 'program'; (*b*) local origin is replaced by a legend of migration; (*c*) the *praśasti* now includes a claiṃ of divine origin by the royal family; (*d*) the regnal years are counted in the Aṅka-System; (*e*) the kings become the viceroys (*rāutta*) of Jagannāth of Puri.
18. Inscriptions of the time of the Imperial Gaṅgas (1078-1434) can be divided roughly into two overlapping categories: One contains long *praśastis*, with genealogies usually going back to the gods, while the other does not care much about ancestors, but rather describes in detail the martial valour of the person who issued it. In the *praśasti* of the Imperial Gaṅgas, which has still to be edited and provides plenty of space, both topics occur, but even here, the heroic theme is subordinate to the genealogical intent of the record.
19. There are a few older hybrid examples, the most significant is the *Dirghasi Inscription of Vanapati* (IO 3/i, No. 15), dated AD 1075. Here, the commander-in-chief of king Rājarāja, son of Vajrahasta III and father of Coḍagaṅga Anatavarman, tells the story of his achievements as an army commander. From the thirteenth century, the long genealogies become popular among the little kings of the Gaṅgas. The Matsyas of Oḍḍādi, for instance, have a line going back to Brahma and comprises 23 generations on earth (Kielhorn 1898).
20. Murthy (1982: 213ff.) mentions special temples for the rite of self-immolation. 'It was also believed that those who performed the rite in the presence of Bhairava, Vīrabhadra, Bhadrakāḷī or Durgā would go to heaven.'
21. The theme of self-sacrifice, which is completely absent in the Kaliṅga inscriptions, can be found in an extreme form in Anavēma's inscription on a pillar of the *vīraśiromaṇḍapa*. As an illustration, I quote from Sharma's translation (in Murthy 1982: 215): 'How wonderful is it that here in this maṇṭapa hosts of Ekāṅgavīras, who proudly make a votive offering of their eyes, hands, heads and tongues, by cutting them off, attain instantaneously a brilliant body of blessed limbs. The next moment, endowed with three eyes, ten arms, five faces (heads) and five tongues, they shine as if they were aṣṭamūrtis (eight-bodies Śivas).'
22. The Gaṅga empire was a stronghold of Vaiṣṇavism which had in the worship of Jagannāth and the mother goddesses a means of encompassing violence within the chief regional cult. Violent male gods like the *girija* Narasimha, Bhairava, Śarabha (the form of Śiva which kills Narasiṃha) exist in Orissa as well (e.g. in Bhubaneswar; Eschmann 1978: 110), but either never rise to prominence or are, as in the case of Narasiṃha, pacified (Siṃhācalam) or incorporated (Jagannāth).
23. These cults are widespread among the immigrant agriculturist castes, but not among the indigenous Kaliṅga population, whose popular deity is Siṃhādri Appanna, alias Varāha-Narasiṃha of Siṃhācalam. The recent cults of Kaliṅga are much less violent than their counterparts in medieval Andhra. The term *vīrulu* (heroes) is nowadays understood to refer to the children who die an untimely death before puberty. Small shrines dedicated

to them can be seen in the fields outside of villages, especially in Reḍḍi and Kamma communities. A *vīruḍu* possesses members of his family to demonstrate his power and forces his still living relatives to worship him. The best known examples are the *vīrulu* worshipped in connection with the Vīrabhadra cult (Knipe 1989).

24. There probably was one attempt to introduce the more heroic types of Hindu worship in the Sūryavaṃśi empire around 1460. Hamvīra, the crown prince and commander-in-chief of Kapilendra Gajapati, who had successfully installed himself on the throne at Cuttack in 1434 seems to have tried to sever the ties between the throne of the Gajapati and the cult of Jagannāth. He, his sons and the relatives, who had spent their whole life on the battlefields of Andhra, preferred southern deities to Jagannāth in their inscriptions. The *Māḍalā Pāñji* (*Kaṭakarājavaṃśāvali*, Ch. 61) alludes to this conflict in the narration of a dream and an ordeal in which Jagannāth himself chose Hamvīra's youngest brother Puruṣottama as Kapilendra's successor. Kapilendra and Puruṣottama won a decisive battle over the rebels near Kuṇḍajori in the Krishna-Godavari delta. After this failure, the southern cults had no chance to become part of the religious policy of the Sūryavaṃśi kings.
25. Examples are the *malliki mardan khaṇḍa* which was used to behead a Muslim officer called Mallik Khan in the battle of Malkangiri (Berkemer 1993: 282 ff.) and the fight between the Zamindārs of Tekkali and Tarla over water rights, in which the Tarla ruler was beheaded and his head buried in the anicut of a tank (*Tekkali Tālūkā Jamīṃdārla Vaṃśāvalī*).
26. There are about half a dozen sources in Telugu about this war. They can be roughly divided into written accounts (*vaṃśāvalī*) and originally oral epics (*kathā*). There is also a source in English by R. Orme and a short passage from Ananda Ranga Pillary's diary (for details see Berkemer 1993: 55 and Narayana Rao 1986).

REFERENCES

Banerjee, R.D. 1921. Andhra Inscriptions of the Time of Rudradāman. *Epigraphia Indica* 16: 19-25.

Berkemer, G. 1993. *Little Kingdoms in Kaliṅga. Ideologie, Legitimation und Politik regionaler Eliten*. Stuttgart: Steiner.

Blackburn, S.H. 1984. Death and Deification: Folk Cults in Hinduism. *History of Religion* 24: 255-74.

Dattatreya Sarma, A.V. ('Vijaya Datt'). 1983. *Vijayanagaraṃ Jillā-Caritra-saṃskṛti.* Vizianagaram: Mansas.

Eschmann, A.C. 1978. The Vaiṣṇava Typology of Hinduization. In A.C. Eschmann, H. Kulke, G.C. Tripathi (eds.), *The Cult of Jagannāth and the Regional Tradition of Orissa.* Delhi: Manohar.

Henige, David P. 1975. Some Phantom Dynasties of Early and Medieval India: Epigraphic Evidence and the Abhorrence of Vacuum. *Bulletin of the School of Oriental and African Studies* 38: 525-49.

Inscriptions of Orissa
1958. *Inscriptions of Orissa,* Vol. I/2. (S.N. Rajaguru, ed.) Bhubaneswar, Govt. of Orissa.
1960. *Inscriptions of Orissa,* Vol. II. (S.N. Rajaguru, ed.) Bhubaneswar, Govt. of Orissa.
1961. *Inscriptions of Orissa,* Vol. III/1 (S.N. Rajaguru, ed.) Bhubaneswar, Govt. of Orissa.
Kaṭakarājavaṃśāvalī
1987. *Kaṭakarājavaṃśāvalī.* A Traditional History of Orissa. ed. H. Kulke and G.S. Tripathi. Allahabad: Vohra Publ.
Kielhorn, F. 1898. Dibbida Plates of Arjuna of the Matsya Family; Saka-Samvat 1191. *EI* 5: 106-13.
———. 1900 . Aihole Inscription of Pulakesin II.; Saka-Samvat 556. *EI* 6: 1-12.
Knipe, D. 1989. Night of the Growing Dead: A Cult of Vīrabhadra in Coastal Andhra. In A. Hiltebeitel (ed.), *Criminal Gods and Demon Devotees.* Albany: State University of New York Press.
Konow, S. 1911. Narasapatnam Plates of Vajrahasta III; Saka-Samvat 967. *EI* 11: 147-53.
Kulke, H. and D. Rothermund, 1986. *A History of India.* London and Sidney: Croom Helm.
Majumdar, R.C. 1967. Foundation of the Gupta Empire. In R.C. Majumdar and A.S. Altekar (eds.), *The Vākāṭaka-Gupta Age.* Delhi: Motilal Banarsidass.
Mirashi, V.V. 1978. Daulatpur Inscription of the Reign of Caṇḍana: Year 6. *Journal of the Oriental Institute,* Baroda 28(2): 34-7.
Murthy, M.L.K. 1982. Memorial Stones in Andhra Pradesh. In S. Settar and G.D. Sontheimer (eds.), *Memorial Stones.* Dharwad and Heidelberg: Institute of Indian Art History, Karnatak University and South Asia Institute, University of Heidelberg.
Narayana Rao, V. 1986. Epics and Ideologies: Six Telugu Folk Epics. In S.H. Blackburn and A.K. Ramanujan (eds.), *Another Harmony. New Essays on the Folklore of India.* Berkeley: University of California Press.
Nilakanta Sastri, K.A. 1975. *A History of South India.* Madras: Oxford University Press. (4th edition).
Pañcatantra. 1930. *The Pancatantra* I-V. Ed. by Franklin Edgerton. Poona: Oriental Book Agency.
Rajashekhara, S. 1982. Rāṣṭrakūṭa Hero-Stones: A Study. In S. Settar and G.D. Sontheimer (eds.), *Memorial Stones.* Dharwad and Heidelberg: Institute of Indian Art History, Karnatak University/South Asia Institute, University of Heidelberg.
Settar, S. and G.D. Sontheimer, (eds.). 1982. *Memorial Stones.* Dharwad and Heidelberg: Institute of Indian Art History, Karnatak University and South Asia Institute, University of Heidelberg.
Sharma, M.S. 1948. *History of the Reddi Kingdom.* Waltair: Andhra University.
Subrahmanyam, R. 1986. *Inscriptions of the Sūryavaṃśi Gajapatis of Orissa.* New Delhi and Delhi: ICHR and Agam.
Venkatakrishna Rao, Bhavaraju. 1973. *History of the Eastern Calukyas of Vengi (619-1210 AD).* Hyderabad: Andhra Pradesh Sahitya Akademi.

A Note on Death and the Holy Man in South Asia

HUGH VAN SKYHAWK

The reversal of the norms applicable to ordinary human beings often characterizes the life of a holy man, especially in South Asia. One of the most succinct expressions of the fundamental polarity between the human being in his inherent condition and the saint is found in the *Bhagavad Gītā*, 2.69:

yā niśā sarvabhūtānām tasyāṃ jāgarti saṃyamī
yasyāṃ jāgrati bhūtāni sā niśā paśyato muneḥ[1]

Similarly, the mystics of Islam, the Ṣūfīs, teach that there are two lives and two deaths for the holy man: '. . . the life in this world and the life "in reality", the physical death and death "in reality". The death "in reality" is related to the life in this world. The life "in reality" is proclaimed to be achieved only after the physical death. It is described as being alive "really' and "eternally". . .' (Hussaini 1985: 43).

In practice, the saint's rejection of the 'life in this world' meant the abstention from the attachment to sensual experiences and the concentration on the eternal, unchanging authentic being of man (*ātman*), or, in the case of the Ṣūfīs, on the experience of the Divine Unity of Allāh (*at-Tawḥīd*). As, in the case of the Hindu holy man, the abstention from sensual experiences prevented the accumulation of transcendental dirt in the form of particles of subtle matter known as *karman* in his subtle body [s. *sūkṣma-śarīra*, u. *latīf-jisma*], his gross material or physical body was also believed to be pure and free of decay. Similarly, the physical body of the *walī*, the Muslim 'Friend of God', was perceived to be pure and free of decay by virtue of the fact that every *walī* has access to the throne and purifying presence of Allāh.

There are innumerable folk-tales that confirm the popular belief in the immunity of the saint's corpse to decay, such as in the well-known tale of the upper Punjab 'Essera and Canessera':

The party which now approached was a gang of notorious robbers, seven in number, one of whom was blind of an eye. Catching sight of the body in the old tomb, they examined it with great care, and exclaimed: 'See, this must be some famous saint! He has come out of his grave, and his body is perfectly fresh. Let us pray to him for favour and good luck!' So they one and all fell down on their knees and besought his assistance. . . . (Swynnerton 1987: 54)

In life, the divine power inherent in the asceticism of the saint was perceived to be of the nature of subtle matter and thus transferable in part to ordinary human beings by a material object that had been in contact with the saint—most often by food that he had eaten or, at least, touched. Such a transfer and the material object that effected it came to be known as *prasād* [s. 'brightness, purity, favour, blessing'] or, in the case of a Muslim holy man, *tabarrukan* [a. 'for the sake of blessing']. Thus, the reversal of individual norms that the saint had practised with regard to his thoughts, words, and deeds resulted in the reversal of the social norms applicable to his person and physical body. That which he left as a physical remainder, his '*ucchiṣṭa*', came to be regarded as the opposite to the highly polluting material leavings of ordinary human beings.

Incidents of the transfer of spiritual knowledge and even salvation by the saliva, the untouched remainder of a meal (*anucchiṣṭa*), the partially chewed food (*ucchiṣṭa*), or *pān* [betel leaves] of Hindu/Muslim saints in South Asia can be found in hagiographical accounts, in Purāṇas,[2] in folk-tales, and even in the *ḥadīth* or traditions of the deeds of the Holy Prophet.[3] The connection of *ucchiṣṭa* as the apotheosized remainder of the Vedic sacrifice as described at length in *Atharvaveda*, 11.7.1-27, and the spiritually potent material remainders left by holy men may be a result of the historical development of the notion of the interiorization of the sacrifice as an ascetic practice.[4] The well-known practice of shattering the skull of a dead *yogī* in order to release his imprisoned *jīva* and the consumption by the participants and observers of this ritual of the pieces of the coconuts shattered on his head as *prasād* points to the perception of the dead *yogī's* body as the material remainder of his interiorized sacrifice, that is, of the asceticism he practised in life.[5]

By far the greatest remainder or '*ucchiṣṭa*' that any human being leaves behind is his corpse. While in the case of an ordinary human being, the corpse is a noxious, potentially dangerous object that must be disposed of quickly and with ritual precision, the corpse of a saint is an object of worship, a tangible repository of the divine power inherent in the saint's asceticism, or in his close relationship to the divine. The same purifying spiritual potency that inheres in the saint's *ucchiṣṭa* in life remains forever in the dust of his bones. In this connection the pilgrimage of singers to the grave of Tānsen at Gwalior, whose heavenly voice was said to be the gift of Muḥammad Ghaws[6] Gwāliyārī (d. 970/1562-3) is especially striking as Muḥammad Ghaws' gift is believed to be transmitted to the pilgrim vicariously by the leaves of the tamarind tree growing on Tānsen's grave.

While the taking of the dust of a saint's tomb for spiritual or medicinal purposes is a common feature of folk piety throughout South Asia, the most striking example of the saint's mortal remains as potent '*ucchiṣṭa*' occurred in the church of St. Paul's College in Goa, where in 1554 a female devotee of St. Francis Xavier (d. 1552), Doña Isabel de Carom, in the passion of her devotion bit off the little toe of the right foot of the saint in an attempt to obtain the salvific power contained in his holy body.[7]

The belief in the potency of a saint's mortal remains for the good of the community even led the people of Gilgit to kill a certain saint who had successfully rid the region of a dangerous spirit, a female *yach* [Burúšaski: *yach*, s. *yakṣa*], lest he wander away, die and be buried elsewhere and thus allow the female *yach* to resume her predations.[8] Similarly, the potency of Sayyid Šāh Walī's mortal remains led the people of Ghulmét (Nagér) to steal his body from the people of Thol and re-bury it in their own village.[9]

Just as the norms of the avoidance of contact are reversed in the case of a saint's mortal remains, so also are the rituals that are intended to transport speedily the spirit of the deceased into the world of the ancestors, or, in the case of Muslims, into the grave to await the Day of Judgement. While in medieval Muslim families the corpse was often removed through a window or even a hole in the wall made especially for that purpose in order that the spirit of the deceased person not find its way back into the family home—Šāh Jahān's and Auraṅgzīb's corpses were removed from the houses in which they died in this manner[10]—, the spirit of a deceased saint is prayed to remain among his devotees by hymns of praise [*qawwālī*], burning of incense, offerings of food (see below), flowers, fine cloths for covering the grave, and by the constant petitions of the devotees who visit his *dargāh*. Indeed, many devotees believe that the saint is physically alive inside his tomb, that he can and does intercede in the affairs of the world on behalf of his devotees. Instead of the funerary rituals of an ordinary human being, a Muslim saint who has died physically is 'married to God'. His wedding or '*urs*[11] with the Divine Beloved is celebrated. In keeping with the spirit of a wedding, his *dargāh* is not a place of despair, but of hope and rejoicing. In this connection the Ṣūfīs cite the *ḥadīth-nabāwī*: 'Truly, the friends of God do not die. Rather, they move from one house to another. . . .'[12]

Just as the Muslim saint himself is wedded to God in his new house, the *dargāh*, so also in India female devotees or even Hindu goddesses are married each year to certain *pīrs*. Striking examples of this are the marriage of Zahrā or Zohrā Bībī, a blind girl, to Sālār Masūd Ghāzī Miyā̃ at Bahraich in Uttar Pradesh every year during the '*urs* on the first Sunday in the Hindu month of *Jeṭh* (May-June),[13] or the marriage of Yoga-māyā of Mehrauli (south Delhi) to Haẓrat Sayyid Quṭb ud-Dīn Bakhtiyār Kākī.[14]

The living presence of the *pīr* in his *dargāh* or 'royal court' is expressed by the observance of etiquette derived from the traditions of the Mughal court: devotees bow and *salām* to the *pīr* in the *mazār*, even prostrate themselves from a distance as was customary when approaching the *bādśāh* at the Mughal court. One should never turn one's back to the *mazār*, but take leave facing the *pīr* or by turning one's right side to him and slowly withdrawing offering repeated *salāms*. Unlike the temporal ruler, whose power after death is often not even sufficient to protect his own grave from plunder and desecration, the power of the *pīr* increases after his physical death. Often palace-like *dargāhs* are built with a labyrinth of corridors that eventually lead to the *mazār* itself. In the case of *dargāhs* built outside cities the surrounding countryside can become known as the *jāgīr* of the *pīr*, whose authority and protection then extends to all who come within this area and not only to devotees. An example of this type of living presence is the *jāgīr* of Afzal Śāh Biyābānī of Kazi Peth (Dt. Warangal), which lies between the borders of four hills on each of which Afzal Šāh Biyābānī is said to have practised asceticism for twelve years.[15]

The power of the *pīr* to protect all who come to his *jāgīr* or *dargāh* for sanctuary is expressed most often in the form of punishments for those who violate this sanctuary. An example of such punishment is found in a traditional account of events that took place in the *dargāh* of Šams-i-Ṭālib in the Gojal region of Hunza in 1887. Bībī Śāh, the milk-mother of a young prince of Hunza, Jahandar Šāh, took refuge in the *dargāh* of Šams-i-Ṭālib as a last resort to save her foster child from an assassin sent by the supporters of a rival prince, Safdar Ali, who was seeking to remain *mīr* of Hunza by killing all other contenders for the throne. The assassin violated the sanctity of the *dargāh*, took out mother and child, and killed them by throwing them from a precipice.[16] According to an oral tradition of Hunza, one year later to the day, the assassin was riding on his horse near the *dargāh* of Šams-i-Ṭālib when suddenly the mountainside gave way under him and plunged him to his death under a mountain of earth and stone.

As recently as 1984, following the murder of Indira Gandhi by her own Sikh bodyguards, more than a hundred Sikhs of Delhi succeeded in saving their lives when pursued by frenzied mobs by taking refuge at the *dargāh* of Nizām ud-Dīn Awliyā. Though there were no police, army, or other visible power to prevent the mobs from killing their victims within the shrine itself, they stopped short at the gates of the *dargāh* and did not violate its sanctity.

The saint's protection of the living who come within the precincts of his *dargāh* or *jāgīr* extends also to those who are born or die near him or those whose mortal remains are brought for burial to the *dargāh*. The protection of the saint Šaykh Selīm Čištī in whose *khānqāh* the future Jehāngīr had been born, restrained Akbar in 1602 from having his son and heir executed for the murder of his close friend and adviser Abu Fazl, who had been beheaded by Bīr Singh Deo of Orcha on Prince Selīm's orders. Though Akbar ordered that all living creatures including livestock within the small kingdom of Orcha be killed because of their supposed complicity in Abu Fazl's death, he stopped short of executing the future Jehāngīr when reminded that Prince Selīm's life was under the protection of Šay<u>kh</u> Selīm Čištī.

One of Prince Dārā Šikūh's final acts was to send the body of his beloved wife, Nādirā Begum, from the Ran of Kutch to the *dargāh* of Miyā̃ Mīr in Lahore, accompanied by his remaining troops, so that she might be protected by Miyā̃ Mīr until the Day of Judgement. Even today, devotees of Miyā̃ Mīr in Lahore bring the bodies of their deceased loved ones to the *dargāh* before burial in a nearby cemetery.

Similarly, Sahībā Jahānārā, Šāh Jehān's elder daughter and the sister of Dārā Šikūh and Auraṅgzīb, herself a Ṣūfī of the *Qādirī-silsilā*, found comfort in the presence of Hazrat Nizām ud-Dīn Awliyā during her unhappy life and solace in the assurance that she would be buried near him in the courtyard of the *dargāh* of Nizām ud-Dīn. Even the stern Auraṅgzīb, hardened by fifty years of continuous war, wrote in the first sentence of his last will and testament:

> That they should shroud and carry this sinner drenched in sins to the neighborhood of the holy Chistī tomb of the revered leader, Sayyid and Shaykh, Zayn al-Dīn Dā'ūd Shīrāzī, since without the protection of that court [of the saints], which is the refuge of forgiveness, there is no refuge for those drowned in the ocean of sin. (Ernst 1992: 224 and note 106).[17]

Roughly forty years later, in 1748, the repentant playboy-emperor Muḥammad Šāh Rāṅgīlā, who, in 1739, had seen the people of Delhi slaughtered and his kingdom pillaged by the armies of Nādir Šāh of Persia, had himself buried near Nizām ud-Dīn in hopes of obtaining the saint's forgiveness and protection.

Not only at the end of life but also at its beginning the protection of the saint is sought by visiting his *dargāh*. In hopes that their children will grow up healthy and live long and prosperous lives, mothers in the vicinity of Aurangabad bring their babies to the *dargāh* of Azam Šāh Biyābānī in the Šāha Gunj precinct of Aurangabad. Holding their babies in their arms they sing cradle songs in front of the *mazār*. Only then is the baby given its name.

While the *pīr* usually manifests himself in a benevolent form in his *dargāh*, there are *pīrs* who, in addition to their benevolent form, can also, for reasons that are not always apparent, manifest themselves in an aggressive or malevolent form. A striking example of this type of *pīr*, known as a *jalālī-pīr*, a *pīr* in which the *mysterium tremendum* of God has found its expression,[18] can be found in Shimshal (in the Gojal region of Hunza) at the *dargāh* of Šams ud-Dīn Tabrīzī, the famous Šay<u>kh</u> of Jalāl ud-Dīn Rūmī, who protects Shimshal from the predations of evil spirits and ensures its fertility, but, at the same time, has been known to blind devotees when they are struggling up the 4,000 metre high scree slope that leads to his *dargāh* and cause them to fall, or to cause rockslides that plunge devotees headlong to their deaths. Each visit to Šams ud-Dīn involves a confrontation with one's own death, in which the *pīr* may play a benevolent or malevolent role. Most devotees offer their *salām* from the riverbank, about 300 metres below the *dargāh*.

According to an oral tradition of Gulbarga, a devotee who knocks with a stick on the *mazār* of Tīgh Barahna ('naked sword'), a saint of the thirteenth century,[19] may meet his death in the form of a sword that emerges from the grave held by an unseen hand and relentlessly pursues its victim until it inflicts a grave wound. No less a personage than a grandson of Ḥaẓrat Bandā Nawāz Gīsūdirāz of Gulbarga once doubted the truth of this tradition and knocked on the *mazār* with a stick. At once the sword emerged and pursued the terrified youth from the eastern wall of the fort of Gulbarga to Gīsūdirāz' *khānqāh* (hospice) near the western wall. Only there, on Gīsūdirāz' order, did the sword make only a slight wound on the boy and then return to its resting place in Tīgh Barahna's *mazār*. Up to this day, no one has been known to have knocked again with a stick on Tīgh Barahna's *mazār*.

At the *dargāh/samādhi* of Ajñānasiddha in Narenda (Dt. Kolhapur), the devotee desiring to have *darśan* of the *svarūp* of Ajñānasiddha must first ritually wash himself at the *ghusl-khānā* near the saint's shrine, pray *al-Fātiḥa*, the first *sūra* of the Holy Qur'ān, and then descend by means of a narrow shaft two metres into the earth beneath the *pādukā* of Ajñānasiddha into a horizontal vault dug at a right angle to the shaft—which is remarkably similar to the side-chamber grave used by Muslims in south Asia—where a *nāg* (cobra) will first appear and then the human form of Ajñānasiddha. Devotees must enter the underground vault alone and—if successful in their quest—are re-born spiritually when they emerge from the saint's grave.

A similar ritual of death and re-birth—but with the point of departure and the destination reversed—is practised by the devotees of Kāniphnāth/Šāh Ramzān of Maḍhī (Dt. Ahmadnagar), who descend into a shaft near the saint's *mazār/samādhi* and then crawl laterally through the mountain underneath the *mazār* in order to reach a *liṅga*-shrine at which Kāniphnāth/Šāh Ramzān is said to have practised *yoga*.

The unique potential of human beings to overcome death is one of the recurring themes of devotional religion or *bhakti* in South Asia. At the same time, the short duration of human life and the . . . 'hovering presence of death (*kāl*) . . . give to the warnings of [*bhakti*-poets such as Kabīr] a tragic intensity . . .' (Vaudeville 1987: 26):

Kabīr, for a little bit of life
people make a grand display-
Yet they all stand on the same road,
be they sultan, prince or tramp! [KG, *sākhī,* 15.43]

Kabīr, do not pride yourself:
kāl holds you by the hair.
Who knows where he will strike you,
Whether at home or abroad? [KG, *sākhī,* 15.44]

Today or tomorrow or in five days
you will rest in the jungle:
Cattle will stray over your head
eating the grass. [KG, *sākhī,* 15.67]

On the other hand, the *sants* can also have great humour with regard to death as in the hagiographical account of the death of Śrī Sant Ekanāth by the Rāmdāsī hagiographer Bhīmasvāmī Śirgāvkar (d. 1797). According to Bhīmasvāmī Śirgāvkar, Ekanāth decided one day to depart this world of mortals and enter *samādhi* forever. He went to the banks of the Godāvarī, sat down in meditation, and soon reached *samādhi.* Hearing of this, his disciples were alarmed and hurried to their king of gurus:

> *Svāmī*! An evil person on the way told us that you had died! The *svāmī* spoke: ' "Who has died?" they (i.e. people) ask. But who knows the deathless Knower [i.e. the *ātman*]?' When they had made their obeisances, Ekanāth departed in truth.[20]

Bhīmasvāmī's version of Ekanāth's death is perhaps more in keeping with the humour and self-effacement that characterizes the ocean of literature that Ekanāth wrote than the larger-than-life portrayal of ecstatic Vaiṣṇava piety by his contemporary, the *Vārkarī-saṃpradāya* hagiographer Mahīpatibūvā Tāharābādkar (1715-90), whose *Bhakta-līlāmṛta* (1774) is the textual source of popular renditions of Ekanāth's death, such as in the *Amar-citra-kathā* comic books.

Though Ekanāth, like most *bhakti-sants,* left behind no tomb or mortal remains, devotees none-the-less seek to purify themselves by touching the pillar in his house on which he is said to have leaned while writing, or his *pādukās* (marble replicas of his feet) when they are carried in a palanquin in a procession through Paiṭhaṇ (*nagara-pradakṣiṇā*) during his death-anniversary celebrations (*puṇya-tithi*). Even more striking is the worship of Ekanāth in the person of a descendant, a young man who is thought to resemble his saintly ancestor, who during the celebrations of *Ekanāth-ṣaṣṭhī,* dresses like Ekanāth and walks in a festive procession from the saint's house to the *Ekanāth-mandir.* All along the way devotees attempt to touch his feet, while police and community volunteers attempt to prevent them by forming a protective circle around him. The most conspicuous example of the belief in the material transfer of divine power takes place on the seventh and final day of the *Ekanāth-ṣaṣṭhī*, on *Phālgun vādya* eighth[21] and is called *dahīhaṇḍī* (the vessel of curds', or 'balls of rice and curds') or *kālā* ('the termination'). The custom as it is practised today involves a large bundle of balls of sesame seeds and jaggery (*tīḷgūḷ*) that is suspended in the air from the veranda of the second story of the *Ekanāth-mandir.* Ekanāth, in the person of his descendant, who stands on the veranda of the second storey of the temple, then strikes the bundle with a stick, while as many devotees as can find a place underneath the *tīḷgūḷ* scramble to get some piece of the *prasād* that falls in all directions among the multitude. For many devotees, Ekanāth manifests himself every year on his death anniversary in the person of his descendant, who is thus a living proof of the saint's victory over death.

One of the most frequently used metaphors describing the physical death and subsequent life of a Muslim saint is 'to go behind the curtain' or 'sit behind the curtain'.[22] At *āstāna* or shrines where the *gādī* (teaching chair or cushion) of the saint forms the focal point of devotion, as at the *āstānaye Biyābānī* in Puṇe, a curtain is drawn between the mundane world and the sphere of the saint at all times except the five times of daily prayer and during religious observances. When the curtain is drawn devotees may go behind the curtain to pray, sit and talk to the *pīr.* Food, drink, *pān,* flowers, incense, and fine silk cloths are offered to the *pīr* sitting behind the curtain, and it is believed that he eats, drinks, and enjoys such offerings. As in the *dargāh,* so also in the *āstāna,* forms of etiquette taken from the Mughal court are observed with regard to the *gādī.*

Love of God and love of man are at the heart of Ṣūfism. Through the love of God or *ishq* the Ṣūfī kills all that within himself that is not God. His *khūdī* or empirical individuality is merged completely with the Will of *Khudā,* that is, God, Allāh, the Divine. Thus he dies before his death. At the moment of his death as an individual he gains a new life in the experience of the Divine Unity [*at-Tawhīd*]. The material analogy to this is the physical death of his body, and the new life he is given as the *pīr* who has 'gone behind the curtain'. The insight into the esoteric meaning of dying before one's death as expressed in a verse from Šaykh Ahmad of Jam (d. Muharram 536/August 1141) sent the great Čištī Šaykh Quṭb ud-Dīn Bakhtiyār Kākī into ecstasy for five days and nights before his physical death on 14 Rabi I, 633/27 November 1235:

> The martyrs of the knife of *taslīm* (surrender) each moment get a new life from the Unseen World. (Rizvi 1978: 137 and note 5)

Each time Qutb ud-Dīn returned to mundane consciousness the verse was repeated by the *qawwāls,* and he was again sent into divine ecstasy until, at the end of five days and nights, he departed his physical body forever.

The certainty of the victory over death infuses later Ṣūfīsm with indomitable optimism. We would be hard pressed to find a more inspiring expression of hope for suffering mortals than the following verses from Jalāl ud-Dīn Rūmī's *Diwān-i-Śams ud-Dīn Tabrīzī*, in which the *dargāh* of a deceased saint is conceived to be a place at which both death and social differences are transcended:[23]

> Come, come! Whatever you are, it doesn't matter.
> Whether you are a Kafir, an idolator, or a fire-worshipper.
> Come, our *dargāh* is not a place of despair!
> Come, even if you have broken your vows a hundred times, come again!

NOTES

1. 'During that which is night for all living creatures the ascetic is awake. That in which the beings are awake is night for the seeing seer' (my translation).
2. That the consumption of the material leavings of a holy man can mean the outright reversal of social norms, i.e. eating the highly impure, partially chewed '*juṭhā*' of a meal, and not just a symbolic or partial exception to the rules of ritual purity is made clear by the use of the compositum '*ucchiṣṭa-lepa*' ['the impure leavings' or 'the impurities that are the remainders (of a meal)'] in *Bhāgavata Purāṇa (BhP)* 1.5.25:
   ucchiṣṭalepānanumodito dvijaiḥ sakṛtsma buñje tadapāstakilbiṣaḥ /
   evaṃ pravṛttasya viśuddhacetasastaddharma evātmarucih prajāyate //
   ['As one who had been granted by the Twice-Born (i.e. the brahmin sages) the impure leavings (of their meal) I once ate (and became) one whose faults had been cast off. For (me) who was thus engaged, whose mental activities (had become) pure, there arose a liking for their *dharma* (that was of the nature of the) *ātman*.'] (my translation). On related terminology for less impure remainders of food, some of which do not entail the consumption of partially eaten pieces of food but the ingestion of comestibles taken from a partially used stock of uncooked foods or an untouched portion of a cooked meal see Wezler (1978: 78f. and note 238; 118 and note 318). Unfortunately, in my study of the Bhakti of Śrī Sant Ekanāth, I overlooked the passage *BhP* 1.5.25 in the discussion of the role of *ucchiṣṭa* as a means of conveying spiritual knowledge from master to disciple. However, in this passage too, it is a 'liking for the *dharma*' of the Bhāgavatas that is conveyed by the *ucchiṣṭa* of the unnamed *ṛṣis,* and not specifically the spiritual knowledge of the guru (see van Skyhawk 1990: 63-7).
3. The first reference in Islamic tradition to the power of a holy man's saliva occurs in the traditional account of an event in the life of the Holy Prophet. In the battle of Qamūs (AD May-June 628), Muḥammad (S.) is said to have stopped the pain caused by an arrow that had pierced his son-in-law's ('Alī ibn Abī Ṭālib's) eye by applying his saliva to the wound (see Rizvi 1986: 15).
4. On the identification of the Vedic sacrifice with asceticism (tapas) as the 'inner sacrifice' in the Upaniṣads see Eliade (1978: 217ff.).

5. On the burial practices of *haṭha-yogīs* see Oman (1903: 157).
6. For technical reasons the Arabic consonant *ghain* must be represented by 'gh', the Arabic '*ain* by an apostrophe ''', and the Perso-Urdū palatal sibilant *śīn* by 'Ś'.
7. The manner in which Doña Isabel de Carom obtained this part of the mortal remains of St. Francis Xavier differs clearly from later clinical amputations and dissections of the saint's body in order to provide holy reliquiae for the devotees of St. Francis in various parts of Asia. On the pious mutilations of St. Francis Xavier's mortal remains see Rayanna (1964: 155ff.). I am grateful to Wilhelm Halbfass for his insights into the incident involving St. Francis Xavier's toe [personal communication in Heidelberg, May 1993].
8. This myth is clearly an example of the overlayering of an autochthonous shaman cult with the story of a later Muslim saint, who possibly came from Kashmir. In the Hunza version of the myth recorded by Hermann Berger the saint is described as a '... pious, learned man from far away...' (Berger Ms.). See Müller-Stellrecht (1980: 55 ff. and note 129).
9. See Müller-Stellrecht (1979: 249).
10. See Sharif (1972: 96).
11. On the derivation of the word *'urs* from an Arabic word for marriage see Hussaini (1985: 43).
12. Ibid.
13. See Schwerin (1984: 148f.) and Mahmood (1989: 35).
14. According to a descendant of Quṭb ud-Dīn, the *dargāh mutawalī* Islām ud-Dīn, the popular tradition of the marriage of Yoga-māyā and Quṭb ud-Dīn may have originated when the Mughal emperor, Bahādur Śāh II (reigned 1837-57, died 1862; better known by his pen-name, 'Ẓafar'), in order to strengthen the solidarity of Delhi's multi-religious population against the interference of the British resident in local politics, gave royal support to the Hindu-Muslim festival 'Phūl valoñ kī sair', ['The procession of the flower vendors'], during which the Mughal emperor, whose summer residence was adjacent to Quṭb ud-Dīn's shrine, first performed *ziyārat* at the *dargāh*, then, on the following day, had *darśan* of Yoga-māyā (a Śaktic goddess in whom attributes of Durgā and Lakṣmī are combined) in her temple nearby the Quṭb Minar (for a summary of the historical situation see Varma 1992: 42f.). Though today only the ceremonial fans (*paṅkhā*) of Yoga-māyā are carried to Quṭb ud-Dīn's *dargāh* during the festival, some Hindu devotees of Quṭb ud-Dīn still believe that Yoga-māyā and Quṭb ud-Dīn are divine marriage partners [personal communication in Mehrauli, 1 March 1994]. In an enclosed grave plot near the 'Ẓafar Mahal' (the ruins of a three-storey palace built by the emperor Akbar II [1806-37], the portal of which Bahādur Śāh II had restored), near the west or 'Ajmerī' gate to Quṭb ud-Dīn's *dargāh*, in a row of graves of members of the royal family, an open, empty grave still bears silent witness to the last Mughal's devotion to Quṭb ud-Dīn, the *dargāh*, and his beloved Hindustān. Here one can see the 'six feet of earth in the lane of the Beloved' ('... *do gaz zamīn* ... *kū-yi yār mẽ*'), for lack of which the exiled poet-emperor pined away in Rangoon during the final years of his life. During the final months of his life, in 1947,

Mahātmā Gandhi—who was well aware of the symbolic significance of Quṭb ud-Dīn's *dargāh* for the multi-religious society of the new, democratic India—saved the shrine from destruction by inducing hundreds of illegal occupants, who had taken possession of it in the chaotic situation that followed upon independence and the end of British rule, to leave the holy precincts peaceably (a photograph of Gandhi leading the squatters out of the *dargāh* is in my possession).

15. Twelve years is the traditional period of a *mahātapa* of a Hindu ascetic.
16. See Müller-Stellrecht (1979: 242).
17. Ernst quotes a translation of Auraṅgzīb's *Testament of Twelve Articles*, published in *Municipal Gazette*, Lahore, 1908.
18. On the two aspects of the 'beauty and goodness of Allāh' [*ǧamāl* and *ǧalāl*], the *mysterium fascinans* and the *mysterium tremendum*, see Schimmel (1990: 183f.).
19. Saiyid Ḥusām Al-Dīn Tīgh Barahna (d. 1281). Cf. Eaton 1978: 32.
20. *Svāmī tumhī melā mhaṇun vāṭesī duṣṭānem̦ ahmāsī nīvedīlem̦. Svāmī mhaṇem̦ koṇī melem̦ hī mhaṇatī. Amara jāṇatī jñānī koṇī. Nāthāsī namana karonī . . .* [illegible word] *taya kaḷe Nātha gele satya.* From *Bhīmasvāmī-Śirgāvkar-kṛta Bhaktalīlāmṛta. Ekanātha-caritra,* 40.11-13.
21. The eighth day of the dark half of the lunar month *Phālgun*.
22. Marāṭhī: *paḍadyām̦t jāṇe or paḍadyām̦t basṇe.*
23. I am grateful to Professor Fateh Mohammed Malik making me aware of the textual source of this famous exhortation of Rūmī.

REFERENCES

PRIMARY SOURCES

Śirgāvkar, Bhīmasvāmī. 1797. *Bhīmasvāmī-Śirgāvkar-kṛta-bhaktalīlāmṛta.* Manuscript accessible in the library of the *Satkāryom̦ttejaka-sabhā,* Dhuḷe (Maharashtra), under manuscript bundle number 541, in *vahī* (account book) format.

———. 1979. *Śrīmadbhagavadgītā.* Edited by Swami Chidbhavananda. Tirupparaitturai.

———. 1983. *Śrīmadbhāgavatamahāpurāṇam.* Edited by J.L. Shastri. Delhi: Manohar.

SECONDARY SOURCES

Eaton, Richard Maxwell. 1978. *Sufis of Bijapur, 1300-1700. Social roles of Sufis in medieval India.* Princeton: Princeton University Press.

Eliade, Mircea. 1978. *Geschichte der religiösen Ideen, 1. Von der Steinzeit bis zu den Mysterien von Eleusis.* Freiburg: Herder Verlag. Translated from the French by Elisabeth Darlap. Title of the original edition: *Histoire des croyances et des idées religieuses. 1. De l'age de la pierre aux mystères d'Eleusis,* Paris: Editions Payot. 1976.

Ernst, Carl W. 1992. *Eternal Garden. Mysticism, History, and Politics at a South Asian Sufi Center.* Albany: State University of New York Press.

Hussaini, Syed Shah Khusro. 1985. Die Bedeutung des 'urs-Festes im Sufitum.

Asien (Hamburg) 17(3): 43-54; translated from English into German by Hugh van Skyhawk.

Mahmood, Tahir. 1989. The Dargah of Sayyid Salar Mas'ud Ghazi in Bahraich: Legend, Tradition and Reality. In Christian Troll (ed.), *Muslim Shrines in India: Their Character, History and Significance*, pp. 24-43. New Delhi: Oxford University Press.

Müller-Stellrecht, Irmtraud (ed.). 1979. *Materialien zur Ethnographie von Dardistan (Pakistan). Teil I. Hunza. Aus den nachgelassenen Aufzeichnungen von D. L. R. Lorimer.* Published in the series: Karl Jettmar (general editor), *Bergvölker im Hindukusch und Karakorum.* 3.I. Graz: Akademische Druck- und Verlagsanstalt.

———. 1980. *Materialien zur Ethnographie von Dardistan (Pakistan). Teil II. Gilgit. Teil III. Chitral und Yasin. Aus den nachgelassenen Aufzeichnungen von D. L. R. Lorimer.* Published in the series: Karl Jettmar (general editor), *Bergvölker im Hindukusch und Karakorum.* 3.II and 3.III. Graz: Akademische Druck- und Verlagsanstalt.

Oman, John Campbell. 1903. *The Mystics, Ascetics, and Saints of India.* London.

Rayanna, P. [Society of Jesus]. 1982. *St. Francis Xavier and his Shrine.* Goa, 1964; revised reprint.

Rizvi, Sayid Athar Abbas. 1978. *A History of Sufism in India,* I. New Delhi: Munshiram Manoharlal.

———. 1986. *A Socio-Intellectual History of the Isnā-'Asharī Sh'īs in India.* I. Canberra/ Delhi: Munshiram Manoharlal.

Schimmel, Annemarie. 1990. *Der Islam. III. Islamische Kultur. Zeitgenössische Strömungen. Volksfrömmigkeit.* Published in the series Christel Matthias Schröder (general editor), *Die Religionen der Menschheit,* 25.3. Stuttgart: Kohlhammer.

Schwerin, Kerrin Gräfin von. 1984. Saint worship in Indian Islam: the legend of the martyr Salar Masud Ghazi. In Ahmad, Imtiaz (ed.), *Ritual and Religion among Muslims of the Sub-continent,* pp. 143-61; New Delhi: Manohar.

Sharif, Jafar. 1972. *Qānūn-i-Islām* Translated from the Persian by Herklots, G.A., and published under the title *Islam in India.* Oxford: Oxford University Press, 1921; reprinted in Delhi.

Skyhawk, Hugh van. 1990. *Bhakti und Bhakta. Religionsgeschichtliche Untersuchungen zum Heilsbegriff und zur religiösen Umwelt des Śrī Sant Ekanāth.* Stuttgart: Franz Steiner Verlag.

———. 1991. Ṣūfī Influence in the *Eknāthī-bhāgavat*: Some Observations on the Text and its Historical Context. In R.S. McGregor (ed.), *Devotional literature in South Asia.* Current research, 1985-8. University of Cambridge, Oriental Publications 46. Cambridge: Cambridge University Press.

———. 1993. Nasīruddīn and Ādināth, Nizāmuddin and Kāniphnāth: Hindu-Muslim religious syncretism in the folk literature of the Deccan. In Heidrun Brückner, Lothar Lutze, Aditya Malik (eds.), *Flags of Fame. Studies in South Asian Folk Culture.* South Asian Studies No. XXVII, New Delhi: Manohar.

———. 1994. Nāgnāth and Nasīruddīn: *Pīr*-worship and *Śaiva-Bhakti* in the literature of the *Nāgeś Sampradāy.* In Alan W. Entwistle and Françoise Mallison (eds), *Studies in South Asian Devotional Literature.* New Delhi: Manohar.

Skyhawk, Hugh van. 1996. Hinduismus und Hindutva. *Zeitschrift der Deutschen Morgenländischen Gesellschaft* 146 (1): 112-27.

Swynnerton, Charles (Reverend). 1987. *Folk-Tales of the Upper Indus.* London, 1893; reprinted in Islamabad: Lok Virsa.

Varma, Pavan K. 1992. *Ghalib: The Man, The Times.* New Delhi: Penguin Books. 1989; reprint.

Vaudeville, Charlotte. 1987. Sant Mat: Santism as the Universal Path to Sanctity. In Karine Schomer and W.H. McLeod (eds.), *The Sants. Studies in a Devotional Tradition of India,* pp. 21-40. New Delhi: Motilal Banarsidass.

Wezler, Albrecht. 1978. *Die wahren 'Speiseresteesser'* (Skt. *vighasāśin*) ['The true eaters of the remnants of food']. *Beiträge zur Kenntnis der indischen Kultur- und Religionsgeschichte.* Mainz: Akademie der Wissenschaften und der Literatur.

PART III

THE NARRATION AND PERFORMANCE OF DEATH

An Indian Myth of the Creation of Death and Life

CLAUS PETER ZOLLER

He who gives life, who gives strength,
whose command all the gods, his own, obey;
his shadow is immortality—and death.
Who is the god whom we should worship with oblation?
Ṛgveda 10.121 (Doniger 1984: 27)

Goddess Durgā asking Śiva:
'Why is it, my Lord, that thou art immortal,
and mortal am I?'
Gorakṣa Vijaya (Eliade 1970: 270)

It would appear somehow out of place to discuss a creation myth in a book devoted to death in South Asia, except for the observation that many cosmogonic myths around the world indeed also describe a primeval creation of death as an indispensable prerequisite for all existence (Eliade 1987, 4: 98). Thus, it is not only very widely accepted that being and life can only be experienced before a horizon of non-being and death. It has also become almost popular knowledge in the West that all order-producing life processes happen only at the *cost* of the production of a significantly higher amount of disorganization (entropy). Again, this insight into an intimate connection and complementary relation between order and chaos is certainly not new. Kuiper (1983: 19) says about the Vedic Indians that for them the 'world order . . . was a precarious balance between the powers of cosmos and chaos', and Lincoln (1986: 217, note 23) reconstructs the following aspect of Indo-European cosmology:

> One is tempted to say that there is no creation without a destruction, but this formulation is a serious over-simplification. In truth, every act of creation is simultaneously an act of destruction: when a living organism is created, the cosmos is in that measure destroyed or de-created, and conversely, when the cosmos is created or its material substance renewed, a living organism is destroyed or de-created.

Lincoln's statement is, of course, very generalizing, but we find the idea again in the time-honoured Indian concept of creation through (self)-sacrifice (cf. the *Puruṣa Sūkta, Ṛgveda* 10.90), where 'Sacrifice is a preeminently creative act' (Parry 1989: 503). This is also seen by Shulman when he says about the 'creative sacrifice' in south India that, 'In the sacrificial cult, a controlled act of slaughter is intended to produce new life and strength for the participants' (1979: 35). Thus, death and cosmogony cannot be separated from each other in South Asia, and it is certainly significant that the most famous cremation ground in India—the *Maṇikarṇika Ghāṭ* in Varanasi—where the corpses are burned as sacrifices, is simultaneously the place where the universe was created (Parry 1994: 31). This idea of a reciprocal conditioning of creation and destruction is reflected in Hindu cosmological concepts, social institutions, and symmetrical designs between cremation rituals and ideas about the procreation, growth and birth of living beings, as well as in homologizations of the cosmos and the human body (Parry 1989, 1994: 11-15, 30-2).

My intention, however, is not to continue producing further 'evidence' for such insights but to introduce here around twenty variants of a myth which describes the creation of death and life. All the variants, which stem from different areas and times of South Asia (some are several hundred years old), appear sufficiently similar to me that I think it is possible to speak of the variants of one myth. The fact that this myth reappears in a large number of different social and cultural settings suggests a noticeable persistent stability against repeated processes of entextualization and recontextualization. This stability thus cannot be exhaustively explained as conditioned by the contexts.

However, stability here does not mean inflexibility. Of course, many variants do contain motifs and other elements which are shared only by a few other variants or which may even be limited to one version. However, the central elements of the myth (most of which appear in all variants) vary, as we will see, only in terms of a limited set of simple binary, ternary or similar oppositions. This myth's partial independence from an all too natural sense of ownership and from an all too direct or 'obvious' interpretation through the communities where it is handed down means (*a*) that it possesses a 'sense' which does not necessarily coincide with the interpretations and sense(s) given to it by the respective communities, and (*b*) that no academic approach that explains the myth as a function of the social context in which it is handed down, can be exhaustive. Neither the senses given a myth by the various communities, nor the academic interpretation in terms of social contexts can be said to be 'wrong'. But it would be wrong to reduce the myth to a reflection of sense-relations external to it.

Myths (and related forms of verbal art and poetry) are, I believe, autonomous to some extent with regard to the conditions of and 'intentions' behind their production. They may, to give one example, develop 'unintended' new meanings, forms and functions as a consequence not of social realities but of aesthetic considerations.

Still, what I will be able to say about the 'sense', structures and functions of this myth after presenting the data is rather preliminary for two reasons.[1] First, the actual number of its versions is certainly much higher than the twenty introduced below, and it would require extensive fieldwork to get a more comprehensive picture. And second, most of the versions below have been collected from secondary sources. In many cases very little information about the contexts is given, and the reliability of the translations can hardly be judged.

Variants of the myth I am going to discuss are known to me mainly from three regions of India. These regions correspond to three groups of sub-variants of the myth: (*a*) Karnataka and Tamil Nadu, (*b*) Bengal and Assam, (*c*) Himachal Pradesh and Garhwal. Though the myth is not an integral part of the classical tradition, it is not just a 'folk-myth' either. It also appears in the literature of some ascetic orders (*d*) and is even mentioned in some Purāṇas (*e*).

The Primeval Goddess, usually called Ādyā or Ādi Śakti, and the Triad (the *Ṭrimūrti* of Brahmā, Viṣṇu and Śiva) are of crucial importance in it. Besides, we will see that a second myth (-cycle), usually centering on Śiva and Pārvatī, was originally appended to the creation myth.[2] The second cycle has been well preserved in Garhwal (see Sax 1991), but in the textual sources from the other areas only vestiges are found. Moreover, we will see that in most cases the Primeval Goddess of the creation myth is said to be isomorphic with a regional folk-goddess. As a consequence, the folk-goddess is frequently addressed, not only with her original name, but also as Ādi Śakti and as Pārvatī/Umā/Durgā. Thus, we can say about the cosmogonical myth's functions: (1) it links regionally limited folk traditions to regional shapings of classical Purāṇic traditions with a pan-Indian background; and (2) an identification of a regional folk-goddess with the Ādi Śakti and with Pārvatī (who are identified beforehand) serves the purpose of *universalizing* the regional goddess in a twofold manner: she is the *Primeval Goddess* and she is the goddess of a prestigious tradition.

In almost all the versions the Ādi Śakti creates the Triad, and very frequently she is involved in cycles of creation and destruction. Thus, Durgā's above question to Śiva, why she is mortal, and not immortal like him—a question which seems to contradict a standard contrast in Hinduism between immortal gods and mortal men—is profounder than the immediate context tries to suggest. Her question gives Śiva the opportunity to reveal Haṭha Yoga (Eliade 1970: 270), a system through which immortality can be achieved. But, in view of the many treatises on yoga which manage without such a strange statement, it is likely that her question is more than just a rhetorical device.

The other quotation at the head of this paper is intended to call attention to another prominent figure appearing in many, though not all the versions of the myth: an ambivalent, trickster-like demiurge, who is frequently the creator of the Goddess and who assumes in some versions the countenance of 'supreme death'. What again may appear like a contradiction: creation of a primeval goddess, in fact, means that she has a beginning. She is *ādi*, 'primeval', she is not *anādi*, 'beginningless', like the Lord of the Universe. But let us now start with brief summaries of the variants.

The first of the five variants of the south Indian subgroup is a 'Creation Myth in a Folk Purāṇa' from Karnataka, published by A.K. Ramanujan (1993: 107-20). It forms the beginning of a folk narrative called *Maleya Madeshvara* and tells the adventures of 'a god/hero/saint . . . [who is] in pursuit of an evil Bali-like demon king (who has imprisoned all the celestials and set even Pārvatī to menial tasks)' (Ramanujan 1993: 101f.).[3]

(a1):
Ādi Śakti comes into being. As time passes, she attains puberty. Since she cannot find a partner to satisfy her passion, she gives birth to Brahmā and asks him to marry her. He rejects her proposal, pointing out that she is his mother. The Ādi Śakti, in turn, puts her hand, in which is an eye of fire, on his head and burns him to ashes. Then she gives birth to Mahāviṣṇu, and the same happens with him, at the end he is burned to ashes. Finally, she begets Śiva. At first he rejects her proposal, saying '*dharma* will be in ruins, *karma* will increase', but she retorts that, if they do not marry, the world cannot come into being. He is still not ready to accept her argument, and tries to postpone the marriage through various demands. Then he asks her to test who is the greater, she or he. If she defeats him, he will marry her. Both start dancing, and she repeats each of his movements. When he puts his hand on his head she repeats the gesture and goes up in flames. Śiva now revives Brahmā and Viṣṇu and shows them the heap of ashes of Ādi Śakti. Now Śiva suggests that they should create the universe, but: 'If all this is to be done, we need women.' The three gods divide the heap of ashes of their mother in three parts, and out of them emerge Pārvatī, Sarasvatī and Lakṣmī, who are married by Śiva, Brahmā, and Viṣṇu respectively. Then Śiva creates heaven and three paradises, and all gods and demons, men, animals and plants. Since nobody eats anything, no one dies. But due to some enticing behaviour of a snake, men start to eat, and as a punishment Brahmā creates the earth for the men and the underworld for the snake, and they now have to live in their respective realms. The snake however secures for herself a boon, and Śiva tells her, 'I'll let you be in two places, in the netherworld and also round my neck.'

A rather awkward way of creating the world! Ramanujan interprets the beginning of this folk Purāṇa in contrast to the Sanskrit Purāṇas, applying principles which he developed several years earlier (1986: 64-7). Thus, he observes (1993: 106), 'in terms of Sanskritic Epics and Purāṇas, folklore in general, and folk Purāṇas in particular, present an alternative world; they are what we may call counter-texts to their better-known "classical" analogues.' In this way he describes a number of motifs of the myth as inversions of classical motifs. For instance, he sees in the incestuous attempts of the Ādi Śakti an inversion of the story of Brahmā, who goes after his daughter, a myth found in the Vedas and other classical texts (1993: 120). And in the self-burning of the Ādi Śakti he sees an inversion of the classical story of Bhasmāsura and Viṣṇu as Mohinī (ibid.). This, he goes on to argue, 'suggest[s] the way the folk Purāṇa reworks motifs from the Purāṇic pool. The myth here, like other women-centered folk materials, also suggests a very feminine (even a feminist) view of the Hindu pantheon.' And in the mischievous snake he sees a reflex of 'Biblical motifs (spread, no doubt, by local missionaries)', motifs which 'are part of the intertextual weave'.

This creation myth in fact may appear like the expression of a feminist anti-establishment counterdiscourse, especially when we recall Doninger's observation (1980a: 28) that in Sanskrit literature one finds many references to 'male unilateral creation', but that 'it does not happen that some woman or goddess . . . becomes able to produce children all by herself'. However, let us first look at the other versions before we reconsider Ramanujan's hypothesis.

The next version from the south is the story of the goddess Aṅkāḷamaparamēcuvari from Tamil Nadu (Meyer 1986: 6-9), who is here 'identified' with the Ādi Śakti and with Umā Parameśvarī:

(a2):
In the beginning there is an egg in which the goddess Umā Parameśvarī takes the form of an embryo. She is born in the egg and forms the universe out of it. Then she takes on the form of a snake 'in order to create the world' (Meyer 1986: 6) and creates, among other beings, a huge number of women, and then the Triad. The three gods realize that their 'mother' wants to become their wife. When they refuse to comply they are burned to ashes, and with them also the women. Then the goddess thinks of Kṛṣṇa, 'who is the master of deceitful plays, who is her elder brother, who knows all that has happened before and all that is going to happen in the future', but who was born *after* she had created the Triad (Meyer 1986: 7). Kṛṣṇa advises her to recreate the Triad out of one of three heaps of ashes and tells Śiva (Rudra) to marry the Goddess, and ask from her, among other things, her third eye. Then he tells Śiva to burn the goddess with the

eye, and Śiva does so. Out of her ashes Kṛṣṇa and Śiva create three goddesses. Then, again, they create the Triad (the third time!), and the three worlds.

A second version presented by Meyer (1986: 43-4) mainly deviates from the first in that the ashes of the Goddess are divided into three parts, which are given to the Triad and out of which emerge their three wives. This mythologeme appears also in the Kanarese version (a1) and in the version of the Kabīr-panth (d3). A theriomorph appearance of the Goddess is mentioned also in (a3) and (a4), but it seems to be limited to the south.

Meyer (1986: 47) relates the myth to gender issues and points out that it describes the goddess' transformation into a suitable marriage partner. We have seen, however, the Goddess in the Kanarese version explicitly stating that she wants to have intercourse with one of her sons in order to continue the creation of the world. Meyer also comments on connections with features of Aṅkāḷamman, a goddess of the cremation ground, who is 'created' from the ashes of burned bodies and who herself is 'the sacrifice, the food offered to fire (or hunger), and her sacrifice is a prerequisite for the renewal of life' (ibid.). Meyer's guess, however, that the myth is 'confusing' because 'Rudra and Visnu create the Trimurti', a motif which 'may be due to the narrator's attempt to weld different cosmogonies' (ibid.) is not convincing. Myth (a1) has already shown that the mother of the three gods can easily metamorphose herself into their three wives.

The burning of the Goddess, mentioned in (a1) and in many other versions, is not an inversion of a classical myth, but is quite a central element of the creation myth. The similarity with the Bhasmāsura-Mohinī myth in (a1), suggested by Ramanujan, is thus either accidental or a sort of adjustment of a more basic mythological structure to a well-known Hindu myth.

The next version was published by Oppert more than hundred years ago (1893: 464-6). Here the popular south Indian goddess Ellamma is equated with the Ādi Śakti:

(a3):

The Ādi Śakti is born out of the earth, a virgin. But before she was born, the great sage Ādijambuvu is born six months before the Kaliyuga. He, with the help of his mantras, causes Ellamma to be born. Within hours she attains puberty and desires to have intercourse with the sage, her 'grandfather'. He, however, says, 'That cannot be', and gives her a root to be planted on a hill. She has to worship the emerging tree, from whose roots a cock appears. When she sees him, she changes into a hen and lays three eggs. The first two become underworlds of the snakes and of King

Bali, and from the third egg is born the Triad. After their birth she again becomes a woman. Now she wants to marry them; they flee to Ādijambuvu, who says that she is only after Śiva. He advises Śiva to ask her to give him her third eye. Then she returns to the hill, and people come to worship her.

Here it is not mentioned that the goddess is burned to ashes. But we find a new element, not mentioned in the previous variants, which frequently appears in other variants below: an (attempted) incestual contact between the Goddess and her creator.

In the fourth variant the Ādi Śakti is identified with the popular goddess Mariamman or Peddamma. This is also presented by Oppert (1893: 472-4):

(a4):
In the beginning there is water in which there is a light. The light gets transformed into a woman. The woman creates an island with a garden, a well, a mangrove tree, and an ant-hill. Then she desires to have a man, plucks a flower from a 'jessamine' bough, and places it in a lotus flower in the well. Then she changes into a roller bird and broods over the flower. She becomes pregnant and lays three eggs. Out of the first egg the world is created and the Triad is born, and out of the two other eggs the demons. Then she lusts after the three gods. Only Viṣṇu pretends to agree, but first asks various things from her. He gets her (third) eye, which he gives to Śiva. Then, however, she loses all her strength and vigour, and the memory of her desire, and she decides to fight against the demons.

In the version from Tamil Nadu published by Whitehead (1921: 126-38), the Goddess is Ammavaru or Aṅkamma. The elements of the creation myth are woven here into a long story, most of which has nothing to do with my present subject. The story is recited 'by Asādis during the annual festivals' (Whitehead 1921: 127). In order to avoid recapitulating this twelve-page-long story I am simply picking out the relevant passages:

(a5):
When Ammavaru comes into existence, she lays three eggs in the sea of milk, one by one in three successive ages. The egg laid first gets spoilt, the next fills with air, and only the third is hatched. This egg has three compartments, from which comes the *Trimūrti*, Brahmā, Viṣṇu and Śiva (p. 127). She builds four cities for her sons and herself, but when she hears that her sons are neglecting her worship she decides to destroy their towns (p. 128). She is very successful in this enterprise, and cuts off the heads of 'the kings' Brahmā, Viṣṇu and Śiva and the heads of seven other kings, but puts them all on again (p. 130). A little later (p. 132), the Goddess tells

a story about Śiva and Pārvatī and their marriage, during which Śiva decapitates the lustful Brahmā. On the next pages (133-4) Ammavaru then relates how she herself had desired to marry Viṣṇu. He, however, sent her to Brahmā, who passed her on to Śiva. When she danced before Śiva he promised to fulfil her wish, if she would give him the three valuable things she possessed—a rug, betel leaves and her third eye. She gave these things to Śiva, who used the third eye to reduce her and all womankind to ashes.[4] However, he regretted his deed, collected the ashes and made them into the form of three women, who became the wives of Śiva, Viṣṇu and Brahmā.

We find here again the motif of the birth of the Triad from an egg and an indication of some attempts at incest. Here the Goddess is burned to ashes, whereas her sons are decapitated (cp. version c4, where she decapitates herself).

It is worth mentioning Whitehead's evaluation of this myth. For him it is full of 'absurdity and extravagance' (p. 137), and 'is a strange, rambling tale, full of weird details, describing the birth of the newer deities, Brahmā, Śiva and Viṣṇu, and the struggle that ensued between the rival religions. It is not improbable that it describes an attempt on the part of the Brāhmaṇs to supplant the worship of the village deity by the new cults and the revival of the primitive religion through some epidemics or other disasters' (p. 127).

We can see that among the five south Indian variants (a1), (a2) and (a5), and (a3) and (a4) are respectively more closely related. However, all five variants share the mythologeme of the birth of the Triad through the Goddess and her consequent lusting for her children, and the children's attempt to escape her advances. Some variants indicate that she wants the intercourse for the sake of creation. In the versions (a1) and (a2) (and, less clearly, in (a5)) the refusal of incest leads to a burning to ashes. In (a1) she first burns Brahmā and Viṣṇu and then burns herself to ashes. Thereafter, it is Śiva who occupies the position of creator, and who recreates out of this *primordial death* his two brothers and his mother. In this way Śiva becomes the 'father' of his mother and his brothers, and she becomes the three wives of the three gods. In (a2) the number of mutual burnings and recreations gets doubled: the Goddess recreates the triad out of ashes, then she is burned to ashes by Śiva, and recreated by him and Kṛṣṇa into the form of three goddesses. Then, in order 'to create, maintain and destroy' (Meyer 1986: 8) the two gods again create the Triad! Since the results of (a1) and (a2) are, nevertheless, the same, we conclude that the myth contains structural elements, which can be multiplied without changing its basic 'meaning'. Such multiplications necessarily lead to a splitting of actor and figure (Turner 1977: 154). The Goddess, for instance, is multiplied, so to say, into Goddess^1 and Goddess^2 (e.g.

Umā, Lakṣmī) or the Triad into Triad[1] and Triad[2]. Thus, the myth 'says' that creation involves a sort of self-multiplication of the creator(s) into the creation. We also see that the original fear of incest disappears after the acts of burning. This must have something to do with the fact that creation out of ashes is an *asexual* type of creation. I will return to this point towards the end of this paper.

In the versions (a3) and (a4) no death or burning to ashes is mentioned, but the Goddess transforms herself into a bird in order to give birth to the Triad. Her sexual desire for her children, however, leads neither to an incestuous act nor to a killing. Thus, we can distinguish 'softer' from 'harder' versions of the myth. Death is nevertheless introduced here as well, because out of two of the three eggs, underworlds or underworldly or demonic beings, are created, and in (a4) it is said that the Goddess sets out to slay the demons.

A fact common to all the versions in South Asia is that the Goddess, although she is called the primeval power, is said *to have come into existence.* In other words, she has a beginning. In (a2) and (a4) she is born out of an egg or out of a light in the primeval water.[5] But in (a2) it is also said that she has an elder brother, Kṛṣṇa, 'who is the master of deceitful plays'. In three of the southern versions no creator of the Goddess is mentioned, but in (a5) she is said to be the daughter of a person named 'Kasi-gotna' (Whitehead 1921: 135) and in (a3) she is the granddaughter of the sage Ādijambuvu. The sage's name probably means 'the primordial rose apple tree'.

* * *

The second subgroup is geographically located in and around Bengal. There the Ādi Śakti is mostly connected with the myth cycles of the regional snake-goddess Manasā. The first version is from the so-called *Śūnya-Purāṇ* of Ramai Pandit, a medieval Bengali text belonging to the Dharma and Manasā cults, which are still quite popular in parts of Bengal, Assam and Orissa.[6] There exist different manuscripts and editions of the *Śūnya Purāṇ*, and consequently the various renderings into English also differ. First a short summary of Dasgupta's presentation (1969: 311ff.).

(b1):

In the beginning the Lord alone moves in the great void. He creates various emanations,[7] and then Nirañjan (also called Dharma). Nirañjan meditates for fourteen years, yawns and out comes the bird Ulluka. He meditates sitting on the back of the bird, and out of some fluid of his mouth the primeval waters emerge. Then other animals come into being successively, on whose backs he meditates as well: a swan and a tortoise. Since all these animals get tired under his weight, he creates the world on the head of the serpent Vāsukī. When he roams about in the world he becomes tired and starts to perspire. From the sweat of his body Ādyā Śakti is produced. When her sexual passion awakes after some time, she produces Kāma and sends him to the Lord. The Lord puts Kāma into a pot where he gets transformed into poison. When Ādyā is unable to bear her passion any more she wants to commit suicide by swallowing the poison. However, she becomes pregnant and gives birth to Śiva, Viṣṇu and Brahmā. The Lord then tests the three: he takes on the form of a corpse floating on water. Only Śiva is able to recognize him in this disguise, which satisfies the Lord. Then he entrusts the three with the task of creation and asks Ādyā Śakti to be the wife of Śiva. Thereafter the Lord returns into the void seated on his mount Ulluka.

Other versions (see (b[2]) and (b4)) say that this test in fact only determines Śiva to become creator and continue creation. Here and in many other versions below no sharp distinction is drawn between the Lord and his 'son' Nirañjan. However, in those versions where the distinction is stressed, it is one of a transcendent God *vs.* an ambivalent demiurge or trickster. The demiurge is closely associated with death and thus occasionally identified with Yama or Dharma Rāja, the Lord of the Dead. His appearance in the version above as a corpse is thus a powerful image suggesting his being 'supreme death'. The mythologeme of the selection of a creator-successor appears also in the Bangani version and in the Himachali version (c3); the creation of various emanations before the creation of the demiurge has a parallel in (d3). The other Bengali versions differ in the following major points:

(b2 [1]):
Nirañjan Dharma is said to be the body of the Lord and not his offspring.[8] After creating the world he perspires, and from his sweat Ādyā Śakti is born. He leaves her, goes meditating and returns when she is grown up. He wants to seek a husband for her, and leaves with her a jar of honey and a jar of poison. She wants to kill herself and drinks the poison, etc. (A. Bhattacaryya 1977: 111-13, 1978: 17-19).

Also here Nirañjan and the Lord are not very clearly separated. Now the next version:

(b2 [2]):
The liquid which Ādyā drinks in order to commit suicide, and which she thinks is poison, is, in fact, the seed shed by Dharma. The owl collects the seed in a pot, brings it to Ādyā and tells her to guard it well, because it contains 'poisonous honey (*viṣa-madhu*)'.[9] After the birth of the Triad, Dharma marries her and tests the three gods. Śiva proves to be

the best, Dharma tells him to marry Ādyā, and then Dharma dies (Maity 1966: 198-9).

Thus, we see that whether the Śakti 'marries' her direct or indirect progenitor depends on how clearly the two figures are distinguished. But in all the variants in which a progenitor of her is mentioned, she first desires to marry him (or he her) and only thereafter does she cast an eye on her sons. The radical ambivalence of this creation, namely the production both of life and death, is also contained in the word *viṣa-madhu*, 'poisonous honey', for Dharma's sperm. She drinks it in order to end her life, but instead gives birth to the Triad. The word *viṣa-madhu* is clearly synonymous with 'death and life' or 'death and immortality', and reminds us of the line from *Ṛgveda* 10.121 quoted at the beginning: 'whose shadow is immortality and death' (*yasya chāyāmṛtaṃ yasya mṛtyuḥ*).

The myth appears also in Bengali oral folk poetry, and in various *maṅgal* texts. There it is sometimes the progenitor of the Goddess who takes the sexual initiative. This situation is identical with the Vedic story of Brahmā's incest with his daughter, which Ramanujan wants to classify only as classical. When the progenitor takes the initiative, she regularly starts panicking and tries to flee. Nevertheless, the intercourse takes place.

So, for instance, in the *maṅgal* quoted by Dasgupta (1969: 314), where a direct physical incestuous contact is proposed by Nirañjan or the Lord, but impulsively rejected by Ādyā:

(b3):
The proposal appeared obnoxiously repulsive to Ādyā, who tried to flee away in all the directions; but at last she had to give way and the marriage took place in the void through the mediation of Ulluka.

More or less the same is said in the *Nīla-pūjā* song (Dasgupta 1969: 317). Interestingly, it states, 'Dharma-raja . . . perspired and from his sweat a phantom was produced . . . [which] became magically transformed into a girl', because here 'phantom' is a translation of *chāyā*, 'shadow'.

Several versions say that the primeval incestuous act (whether it is conducted or not) between the Goddess and either her indirect progenitor or her son is mediated by someone. In (b3) it is the owl (Ulluka), and in other versions it is Dharma, Nārāyaṇa or Kṛṣṇa. In other words, the 'marriage broker' (a trickster or demiurge) appears either in a more Shaivite (Nirañjan-Dharma) or a more Vaishnavite outfit (Nārāyaṇa or Kṛṣṇa, but also the owl Ulluka, a theriomorphic embodiment of Viṣṇu). Thus, there is at least a tendency, according to which there is a mutual conditioning in the 'sectarian' shaping of the marriage broker and the Lord (if it is made explicit): when the mediator is a Vaishnavite figure then the Lord is or tends to be a Śiva-like person and *vice versa*.

In the *Gorakṣa-vijaya*, a Bengali poem belonging to the Nāth sect (Dasgupta 1969: 320), the following version appears:

(d1):
The Lord (*Kartār*) tries to capture the Goddess. She wants to flee, but is taken by force, and through their union the world is created. From the Lord come into existence Brahmā and Viṣṇu. From different body parts of *Anādya* (Dharma) emerge Śiva and Gaurī. The Lord wants for someone to marry Gaurī. 'All bent their head out of shame.' The Lord then orders Śiva to marry Gaurī.

This is an example of the connection between the Goddess and Pārvatī (here called Gaurī).[10] The version does not say how Dharma is created. But here the initiative for the primeval sexual act and for the creation of the gods of the 'second generation' is very much on the male side. This inversion—the Triad is not created by the female but by the male partner—is also described in the *Manasākāvya* of the mid-seventeenth century poet Jagajjiban (Maity 1966: 199-200):

(b4):
Dharma first creates the Triad, then he creates the Goddess from his sight. She is called Manasā. He sleeps with her, but then feels so guilty that he wants to commit suicide. Before he ends his life he tests the Triad, finds Śiva superior, tells him that Manasā will be his wife and enters his mouth. She throws herself upon a funeral pyre, changes into a baby, is put adrift on a river in an iron box, then found by the sage Hemanta, under whom she (now named Durgā) grows up until she marries Śiva.

Several versions reproduced in this paper mentions that the Lord (or Nirañjan) retreats (e.g. into the void) when creation has been set into motion. The saliva of Śiva's mouth, into which Dharma enters, equals the primeval waters (see myth (b1)). This means that Dharma's 'suicide' here is a 'death' which is different from the deaths of the Goddess and the Triad. The Lord and his demiurge are not born, and thus Dharma rather retreats into a primeval state beyond existence and non-existence. On the other hand, all the myth's versions say that the Goddess is born, and so is the Triad. Consequently, she can be burned to ashes (as her children can be), she can be cremated, and can be recreated (as her children can be), and she can be reborn as Pārvatī. It is in this sense that the Goddess is mortal and the Lord immortal.

In the following final version from Bengal, which belongs to the Nāths (Dasgupta 1969: 319), both Dharma and the Goddess are the children of the Lord:

(d2):
Nirañjan Gosāmi creates *Anādi Dharma-nāth* and the goddess Kaketukā.[11] She is then put to death under the pressure of the feet of *Anādi*, but revived again by the Lord. He instructs to create the universe with her. From the fist of *Anādi Dharma-nāth* the Triad emerges.

Here, again, we have the polarization of the immortal creator(s) *vs.* the mortal Goddess.[12]

* * *

Let us now turn to Himachal Pradesh. In contrast to the myth's variants in neighbouring Garhwal, here the goddess is called Mansā Debī in all the versions. Since, however, Mansā Debī is worshipped practically nowhere in this region, it is possible that the Himachali variants have been imported from eastern India not too long ago. This hypothesis is corroborated by the fact that in most cases the myth is connected with a regional goddess, whereas, in the sources from which the following versions are quoted, it appears as if they are rather isolated stories, not integrated into greater myth cycles.

However, there is one exception. At the so-called Blāj (resp. Barlāj, Balrāj) festival in eastern Himachal Pradesh, the myth is connected with the myth of the conquering of king Bali by Viṣṇu in his dwarf incarnation.[13] In some parts of Himachal Pradesh this festival is also associated with the Pāṇḍavas (B.R. Sharma 1993: 33f.). This is significant, because the Garhwali versions of the creation myth are more or less explicitly linked with regional *Mahābhārata* traditions. Here is a summary of Joshi's translation (1911: 272-5):

(c1):
Mansā Debī is born out of the spirit of Nārāyaṇa. He tells her to protect the earth and gives her seven jars (*kalaś*) to keep in a store-room for nine months. From the first jar she breaks Brahmā emerges. She wants to marry him, he refuses, and is burned to ashes by her. The same happens to Viṣṇu. When she asks Śiva, he first wants his two brothers revived. Then Brahmā and Viṣṇu say that they will conduct the marriage rites after completing creation. After the first attempts they create Kāma, whose descendants rule happily. One of the descendants is Bali. Then follows the Bali-Vāmana story (see Doniger 1982: 178f.): The first step of the dwarf covers the half world, the second the whole and with the third Nārāyaṇa pushes Bali down into the seventh hell.

It is remarkable that here the trickster Nārāyaṇa is equated with Viṣṇu as Vāmana. This variant resembles the one from Karnataka and (a5) from

Tamil Nadu regarding the attempt to postpone the marriage between the Goddess and Śiva.

In the following two versions unfortunately no contexts have been provided by the authors. The first is from Ranchan and Justa (1981: 10), who say that the myth is sung as a ballad in the Kulu and Simla districts (ibid.):

(c2):
Mansā Devī is 'born from the mind of Lord Nārāyaṇa'. She collects mustard seeds from bushes which had grown from seeds strewn by the Lord. She keeps them in vessels, and after the usual amount of time the three gods are born. She wants to marry one after the other, burns Brahmā and Viṣṇu to ashes. Śiva agrees to marry her, but he wants to have his brothers revived. She revives them.

Whereas in this version the progenitor is a Vaishnavite figure, he is a Shaivite deity in the next, published by G. Sharma (1991: 19-21):

(c3):
The 'Guru' besmears himself with ashes from his *dhuni*-fire. This he rubs off and out of it creates a figure into which he breathes life: Mansā Devī. When she is twelve, she takes a bath in the river, the Guru sees her and his sight impregnates her. She gives birth to the Triad. The Guru wants someone to take over creation. Brahmā and Viṣṇu fail, but not Śiva. Brahmā is cursed to be reborn as a poor Brāhmaṇ, and Viṣṇu as an Acharaj, 'a collector of shrouds in the cremation ground'; Śiva then creates man and the other living beings.

* * *

Let us now turn to Garhwal. Besides my own material from Bangan in western Garhwal, to which I will return below, Sax (1991: 18-22) has published a version from the catchment area of the Alaknanda valley. Here, near the headwaters of India's holiest river, we find the myth integrated into the cult of the mountain goddess Nandā Devī.

Sax, who points out a connection between the creation myth of Nandā Devī and the one published by Ramanujan (Sax 1991: 31), does not present the translation of the myth right from the beginning. He says, however, that the 'primordial goddess named "Ādisakti". . . has given birth to the goddess Pārvatī, who has given birth to the woman Nalina, who has given birth, in turn, to the bird Pankhina' (Sax 1991: 18). The very first (unpublished) part of the myth is indeed not very clear.[14] But there is another Nandā Devī story collected by Sax from an old Bhotiya man, where the following is said: 'In the beginning when earth was *jalākār* . . . the water was spinning around and around and around, it became a pupil.[15] It made foam, and this pupil was born from that foam. And *Śakti* was born in the pupil. . . .' Now a short summary of Sax's published version:

(c4):
Ādi Śakti realizes after creating the whole world that she needs a husband. She 'enveloped the ocean', and out of her menstrual blood Brahmā is born. She wants to have him as husband; he refuses, and she creates *Brahmā-loka* for him. The second, very similar scene is with Śiva (here called *Jaṭīlo Bagyelo*, p. 19), whom she makes king of the wilderness. The third scene is with the blacksmith Kalia Lohār (who is the weapon smith of the Pāṇḍavas in many local legends). She asks him to 'forge seven iron knives'. She takes the seven knives, visits various places, and asks herself, 'who will rid me of my sorrow?' (Sax 1991: 22). She then decapitates herself, her head flies to Mount Kailāś and her trunk falls down into Rishasau town. The head gets transformed into Śiva, and in Rishasau she is born as Gauradevī in the place of the old sage Hemant.

Now Gauradevī is the name both of Nandā Devī and of Pārvatī, and, in fact, Nandā Devī is a regional incarnation of Pārvatī. This myth shows some remarkable similarities with the Tamil version (a5): in both versions the Goddess provides her sons with kingdoms, and in both there is an allusion to myths about Śiva and Pārvatī, and some beheading takes place. But it is interesting that here her third son is not Viṣṇu, but the weapon smith of the Pāṇḍavas, Kalia Lohār. This may suggest a connection between the creation myth and regional *Mahābhārata* traditions, a connection which is clearly expressed in songs from Bangan (see p. 220).

The motif of the Goddess enveloping the ocean and the consequent birth of the Triad out of her menstrual blood has to be seen in connection with versions like (a4), where she is born out of water and light, or Sax's version from the Bhotiya, where the primeval water is transformed into foam and into a pupil of the eye, out of which she is born.[16] Moreover, a connection (or rather homology) among primeval water, light and menstrual blood is observed by Salomon (1991: 283f.) in the tradition of the Bauls. She says that the famous Baul poet-saint Lalan equates light with water in his cosmogonic songs, and that 'Lalan may mean that light . . . is the śakti in menstrual blood'. And about Nirañjan, whom we will meet again below, she says (p. 284), 'In *dehatattva* terms, Niranjan floating in an egg on the cosmic waters is the *adhar mānuṣ*, the active form of the Supreme, who appears in the egg sac of menstrual blood.' Consequently, she interprets Lalan's line 'Find out about the light that surrounds Niranjan' (ibid.) thus: 'The 'light' here signifies menstrual blood' (ibid.). I think the beginning of Sax's creation myth (c4) has to be seen in this context.

Sax connects this creation myth with gender issues. First step: inversion of male dominance, because the Goddess is the original power; second step: reestablishment of male dominance through transformation of her head into Śiva on Mount Kailāś. But besides this aspect, the Goddess' self-killing is strongly motivated, as in the other versions above, by her incestuous desire. She expresses her desperation when she says to one of her sons that she is suffering (Sax 1991: 20) or when she says to herself (Sax 1991: 22), 'I am alone, a brokenhearted girl, and who will rid me of my sorrow?'

The last folk-version of the myth I want to introduce here stems from Bangan, from the valley of the Tons river in western Garhwal. It is part of a song called *Iśe ka Bakhaṇ* 'The Saying of the Lord'. It is performed annually in February during a five-day festival called *Ḍaknatsaṇ*, 'dance of the bards'. In this region the myth is not connected with the cult of a god or goddess,[17] but with a regional version of the *Mahābhārata* epic, locally called *Paṇḍuaṇ*. According to 'The Saying of the Lord' the goddess *Śibśakti* (or *Mātā Pailua*, 'the first mother') is born. Then she creates three lumps, out of which the three gods are successively born. Brahmā and Viṣṇu refuse to marry her and are reduced to ashes.[18] When she asks Īśvar Śambhu or Īśvar Jagannāth, he burns her to ashes. This resembles the above myths (a1) and (a2), where there is also a strong identification between Śiva (the 'son' of the Goddess) and the Lord of the World (the Goddess' 'father').

However, that Śiva and the Lord are not exactly the same becomes clear in a later part of the Bangani song. It continues describing how the Lord creates the world: He pulls her apart like a rice cake (which puffs up in hot oil), then he gives the heavy earth to a giant whose name is 'tortoise', and asks him to hold her a short while until he returns.[19] The giant gets tired, puts the earth down and runs behind the Lord. The Lord gets frightened, and some beads of sweat fall down, out of which 'the wise child Nārāyaṇ' is born. Nārāyaṇ puts the earth upon a pillar, which, in turn, is put upon the back of the kneeling giant 'tortoise'.

Also here we find our hypothesis corroborated that, when the Lord of the Universe has a Shaivite nature, his 'son' is a Vaishnavite deity. The 'Saying of the Lord' does not state explicitly by whom 'the primeval mother' was created; and Pārvatī, whom the Lord now desires to marry, is not described as her reincarnation. Rather, Pārvatī is said to be the daughter of queen Mainā and king 'Lord of the Snow' (Impti Raja). This king is, of course, none other than the Himalaya, who is none other than the sage Hemant, mentioned in the myths (b4) and (c4), under whom Pārvatī grows up. According to Bangani traditions, Pārvatī has two sisters, Kuntī and Gāndhārī, who are the mothers of the Pāṇḍavas and the Kauravas.[20] However, queen Mainā is not happy with the Lord, who arrives in the palace like a beggar; she wants to give her daughter to one 'who is like Brahmā, Viṣṇu or Śiva'. Nevertheless, the two marry.

All the myth's versions presented so far belong to folk traditions. But there are also at least two short Purāṇic versions. It is, however, quite likely that the myth did not originate directly from a Sanskrit Purāṇa. The first Purāṇic version is from the *Mahābhāgavata Purāṇa* 3.15-70:

'Devī created Brahmā, Viṣṇu and Śiva. Then she divided herself into three parts and promised to become the wife of each of them . . . and to test them Devī assumed a terrifying form' (Doniger 1981: 98). She is pleased only with Śiva, whom she promises that she will become Sati in order to marry him (ibid.).

The second version is from the *Bṛhaddharma Purāṇa,* which says that she appears before the three gods 'in the form of a worm-infested corpse' (Doniger 1981: 99). Here it is the Goddess and not the Lord (who is not mentioned at all) who tests the triad. The *Mahābhāgavata Purāṇa* also suggests a close relation between the Goddess of creation and Pārvatī. Before I now turn to another aspect of the creation myth, let me point out that the folk myth cycles of Śiva and Pārvatī contain a fact not found in the classical Purāṇic myths: Śiva and Pārvatī are 'consanguines'.

I have pointed out above that several versions mention a 'marriage broker' who has an ambivalent, sometimes even sinister character. In Bengal he is called Nirañjan and he wants to arrange the marriage between the Lord and the Goddess. In Bangan this son of the Lord is 'the wise child Nārāyaṇa', a Viṣṇu-like figure who rides on his Garuḍa and who also appears in the regional version of the *Mahābhārata,* where he acts as a trickster (Zoller forthcoming). In a story from Himachal Pradesh, he arranges the marriage between Śiva and Pārvatī, and also there his 'love of suggestions and trickery' (Ranchan and Justa 1981: 75) is stressed. And in the Tamil myth (a2) Kṛṣṇa, '[t]he master of deceitful plays', arranges the marriage between Pārvatī (*alias* Aṅkalamai, *alias* Ādi Śakti) and Rudra (Śiva) (Meyer 1986: 7-8). In Tamil Nadu he is said to be the elder brother of the goddess (Meyer 1986: 8). To my knowledge, this is not said in the classical Sanskrit literature, but it tallies perfectly with the following preliminary outline of the prototypical structure of the creation myth:

Lord
↓
Demiurge/Trickster
↓
Goddess
↓
Triad

I will return to this scheme later. I have chosen the word 'demiurge' for the 'son' of the Lord, because it can mean a subordinate creator of the world and even the author of evil. Of course, the role of creator can be taken over by any being on the four 'levels' indicated in the scheme above, as we have seen, but the ambivalent character is typical only of him.

Whereas the figures of Goddess and Triad (and usually the attempted incest) are essential to the myth, the Lord and the Demiurge are not manifest in all versions. However, they are met with in all three regions. In (a3) the Goddess is created by her 'grandfather' Ādijambuvu, and in (a2) her elder brother is Kṛṣṇa. The snake in (a1) is probably not a biblical motif, as Ramanujan thinks, but a theriomorph figure of Viṣṇu: the snake behaves like a trickster and, moreover, is related to the two realms of heaven and underworld, as Viṣṇu is. We have seen that, whether the trickster/demiurge is more a Shaivite or a Vaishnavite god tends to depend on the character of the Lord: the two figures must be complementary. The Shaivite and Vaishnavite forms of the 'son' are, however, not exactly symmetrical, and Nirañjan/Dharma rather stresses the aspect of the demiurge, whereas Nārāyaṇ/Kṛṣṇa appears more like a trickster. Nevertheless, the version from Bangan illustrates that Nārāyaṇ too (as 'son' of the Lord of the World) can be engaged in the business of creating and establishing the world. And the trickster-like aspect of Nirañjan becomes apparent where he is described as the creator of *bhavajāla*, 'the snares of the world'.

The rather gloomy nature of Nirañjan is probably responsible for his occasional identification with the epic and Purāṇic Dharma Rāja, that is, Yama, the god of the dead, 'the first ever to die' (F. Bhattacarya 1994: 347, 350). F. Bhattacarya formulates the god's other aspects in the following way: 'he is a superior form of the Creator' (1994: 346); he 'is present both at the beginning and at the end of a cosmic cycle, as also at the birth and at the death of individuals' (1994: 347); and, very important, he deals with his devotees in an 'ambivalent way' (1994: 353).

* * *

Especially the Dharma Das branch of the modern Kabīr panth has a rich cosmology based on the same creation myth. Here is a brief summary of the three-page version published by Keay (1995: 135-7):

(d3):
Sat Puruṣ, 'the true being', is the highest Lord. He creates six emanations (or Brahmans) *sahaj, omkar, akṣar,* etc.[21] Out of *akṣar* emanates an egg, and out of the egg a terrible being named Nirañjan emerges.[22] Nirañjan (also called *Kāl Puruṣ,* with *Kāl* meaning 'time' or 'black') obtains from

Sat Puruṣ the boon that he will rule the three worlds. A tortoise holds the material for the creation. A fight ensues between the tortoise and the demiurge. Nirañjan cuts off sixteen of the tortoise's heads, and the sun, the moon and the other necessary materials are set free. Now *Sat Puruṣ* and Nirañjan fall out with each other, the Lord cuts himself off, and Nirañjan is unable to continue the creation. Therefore, the Lord creates for him the Ādyā (Śakti). She gives birth to the Triad, and thereafter Nirañjan becomes invisible as well. Ādyā creates three daughters for her three sons. They are, however, drowned in the ocean. The Triad churns the ocean and recovers them again. Brahmā creates the present world and people start to worship the Triad. As a sort of countermeasure, their mother again creates three women, who are the originators of music and singing.

The myth continues describing how the saviour Kabīr helps people to escape the snatches of Nirañjan and reach the *Sat Puruṣ*. Then follows a description of the great deluge, which takes place as an exact reversal of creation, and which will be followed by the next creation, when Nirañjan again will 'spread out the creation on the back of the Tortoise' (Keay 1995: 137).[23] In this version the theme of incest is subdued, but the repeated creation of the three 'daughters' of Ādyā strongly reminds one of the repeated creation of the Triad in (a1) and (a2).

Here one is amazed at the sharp polarization between Lord and demiurge, which does not seem to be widely known outside the Kabīr panth.[24] On the other hand, we have seen that sometimes the two seem barely distinguishable. Thus, it is hardly surprising to observe a good deal of confusion in the interpretation and understanding of Nirañjan.

Hazariprasad Dvivedi has named the fifth chapter of his book on Kabīr, 'Who is Nirañjan?'[25] He raises this question because he observes the following: in the middle ages, especially in the surroundings of the Nāths, Nirañjan first was regarded as 'the highest principle' (*param tattva*), and his realization was the highest state (*nirañjan kā sākṣātkār hī param pad*). Later on, however, a great misfortune (*baṛī durgatī*) occurred to Nirañjan in the Kabīr panth, because he was made into a full-fledged devil (*Nirañjan vahāṁ pakkā śaitān banā diyā gayā hai*) (Dvivedi 1960: 53-4). However, taking into consideration what we have learned from our creation myth, this is not at all surprising. Dvivedi was not aware of the fact that he was not describing a change in the nature of a god, but that he was touching on an Indian tradition in which a Lord of the Universe was distinguished from a demiurge—distinguished, however, not always very sharply. This confusion was also due to the fact that both could (or can) be addressed with the same name.

In the tradition of the Nāth Yogis and the Sants the demiurge, the creator of the *bhavajāla*, 'the snares of the world', was and is valued very negatively and occasionally even identified with Yama, the lord of the dead (Dvivedi 1960: 64). The same identification (but without this negative assessment) is also found, as already pointed out, among the followers of Nirañjan/Dharma in Bengal.[26] All this seems to almost suggest a world-view in which this world is the realm of death, and the other world the realm of life.

Other Kabīr-panthi texts which contain close variants of the above-sketched cosmogony, are, for instance, the *Kabīr-i-manśūr* (an account of Kabīr's life and 'a manual of theology of the Kabīr Panth' written in 1887 in Urdu [Keay 1995:131]) and the *Nirañjan Bodh.* Both describe Nirañjan in very negative terms. The *Kabīr-i-manśūr* says that Nirañjan, *alias Kāl Puruṣ,* is a very terrible, ardent and arrogant being (Dvivedi 1960: 54: *durdamanīya kālpuruṣ nirañjan . . . yā kālpuruṣ baṛā pracaṇḍ, abhimānī aur pratāpī huā*), and according to the *Nirañjan Bodh* he is 'terrible in appearance' (Keay 1995: 127). When Ādyā Śakti, the Triad and the world are created, Nirañjan disappears, but tells the Goddess before that she should not disclose his existence to the Triad (Dvivedi 1960: 55).

A very similar version of the myth current in the Dāmā Kheṛā monastery in Chattisgarh is quoted by Varma (1972: 68-71). The noteworthy points of deviation from (d3) are: When *Sat Puruṣ* has created the six Brahmās, they are supposed to create worlds, but all fail (cp. [c3]). He sends the Brahmā *Akṣar* asleep, and when he wakes up again an egg is floating on the ocean (see p. 219 the tradition of the Bauls), out of which the haughty Nirañjan emerges. Then *Sat Puruṣ* creates the woman Māyā, who falls in love with him, but finally agrees to unite with Nirañjan. The Triad is born and Nirañjan becomes invisible. Māyā indicates Brahmā her incestual desire which he rejects, etc.

Thus, here also we have the 'classical' scheme of Lord—Demiurge—Goddess—Triad, and Nirañjan's above-mentioned withdrawal (b2 [2], b4). The 'confusion' between Nirañjan as Lord and as demiurge has also been noticed by Dwyer: 'In other sects more or less contemporary with Kabīr *niranjan* is seen variously as something akin to the demiurge of the Gnostic sects, playing a subordinate role in creation' (1981: 111). But instead of considering the historical dimensions (after all, the sinister Nirañjan is also mentioned in early texts of the Kabīr panth) Dwyer tries to 'solve' the problem with arguments of textual criticism: 'Kabir . . . true to his chameleonlike habit of adopting terms according to changing contexts, simply called God *niranjan*' (1981: 111f.). And, 'I do not think it likely that Kabir would have used a technical term like *niranjan* in contradictory senses and hence where it is found in the meaning of the god of death I would suspect the authenticity of the reading' (ibid.).

Apart from the fact that I am not really sure that Kabīr could never take the liberty to make contradictory statements, Dwyer's argument, of course, depends on his central notion of 'authenticity' (1981: 273-80).[27]

For our purposes, however, it suffices to show that the myth (which describes the creation of life and of death), together with the concept of the demiurge, is also found in the Sant tradition. Here are two quotations from earlier sources. The first is a *śabd* from the *Kabīrvāṇī* found in Dvivedī (1960: 59):

avadhu niranjana jal pasāra /
svarga-pātāla-jīva-mṛta maṇḍala tīna loka bistāra //

The yogi Nirañjan cast the net /
he spread the spheres of heaven and underworld, of life and death, and the three worlds //

The other passage is the rather allegorical *śabd* 114 from the *Bījak*:

ādi puruṣa ika vṛccha hai nirañjana dāra ho /
tiri deva sākhā bhaye patta saṁsāra ho //

The primeval man is a tree, Nirañjan is his branches /
the three gods became its twigs, its leaves are the worldly illusion //

This second verse is also found in the *Kabīr Granthāvalī* (*Pad* 152.1-4), where instead of *nirañjana* the word *yama* 'god of the dead' is used!

* * *

A recapitulation: This Indian myth about the creation of death and life displays a striking structural stability over a sizeable geographical area and a significant period of time. It does not seem to appear in tribal traditions, and it is only very loosely connected with classical Sanskrit texts. This does not tally with the standard concepts of a pan-Indian great tradition interacting with regional little traditions. However, Blackburn and Ramanujan (1986: 19) have pointed out 'the possibility that local, folk traditions need not be derived from a great tradition, nor be independent of each other, as is often assumed'. Moreover, I do not think that the often-stressed opposition between oral and written transmission is of great relevance in our context, although Dimock has suggested (1966: 198) a succession of oral → written → oral, etc., in case of the Bengali Mansā-*maṅgals*. Except in the case of the Himachali versions, which seem to suggest a borrowing from eastern India, both the local/genetic origin as well as the historical connections and influences between the various 'centres' of this myth presently remain obscure.[28] But at least in northern India there seem to be close connections between the myth and ascetic orders like Vairāgis, Nāths, and the followers of Kabīr. Directly after the myth's performance at the Blāj fair in some places in Himachal Pradesh,

Vairāgis appear and present plays (Joshi 1911: 270), and the bards who sing the 'Saying of the Lord' in western Garhwal, also exhibit a number of features strongly suggesting old connections with the Nāths (Zoller, forthcoming).

We have seen that in many regional traditions this myth is employed as an instrument in order to universalize regional deities. Moreover, Sax and Ramanujan stress the myth's connection with gender issues and the concept of counterdiscourses. However, it may be sometimes difficult to connect the contents of myths, which are widely removed from the sphere of everyday experience of the communities, with social issues and conflicts. Nevertheless, these are important perspectives, because they show how people 'make sense' out of such myths. However, we should not forget that the opposite of this perspective is relevant as well. McDowell (in Bauman and Briggs 1990: 63) has stressed the fact that it is indeed just the *suppression* of a (direct) referential function that makes myths 'efficacious'.

I want to suggest here that all the variants of the creation myth are variants of one prototype. In Holenstein's sense, a prototype is not an 'emic' invariant unit (Hiiemäe and Krikmann 1992: 134), but an *optimal representative* within the group it belongs to (Holenstein 1985: 194). This optimal representative is surrounded by variants up to a periphery which cannot be exactly demarcated. This concept differs from that of the polythetic groups insofar as here the members belonging to a prototypical group must not always share many characteristic features (ibid.). According to Holenstein, it is not necessary that a prototype coincide with a realized or actual form; it can also be an *ideal type* both in the sense of 'optimal' and 'unreal'. In such cases it is a mental or theoretical construct which combines all characteristic features, features which in reality always only appear in varying combinations (Holenstein 1985: 204).

The construction of the following prototype is mainly based on a limited number of secondary sources. Therefore, it is preliminary and may have to be modified in the future. Not all the versions mention a progenitor of the Goddess or a Lord and a demiurge. But in all three regions variants do exist which mention a creator of the Goddess, and in any case have we seen that the Goddess is in all the variants said to have *come into existence.*

Since, however, the Goddess is not always created by the demiurge, but can also be his 'sister' ([d2] and the Chattisgarh version of [d3]), it seems better to characterize the myth's prototype as consisting of two essential triads (to which more Triads might be added):

(1) Lord – Demiurge/Trickster – Goddess
(2) Brahmā – Viṣṇu – Śiva

The two triads of the prototype realize two distinct steps of creation:

the first is characterized by parthenogenesis, where the 'child' is a 'shadow' or 'phantom' or emerges out of a 'pupil of the eye', and the second is characterized by a more or less overt or covert sexual (and inevitably incestuous) creation, where the children emerge from 'balls': thus the Triad emerges from eggs, jars, lumps, or a fist. In the first Triad, there is no sharp generational differentiation between the three actors. On the other hand, the members of the Triad are always the children of the Goddess (and the demiurge) and they only can take over and continue the work of creation (after undergoing some test). The fulcrum of both the triangles is the Goddess, who is created asexually, but who creates sexually.

These two steps of creation resemble the Hindu concept of the *yugas*, according to which reproduction in the first *yugas* happened asexually, and reproduction became sexual only later on (Parry 1989: 496f.). An important difference between this concept of the *yugas* and the creation myth, however, is, that in the former the process of creation and the 'arrow of time' follow an unidirectional (and cyclical) 'downward'-movement, with destruction following creation after the completion of one cycle of four ages. The myth describes a much more original or basic reality: there does not yet exist a unidirectional temporal movement. Consequently, the Goddess can turn back towards her creator or forward towards her sons in order to carry out a creative sexual act—but she also can be the 'sister' of the creator god. Moreover, non-sexual acts of creation can *follow* sexual acts (see [a2]). Another consequence of this 'pre-temporal' level is the tendency to separate actor and figure. This leads to such apparent paradoxes as Śiva's creation of the Triad. And this has also forced me to characterize deities as 'more Shaivite' or 'more Vaishnavite'.

The essential structure of this myth, the pair of triangles, is expanded in some versions by various types of other Triads. Some of them are repetitions or continuations of the same creative acts: the three 'daughters' of the Goddess, mentioned in (a1) and in the versions from the Kabīr panth, who, like the Triad, can be destroyed and then recreated. Others, like the three eggs in the Tamil versions, the three worlds, or the three animals (owl, swan, tortoise) created in the beginning (a2), appear rather to have a conventional background.

Without trying to be exhaustive, let me suggest some ways how the oppositions of sexual *v.* asexual generation and sexual *v.* asexual relationship are structured in this myth.

(*a*) An actual act of incest can happen only between actors who have been created asexually. Or, in other words: either asexual generation and sexual relationship or sexual generation and asexual relationship. The first variant we have in the first Triad. There we see that after incest the initiator of that act dies/disappears/commits suicide or at least wishes to do so. If the initiator is a god, he disappears; if it is the Goddess, and if she kills herself, she is reborn. (If incest is not actually committed, then the introduction of death is connected with the second Triad.)

(*b*) In case of the second Triad, we have asexual generation ('egg'-type), and in several versions the expression of desire for an incestuous act. But in *no* version does incest actually take place between the Goddess and (any of) her children. Thus, we have here rather a reversal to the situation in the first Triad, because the *refusal* to commit incest leads here to death. The Goddess can only become 'wife' after she and her children have been burned to ashes and resuscitated. It is only after such a 'desexualization' that the Goddess as Pārvatī can become the wife of Śiva.

CONCLUSION

This myth of the creation of life and death deals, I think, with some central themes of Hindu civilization in a highly concentrate language. It is based on a simple symmetrical structure, which is the reason for its striking stability. It suggests a mirror-image concept of creation and destruction, where cremation ground and 'creation ground' collapse into one (see Parry 1994: 11-15).

The creation of the universe, however, does not start off with a pristine innocence, but, right from the beginning, with fatigue and guilt, with decline and death. A most dramatic embodiment of this mythical theodicy is the figure of the demiurge. In his most sinister aspects, where he comes close to Yama, the king of the dead, he, the ruler of the universe, appears to be presiding over a 'vale of death', thus suggesting that this world is not the realm of life but that of death. The figure of the demiurge and the myth of the creation of death and life appear to belong to non-dominant religious cults. But their frequent occurrence nevertheless shows that they are neither obscure nor absurd, nor peripheral phenomena.

NOTES

1. In the latter part of this paper I will show that the myth's variants are all more or less complete realizations of an ideal *prototype* (in the sense both of 'optimal' and 'unreal'). The notions 'structure' and 'sense' here mean almost the same, because the myth's variants clearly show that they cannot vary at random. Therefore, the 'sense' or the 'meaning' the myth expresses must be in some way identical with its formal linguistic structures.
2. Some versions indicate connections with the demon king Bali or with folk versions of the *Mahābhārata* (see below).

3. This Folk Purāṇa is sung by a group of specialists on 'special days (pilgrimages and occasions)' (Ramanujan 1993: 106). As in the Sanskritic Purāṇas, the creation myth appears right in the beginning.
4. Compare (a2) and (d3).
5. Water and light as primeval substances are also known in the Bengali Baul tradition (Salomon 1991: 282).
6. 'Sunyapuran (Bengali) is an interesting but semiobscure poem propagating a peculiar religious cult of medieval Bengal associated with Dharma worship. The poem, composed not earlier than the sixteenth century, is known after Ramai Pandit who is considered the incarnation of Dharma himself' (Mahapatra 1992: 4086f.). Regarding the Dharma cult see Dasgupta 1969: 259-310 and F. Bhattacarya 1994: 345-62, and regarding the cult of Manasā see Maity 1966.
7. For example, 'vital air', 'compassion', 'illusion', etc. Cp. below version (d3).
8. These are, of course, two closely related concepts. Both can be said to mean that Nirañjan is 'the active form of the Supreme' (Salomon 1991: 284).
9. Similar to Doniger (1975: 275).
10. The Ādi Śakti is said to be Gaurī, Pārvatī, Durgā or Umā in Bengal (see above and below) and in Garhwal (see below). In Tamil Nadu she can be called Umā and Pārvatī (Meyer 1986: 6ff.); and Aṅkalā is said to be Pārvatī, daughter of Parvatarājan (Himalaya) (Meyer 1986: 34).
11. The Goddess' name is perhaps a variant of Ketakā, an epithet of the snake-goddess Manasā (Maity 1966: 203).
12. The same idea is expressed with similar imagery in the creation myth of the *Ḍhol Sāgar*, 'Ocean of the Drum', a text used by Garhwali bards. It deals with the mystical dimensions of their drums, but it too is rooted in Nāth traditions (Catak 1973: 72). About creation it says that Nirākār Gosaiṁ or Ādi Gusaiṁ creates Śiva (*Bhola*) by rubbing his brow and Pārvatī by rubbing his foot (Catak 1973: 73).
13. The festival's name derives from Sanskrit *Bali Rājā* 'king Bali'. A not very clear connection between the creation myth and king Bali is also mentioned in (a1), (a3) and (c3). King Bali's attempt to have intercourse with Pārvatī (Ramanujan 1993: 102) may be compared with the myth cycle of Nandā Devī/Pārvatī, where the buffalo demon Mahiṣāsura tries to achieve the same goal with the same goddess (Sax 1991: 128-35).
14. I am very grateful to him that he has allowed me to see and quote some of his unpublished notes.
15. Of an eye.
16. The pupil may be an 'alloform' for the egg, out of which she is sometimes said to be born.
17. Bangan is a sort of 'goddess-free zone', that is, there are practically no Devī shrines in the area. The reasons and the historical background for this unusual phenomenon are described by me elsewhere (Zoller forthcoming a).
18. However, there is only innuendo about her incestuous desire in this song.
19. In another part of the song it is mentioned that the Lord asks the Triad to find a base where the earth created by him can be safely placed. As in other

versions from Bengal and Himachal Pradesh, mentioned above, Brahmā and Viṣṇu fail and are condemned by the Lord.

20. In my habilitation thesis I am dealing in more detail with the links between the creation myth and the *Paṇḍuaṇ*. In this regional *Mahābhārata* the Pāṇḍavas are connected with immortality and the Kauravas with death, and they continue to vary in ever new ways the great themes of life and death which are seminally formulated in the creation myth.
21. The various emanations (Brahmans) seem to be due to Sufi influences (Keay 1995: 139). See also note 7.
22. Compare the above-mentioned Baul tradition of Nirañjan floating in an egg.
23. Compare this with the Bangani myth above, where Nārāyaṇa places the earth together with the world pillar on the back of the kneeling giant 'tortoise'.
24. Gold (1987: 97) says that the Kabir-panthis homologize the universe and the human head, and 'The head is the seat of Niranjan, as Kabirpanthis often call the (negative) principle of "mind", conceived as a demigod'.
25. *Nirañjan kaun hai*?
26. It hardly needs to be stressed that the mythologies of Nirañjan and Yama/ Dharma Rāja actually have nothing in common.
27. For a down-to-earth assessment of how few of the texts can be attributed with some certaiṇty to Kabir see Vaudeville (1993: 131ff.).
28. As long as no exhaustive stocktaking of this myth exists, my identification of the three main areas has to remain hypothetical and preliminary.

REFERENCES

Bauman, Richard and Charles L. Briggs. 1990. Poetics and Performance as Critical Perspectives on Language and Social Life. In *Annual Review of Anthropology* 19: 59-88.

Bhattacharyya, Asutosh. 1977. *The Sun and the Serpent Lore of Bengal.* Calcutta: Firma K.L. Mukhopadhyay.

———. 1978. *Folklore of Bengal.* New Delhi: National Book Trust.

Bhattacharya, France. 1994. The God Dharma, Human Sacrifice and *Bhakti* in the Dharma Maṅgal. In Alan W. Entwistle and Françoise Mallison (eds.), *Studies in South Asian Devotional Literature.* Research Papers, 1988-91 presented at the Fifth Conference on Devotional Literature in New Indo-Aryan Languages, held at Paris - École Française d'Extrême-Orient. New Delhi: Manohar, Paris: École Française d'Extrême-Orient.

Blackburn, S.H. and A.K. Ramanujan (eds.). 1986. *Another Harmony: New Essays on the Folklore of India.* Berkeley: University of California Press.

Cātak, Govind. 1973. *Gaṛvālī Lokgāthāeṁ.* Dehradun: Pratibha Prakashan.

Dasgupta, Shashibhushan. 1969 (1946). *Obscure Religious Cults.* Calcutta: Firma K.L. Mukhopadhyay.

Dimock, Edward, J., Jr. 1989 (1966). *The Place of the Hidden Moon: Erotic Mysticism in the Vaiṣṇava-Sahajiyā Cult of Bengal.* Chicago: University of Chicago Press.

Doniger, Wendy. 1975. *Asceticism and Eroticism in the Mythology of Śiva.* Delhi: Oxford University Press.

———. 1980a. *Women, Androgynes, and other Mythical Beasts.* Chicago: University of Chicago Press.

———. 1980b. *Karma and Rebirth in Classical Indian Traditions.* Berkeley: University of California Press.

———.1981. *Sexual Metaphors and Animal Symbols in Indian Mythology.* Delhi: Motilal Banarsidass.

———.1982 (1975). *Hindu Myths: A Sourcebook Translated from the Sanskrit.* Harmondsworth: Penguin.

———. 1984 (1981). *The Rig Veda: An Anthology.* Harmondsworth: Penguin.

———. 1993. *Purāṇa Perennis. Reciprocity and Transformation in Hindu and Jaina Texts.* Albany: State University of New York Press.

Dvivedi, Hazariprasad. 1960. *Kabīr: Kabīr ke vyaktitva, sāhitya aur dārśanik vicāroṁ.* Bambaī: Hindī-Granth-Ratnākar.

Dwyer, William J. 1981. *Bhakti in Kabir.* Patna: Associated Book Agency.

Eliade, Mircea. 1970 (1958). *Yoga: Immortality and Freedom.* Princeton: Princeton University Press.

Eliade, Mircea (chief editor). 1987. *The Encyclopedia of Religion.* Vol. 4. New York: Macmillan.

Feher, Michel, Ramona Naddaff and Nadia Tazi (eds.) 1990 (1989). *Fragments for a History of the Human Body.* Part II. New York: Zone.

Gold, Daniel. 1987. *The Lord as Guru. Hindi Sants in North Indian Tradition.* New York, Oxford: Oxford University Press.

Holenstein, Elmar. 1985. *Sprachliche Universalien. Eine Untersuchung zur Natur des menschlichen Geistes.* Bochum: Brockmeyer.

Joshi, Pandit Tika Ram. 1911. Notes on the Ethnography of the Bashahar State, Simla Hills, Punjab. *Journal of the Asiatic Society of Bengal.* September 1911: 525-613.

Keay, F.E. 1995 (1931). *Kabir and his Followers.* New Delhi: Mittal Publications.

Kuiper, F.B.J. 1983. *Ancient Indian Cosmogony.* Essays selected and introduced by John Irvin. Delhi: Vikas Publishing House.

Lincoln, Bruce. 1986. *Myth, Cosmos, and Society: Indo-European Themes of Creation and Destruction.* Cambridge: Cambridge University Press.

Mahapatra, P.K. 1972. *The Folk Cults of Bengal.* Calcutta: Indian Publications.

Mahapatra, T.S. 1992. *Encyclopedia of Indian Literature* (chief editor Mohan Lal), Vol. V. New Delhi: Sahitya Akademy.

Maity, Pradyot Kumar. 1966. *Historical Studies in the Cult of the Goddess Manasā. A Socio-Cultural Study.* Calcutta: Punthi Pustak.

Meyer, Eveline. 1986. *Aṅkāḷaparamēcuvari: a goddess of Tamilnadu; her myths and cult.* Wiesbaden: Steiner.

Oppert, Gustav. 1893. *On the Original Inhabitants of Bharatavarṣa or India.* Westminster: Constable.

Parry, Jonathan. 1989. The End of the Body. In Michel Feher, Ramona Naddaff and Nadia Tazi (eds.), *Fragments for a History of the Human Body.* Part II. New York: Zone, pp. 491-517.

———. 1994. *Death in Banaras.* New Delhi: Cambridge University Press.

Ramanujan, A.K. 1986. Introduction. In Stuart H. Blackburn and A.K. Ramanujan (eds.), *Another Harmony: New Essays on the Folklore of India.* Berkeley: University of California Press, pp. 1-37.

———. 1993. On Folk Mythologies and Folk Purāṇas. In Wendy Doniger (ed.), *Purāṇa Perennis. Reciprocity and Transformation in Hindu and Jaina Texts.* Albany: State University of New York Press.

Ranchan, Som P. and Justa, H.R. 1981. *Folk Tales of Himachal Pradesh.* Bombay: Bharatiya Vidya Bhavan.

Salomon, Carol. 1991. The Cosmogonic Riddles of Lalan Fakir. In Arjun Appadurai, Frank J. Korom, and Margaret A. Mills (eds), *Gender, Genre, and Power in South Asian Expressive Traditions.* Philadelphia: University of Pennsylvania Press.

Sax, William. 1991. *Mountain Goddess: Gender and Politics in a Himalayan Pilgrimage.* New York: Oxford University Press.

Sharma, B.R. 1993. Impact of the *Mahābhārata* on Folk and Tribal Culture of Himachal Pradesh. In K.S. Singh (ed.), *Mahābhārata in the Tribal and Folk Traditions of India.* Shimla: Indian Institute of Advanced Study, and New Delhi: Anthropological Survey of India.

Sharma 'Vyathit', Gautam. 1991 (1984). *Folklore of Himachal Pradesh.* Translated by Mrinal Pande. New Delhi: National Book Trust.

Shulman, David. 1979. Murukaṉ, the Mango and Ekāmbeśvara-Śiva. Fragments of a Tamil Creation Myth? *Indo Iranian Journal* 21: 27-40.

Vaudeville, Charlotte. 1993. *A Weaver named Kabir. Selected Verses with a Detailed Biographical and Historical Introduction.* Delhi: Oxford University Press.

Whitehead, Henry. 1921. *The Village Gods of South India.* Calcutta: Association Press.

Zoller, Claus Peter. 1997. Heroic Ballads and the Biography of a Woman: On Coping with Conflicts in the Western Garhwal Himalayas. In Irmtraud Stellrecht (ed.), *Proceedings-Band.* Mainz (Occasional Papers 3).

———. (forthcoming a). *Himalayan Heroes.*

———. (forthcoming b). *Die Paṇḍuaṇ: Ein mündliches Mahābhārata-Epos aus dem Garhwal-Himalaya.*

Stringing a Necklace of Heads

Sacrifice and Death in the Cult of Devnārāyaṇ[1]

ADITYA MALIK

INTRODUCTORY

Narratives about the Goddess killing a demon are recurrent not only in Sanskrit texts like Purāṇas and Māhātmyas, but also in many local and regional tellings, both written and oral.[2] The core of the story centres around the destruction of a demon or demons who, through the accumulation of supernatural abilities, have upset the balance of power in the universe. Out of all the gods only the Goddess is able to match the demons' potency and restore the cosmic order.[3] The relationship between the Goddess and the demons whom she destroys is not simply one between victor and victim or two warring factions, often there is an underlying quality of eroticism, that is employed to weaken the demon.[4] Sometimes, in a more explicit expression of eroticism, the Goddess *marries* a demon. Thus, for example, during a temple festival dedicated to the Goddess Māriyammaṉ in Kaṉṉapuram in Tamil Nadu, the goddess is wedded to a demon, who at the end of the nine night long ritual proceedings is 'killed'.[5] The myth associated with the ritual somewhat clarifies the reason why the Goddess kills the demon, and explains his erotic feelings towards her. In other contexts eroticism coupled with violence is transformed into intense devotion. The demon's death at the hands of the Goddess results in his conversion and subsequent elevation to the status of a guardian and *bhakta par excellence* of the Goddess.[6] In the *Kālikā Purāṇa*, for example, the buffalo-demon Mahiṣāsura, upon realizing in a dream that he will be beheaded by the Goddess, asks her for two boons: one is a share in the sacrifice, and the other that he remain at her feet forever.[7] The Goddess grants his second wish only, and as is evidenced by splendid miniature paintings and temple reliefs spanning a period of two thousand years, the demon does stay at the Goddess' feet for all time.[8]

In this paper I examine the aforementioned themes of eroticism, sacrifice, and death in the context of the oral epic and cult of Devnārāyaṇ in Rajasthan. There are two broad questions I will raise—one general and the other specific. The more general question is concerned with the idea of death expressed in the narrative: Is death a final, irretrievable, singular event, or is it a constituent element in a series of transmutations and transformations?[9] The other more specific question is concerned about the deaths of the epic's heroes: What is the cause of their death? How do they die? What is the significance of their deaths within the cult in particular and with regard to notions about heroic death in Rajasthan? In the latter context, it is hoped that, on the one hand, while giving a brief outline of the narrative, some parallels with the narrative concerning the Goddess and the demon will become apparent. On the other hand, it is hoped, that certain divergences with respect to the religious ideals of *bhakti*—in particular with regard to the act of 'conversion'[10]—underlying the Purāṇic myth will also become evident.

THE CULT OF DEVNĀRĀYAṆ

The cult of Devnārāyaṇ is one of the most widespread *folk-cults* in Rajasthan. Devnārāyaṇ is worshipped mainly by the pastoral and farming community of the Gūjars, although devotees also belong to members of other communities, such as the Bā̃bhī, Kumahār, and, in some cases, even Rajput. A central element of the cult is the recitation and performance of an oral epic that narrates the life of the deity, and that of his ancestors. Easily one of the longest and most popular oral religious narratives in Rajasthan, the epic is performed by pairs of itinerant singers most often from the Gūjar community,[11] in front of an approximately 8 m long scroll called *paṛ* on which various characters and scenes from the epic are elaborately depicted. Performances always take place at night, usually during nocturnal vigils (*jāgraṇ*) in front of an audience of devotees of Devnārāyaṇ. In addition to reciting episodes from the epic, the singers also dance while playing a stringed instrument (*bīṇ, jantar*) and pointing to sections of the scroll that pictorially correspond to parts of the narrative being told.[12] In fact, the scroll functions as a kind of 'portable temple'[13] In its centre there is an almost life-size representation of Devnārāyaṇ, in front of which a makeshift altar is set up for the duration of the performance. Incense sticks are burnt here and offerings of grain and money are made by devotees throughout the performance.[14]

The epic of Devnārāyaṇ has been classified under the category of 'martial' epics. Such epics are usually 'concerned with power, social obligation, and social unity; they turn on the themes of revenge, regaining lost land, or restoring lost rights . . . (and they) celebrate external—often military or political—conflict and a warrior ethic'. (Blackburn *et al.* 1989: 5). One of the main themes of the epic is the simultaneous kinship and rivalry between Gūjars and Rajputs[15] that is resolved only when Devnārāyaṇ avenges his ancestors' deaths and regains their lost property. The epic has two main parts whose overall thematic and ideological character differs distinctly from one another.[16] The first part called the Bagaṛāvat is about the heroic deeds of twenty-four Gūjar brothers, who are preordained to die at the end of a period of twelve years in a battle against a Rajput chieftain. The second part is about Bhagavān's incarnation as Devnārāyaṇ, the miracles he performs and the revenge he and his four cousins ultimately take on the Rajput chieftain. Whereas the first part is generally said to be marked by suffering (*dukh*), pain, and death, the second is marked by reunion, miracles and divine testimony (*parcyo*). The second part, thus entails a reversal of the first part: death and defeat are followed by birth and creation, finally resulting in the establishment of Devnārāyaṇ's cult amongst his followers.

An important feature of the narrative is that it provides an explanation for various components of Devnārāyaṇ's cult. In other words the narrative tells us why and how the performance came into existence, how the scroll, a lineage of priests and places of worship were created and so on. Epic narrative and cult thus form a self-referential unit. Whereas the cult generates the emergence and re-emergence of the narrative through ritual performance, the narrative legitimizes and explains the emergence and establishment of the cult.

In the following section certain parts of the narrative prior to Devnārāyaṇ's birth are related in summary. After this a discussion of the themes of sacrifice, eroticism, and death will be taken up in the context of the lives, deeds, and deaths of the twenty-four Gūjar heroes.

THE NARRATIVE OF THE BAGAṚĀVATS

The narrative begins at a time when Brahmā is performing a Vedic sacrifice (*jug*)[17] in Pushkar—the famous pilgrim town in the district of Ajmer. Brahmā invites all the gods and Ṛṣis to his sacrifice. Among them is a group of twenty-four Ṛṣis living in the Nāg Pahāḍ, a mountain chain running parallel to Pushkar. The Ṛṣis are disciples of Śaṅkar. Śaṅkar forbids them from attending the sacrifice, but they insist on going because they have received invitations from Brahmā. All of a sudden Śaṅkar grows ravenously hungry. The Ṛṣis suggest he eat the fruits growing in the forest in which they live. But Śaṅkar says this will not satisfy him. He wants more than plain fruit. But what else is available in the forest? There is no cereal or grain either. So what does Śaṅkar do? He turns to his disciples and begins consuming them one after another.[18] After he has eaten them and satiated his hunger, he then visits Brahmā's sacrifice himself. The sacrifice comes to a halt because of the sin Śaṅkar has committed.[19] He asks Brahmā how he should atone for his sin, whereupon Brahmā informs him that the only means would be to offer the Ṛṣis his own body in a future existence, in which the Ṛṣis are to be born as the twenty-four sons of a single father.

The narrative shifts now to a more historical time. It is the reign of King Bisaldev of Ajmer. The populace is being terrorized by a lion that feeds on one individual every night. On one particular night, a Rajput called Hari Rām[20] offers to take the place of a boy whose turn it is to be eaten by the lion. He sets up a trap for the lion and beheads it. Then in order to wash the blood off his sword and to cleanse himself of the sin of slaughter, he goes to the holy lake of Pushkar carrying the lion's head on his shoulder. It is a full moon night (*pūrṇimā*). Exactly at the same time on the opposite bank a Brahman girl who has taken a vow never to see the face of a man is performing ablutions and bathing in the lake. While bathing, she sees the reflection of a man's body with the head of a lion on the surface of the lake, and conceives. She insists that Hari Rām marry her now, but he vacillates saying that such a marriage is not possible because she is a Brahman and he a Kṣatriya. Finally, however, King Bisaldev allows him to marry the Brahman girl. After nine months their son is born. He has the head of a lion and the body of a man, and is named Bāgh Siṃh.[21] Later because of his unusual and fearsome appearance, no one is willing to marry his daughter to him. He lives alone in a garden attended by a Brahman cook. One day on the festival of swings (*ākhā tīj*), a number of young girls of various castes come to the garden attracted by Bāgh Siṃh's silken swing. The Brahman allows them to use the swing on the condition that each of them circumambulate Bāgh Siṃh. While they are doing this, the Brahman performs the necessary engagement rites. Unknowingly they are engaged to Bāgh Siṃh. Later Bāgh Siṃh marries twelve of them. Each of his wives gives birth to two sons who are collectively called the Bagaṛāvats.

The Bagaṛāvats, whose mothers belong to different castes, are all married to Gūjar women. Of the twenty-four Bagaṛāvats, Savāī Bhoj is the most valorous. Each day Savāī Bhoj takes the Bagaṛāvats' cattle herds to graze on the slopes of Nāg Pahāḍ. One of the cows regularly leaves the herd and returns on its own in the evening. One day Savāī Bhoj follows the cow and discovers that it is being milked by the ascetic Rūpnāth. As compensation for milking their cow, Rūpnāth gives Savāī Bhoj a sack full of grain. But the brothers have no use for the small quantity of grain, so they feed it to birds. The next morning, however, they discover that the few grains left sticking to the seam of the sack have turned into gems.[22] They realize their folly and Savāī Bhoj returns to the ascetic to become his disciple. One day Rūpnāth has Savāī Bhoj heat a cauldron of oil and circle it, while he himself follows. While they are circling the cauldron, the ascetic tries pushing Savāī Bhoj into the boiling oil, but Savāī Bhoj leaps over with the help of his cowherd's staff.[23] In the next round Savāī Bhoj follows the ascetic and pushes him into the cauldron. Not so agile, the ascetic falls into the boiling oil. Instantly his body turns into solid gold. While Savāī Bhoj stands there repenting his crime, the ascetic reappears in the hermitage as though nothing had taken place. He explains that the golden image is a gift that will grant the Bagaṛāvats unending wealth for a period of twelve years after which both wealth and life (*māyā-kāyā*) shall come to an end. He also gives Savāī Bhoj the gifts of a mare, a cow, and an elephant, all of which have special powers.[24] Savāī Bhoj returns to his home. The brothers ask Tejājī, the eldest amongst them, what they should do with their newly acquired wealth. Tejājī, whose mother is a Bānyā,[25] advises them to bury the money in the ground and hoard it. Nevājī, one of the youngest brothers, suggests, however, that they do good deeds with the money, i.e. build wells and temples, distribute the wealth and make a name for themselves since both the wealth and their lives will end after twelve years.[26] The brothers choose the latter alternative. Soon their fame spreads far and wide.

In due course they meet their future enemy, the Rajput chieftain of Rāṇ City whose name is Rāṇā (or Rāvjī). The Rāṇā and the Bagaṛāvats become *dharam*-brothers. In an extended drinking session, they overturn jars laden with alcohol onto a hillside flooding the earth to such an extent that the alcohol actually flows down into the kingdom of Basak Nāg, serpent lord of the underworld. Angered, Rājā Basak deposits the Earth temporarily on a bull's horns and goes to Bhagavān's court to complain about the Bagaṛāvats. But neither Basak, nor Hanumān, nor Bhagavān can do anything to remedy the situation because the Bagaṛāvats are so powerful. Finally Bhagavān assumes the form of a mendicant (*jogī*) and visits Sāḍu Mātā, the wife of Savāī Bhoj, begging for alms. Sāḍu, who has just completed performing ablutions and bathing, appears in front of the mendicant covered only by her long tresses. Struck by her devotion, the mendicant (or Bhagavān) grants her a boon. Sāḍu desires that Bhagavān be born as her son. Bhagavān promises to be born as her son on the thirteenth day after the Bagaṛāvats have been killed.

After his return, Bhagavān requests Śakti, who agrees to go to Earth to fulfil the task of destroying the Bagaṛāvats. She manifests herself as an infant girl in a forest where she is discovered by the King of Bhū̃āl, who adopts her. Exactly at the time of her birth, her maidservant Hīrā Dāsī is born in the house of a Mahājan. Śakti grows up unusually fast. And, soon Brahmans are sent out to find a suitable bridegroom for her. She insists that they find someone belonging to a family in which one father has twenty-four sons. After a long and frustrating search the Brahmans find the Bagaṛāvats. They arrange to have the queen married to Savāī Bhoj. But because they already have wives, the Bagaṛāvats suggest that the queen be married to their *dharam*-brother, the Rāṇā. Thus, arrangements are made for the Rāṇā to marry Rāṇī Jaimatī as the queen is called. When the marriage procession sets out, Savāī Bhoj instead of the Rāṇā, leads it. In the meanwhile Rāṇī Jaimatī orders the *toraṇ*[27] to be hung in a high place that the Rāṇā, who is old and feeble[28] cannot reach up to. Instead of the

Rāṇā, Savāī Bhoj strikes down the *toraṇ*. When the marriage procession arrives, the queen pretends she has high fever. She asks her maidservant to bring Savāī Bhoj's sword that is supposed to have healing powers. In the inner chambers of the palace she then circles the sword, thereby secretly marrying Sāvāī Bhoj. In public, however, she marries the Rāṇā. At the end of the ceremonies, when she is to accompany the Rāṇā to her new home, she insists on staying with the Bagaṛāvats. The Bagaṛāvats coax her into going with the Rāṇā, promising to fetch her after a period of six months. Upon arriving in the Rāṇā's palace, however, the queen says she will not play dice[29] with the Rāṇā till he has constructed a new palace for her. The construction of the palace, of course, takes a long time, and six months are soon over. In the meanwhile, the Bagaṛāvats—even against the advice of their wives—prepare to fetch the queen. The queen elopes with the Bagaṛāvats. The Rāṇā is patient, advising the Bagaṛāvats in a brotherly manner to send the queen back to him. But, the Bagaṛāvats stick to their decision. Finally, the Rāṇā gathers together the armies of fifty-two[30] forts on the banks of the Khārī river. Bhavānī, who now has assumed her true form, promises to accompany the Bagaṛāvats only on the condition if they fight the Rāṇā's army one at a time. She also demands that the brothers offer their heads to her. The Bagaṛāvats willingly agree to her grotesque demands. A great war[31] is fought on account of Rāṇī Jaimatī (or Bhavānī). In the battle some of the brothers continue fighting even after their heads have been severed by the Goddess' discus. But in the end all of them are slain and the Rāṇā is victorious. The Goddess assumes her awesome, terrifying form. Amidst the corpses of slain warriors, she squats on the battle ground, dripping with blood, stringing a necklace of the Bagaṛāvats' heads. After their deaths, the heroes' wives with the exception of Savāī Bhoj's wife, Sāḍu Mātā, commit *satī*. Sāḍu Mātā begins severe *tapas* on a hill near the battlefield. After eleven days, when her honour and life is about to be threatened by the Rāṇā, she calls out to Bhagavān, who has promised to be born as her son. Devnārāyaṇ, who is playing a game of dice at the time with Rājā Basak, lord of the underworld, rises up on a stream of water that splits apart the rock on which Sāḍu is seated. Borne on that jet of water in a lotus blossom, the infant Devnārāyaṇ falls into Sāḍu Mātā's lap.

At this juncture the second part of the epic begins.

CONCEPTIONS OF DEATH, MARRIAGE AND EROTICISM

The first point to be discussed is the manner in which death is conceived of in the narrative. There are four instances in which death occurs. In each case it is violent and premature. In the very first instance, the twenty-four Ṛṣis die on account of being eaten alive by Śiva. But this leads to their rebirth in a future life as the twenty-four children of the man-lion, Bāgh Siṃh. Bāgh Siṃh, himself is born as a result of his father's having slain a marauding lion, and encountering the Brahman woman in Puṣkara. His twenty-four sons, the Bagaṛāvats, accrue wealth and fame from the body of the ascetic who has fallen into the cauldron of boiling oil—and presumably dies. Finally, the brothers' death at the hands of the Goddess is coupled with the birth and incarnation of Devnārāyaṇ. In each of the examples violent death is coupled with a creative act either in the form of offspring, wealth and fame, or, in fact, God himself.[32] It appears that a *particular kind* of death is never the end, but a point in a cycle of transmutations and transformations: the twenty-four Ṛṣis become the twenty-four Bagaṛāvats; the slain lion lends shape to the figure of the man-lion, Bāgh Siṃh; the body of the ascetic Rūpnāth turns into a source of unending wealth and prosperity for his disciples; and the brothers' own death is connected with the manifestation of Bhagavān. Thus, it seems as though the 'goods of life'—children, prosperity and fame, divinity itself, are to be churned out of the power released by extraordinary and violent forms of physical cessation.[33]

The second interconnected point is that marital liaisons on the whole are a tricky if not fatal business. All throughout the narrative marriages are the result of either accident or deceit. The marriage between Hari Rām, the Rajput, and the Brahman girl, for example, is the result of an unintentional coincidence. The marriage between Bāgh Siṃh and his twelve wives is unintentional on the part of his wives, but involves deceit on the part of Bāgh Siṃh or rather his Brahman caretaker. The Goddess too, secretly marries Savāī Bhoj by means of a ploy. Their covert marriage finally results in the destruction of the Bagaṛāvats.

Perhaps one reason for the deceit and danger underlying these instances, is the fact that the marriages are between 'unequals', transgressing both the social hierarchy and the hierarchy of beings. Thus, Hari Rām is Rajput and his wife Brahman.[34] Bāgh Siṃh is semi-divine, but his wives are human representing various different caste groups; and, lastly, the Goddess is divine whereas her lover, Savāī Bhoj, is a mortal. Like in the instances of 'violent death', the transgression or 'violence' done to social and natural hierarchy through marriage, once again results in the extraordinary:[35] the birth of Bāgh Siṃh; the birth of the Bagaṛāvats; and finally also the deification of Savāī Bhoj after he has sacrificed himself to his secret spouse, Bhavānī.

The third point is that if we look at the broad pattern of the narrative, it should be clear that it matches the myth about the Goddess and the demon on certain important points. To begin with the Bagaṛāvats' great power and unending wealth is the product of a boon or gift given to them by Śiva on account of their act of extreme sacrifice performed in a previous existence in which they were Ṛṣis. Their deeds of heroic abandon, quintessentially symbolized by the incident in which they pour streams of alcohol onto the Earth's surface and down into the underworld angering Rājā Basak, are similar to those of misbehaving demons. As in the case of demons a complaint regarding their misbehaviour reaches Bhagavān or Viṣṇu, and since various gods are unwilling or unable to destroy the Bagaṛavāts, Bhagavān requests Śakti, who is given the task of killing them. Śakti or Bhavānī succeeds in doing this by taking incarnation as a king's daughter, causing the Bagaṛāvats and the Rajput chieftain to go to war on account of her. She does not kill the Bagaṛāvats outright, but deceives them into getting killed. The means she uses to incite the factions against one another are those of love and marriage, allowing each group to believe that she belongs exclusively to one of them. In reality, however, she makes certain that neither marriage is actually consummated.[36] Thus, during the six months spent with the Rāṇā she refuses to play 'dice' with him, till he has built a new palace for her. And, once she joins the Bagaṛāvats she immediately instigates the quarrel between them and the Rāṇā in which they all die, once again avoiding intimate contact.[37]

THE HEROES' SACRIFICE

It is important also to remember that the Goddess lays down conditions for the Bagaṛāvats, promising to accompany them into battle[38] only if they fulfil the conditions. But, paradoxically the conditions she lays down demand their own destruction. In other words the Goddess will remain with them only if they die. But then they are dead, so how can she stay with them? Perhaps the answer to this question can be found in the cult that has originated about the figure of Savāī Bhoj. In one of the main temples where he is worshipped, there is an image of the Goddess adjacent to his. She remains with him posthumously, so to speak, after he has become a 'hero-deity' (*jhūjhār*).[39] Beneath the overt theme of marrying the queen, there appears to lie a tussle for possession of the Goddess. Ultimately, she belongs only to those who give up their lives for her. The Bagaṛāvats' willingness to go through with the Goddess' demands is tantamount to an act of voluntary self-sacrifice. In a sense this is in continuation of the first episode in which the twenty-four Ṛṣis offer their own bodies to satisfy Śiva's hunger. Unlike in the case of demons, the Bagaṛāvats do not *become* steadfast devotees of Śiva or the Goddess. There is no conversion here, since they are prior to their deaths, already great *bhaktas*.[40] Thus, in contrast to the Purāṇic myth in which the demon is slain because of his arrogance and defiance of the gods' powers, the heroes, in some sense, *choose* to die.

THE MEANING OF THE HEROES' DEATHS

What, then, is the specific meaning of their deaths in this particular context? It appears that the meaning of their deaths cannot be found in connotations related to the simple termination of body or ego, but in the ritual symbolism of offering or gift (*dān*)—an image central not only to this narrative, but many others in Rajasthan.[41] For example, in the story of Jagdev Pũvār,[42] who offers his head on a platter to the Goddess or in the case of the epics of Tejājī and Pābūjī whose heroes both fulfil the Goddess's demands to the point of destroying themselves. The heroes' deaths, are thus linked to the idea and practice of self-sacrifice as an ultimate offering to the deity, and to the notion of battle as sacrificial arena.[43] Moreover, the *voluntary* nature of their deaths, approaches the ideal of a 'good death'[44] typically embodied by the ascetic who renounces gross, physical existence from the time of initiation. To sum up: the heroes' deaths incorporate two seemingly opposed notions: (1) violence, and the relinquishment of control (implying chaos, and a 'bad death'), and (2) choice, self-sacrifice and renunciation (implying order, and a 'good death'). Both these features are concomitant with widespread notions of the heroic found in Rajasthan. Thus, many major and minor narrative traditions dealing with women and men whose deaths are connected with battle naturally have a violent, but also sacrificial component. Furthermore, the particular structure of epic narratives like those of Devnārāyaṇ and Pābūjī, are deeply informed by the central role of the Goddess, who inspires, motivates, and directs the heroes' actions, while simultaneously arranging and demanding their destruction as a singularly awesome token of devotion.[45]

CONCLUSION

Two interrelated perspectives on the meaning of death emerge from the foregoing discussion of the narrative and cult of Devnārāyaṇ.

The first perspective relates to the more universal issue of the continuity of human life, and the social and religious construction of death. In the narrative we find that incidents of death are coupled with rebirth, transformation, and regeneration. The latter provide a means of encompassing disjuncture and physical termination within a framework of continuity and flow. The various incidents of death involving the twenty-four brothers, the ascetic, and the lion all have a marked aetiological dimension. In fact, they all bear a causal function that provides the narrative with a series of specific linkages that move through different time-cycles, generations, and lives. There are no terminal points, no absolute endings, no final tragedies. Ultimately nothing is lost through death.

The second perspective arises from the embeddedness of the notions of death, regeneration, rebirth, and transformation within the specific context provided by Rajasthani (and Indian) culture. Here we find that the heroes' deaths entail a wide range of meanings, and are connected to an important set of overlapping religious themes and patterns. The crucial position occupied by the Goddess in relation to the heroes' lives and deaths provides a striking parallel to Purāṇic narratives about the slaying of demons by the Goddess resulting sometimes in their transformation or 'conversion'. The demon reverts from being an *asura* to becoming a perfect *bhakta.* The slaying itself often contains an undercurrent of *liebestod* in which the Goddess exploits the demon's erotic feelings towards her in order to weaken and finally destroy him. These structural dimensions of the myth are, by and large, also found in the narrative of the Bagaṛāvats. However, there are some important distinctions. First, there is an explicit understanding that the Goddess *is* Savāī Bhoj's *lover.* She chooses to marry his sword secretly in the private chambers of her palace. Second, the twenty-four brothers are continuously aware of the twelve year limit to their lives given to them by the ascetic Rūpnāth *alias* Śaṅkar. They, thus willingly enter into a self-destructive pact with him and later with the Goddess. The battlefield becomes a sacrificial arena for the latter in which the heroes offer up their own lives in the fullest expression of *bhakti.* The violence of the battlefield is thereby contained within a framework of self-sacrifice, renunciation, and devotion. These qualities finally transform the possibility of a 'bad' death generated by violence and prematurity into the 'good' death of heroes.

NOTES

1. Paper read at international interdisciplinary colloquium on: 'The meaning of death in South Asia', Heidelberg 1993. The author wishes to acknowledge the support of the German Research Council in generously funding a research project on the cult of Devnārāyaṇ between 1991-4. The material discussed here is based on fieldwork done in Rajasthan in 1991, 1992, and 1994. Recordings of the two principal sections of the epic (see below, section entitled 'The cult of Devnārāyaṇ') were made on two separate occasions by the author in May 1991 and February 1994. The epic was sung by Śrī Hukmārām Bhopā, and his co-singers, Śrī Moṭārām Gūjar and Śrī Kiṣnārām Gūjar. The version of the epic known to Śrī Hukmārām Bhopā runs into some forty-five hours of recording time.
2. See, for example, Shulman (1976) and Beck (1981) for references on south Indian, Tamil versions of the myth.
3. Essential features of the myth can be found in the *Devī-Māhātmya* of the *Mārkaṇḍeya Purāṇa,* 82.1-68, 83.1-41.
4. The battle between the demon and goddess is often 'preceded by an

episode in which Mahiṣa lusts for the goddess and tries to seduce her; she encourages his desire as a means of weakening him—a classic ploy in Hindu myths' (Shulman 1976: 122).

5. See Beck (1981: 83f.): 'Once in a year, at the small but famous temple for Māriyammaṉ . . . the goddess marries a demon. During a period of more than a week, a tree trunk representing a mysterious spouse stands planted in front of her shrine. Eight days (and nine nights) later that symbol is uprooted and the goddess briefly becomes a widow. . . . During the first period, when the goddess is linked to an unknown male, she is extremely temperamental. Her mood is beneficent and cooling by day, but angry and hot by night. . . . She also possesses her priest and devotees regularly while enjoying those unorthodox wedding rites.'
6. See Erndl (1989: 240) for the case of goddess Vaiṣṇo Devī in Jammu District. In the myths of this goddess, Bhairo plays a central role: 'On the one hand, he represents all that is opposed to Vaiṣṇava ideals of propriety: he is a *tāntric*, a meat eater, a wine drinker, and a lascivious womanizer. On the other hand, he is the ideal devotee whom the virgin goddess Vaiṣṇo Devī rewards by granting two boons, *mokṣa* (liberation) and the homage of pilgrims.'
7. *Kālikā Purāṇa* 60.104-5:
yajñabhāgamahaṃ bhoktumicchāmī tvat-prasādataḥ /
yathā makheṣu sarveṣu pūjyo'haṃ syāṃ tathā kuru //
tvat-pādasevaṃ na tyakṣye yāvatsūryaḥ pravartate /
evaṃ varadvayaṃ dehī yadī deyo varo mama //
8. *Kālikā Purāṇa* 60.106-7:
yajñabhāgāḥ surebhyastu kalpitā vai pṛthak pṛthak /
bhāgo na vidyate cānyo yaṃ dāsyāmī tavādhunā //
kintu tvayī mayā uddhe nihate mahiṣāsur /
naiva tyakṣyasi matpādaṃ satataṃ nātra saṃśayaḥ //
On the iconography of this image, see, for example, Agrawala (1958).
9. This question is linked to the broader cross-cultural issue of how the disjuncture created by physical death is encountered and overcome by the individual and society. Bloch and Parry (1982: 9ff.) argue that it is the religious construction of time as something not irreversible, but repetitive that allows human beings to perceive of life, and, in particular, death as points in a continuous flow of events. In the narrative discussed here, the continuity of individual and group identity is guaranteed not only through successive generations, but also through different ages.
10. See, for example, Smith (1989), and Hiltebeitel (1990: 1): '"Demon Devotees", . . . are perhaps uniquely Indian (though not necessarily Hindu), for their mythologies are shaped by a theology of *bhakti*, or devotion, in which the gods repeatedly convert their demon adversaries—sometimes by defeating them, but more often by killing them (implying the principle of reincarnation)—into their devotees.'
11. In some cases also by members of the Kumahār (potter), or Bābhī (leather worker, weaver) communities.
12. On the nature and spread of pictorial narrative traditions, see Mair (1988). For the special case of of Pābūjī, see Smith (1991: Ch. 3).

13. See, also, Smith (1991: 8ff.).
14. The epic is never performed in its entirety at any one vigil. Usually a single episode is chosen on the basis of the singers' and audience's inclinations. In addition to the performance of the epic during 'night-wakes', Devnārāyaṇ, and his father, Savāī Bhoj are worshipped in temples and shrines. In contrast to the rich visual representations of the deity offered on the *paṛ*, the temples contain rows of large, upright brick slabs (*īṭh*) that are either blank or pasted with red, blue, and yellow tinsel. Although in daily worship, these are understood to be either Devnārāyaṇ, Savāī Bhoj, or sometimes Devnārāyaṇ and his four cousins, in the epic the bricks are said to signify Devnārāyaṇ's wife, Rāṇī Pīpal De. Temple priests carry the title of Dās or Nāth, and have a strong affinity both in terms of outward appearance and religious attitude to the influential Śaivite yogic order, the Nāth Sampradāy.
15. Komal Kothari (personal communication) points out that this actually represents a conflict between pastoralists and agriculturalists (or land-owning groups). The boundaries between Gūjars and Rajputs are, both in the epic, and also in historical (see, for example, Puri 1957) and social terms (see Raheja 1988: 22) overlapping. In fact, the heroes of the first part of the epic cannot claim a 'clear-cut' lineage at all. (See section on 'Conceptions of death, marriage and eroticism'). They are sons of the multi-caste wives of Bāgh Siṃh, a man-lion, who in turn is the product of a 'mixed' marriage between a Rajput and Brahman, or Rajput and Bānyā, or Gūjar and Brahman, depending on which variant of the story one chooses. Furthermore, Savāī Bhoj, the central character of the first part of the epic, is born of Bāgh Siṃh's Rajput wife. The 'appropriation' of the epic's heroes and of the cult itself into a more well-defined caste or group identity seems to occur through the bonds of marriage: the heroes are, without exclusion, wedded to Gūjar women. Moreover, it is Savāī Bhoj's Gūjar wife, Sāḍū Mātā, who bears an incarnation of Bhagavān, Devnārāyaṇ.
16. On the one hand, there are Śaivite themes of asceticism, self-sacrifice, violent offerings to the goddess, and, on the other hand, Vaiṣṇava themes of *bhakti*, incarnation, and divine healing.
17. Brahmā's performance of a (Sanskrit) *yajña* is also the central theme of the Sanskrit *Puṣkara-Māhātmya* that deals with the origins of the pilgrim town. As in the episode narrated below, here too the ritual is disrupted by Śiva. Appearing in the form of a naked, skull-bearing ascetic, he magically lets his impure 'begging-bowl' reduplicate itself to the extent that the entire sacrificial awning is inundated with polluting human skulls. See Malik (1993a: 69-74; 284-8).
18. On the Aghoris, see Parry (1982). On Śiva as an Aghori in the Bagaṛāvat, see Singh (1993: 415).
19. Śiva's interference with Brahmā's sacrifice, echoes the ancient myth of Śiva and Dakṣa's rivalry. In the myth, Śiva, after having been excluded from Dakṣa's sacrifice, proceeds to destroy it and to kill Dakṣa.
20. In one variant, Hari Rām is supposed to be a Gūjar who is later given the title of 'Siṃh' from King Bisaldev because of the selfless act of slaying the man-eating lion. See, also, Malik (1993b: 381ff.)
21. Bāgh means 'lion'.

22. This incident and the one following in which Rūpnāth's body turns into gold, are typical of the large corpus of legends extolling Nāth Yogis' miraculous powers. See Gold (1992).
23. Savāī Bhoj has been forewarned of the Yogi's intent. See Singh (1993: 414).
24. The mare, in fact, is a manifestation of Śakti. The cow is none other than Kāmadhenu, the 'wish-fulfilling cow'. For variants on this, see Singh (1993: 414).
25. Bānyā is the name of a caste of merchants and traders, more known for their dealings with money than for bravery or heroism.
26. This attitude of generosity and fearlessness is considered a typical quality of the life-style adopted by warriors and bandits in Rajasthan.
27. An emblem which is to be struck down by the bridegroom.
28. The Rāṇā is considered to be 120 years old!
29. A euphemism for sexual activity. See Gold (1992: 99, fn. 66).
30. A phrase denoting the vast extent of the Rāṇā's military dominion. The number is used elsewhere too in order to convey greatness. Cp., for example, the 'fifty-two' *ghāṭs* of Puṣkara (Malik 1993a: 7) or the 'fifty-two' forts of Pābujī's kingdom of Koḷu (Smith 1991: 289).
31. The term used here is *mahābhārat.*
32. It should be noted, however, that the ascetic 'component' is persistent throughout the narrative. In all the cases of death discussed, it is an ascetic (or asceticism) that is the agent of transformation. Thus, it is Śiva who promises that his disciples will be reborn as brothers in one family, and Rūpnāth whose own body undergoes an alchemic change. In one recording of the story, the man-eating lion is considered to be a *yogi* who has altered his shape. And, finally, the brothers' death is an act of renunciation that is typical of 'warrior-ascetics'.
33. Cp. Heesterman's (1985b) hypothesis regarding a 'pre-classical' level of the Vedic sacrificial complex. According to him, a shift took place from the antagonistic rite of war, in which 'the goods of life' were obtained through death and physical sacrifice, to the ordered space of the Śrauta rituals, in which an attempt was made to transcend violence and death by reverting to the predictability generated by the use of the rules and regulations of ritual. In the case of Devnārāyaṇ's epic and cult, it appears as though the 'pre-classical' notion of regeneration, rebirth, and immortality through violence, death, and self-sacrifice in battle (and other contexts), has, at least in ideational terms, been continued: No attempt is made here to 'rationalize' and contain the 'negative' aspects of existence.
34. This corresponds to the classical category of a *pratiloma* marriage.
35. Of course, the prototypical case of 'cross-marriages' resulting in the superhuman is to be found in the *Mahābhārata.* Bhīṣma, Karṇa, and the five Pāṇḍavas, for example, are all born of liaisons between deities and humans. See van Buitenen (1973: xix-xxi).
36. The queen, in fact, remains a 'murderous', 'virgin' bride.
37. It is not surprising in this context, that marriages throughout the narrative—far from being happy, romantic events—bristle with deceit, danger, and death!
38. The Goddesses, Durgā (or Bhavānī), Ambā, and Umā are, like their

Babylonian and Assyrian counterparts, Nanā and Istār, not only connected with fertility, marriage, love and the earth, but importantly also with the protection of cities, and with war. See Mukherjee (1969: 11-18).

39. Savāī Bhoj attains 'immortality' through offering his life in a violent, sacrificial act. In his temple he is given ritual offerings such as alcohol that are deemed appropriate for a warrior. Devnārāyaṇ, on the other hand, is only given non-alcoholic and vegetarian offerings.
40. Although scholars like J.D. Smith interpret the demise of Indian folk epic heroes as a deviation from notions of 'conventional *bhakti*', they see a substantiation of the workings of fate in the narratives—a one-way transfer of evil from the gods onto women and men: 'Celestial beings propose to provoke and participate in human conflicts, causing enormous human carnage; and the reasons for doing so are purely to avoid trouble in heaven' (Smith 1989: 183). Unlike Smith my contention here is that the heroes' deaths contain an element of choice. Smith (personal communication) points out that his emphasis in the article quoted above is more on the benefit attained by gods, whereas I emphasize the benefits gained by humans through self-sacrifice. Both perspectives, however, deserve equal attention.
41. Cp. the notion of (Sanskrit) *dāna* as exemplary action for the Kali Yuga.
42. For a variant of this story from Uttar Pradesh, see Raheja (1988: 22-3).
43. The act of offering one's self or specifically one's head has a much wider connotation. Thus, it would also be possible to view the conflict between the Bagaṛāvats and the Rāṇā as an antagonistic rite in which the battlefield is a sacrificial arena where the trophy is death or rather the 'head'. 'The head' as Heesterman writes, 'is associated with and contains a treasure or a secret that is the essence of the universe. Everything depends on obtaining the head, and the gods have to contend for its possession' (1985a: 47). It is interesting, therefore, that in the sacred geography of the Sāvāī Bhoj temple near the town of Āsind in the district of Bhilwara—one of the main pilgrimage centres of the cult—the priest has clear notions about the place where Savāī Bhoj's head fell and where his body fell. It is at the place where his head fell that the Goddess' temple has been constructed. The entire region surrounding the temple is called a *raṇkhet.* (*raṇkhet* in Rajasthani literally means 'battlefield'. The Sanskrit equivalent would be: *raṇa-kṣetra.*). Thus, in a long line of transformations, the battlefield has become a sacred-field. (The other well-known example of a battlefield becoming a centre of pilgrimage is that of Kurukṣetra. The legend of the origin of the sacred town Gayā has a similar sacrificial component: Brahmā or Viṣṇu conducts his sacrifice on the body of the slain demon Gayāsura.)
44. See Bloch and Parry (1982: 15-18).
45. In a recent review of scholarship on the *Rāmāyaṇa, Mahābhārata,* and regional oral epics (particularly 'martial' epics), Hiltebeitel (1995: 31) argues against the position put forth by Blackburn and others (Blackburn *et al.* 1989), who '. . . situate the goddess, and heroines linked with her, as one of the primary contributors to the secondary and tertiary process of deification. . . . By moving goddess and heroines to secondary and tertiary levels of a presumed order of development, scholars . . . have bewilderingly

continued to treat both oral and classical epics as if they originally did without them.' In the present article I have tried to show the nature of the relationship between the twenty-four brothers and the Goddess, rather than lay bear the would be 'historicity' of the heroes and their subsequent deification. As pointed out already, this relationship is defined by qualities of eroticism, devotion, and self-sacrifice.

REFERENCES

Agrawala, R.C. 1958. Goddess Mahiṣamardinī in Early Indian Art. *Artibus Asiae* XXI (2): 123-30.

Beck, Brenda E.F. 1981. The Goddess and the Demon. A Local South Indian Festival and its Wider Context. *Puruṣārtha* 5: 83-136.

Blackburn, S.H. *et al.* (eds.). 1989. *Oral Epics in India.* Berkeley, etc.: University of California Press.

Bloch, M. and Parry, J. (eds.). 1982. *Death and the Regeneration of Life.* Cambridge: Cambridge University Press.

Erndl, Kathleen. 1989. Rapist or Bodyguard, Demon or Devotee? Images of Bhairo in the Mythology and Cult of Vaiṣṇo Devī. In Alf Hiltebeitel (ed.), *Criminal Gods and Demon Devotees.* New York: SUNY.

Gold, Ann Grodzins. 1992. *A Carnival of Parting.* Berkeley, etc.: University of California Press.

Heesterman, J.C. 1985a. The Case of the Severed Head. In J.C. Heesterman, *The Inner Conflict of Tradition.* Chicago: University of Chicago Press.

———. 1985b. Ritual, Revelation, and the Axial Age. In J.C. Heesterman, *The Inner Conflict of Tradition.* Chicago: University of Chicago Press.

Hiltebeitel, Alf (ed.). 1989. *Criminal Gods and Demon Devotees.* New York: SUNY.

———. 1995. Religious Studies and Indian Epic Texts. *Religious Studies Review* 21 (1): 26-32.

Kālikāpurāṇam. Chowkhamba Sanskrit Series Office, Varanasi, 1972. [Bi. Nā. Śāstrī (ed.)]

Mārkaṇḍeya Purāṇa. Bibliotheka Indica, vol. 29, Calcutta, 1862. (Transl. F.E. Pargiter, 1904).

Mair, Victor. 1988. *Painting and Performance.* Honolulu: University of Hawaii Press.

Malik, Aditya. 1993a. *Das Puṣkara-Māhātmya. Ein religionswissenschaftlicher Beitrag zum Wallfahrtsbegriff in Indien.* Stuttgart: Franz Steiner Verlag.

———. 1993b. Avatāra, Avenger, and King: Narrative Themes in the Rājasthānī Oral Epic of Devnārāyaṇ. In Heidrun Brückner, Lothar Lutze, Aditya Malik (eds.), *Flags of Fame. Studies in South Asian Folk Culture.* Delhi: Manohar.

Mukherjee, B.N. 1969. *Nanā on Lion.* Calcutta: The Asiatic Society.

Parry, Jonathan. 1982. Sacrificial Death and the Necrophagous Ascetic. In Maurice Bloch and Jonathan Parry (eds.), *Death and the Regeneration of Life.* London: Cambridge University Press.

Puri, B.N. 1957. *The History of the Gurjara-Pratiharas.* Bombay: Hind Kitabs Ltd.

Raheja, Gloria G. 1988. *The Poison in the Gift.* Chicago: University of Chicago Press.

Shulman, David D. 1976. The Murderous Bride: Tamil Versions of the Myth of Devī and the Buffalo-Demon. *History of Religions* 16: 120-46.

Singh, Bahadur. 1993. The Episode of the Golden Śiva Image in the Bagaṛāvat. In Heidrun Brückner, Lothar Lutze, Aditya Malik (eds.), *Flags of Fame. Studies in South Asian Folk Culture.* Delhi: Manohar.

Smith, John D. 1989. Scapegoats of the Gods: The Ideology of the Indian Epics. In Stuart H. Blackburn *et al.* (eds.), *Oral Epics in India.* Berkeley, etc.: University of California Press.

———. 1991. *The Epic of Pābūjī.* Cambridge: Cambridge University Press.

Van Buitenen, J.A.B. 1973. *The Mahābhārata.* Book 1. Chicago: University of Chicago Press.

Narrated and Dramatized Death in Tuḷu Culture

HEIDRUN BRUCKNER

I. INTRODUCTORY

The present article approaches the theme of death in the context of oral narratives and ritual dramas of Tuḷu folk culture as found in coastal Karnataka (South Kanara District) on the west coast of south India. I shall examine the role of death in myths as well as rituals, since death is present in both, the stylized dramatizations of the annual festival rituals for the local deities and the oral texts recited during these rituals. The point I want to make is that in these folk religious cults death forms an important link between the textual and the ritual dimension, although the extent to which narrated and dramatized death correspond to each other differs in the various configurations of the cults. The treatment of the central issue also involves other questions, such as the relationship of death to violence and fertility and the function of death in processes of deification and in the very establishment of religious cults.[1]

Widening my perspective, I also want to look at the difference between death inflicted by a protagonist on others and death suffered by the protagonist himself or herself. In instances of suicide, both perspectives on death coincide. Placed in a larger framework, these observations may help our understanding of the range and function of death and 'styles of dying' (Richard Burghart) within Hinduism and its local and regional transformations. Considering the religious importance of death and violence, Tuḷu notions of the divine share many features with popular Hinduism in other parts of India. All through south India and the Deccan, the worship of the deified dead plays an important role. Especially in the case of deified heroes, the martial outlook and the focus on fighting link their cults to those of famous gods of Purāṇic, epic or classical Dravidian descent in whose annual festival rituals their victorious fights against demonic counterparts are celebrated (cf. Hiltebeitel 1989; Sontheimer 1981, 1989).

Whereas in the latter instances the focus is on the attacking, aggressive deity, in the cults of the deified dead it is the victims of violence whose life and death are commemorated. In both patterns, elements of violence and antagonism play a central role in myth as well as ritual. This may have to do with the importance assigned to death for the regeneration and renewal of life and fertility (cf. Bloch and Parry 1982). It is a widespread popular notion that a violent death in particular sets free powers which can become resources of life for the living (cf. Blackburn 1985, 1988)..[2]

It is against this background that I want to look at the material from coastal Karnataka. Tuḷu oral literature and religious practice provide a wide range of notions about death and the divine which also include texts and ritual dramatizations situated halfway between the two patterns. In examining several examples of Tuḷu texts and festival rituals, my central questions are: How is the event of death described in the texts and to what extent do the social identity, personality and deeds of the hero determine his 'style of dying'? In what way is death, or rather the act of being killed, 'staged' in ritual drama in different cult configurations? How do epic or mythological narrative and ritual dramatization relate to each other with respect to death, and how are the powers of death made accessible?

In the next section (II), I shall summarize and discuss a number of exemplary texts about deified humans and the corresponding ritual dramatizations. In section III, I shall relate them to the texts of another group of local deities and the ritual practices connected with them.

II. ACCOSTING DEATH IN NARRATIVE AND RITUAL: BASIC PATTERNS

Although the Tuḷu cultural region of coastal Karnataka is small, social as well as sub-regional and local variation is considerable in the various configurations of cults indigenous mainly to matrilinear castes of agriculturalists, toddy tappers and service castes related to them. Some features seem to link them with folk religious cults in other regions, whereas others appear unique. None of the local deities in question has Sanskrit Māhātmyas or Sthalapurāṇas, nor do any other written texts exist about them. In their little temples they are normally represented only by a sword which marks an absence as much as it may mark a presence. In most temples, no regular worship is conducted during the year. Only during the large-scale annual festivals do the gods publicly become embodied by descending upon their dancers and bards. The festivals are most spectacular events matched only by those of the Teyyam of northern Kerala (see Nambiar 1993, Freeman 1993).

The identity of the deities is reflected in and constituted by their iconographic representations as living icons during the annual festivals, their oral myth-legends recited at the same occasion, the speeches of their priests and singer-dancers made in a possessed state, and, finally, the dramatic enactments during the festival rituals, which include stylized fights and self-mortifications.[3] The divine beings range from deified ex-untouchables to princely figures of unspecified origin. They also include deities of Purāṇic descent as well as theriomorphic beings, such as a tiger-, a buffalo- and a boar-deity. Their worship is often combined with the worship of ancestors.

In accordance with the wide range of superhuman beings within this group of religious cults, their ritual embodiment is taken charge of by several low castes of professional bards and god-dancers. There is a close correspondence between the identity of a deity, the specialist caste in charge and the patrons of a ritual. In the case of two of these specialist castes, the Paravas and the Nalikes, the deities are, in general, either deified humans or beings from a heavenly world. The deities embodied by the Pambadas, the third and supposedly highest of the bardic castes, form a group by themselves (see also section III). They are referred to as 'princely deities', *rājandaivas,* and the Pambadas impersonate them nearly exclusively in festivals patronized by families of the dominant Baṇṭ-caste of agriculturalists. Their priestly media normally belong to the *biruve* caste.[4] In the texts, these *daivas* are situated half way between *bhūtas* (Tuḷu *būta*), spirits, and *dēvas,* gods. They are neither former humans nor are they said to have come down from heaven.

The texts of this group display a peculiar structure of short interlocking narrative episodes in which wanderings of deities through the Tuḷu country figure prominently. Different local sections are added to a set of nuclear portions. They describe the arrival and the deeds of the god at the place of recitation of the text. In contradistinction to this episodic narrative structure, the texts of the other castes generally centre on a larger continuous narrative. Their singers are wandering bards or minstrels who move from place to place with the same, relatively fixed epic text, whereas the Pambadas are more closely attached to certain noble families and their lands.[5] They rather resemble bards appointed at royal courts, the king whose deeds are recited being the deity of the place.

To start with I shall discuss three texts from the Parava and Nalike bardic traditions; the texts deal with the life and death of human beings and their eventual deification.

My first example is an epic recited by Parava singers and god-dancers about a pair of heroic twins of the *biruve* ('toddy tapper') caste, called the Baiderlu. The story of the twin brothers Kōṭi and Cannaya is probably the most well-known, widespread, and popular legend of the Tuḷu country (Tuḷunāḍu). It has first been recorded in the middle of the nineteenth century by the Basel missionary Mögling, who handed it on to A.C. Burnell to form part of Burnell's larger collection. Burnell died before his collection could be published. Taking the help of another Basel missionary, A. Männer, Major Temple had Burnell's texts printed in the *Indian Antiquary* in the 1890s (Burnell 1994-7).[6] This publication contains three versions of the story, the first one appearing to be the most consistent account, especially with respect to the death of the heroes (Burnell 1894: 22-4, 29-49 and 85-91).

The narrative begins with the story of the twins' mother, Dēyi Baidēdi, originally a Brahmin girl who is abandoned by her parents in the forest because she reached puberty while still in their house. She is found by a toddy tapper (*biruve*) who makes her his fictive sister and marries her to his nephew. It is soon found out that Dēyi has a special knowledge of medicinal herbs. People start consulting her as a healer. While she is pregnant with the twins the local ruler, called a Ballāl, gets hurt during a hunting expedition and requires her help. She goes to the manor house and cures him. He promises to look after her children. Dēyi goes into labour right there, and dies in childbirth. The twins, who soon display unusual prowess, get into trouble with their master, who does not fully keep his promises, and especially with his Brahmin minister, whom they finally kill in a fight. Killing several other persons on their way who have not kept their promises to them or not shown them proper respect, they leave the country and enter into the service of the neighbouring Ballāl.[7] They choose wasteland as a gift from him and start cultivating it. They instigate the Ballāl to re-institute the royal hunt and the worship of ancestors, which have both been neglected in the kingdom. During the hunt, a giant boar is killed and falls down on the border of the neighbouring kingdom. Both kings claim the animal and a battle ensues with the neighbouring king's army. After single-handedly killing large numbers of enemies, the elder brother, Kōṭi, is hit on the calf by a poisoned arrow shot from ambush from behind him. He feels he will die and requests that water be poured into his mouth. The Ballāl has him taken to his verandah, where Kōṭi assures him that he and his brother will continue to serve him as warriors even after their death. He should simply plant their swords in the battlefield when required. When the Ballāl himself has poured water into the hero's mouth, 'he leaves his body and goes to Kailāsa'. But the god Bermeru will not admit him without his brother. Meanwhile, the younger brother has committed suicide by hitting his leg (in the other version, his head) against a rock, since life without his elder brother is meaningless to him. Having performed purificatory rituals at the request of Bermeru, they are finally admitted into his temple and stand at his right side. The text concludes by stating that in the world they were honoured like Bermeru himself. It also stresses the honours conferred on the dead bodies by the Ballāl, who has them cremated with great pomp.[8]

I want to stress the following points in the story: The heroes are of mixed descent. In the earlier generation, the focus is on their mother, the father is hardly mentioned. The mother dies after giving birth to the heroes. A Ballāl, a member of a higher caste to which their own caste stands in a service or king-vassal relationship, is obliged to look after them because their mother has rendered him a very special service (saving his life at the cost of her own). The Ballāl fails in his duties towards the twins. They leave his kingdom without committing any direct physical aggression on him. Instead, they kill a number of other people who have failed to keep promises, tried to cheat them or simply denied them respect out of caste pride. The heroes look to the performance of traditional royal duties, go hunting, and kill a boar. All through, they display immense prowess in combination with a strong sense of honour, and perform acts of valour, especially in battle. They are killed from ambush and commit suicide respectively. They have a special connection with the Tulu deity Bermeru.[9]

The hero of my next example, Koḍdabbu (Kordabbu) or Babbu, stems from an ex-untouchable caste, the Muṇḍala, who used to be serfs of castes of agriculturalists. The Koḍdabbu *pāḍdana* and performance tradition has been studied by Claus (1989). My summary of the text is based on his synopsis (1989: 233-5). The text has not been published so far. It is performed in certain contexts by members of the Muṇḍala caste. In public, village-wide, annual festival rituals, it is performed by the Nalike caste of bards, who also act as god-dancers of the deified hero.

The version collected by Claus starts with an account of the life of the hero's mother, Malvedi. She is orphaned at a tender age and brought up in the local manor house. As part of her puberty ceremony, which she is asked to perform according to the rules of her own, low caste, she bathes in the river, sprinkles rice into the water, and says: 'O, fish! As the rice fills your stomachs, may a baby fill mine' (1989: 233). When she actually becomes pregnant the lord of the manor is blamed. Malvedi agrees to undergo several trials to prove she has not had intercourse with any man. Calling upon the help of god Bermeru, she emerges unharmed. On the way home, Malvedi dies in childbirth. Like her, her son Babbu is brought up in the manor house, growing at unusual speed and performing miraculous deeds in the service of his masters. Thus, when asked to keep birds from eating rice laid out in the courtyard to dry, he, still a small child, simply kills them all, but brings them back to life when scolded by his foster mother. By his straightforwardness and fearlessness he later angers a Brahmin, who warns the king of this dangerous low-caste boy. When he is scolded again by his mother he leaves home and has encounters with men of various artisan castes. He learns divination and absconds with coins from a mint. Under some pretext, he is finally asked through the lord of the manor to report at the king's court. The king orders him to go to the bottom of a deep well where no water has been struck. Babbu obeys, although he knows that a trick is being played on him. As soon as he is down in the well, a big boulder is placed over the mouth, leaving him to die. Later on, several heroes passing by and hearing his cries for help are not able to remove the rock. Finally, a young girl, Tani Maniga, hears his cries. When she touches the rock with her silver sickle, invoking the earth and the sky, the rock bursts into pieces. Since the well is very deep, she lowers her sari into it, admonishing Koḍdabbu not to look at her while climbing up. He neglects her warning, but, by declaring that they will hereafter be known as brother and sister, Tani Maniga's chastity is preserved. Claus concludes his synopsis: 'They return to Kaccura Manor as *bhūtas* in *māyā* form and they are honoured and worshiped. The legend goes on to mention that they perform other deeds in other places and also tells how they come to be worshiped in those places'. (1989: 235)

Again, as in the previous example, the protagonist is orphaned at birth and his mother is endowed with special powers. The motif of the orphan brought up in the lord's house is doubled by extending it into the mother's generation. Lack of emphasis on the heroes' father is enhanced in this epic by a supernatural conception brought about—we may assume from other examples in the same and other texts—by the mother's extraordinary power of truth (*satya*), a quality popular with Tuḷuva heroines. By the same power she survives the trials imposed on her by a suspicious society. She undergoes these trials not primarily to prove her own innocence, but to protect the honour of the lord she serves. Similarly, her son Babbu is eager to serve the lord and lady of the manor, though sometimes misinterpreting their wishes or taking them too literally. His extraordinary physical strength and capacities lead to harm, even when he just wants to help.[10]

There is a focus on the lord-vassal scheme here, combined with a relation of fictive kinship. Claus (1978), using an expression applied by Gough with respect to Kerala, speaks of 'relationships of servitude' and comments that these are still seen in Tuḷunāḍu 'in a domestic idiom. The servants are dependents of their lord, and the relationship is expressed in fictive kinship terms. Thus, servants are regarded as the lord's children (*maga*) or younger siblings' (1978: 19). Against this conceptual background, I would suggest that the orphaned state of the heroes serves to emphasize—and test!—claims of fictive kinship by making it more real. In both epics, the promise of protection implied in notions of fictive kinship proves vain when really tested. His lord does not even attempt to protect Koḍdabbu when the king calls him, although he is quite aware of what the king is up to. Like the twins, Koḍdabbu is cheated by a superior power, the king, who believes the hero is getting too dangerous. Unlike the twins, he actually becomes the victim of the king's injustice and nearly loses his life in the well incident. Without the support of his lord he cannot fight or escape the king. The continuation of the story again brings in a female figure endowed with similar powers of truth as those the hero's mother had. It is at this point that he, albeit in a rather innocent way, becomes guilty too. After his rescue, which involves a transgression vis-à-vis his fictive sister, a continuation of earthly life no longer seems possible. The pair escape from the human mode of existence by 'becoming *māya*'. The Sanskrit term *māyā* (Tuḷu *māya*) is used in Tuḷu in the sense of an invisible mode of existence as well as of the power to assume this mode or to transpose others into it. It is this mode in which the local deities are said to exist. The counter-term *jōga* is used for the visible state a being from the *māya* realm can assume. When deities or deified beings are embodied by specialists during rituals this is also called the *jōga* state.[11]

The third major epic text of South Kanara dealing with deified humans and performed, like the Koḍdabbu epic, by bards of the Nalike caste is available in transcription and translation in the old collections.[12] It deals with the mason and sculptor Kalkuda and his twin sister Kallurti and has a number of motifs in common with the two texts summarized above. Since the twins' father is called by the king to work in Śravaṇa Belgola while their mother becomes pregnant with them, they are actually brought up fatherless. Like Koḍdabbu, Kalkuda grows at exceptional speed. He is eager to go and meet his father and work like him. A difference from the other epics is his subsequent encounter with his father, whom he surpasses in skill, building temples and monumental statues for the Jaina kings of the region. The father commits suicide when the son points out a mistake in his work. Other motifs shared with the Koḍdabbu as well as with the Kōṭi-Cannaya epic are a conflict with a jealous and aggressive king, the ruler of Karkal, who—after the completion of the work—does not keep his promise and has Kalkuda's left arm and right leg cut off so that he can do no such excellent work for another master. Kalkuda still manages to get away to the kingdom of Yenur and to do similar work there. The continuation of the story is of interest because it tells us more about the transition to the *māya* state and its motivation. It also provides information about post-*māya* events not available in any detail in the above versions of the other two epics:

Her twin brother Kalkuda having been away for many years, the sister, Kallurti, cannot bear life without him any longer and sets out to look for him. Passing all the places where he has worked, she gradually comes to know about his fate, and, half insane with grief, finally reaches Yenur. On seeing her brother, she makes an oath to revenge herself on the king of Karkal. She convinces her brother that they should not live under such circumstances. They request Mahādeva to make them disappear into the realm of *māya* (*māya malpoḍu*), and they purify themselves in the invisible state. Then they violently take revenge on the king, his family, and the people of his kingdom. After much destruction and affliction which no ordinary magician can properly diagnose or control, they finally enter into an agreement with a master magician: They permit him to control them against his promise of conducting their cult worship etc. the way they want it. They accept a beautiful feast on a grand scale. When they are under control 'every thing became as it was before' (1896: 226). The pair proceeds to various other places where they afflict people and are appeased by the introduction of their cult worship.

Although placed in a different milieu, the basic pattern of social conflict between an unusually talented member of a lower caste and a king who wants to avail himself of his talents is maintained in this text too. The hero is cheated by a royal master who does not keep his promise and is physically destroyed by having one arm and one leg cut off. A woman with special powers, the hero's twin sister, is the one who decides that they cannot live under these circumstances. Like Koḍdabbu and Tanimaniga (Tani Maniga), the brother-sister pair voluntarily give up the visible form of human existence, revenge or the restitution of justice not being possible in the human social setting of a hierarchic caste society. Only as spirits or supernaturals can they execute their revenge and demand the respect and honour refused to them as human beings.

Relying on the narrative material presented so far—with the reservation that other versions exist, but are not available in published form to date—I shall now take up the questions posed initially. Firstly, how do the person of the hero and his style of dying relate to each other? Secondly, how is death staged in ritual drama? And, thirdly, to what extent do narrative and ritual depiction of death correspond to each other?

The first question is answered most easily with respect to the first text. The twin brothers Kōṭi and Cannaya are martial heroes and at least the elder one dies on the battlefield—an apt way of dying for a warrior, were it not that he is killed from ambush. But this aspect, too, is in accord with one of the major themes of the brothers' life: being cheated by others who are jealous and envious of them. The death of the second twin is different. Here, the focus is on the inseparability of the pair. The younger cannot live without his elder brother. Killing one of them means killing both, even though the second one himself executes his death. Not using any weapon, he slaughters himself in a strange, crude way by hitting his head (in the other version: his leg) against a rock. There is no mention of revenge, fury or frenzy. Kōṭi assures the king that he and his brother will help him in battle even after their death if their swords are planted in the battlefield. Except for joining the god Bermeru, no post-mortal activities are mentioned in the accessible versions of the epic. They basically end with the death of the heroes and, perhaps significantly, with the execution of their funerary rites. It may be worthy of note in this context, that, strictly speaking, the brothers are not classed as *bhūtas*, spirits, but form a category by themselves, the Baiderlu, a name referring to their caste.[13]

In the grand annual festival rituals of their cult worship held by members of their own community, the *biruverū*, but also joined by people of other castes, the twins appear on the bodies of costumed Parava dancers who are at the same time their bards, as well as on the bodies of their priestly media. As in most all-night festival rituals for the local deities, their presence is built up in three stages. After an invocation, they make their preliminary appearance on the bodies of their dancers, who put on sacred anklets and recite portions of the narrative. They then present themselves in the light of torches, the dancers exposing their bare chests to the fire in order to show the deities' power. In the second stage, the supernaturals descend upon their priestly media who carry their swords. Through these media, they give speeches containing references to the narrative as well as blessings and assurance of protection. In the final stage, the twins again appear on the bodies of their dancers, who are now costumed more elaborately, carry swords, and give speeches and blessings as well. This is considered to be the most complete representation of the deities. Portions of the *pāḍdana*-narrative are recited at different points before and during the rituals. First as a preliminary invocation, then during make-up, then again in the initial stage, sometimes in between stages, and again for the final stage. As we shall see, the usage partly differs in other configurations of the local cults.

A scene which may be taken to refer to the 'death' of the twins is enacted twice, first by the priestly media and later by the Parava dancers. Dramatic action starts with movements to the accompaniment of an orchestra. They hold their swords by the sharp edges and direct them to their own chests. The priests, and later the dancers, finally cut their chests with the weapons and leave the points of the swords in their skin for quite sometime. When they are pulled out again, a leaf with sandalpaste is put on the wound to stop the bleeding, and the media sink back into the arms of helpers. These are the most intense moments of the ritual, or, to use an expression suggested by Blackburn, the moments of the greatest 'ritual depth'.

If we compare this scene with the description of the twins' death in the narrative, the differences are obvious. In ritual drama, the twins' action is simultaneous and identical. Their self-mutilation has the appearance of suicide. But it is different from Cannaya's suicide in the narrative. The weapons used in the ritual also differ from the weapon by which Kōṭi is killed in the narrative, i.e. an arrow shot from ambush. Therefore, the scene of the ritual is not theatrical in the sense of staging what is scripted by the narrative. My feeling is that it is much more: central notions of the narrative and of the cult are focused and translated into action. Ritual does not simply repeat what narrative tells but shows what narrative cannot tell. Ritual action maintains the brothers' agency as martial heroes, shows their 'being killed' without any reference to an ultimately irrelevant external agent, and, finally, dramatizes the brothers' self-sacrificial readiness to fight and die for their warlord as well as—in the cult—for their followers. It is by blending these three aspects that the scene takes on its ritual depth.

The available summary of the Koḍdabbu *pāḍdana* deals with the 'dying scene' very briefly. Claus 1986 does not describe or discuss its ritual enactment in any detail either. I am filling this gap from my own fieldnotes taken in 1986. The *pāḍdana* recorded at that time roughly corresponds to Claus' summary but the recording unfortunately does not contain the last portion of the text. I have to offer the following observations on narrative and ritual on the narrow basis of the data available to me. The story of Koḍdabbu and Tanimaniga can be read as two narratives blended in one. The first one ends with the intended killing of the hero who is left to die in a well. Considering the task assigned to him, to make water flow from a well which has not struck water, the incident takes on an air of human sacrifice for the renewal of fertility. The 'untouchable' hero is made to fulfil the express task of providing water in quite a different way, by giving up his life. Babbu, although aware of being cheated, places his obligation to serve and obey the king higher than his own life—in spite of the injustice done to him and the refusal of protection by his elders, in particular his foster father. In this sense, his behaviour amounts to self-sacrifice. His end would have been tragic.

The second narrative starts with the appearance of Tanimaniga, leading to Koḍdabbu's rescue from the well and his breaking the promise he gave her. The hero's double tragedy, first being a victim of injustice left all alone to die in a well, and then involuntarily committing an offence against his newly gained 'sister', collapses into the impossibility of living on. The second tragedy, though, has one definite advantage over the first: the hero's agency is restored. His self-punishment not only shows that he takes responsibility for the offence he committed, but also permits the display of central features of his personality, such as courage and power. It is this aspect that the ritual attempts to dramatize. At the same time, there is a shift from inter-caste conflict in the first narrative to a male-female encounter in the second one.

In the annual Koḍdabbu *kōla* festivals, the hero and his fictive sister are impersonated by professional bards and dancers of the Nalike caste. In the performance I witnessed in 1986, the initial portions of the *pāḍdana*, dealing mainly with the hero's mother, were recited in the first stage of the rituals for nearly an hour. After the stage of possession of the priestly media—who belong, like the hero, to the Muṇḍala caste—Koḍdabbu's Nalike dancer reappeared along with Tanimaniga, who danced first on her own and then together with Koḍdabbu.[14] After a procession, another portion of the narrative was recited. The staggered sequence of appearance of Koḍdabbu and Tanimaniga corresponds to the structure of the 'double' narrative. The last stage began with Koḍdabbu's dancer appearing in the full attire of the deified hero, including his 'face', a metal mask tied on top of the head, and dancing with torches in his hands. After the mask had been removed, the 'well-incident' was enacted. In front of the chief patron, the former landlord of the Muṇḍala participants, and representatives of their own caste, Tanimaniga marked a spot on the ground where a banana leaf was placed and Koḍdabbu's head ornaments deposited. Tanimaniga put some drops of oil onto his untied hair. Having taken the patrons' permission, Koḍdabbu was given an iron sword and started hitting his own head with it. He cut his forehead until some blood flowed from the wound and dramatically continued his self-injuring action until the patrons pleaded with him to stop and the priests interfered. Tanimaniga rubbed his bleeding forehead with a leaf containing some sandalpaste.[15] Then the pair blessed the patrons and audience.

Whereas in the narrative Koḍdabbu's breach of promise and his wish to atone for it are referred to only briefly, the stylized enactment of his atonement becomes a central scene in ritual drama. Here, Koḍdabbu's 'play with death'[16] takes on dimensions of self-sacrifice that go beyond the narrative context of the epic, and at the same time, signal his power of protection.[17]

In the case of Kalkuda and Kallurti, I am not aware of any particular incident from the narrative being dramatized in ritual. As in the case of most of the other deities of the local pantheon, Kalkuda's dancers and priestly media carry a sword. His sister, Kallurti, also called Kālamma, wears black facial make-up with white ornamentation, carries a stick, and takes burning embers on her tongue to show her special power. She is said to throw stones on houses and can cause fires. In spite of the scarce data available to me I have included the pair among my examples because their story provides evidence of revenge and frenzied aggression of victimized persons not mentioned in the stories of the other deified heroes. It is only after a transition into the *māya* state, though, that Kālamma and her brother can fully display the power of their anger. In the acts of destruction they are said to have performed there is an element of compensation for the unjustice they suffered in their lifetime, and a restitution of dignity and agency. The state of *māya*, the disappearance from the visible world, becomes the starting point to negotiate re-entry into the social world under their own terms and conditions. With a master magician as mediator whom they finally permit to control them, they can re-establish their relationship with society under new premises. Ironically, it is by means of the invisible state and power of *māya* that the protagonists become socially visible beyond the borders of their own caste and establish relationships with a wide range of worshippers. Through ritual, the power of their uncontrolled rage is transformed from destructive into protective energy and made accessible to individual worshippers as well as to the community as a whole.

III. TRANSFORMATIONS

How are these patterns continued or transformed as we move on to texts and rituals of the Pambada bards which form part of a different cult configuration? One major change is that most of the texts do not centre on the life stories of humans any more but on the acts and wanderings of beings who already enter the scene as supernaturals. In a way, these texts start where those of the deified dead end. Thus, both in the *pāḍdanas* of Koḍdabbu and Tanimaniga as well as in those of Kalkuda and Kallurti, there are concluding sections which speak of their going to different places and obtaining worship.

Among the roughly twenty Pambada texts of my collection (Brückner 1995), there are only two focusing on the life of a human being and ending with his deification. Only these two short texts are named after the deified human. Cult-worship, in both cases, is restricted to one place, or to two closely related places only. In a third instance, the text is not explicit about deification. In general, there is a shift of emphasis from narrative to ritual. The narrative *pāḍdana* texts used in rituals of this configuration are shorter and their recitation normally is confined to an invocatory portion recited by the bard and god-dancer in front of the temple before starting his make-up and a section recited in full costume at the beginning of the third stage of the rituals. Most of these texts have ceased to exist and to be performed independently of ritual. Their episodic structure serves to create or reflect a network of interrelating groups of agriculturalists of the dominant Baṇṭ caste and their landed property. Thus text structure is closely tied up with socio-political organization as well as with kinship and, to some extent, genealogy.

The process leading from one type of text to the other can be exemplified by a story transmitted in ritual as well as non-ritual performance traditions. It is used in the male ritual performance tradition of the Pambadas under the name of the deity Kānṭēri Jumādi and consists of just one short episode: a young hero, Dēvu Pūñja, holds a grand festival for his deity, Jumādi. The hero does not arrive on time for the festival rituals and is cursed by the deity to be killed in a subsequent battle. The narrative is also known in the female fieldsong tradition and among Parava bards. In both these traditions, the texts are much longer than with the Pambadas. With the women, the *pāḍdana* is known under the name of the human hero who represents an important family of Baṇṭ manor lords.[18] These texts deal with family history and with the entire life of Dēvu Pūñja, starting from his childhood. There is a focus on kinship relations, marriage alliances, and the unusual qualities of the young boy, who acts in a courageous and independent way.

When his father dies, the right to their estate goes back to the king, who declares that the rights will be given to the warrior victorious in a battle the king has to fight. Since there is no other male in the family capable of leading the batallion to battle, Dēvu Pūñja wants to save the honour of his family and regain the rights to the estate himself. He quickly learns warfare from his maternal uncle, gets his father's weapons repaired, and is assured of the help of the family deity, Jumādi, by his uncle. Thus equipped, he reports to the king and excels in the battle. But, under the influence of Dēvu's cousin, the king does not keep his promise to give Pēriñja estate to Dēvu. Instead, he demands more victories in other battles to come. Dēvu feels cheated. His sense of honour does not permit him to stay in Pēriñja manor any longer. Along with his mother and the tenants, he leaves the estate and settles on the territory of another king. When Dēvu does not give him his proper share of the harvest,[19] the king wants to ruin him with the help of the local harlot. He suggests that Dēvu should have a festival for his family *daiva* Jumādi. When he goes to Bantval market to get plantains for the feast, the harlot has gotten all the shops closed and lures him into playing a game of chess (or

CENNE)[20] with her. Cheating him, she robs him completely of his rich clothes and ornaments and humiliates him. During the game, several messengers arrive one after the other to urge Dēvu to come for the rituals. Finally, he arrives with only a cheap loincloth left on his body. For being late, Jumādi curses him to die. Shortly after, the king has village youths cut off Dēvu's head in the fort of Uccila, having used some pretext to get him there.[21]

Just like the longer epic *pāḍdanas* treated above and ending with the deification of the heroes, these texts, too, tell the life story of an unusual heroic personality, though starting not with his birth but only with his childhood. Even as a boy, the hero is uncompromising, fearless and straightforward. There is an emphasis on his sense of honour and on his pride. He loses his father at a tender age. The hero's major counterpart is a king who makes use of him but does not keep his promises. At a later point the hero, too, fails vis-à-vis a king and vis-à-vis his own family deity. It is the latter failure, in the first place, for which he has to pay with his head. The motif of cheating is shared with Koḍdabbu. But, in both instances, the moral dimension of the cheating does not appear to be causally connected with the death of the hero. The heroes' encounters with women stand in opposition to each other, Koḍdabbu's meeting with Tanimaniga leading to a brother-sister alliance that continues even after death, whereas in Dēvu's encounter with the prostitute and the game they play, stress is laid on the antagonistic component. The harlot is the moral opposite of the *satya*-female Tanimaniga. Socially, we move up one or even several steps in the caste hierarchy, Dēvu belonging to a family of the dominant caste of Baṇṭ agriculturalists eligible for the headmanship of *guttu*-estates on feudal tenure.

The longest and most interesting version of the story accessible to me presumably belongs to the male performance tradition of the Paravas; it was noted down for Basel missionaries, most probably Weigle or Mögling, in the 1840s.[22] It forms part of a collection of four interconnected texts, three of them dealing with the *daiva* Jumāvadi (Jumādi) Bāvano and the fourth with the deity Malarāya. The first and the last describe the (similar) origin of the two deities and the way their worship was established. The two remaining texts are longer. One of them tells the story of Dēvu Pūñja, and the other narrates events in the previous generation.

As compared to the version(s) summarized earlier, these versions put more emphasis on the role of the *daiva*. Martial and political events figure more prominently than kinship relations, marriage alliances, etc., especially in the Dēvu Pūñja story proper. These shifts mark the transition from the non-ritual fieldsong traditions to the textual traditions of the bardic castes.

The first narrative introduces a man called Saṅkara Atikāri who is killed (decapitated) in battle after his *daiva* Jumādi has warned him by showing bad omina which he has ignored. After his death, his four sons are assigned estates (*guttu*) by the king Kāmarāya Baṅga. The youngest son gets Bolluru *guttu* and marries Dēvu Pūñja's sister Dāramu of Pēriñja *guttu*. As in the above-quoted version, Dāramu takes away some coins to bring to her father during her first visit home. Jumādi, the *daiva* of the estate, follows her and punishes her by causing her father to die. When the reason is found out, the children's uncle Kānta Atikāri conducts a festival ritual for Jumādi. The *daiva* decides to follow him to his estate. He informs Kānta in a dream that he wants to be worshiped by him and becomes the *daiva* of his house.

In the perspective of this text, the main function of the story is to explain how the *daiva* came to be associated with Kānta Atikāri, a piece of information not provided by any of the above-mentioned versions. In fact, it is as Kānta Atikāri's *daiva* that this form of Jumādi has become known in the region to this day, even though later on the *daiva's* temple at Panambūru on the coast became more famous.

The other text of the Tübingen manuscript tells Dēvu Pūñja's story proper, first focusing on two well-known rival kings, Kāmarāya Baṅga and Timmanna Ajila, and a conflict between them which leads to a war.

Before the battle, the Ajila king realises that no troops have come from Pēriñja guttu. Maju Pūñja's nephew uses his uncle's death as a pretext not to join the battle. Maju's young son Dēvu learns about this shameful behaviour from his mother, who is in complete despair. The young boy promises the king to fight if he gets the headmanship of Pēriñja in return. The king agrees and makes a promise. Dēvu qickly gets trained by his uncle, who also gives him his *daiva* Jumādi Bāvano to help him.

The battle is described in more detail than in the female version. An important difference is that Dēvu first gets into great difficulty and succeeds only when he remembers his *daiva*. The ensuing conflict with the Ajila king, who refuses to keep his promise and makes new demands instead, is described more elaborately in this version, mentioning the mutual threats in cruel detail. Next, Dēvu does not simply leave home wandering aimlessly, but goes straight to the Ajila's major enemy, king Kāmarāya Baṅga, with the intention of joining him in order to take revenge on the Ajila.

Kāmarāya is happy and confers headmanship on him. In the next battle, Dēvu defeats the Ajila's army and humiliates him personally exactly the way he has threatened to do. He receives more titles of honour from the Baṅga king and is entrusted with the accounts and the collection of taxes. But soon he gets into trouble, being suspected of taking bribes. In this situation, Dēvu appeals to his *daiva*, promising him a grand feast if he helps him out. The *daiva* saves him. The king becomes suspicious about the supernatural assistance Dēvu gets, and wants to deprive him of it. As in the above versions, a prostitute, Siddu, helps him make Dēvu neglect his duties vis-à-vis his *daiva*. She holds him up at Bantval with a game of dice, cheats, and robs, and humiliates him. When he finally arrives at the festival area, the offended and jealous *daiva* Jumādi enters into a lengthy dialogue with him, recounting all the help he has given him. Only then does he curse him to die.

The final scene again differs from the female versions:

After some time, the Cauṭa kings of Ullala attack the Baṅgas, and Dēvu is asked to fight them. In the battle, he is hit from behind by a spear which chops off his head. The Cauṭa chieftain to whom the head is taken mourns the disfigurement of such a hero. The text ends: 'When saying thus, Jumādi trembled in the tip of Dēvattikāri's [i.e. Dēvu's, H.B.] moustache.'

The text of the Tübingen manuscript does not describe Dēvu Pūñja's childhood the way the female versions do, but focuses on his martial activities. Here too, though, his young age and special talents for warfare are mentioned. Like Kōṭi and Cannaya, Dēvu Pūñja gets into a conflict with the ruler of the realm, who does not keep his promise, and Dēvu seeks an alliance with another overlord. Like the twins, he has a double affiliation, with the king and with a deity, but, in Dēvu Pūñja's case, the royal and supernatural realms are not as clearly spatially separated as with Kōṭi and Cannaya, and Jumādi appears to be much less aloof from human concerns than Bermeru is. Like Kōṭi, Dēvu is killed from ambush and hit from behind, but this tragic end is considered a consequence of his *daiva's* curse.

His sister, whose birth, etc., are described in the fieldsong tradition, is introduced here from a very different angle. The scene is shifted to Bolluru, where her future husband prepares his proposal. The focus is on her behaviour after marriage, which leads to her father's death. The death is caused—as a punishment for her—by her husband's family *daiva*, Jumādi. Ultimately, she becomes a mere medium for the *daiva* Jumādi taking him from Bolluru via Pēriñja to the estate of Kānta Atikāri.

The Tübingen version of the Dēvu Pūñja story provides an important link between two extreme perspectives, that of the female fieldsong tradition and that of the male ritual performance tradition of the Pambada caste patronized by Banṭ agriculturalists. As in the case of Kōṭi-Cannaya and Koḍdabbu, the human hero of the narrative is a member of the patron caste, here a Banṭ. A major difference is that the hero is not deified, and hence the festival is held not primarily in his honour, but in honour of the deity considered responsible for his success and downfall. With respect to Dēvu's fate there is a shift from human to supernatural agency.

The last version of the Dēvu Pūñja story to be discussed is that of the Pambada bards. It is by far the shortest text, focusing nearly exclusively on Dēvu's relation to his *daiva*. It covers only the last portion of the narrative of the other texts and consists of just eighty-three sentences.[23] It can be taken to exemplify the peculiar emphases of the Pambada-Banṭ-*rājandaiva* performance tradition.

Dēvu Pūñja is introduced as living in Bolluru manor. He wants to have a *nēma* festival for his *daiva*, Jumādi, and dresses up to go to Bantval market and buy some items for the festival. There, the prostitute Siddu persuades him to play a game of *cenne* with her. Dēvu loses three times. While the game is going on, messengers arrive, urging Dēvu to come for the rituals, which have already begun. When Jumādi himself finally sends the third messenger, Dēvu has been completely robbed and humiliated by the prostitute. He sneaks into the festival arena through the back entrance. Angry and jealous, Jumādi summons him and curses him to die. Dēvu stands there weeping in distress. The second part consists of two short episodes. In the first one, a battle with the Baṅgas is mentioned in which Dēvu first is victorious but then is killed by Jumādi himself. The *daiva* is said to tie Dēvu's head on his, the *daiva's*, back. Soon, the family again give a festival for Jumādi at Bolluru, as Dēvu is dead. The last portion describes Jumādi's wanderings and his establishment at a place called Panambūru Sārāla Paṭṭa.[24]

In this carefully structured telling of the story, there is perfect symmetry between the progress of the festival with its various stages and the gradual defeat of Dēvu by the prostitute in the game of *cenne*. The narrative focuses on three major themes which are prominent in many texts recited by the Pambadas in the context of festival rituals: First, the description of the very rituals at which the text is recited; second, the narration of an offence committed vis-à-vis the deity celebrated in the rituals, and the punishment by the deity; and, third, the theme of the violent death of a human protagonist. This last theme is reinforced by having the hero's head chopped off and by Jumādi tying it onto his back.

By virtue of the fact that the texts are recited as part of the festival and the fact that the description of festivals forms part of most texts, the ongoing ritual is mirrored in its verbal description and, *vice versa*, the verbal description in the ongoing ritual. Text and ritual include and thereby reinforce each other. Because narrative episodes are linked by the wanderings of the deities through the Tuḷu country, the narrative recited and the act of recitation also link the ongoing festival and its arena to other places visited by the god and to other festivals he obtained at those places. His earlier history is made part of the present moment and locale, creating a spatial and temporal continuity. These functions of the *pāḍdanas* are complemented, reflected and reinforced by other genres of formal utterances in the rituals, such as the god's speeches, blessings and accounts of his deeds in a peculiar prose diction (*nuḍi* and *kaṭṭŭ*). Whereas the *pāḍdanas* use a third person narrative form, *nuḍi* and *kaṭṭŭ* are made more dramatic and immediate by using the first and second persons. The people present are directly addressed by the deity and can respond to him. In this way, narrative becomes part of the actual situation and the present moment is made part of the narrative. Similarly, when the deity addresses the patrons by the names of their ancestors, they are placed in line with patrons of earlier generations who formerly stood in front of the god as their descendants do now, and, the ancestors become part of the ongoing ritual. There is a constant oscillation between past and present, identity and difference, the truth of the narrative and the validity of ritual action, the realm of the gods and the realm of humans, which has a peculiar impact in the case of narrated and dramatized death.

Whereas the human heroes of our earlier texts become deities generated from 'within' a particular locality and social setting, the *rājandaivas* are viewed as arriving from outside. This involves the linking of narrative episodes by means of two basic patterns. Either a deity already established at some other place chooses to follow a person attending his festival to the person's own locality. Or an initially unidentified deity comes on his own and makes his presence felt by afflicting animals or children or by possessing a person, preferably a *biruve*. The establishment of a cult often involves a conflict between a *biruve* tenant and his Baṇṭ landlord. The attitude of the Baṇṭ farmers towards this being is at first contemptuous and aggressive. This is in accord with the pride and impatience which are ascribed to their character along with courage and a martial spirit. In the texts, the farmers provocatively refer to the spirit as *kāṭŭ būta*, 'wild *būta*' or 'forest *būta*', or as *biruve būta*, meaning 'the *būta* of a toddy tapper'. They punish the possessed toddy tapper by hitting him with thorny twigs. Especially when a king is involved, the *biruve* often has to undergo an ordeal. The spirit then demonstrates its power by rescuing the toddy tapper in a miraculous way. It is left open whether the person survives this 'rescue'.

By means of deeds which are often destructive, the spirit commands respect and obtains worship. He then grants protection and prosperity. By being established at the estate and the manorial house, he turns from a *būta* into a *daiva*, and the toddy tapper becomes his possession priest. To attain the position of a *rājandaiva*, the *daiva* must first become the lord of powerful landholders. The deified dead of lower castes still associated with their former social status are not eligible to become family deities of the landed nobility and the 'rulers' of the land. But the narratives point to a way in which the powers of such beings can still be appropriated. Although the deification of a killed or violated person is not part of the stories, the death described in the texts has an impact on the identity of the *daiva* which is modified by such an event. Thus, *daivas* often adopt the name of the place where such an event is said to have occurred. It is either added to their former name or the latter is fully replaced by a new one derived from the place name. This is one way of absorbing or integrating the powers set free by a violent death. It is closely related to the process of deification of the dead but—for certain reasons—does not go as far. The *biruverŭ*, who look back on a martial tradition as well, have in the texts a double affiliation with a human as well as with a superhuman power and finally turn into mediators between the two. In the cult, they become media of the deities. The uncontrolled possession of the narrative, sometimes occurring on the top of a palm tree, is processed as it were and elaborated into controlled and artfully choreographed ritual possession that lasts for twelve to sixteen hours and involves two different media, the *biruve*-priest and the costumed god-dancer, who becomes the living and speaking icon of the deity, endowed with its royal and martial attributes. Against this background, the *rājandaivas* cannot be viewed exclusively as powers from outside but appear as a blend of internal and external, human and superhuman forces.

Although, in ritual, human and divine powers control each other and a setting is created in which destructive forces can be turned into productive ones, the 'play with death' remains an important dimension in the rituals of most *daivas,* even if there is no reference to a particular scene described in the narrative. Especially the boar deity Pañjurli and the 'wild' form of princely Jumādi (Marlu Jumādi) enter into a state of frenzy, remove their head ornaments, and hack their foreheads with a sword, like Koḍdabbu. In the course of this scene, they try to escape from the ritual arena, and they have to be hunted and brought under control again by their priests and young men from the audience. Pañjurli is a boar and a prototypical warrior at the same time. In spite of his originally being an animal, his narrative has some elements in common with the story of Kōṭi and Cannaya and that of Koḍdabbu. Śiva, who in this *pāḍdana* resembles a Tuḷu agriculturalist, had gone hunting and killed a boar and his sow, unaware of her young ones. When he finds them, he takes them back to Pārvatī, who brings them up. After sometime, they start destroying the garden and are cursed and sent off by Śiva to obtain a living from people. As with our deified heroes, a socially superior person is responsible for the death of their parent(s), and, in compensation, brings up the orphaned offspring. Unable to control the offspring, the person abandons the offspring, or the offspring leave on their own, finally obtaining worship from people.

Ritually, Jumādi's assistant *daiva* Baṇṭe, whose name marks him as a representative of the Baṇṭ caste, is the continuation of Pañjurli. He is the prototypical warrior-vassal, forming a king-vassal pair with princely Jumādi. Riding a horse, he wears the mask or face of a boar. In contradistinction to Pañjurli, he has no *pāḍdana* narrative of his own and is said to be dumb. An explanation is given in a widespread *pāḍdana* of Jumādi (Sārāla Jumādi, the powerful 'Jumādi of a thousand'). According to this text, Baṇṭe once tried to overpower Jumādi. The latter subdued him and locked his mouth. That is why he is dumb in the presence of Jumādi but can speak when he is alone, as Pañjurli. In a central scene of the festival rituals, Baṇṭe grabs an iron sword from the altar, throws off his head ornaments, and hacks at his forehead with it, just like Pañjurli, Marlu Jumādi, and Koḍdabbu. Whereas in the case of Koḍdabbu this action is supposedly addressed to Tanimaniga and meant as an atonement, Baṇṭe's action is directed towards Jumādi, who finally orders the priests to stop him, or, at some places, addresses him and 'revives' him when he is already lying on the ground unconscious. These parallels in ritual action, dramatizing a 'play with death', suggest a strong conceptual continuity, even though we hardly find corresponding narrative parallels with reference to these scenes. This conceptual continuity consists in a focus on self-sacrifice in the context of 'relationships of servitude'.

As compared to the self-injuring play with the sword, fighting scenes involving two protagonists do not acquire the same dimension of ritual depth. Thus, in the rituals connected with the short Pambada-version of the Dēvu Pūñja story (see pp. 260-1), a fighting scene and the tying of Dēvu's head are dramatized by the god-dancers of Jumādi and his assistant *daiva* Baṇṭe. Ritual drama stages a stylized, playful mock-fight which also serves to entertain and is especially appreciated by the children in the audience. Finally, the divine pair throw away their crude cane bows and arrows beyond the ritual arena and start a graceful dance.

IV. SUMMARY AND CONCLUSION

I have first examined three oral Tuḷu texts of epic dimension about former humans who eventually came to be deified. They receive a form of worship in which they are embodied by specialists and certain scenes from their lives are enacted. My focus has been on the relationship of narrative text to ritual drama, especially with respect to death and dying. The analysis has shown that certain aspects and elements of the oral narratives are selected for dramatic representation and that even these are not simply used as scripts or textbooks for enactment. They are transformed, continued, reacted to, complemented or elaborated on. Only narrative and ritual drama taken together seem to present the 'entire story' of the protagonist, although the two can exist independently of each other. Concerning modes of dying, the material seems to suggest that ritual drama restores the agency of the protagonists victimized in the texts. In the ritual, they enact their readiness to die by inflicting wounds on themselves with swords. Such acts assume a wider meaning in the ritual by being addressed not only to the warlord of the narrative, e.g. of Kōṭi and Cannaya, but to the entire community of worshippers present during the rituals. With Koḍdabbu, the hero of my second example, atonement and self-sacrifice are blended and elaborated in ritual drama.

In section III I have moved on to a different configuration of texts and rituals based on a corpus of twenty texts collected from Pambada bards, only two of which deal with deified humans. My intention was to check whether my observations on the relationship of narrated to dramatized death would be valid in slightly different settings as well. Textually, the difference from my earlier examples is that the human protagonists are transposed to the invisible state of *māya* in the one case by a *daiva*, in the other by a god. They are not victims of human violence or cheating. In both cases, the transposition amounts to the physical death of the human being and takes place against his will as an act of divine aggression compensated for by accommodation in the deities' realm. In ritual drama, no self-sacrificial action or self-injury is shown. In one case, the focus is on the deity transposing a herd of buffaloes and the herdsman into *māya*. This is shown by the priest taking away the herdsman's stick.[25] In the other case, the hero, Balavāndi, who had offended the deity Bemmeru in the text, performs another stylized act of aggression in the course of the festival rituals. It is the climax of the ritual drama when he mounts his wooden horse, approaches the shrine of Bemmeru housed in the same complex, and throws hair from his moustache against Bemmeru three times (cp. Brückner 1995, Ch. 5.3). The worship of these two deified persons is restricted to one place for each, whereas the deified heroes discussed above are worshipped throughout the Tuḷu region.

The comparison may lead us to assume that only a protagonist described as a victim of human violence in the narrative will enact self-sacrificial feats in ritual drama. But this is not a general rule. Looking at the festival rituals of some of the *rājandaivas*, the 'princely deities' patronized by Baṇṭs and embodied by Pambadas, we see very similar scenes of self-injury with swords without corresponding narrative references to human violence (see p. 267). To stop the frenzy of the deities hacking their foreheads with their swords, the priests try to substitute a live chicken to divert their aggression to another victim. This is not done at this point with deified humans. Nevertheless, there is a continuity in ritual drama which indicates the basic importance of self-injury and self-sacrifice as a display and assurance of the power of the deity, independent of the narrative text. Although ritual acts do not seem to be directly determined by the narrative, drama and narrative are coordinated in the sense that they jointly characterize a deity in a particular way, the third component being the iconography of the embodied deity. Thus, these 'wild', powerful figures are distinguished from kingly deities, who display a more dignified and ceremonial behaviour in ritual drama.

In examining the relationship between narrative and dramatization we also have to distinguish between the enactment of a particular narrative content, such as Koḍdabbu's atonement after the well incident, a more general thematic connection between narrative and ritual, and the modes of performance, i.e. recitation of the narrative in the rituals. I have exemplified with the shortest of several versions of the Dēvu Pūñja story—the only one which has come to be preserved in a ritual performance tradition—how text and ritual are thematically interwoven. The text focuses on the very rituals during which it is recited; on an offence against and punishment by a *daiva*; and, finally, on the violent death of the human protagonist, Dēvu Pūñja, brought about by the *daiva*. The story is part of the *daiva*'s cult and has not led to the deification of Dēvu Pūñja. My comparison with longer versions of the text which have not been preserved in the Pambada performance tradition has shown that the focus on the punishing *daiva* is the result of a gradual shift.

The transition from the deification of a human to the celebration of a punishing deity within a closely interrelated group of local cults invites comparison with patterns encountered in texts and performances of other cults of south India and the Deccan that were mentioned at the beginning of this paper. We should keep in mind that in the Tuḷu material there is a textual focus on inter-caste social conflict and a ritual one on the dramatization of self-sacrifice. As we move on from narratives about the deified dead to those about princely *daivas*, supernatural intervention in human conflicts increases. In both cases, ritual drama is performed by professionals and takes place in the spatial and conceptual centre of the annual festivals. Another important component of the village level festival rituals of local deities consists in antagonistic rituals between the male youths of two villages. Such competitions and playful group fights use torches or take the form of ritual football matches.

In folk religious cults of male royal deities of the Deccan, such as Khaṇḍobā-Mailāra-Mallanna, oral narrative gives way to Sanskritic myths dealing with conflicts between gods and demons on a cosmic level. In the case of Mailāra of North Karnataka, dramatic enactments during festivals stage stylized fights between a divine protagonist and his demonic antagonist, both represented by images or invisibly riding horses. They are accompanied by the masses of their worshippers, who form their troupes. The climax of the festival is the killing of the demon by the deity on the fields near the temple. In contradistinction to the Vedic paradigm of *deva-asura* fighting, medieval concepts of *bhakti* have had their impact on the fate of the demon in folk religion. He turns into a devotee and becomes the doorkeeper of the deity's temple (cp. Hiltebeitel 1989). His killing takes on an eschatological dimension. Although this dimension is not made explicit in most of our Tuḷu material, there are instances where human death caused by the *daiva* is viewed as 'saving' the person, mostly from human persecution (see p. 265). Dēvu Pūñja of our sample text is not deified, but he is made part of the cult by being represented iconographically in the *daiva*'s shrine and in ritual drama. His family continue to be devoted to the *daiva*. The major contrast to the death of the deified hero seems to be that the hero's death is not inflicted as a divine punishment but appears as a human tragedy. He dies as a victim of injustice and violence, or his death is self-inflicted or self-induced as a consequence of such human behaviour.[26]

In the context of the folk-religious cults studied by Sontheimer (e.g. 1981, 1989), acts of valour and self-injury are not performed 'centre stage' by professionals, but in a less formal setting by individual devotees who often belong to particular groups or communities. Their feats include breaking chains, acting as the horse of the god and beating themselves with whips, piercing the calves of their legs with pointed pegs, etc. The low-caste Kañcavīras perform such feats at Devaraguḍḍa and other places. Sontheimer comments: '. . . these *vīras* through their fury and exertion arrive at a stage where sacred energy is produced, resulting in the presence of God. . . .' The power to incorporate the gods 'is also obtained in the excitement of initiatory military combat' (1981: 15). Sontheimer speaks of 'a play with death' and explains: 'They invoke the god with their feats and the spectators enjoy the spectacle and at the same time feel reinforced and relieved by the close association with their god, mediated by people who by their very outlandishness and devotion are closer to the god' (1981: 16).

Sontheimer observes that 'the play with death' is characteristic of tribal festival rituals and has subsequently been integrated into the larger multi-caste folk-religious cults: 'The "play with death" is common in Dhangar and Kuruba *jatrās* and has entered from there into popular *jatrās* of gods worshipped by all communities, like in the case of the Mhaskobā cult of Vīr in Maharashtra. The Dhangar *devṛṣi* ('shaman') would belabour his stomach with a (rather blunt) sword, or dance holding the sword tip pressed against his mouth, tongue and teeth, as in the Mhaskobā *jatrā* at Vīr. Or, in the *kheḷ* of the Dhangars, the dancing *devṛṣi* would lean with his bent body on a stick or sword the grip of which is placed on the floor. This reminds us of the Varabhaṭṭas of Mailāra impaling themselves on spears. These rites and the Dasarā festival at Devaraguḍḍa show that the gruesome self-sacrifices of earlier times resulting in death have been brought under control by a performance which tends to be ritualized and stylized by more or less symbolic actions' (1981: 20).

In his concluding remarks, Sontheimer gives an example of the actual threat to life contained in ritual drama: 'The ambivalence and danger of the god, if ill-controlled, is well expressed by an incident told by a Dhangar shepherd: *A Dhangar siddha 'playing with the sword' danced and became possessed by the god Birobā [the great pastoral god of the Deccan]. A rival of the siddha had evil intentions in his mind. He made the drummers suddenly change the rhythm. The [indispensible] drum (dhoḷ) and the siddha fell on the floor. His vital breath (prāṇ) left him.* . . . It is the well-ordered rhythm of drum which holds Death under control, or pleases the god, and turns the powers of the god into the beneficial' (1981: 21).

The descriptions Sontheimer gives remind us of some of the central scenes in the festival rituals for the deified dead in Tuḷu religion. But unlike the Tuḷu material, there seem to be no specific narrative reference texts to which these acts of valour are linked. It is culturally understood that they display the power and greatness of the deity as well as the faith of the devotee. The comparison should caution us to ascribe fixed, identical meanings to acts of similar appearance. It may be a truism by now, but it deserves to be restated, that individual acts may change their meaning with the slightest shift of context. What in a tribal setting may be a way to force the coming of the deity takes on a whole set of additional meanings when transferred to a multi-caste setting like the Tuḷu one, in which 'relationships of servitude' are of primary importance. In the folk-religious cults of the Deccan, these heroic performances of self-injuring acts coexist with the enactment of the *deva-asura* fight.

In narratives connected with south Indian village goddess cults, the demon killed by the goddess as a punishment also turns into a demon devotee acknowledging the supreme power of the goddess. But, at the same time, oral traditions identify the village goddess with female victims of injustice and violence. In their annual festivals, these deified females are viewed as divine slayers of a demonic antagonist, identified with Mahiṣāsuramardinī, Durgā as the slayer of the buffalo demon. The ritual here appears as a continuation of the oral narrative, scripted by a Sanskritic pattern. The double identity as deified victim of violence and victorious slayer of a demonic aggressor blends patterns of oral and Sanskritic traditions (cp. Brückner 1996).

Whereas Sontheimer's examples provide ritual drama without a narrative text, the village goddess cults provide oral texts without corresponding ritual enactments. In both cases, potential for social conflict and re-negotiation is de-emphasized in favour of an abstracted mythological pattern on which general consensus is easily obtained. In the Tuḷu material, we often have texts and ritual dramas, although the extent to which narrative and ritual correspond to each other varies considerably from case to case. All through the groups of texts examined here, social conflict forms an important constituent of the narrative. There is aggression or injustice on the part of the socially superior, and dedicated service, voluntary self-sacrifice, but also rebellious action of and trials imposed upon the socially weaker. Between the narratives of the deified dead and those of the *rājandaivas* there are important shifts from human to supernatural agency. These 'plots' all result in the establishment of religious cults which, again, dramatize 'relationships of servitude' with special reference to their self-sacrificial dimension. The festival rituals also provide an important forum to negotiate village, caste and family affairs. As compared to the narrative texts, in ritual drama the pattern of the relationship of servitude is multiplied, reversed, inverted, and reciprocated, extending to relationships between gods and men. Narrated and dramatized death appear as two sides of the same coin. Whereas narrative death stresses the suffering and tragedy of the victim of injustice and aggression, dramatized death is a self-induced, breath-taking 'play with death' which stresses—and, in the case of formerly human victims, restores—agency. Playing with death generates powers which have to get out of control to prove their own force. Ritual drama provides a setting to control the uncontrollable and to turn its powers into resources for life.

NOTES

1. I wish to thank Veena Das, New Delhi, for her kind interest in an earlier draft of this paper. Discussions with her greatly helped me to clarify my points. My thanks are also due to Anne Feldhaus, Tempe, for improving the English style.
2. In south Indian village goddess cults, both patterns—that of the demon-killing deity and that of the deified victim of violence—appear to be blended, but, to my knowledge, it has not been shown in any detail so far how they are linked in actual narrative and in ritual practice.
3. These are not executed by the devotees, as in many of the folk cults of the Deccan, but by the professional god-dancers.
4. *Biruve*, literally 'bow-man', plural *biruverŭ* is the Tuḷu name of the so-called 'toddy tapper' caste. In much of the standard literature, such as Thurston's *Castes and Tribes of Southern India*, the Kannaḍa term 'Billava' is used to refer to them. The final *ŭ* with the half-circle above is used to transcribe an unrounded voiced *ŭ*.
5. The texts of all groups are uniformly termed *pāḍdana* in Tuḷu, a term derived from the Dravidian root *pāḍ-*, to sing.
6. The Tuḷu originals of some of these translations were printed by the Basel Mission Press, Mangalore, in 1886 for internal use of the mission only. See Brückner and Poti 1992 for an account and comparison of the two collections and an attempt to re-contextualize them.
7. On their way through the forest to the other kingdom they have an encounter with the god Bermeru. See Claus (1978: 7-9), whose summary of the story focuses on this event. He does not mention the death scene.
8. In the second version (Burnell 1895: 114-21, 141-53, 211-15, 242-4 and 267-72), the death scene (1895: 271/72) is a little briefer and less consistent but basically resembles the one summarized here. In the third version, added by Männer (Burnell 1896: 295-310 and 328-42), the death scene (1896: 342) is again very similar, but appears to be merely a summary of the first version. It ends: 'So the brothers who were together in life were together in death also' and adds the comment: 'Therefore the people, and especially the Billavars [i.e. *biruverŭ*, toddy tappers, H.B.], believe that these heroes are still powerful in the other world, and worship them.'
9. For this last point see Claus 1978.
10. These traits Baḅbu shares with many of the local deities.
11. See Brückner 1995: 247-50 and passim as well as the literature cited there.
12. Burnell 1896: 61-3 'Kalkuda' and 216-27 'Kallurti'; cf. Männer 1886, texts nos. 9 and 10.
13. Derived from a form of the word *baid[y]e/vaidye*, also referring to a member of the *biruve*-caste, with the honorific and plural suffixes *-ru* and *-lu*.

Similarly, the Siri deities of South Kanara are not classed with any other group of spirits or deities.

14. Females are embodied by male dancers dressed as females.
15. A very similar scene showing the cutting of the forehead by Koḍdabbu is recorded on a short documentary film shot by B.V. Karanth for the Sahitya Akademi, New Delhi. Claus (1989) refers to the well incident in the context of a ceremony called *parake darśana,* a day-time possession session for the consultation of deities, during which Koḍdabbu and Tanimaniga are present in the bodies of their priestly media of the Muṇḍala caste. In this context, the *pāḍdana* narrative is not recited: 'As the possession priests enact portions of the story, the possession builds up to a crescendo with the enactment of the episode at the end of the story in which Tani Maniga saves Kordabbu from the well and Kordabbu threatens to destroy himself for having broken his vow not to look at her when she is naked. This scene of Kordabbu beating his stomach with a sword is the centerpiece of the day's ritual activity. Villagers of all castes then come before the spirits and pay their respects or seek the spirits' aid in solving troubles' (1989: 62).
16. I have adopted this expression and the one 'play with sword' used below from Sontheimer 1981.
17. Cf. Claus' remarks about the 'message' of Koḍdabbu's *parake darśana* ceremony: 'First there is the long and detailed statement of Kordabbu's able service to the Mundala community. Then there is his vow to uphold the hierarchical principles of the caste system and to protect women (illustrated by his self-chastisement after his initial mistreatment of Tani Maniga). These are the more public messages, with Kordabbu himself representing the Mundala to the community at large' (1989: 63).
18. I am grateful to Peter J. Claus, Berkeley, who graciously gave me copies of several female versions of the text from his unpublished collection.
19. Other versions mention no such offence on the part of Dēvu, but motivate the plotting by the king's jealousy of the valiant young warrior. In yet other versions, the king is the one whose army had been defeated by Dēvu and who wants to take revenge on him.
20. On the meanings of this game, see Claus 1986.
21. In another version, Jumādi himself appears at the fort and cuts off Dēvu's head.
22. These are the earliest available transcriptions of Tuḷu *pāḍdana* texts, a total of sixty-one pages, closely written in an older variety of the Kannaḍa script. They were identified only in 1988 by Viveka Rai and me in the Tübingen University library in the legacy of the missionary Hermann Gundert, where they had been catalogued along with a sketch for a German Kannaḍa grammar and labelled *daivahuttu,* 'the origin (or: birth) of *daiva*' on the index card (Ma I 818). The text had mistakenly been classified as a Christian tract. Viveka Rai and I are presently preparing to publish the original Tuḷu texts with English translations and an introductory study. The first draft was prepared at Tübingen in summer 1993 with the help of a grant from the German Academic Exchange Service (DAAD) to Dr. Rai.
23. Cf. Brückner 1995: 177-81; Tuḷu text 352-5, German translation 471-4, plates 46-9, musical notation p. 176.

24. Here the recorded version used to be recited by Aitappa Pambada as an invocation *pāḍdana* during the annual festival rituals, up to the construction of modern Panambur harbour. For the harbour project, land was acquired by the government and Jumādi's patrons were given property in a different place. The temple, too, was shifted to the new locality.
25. Text and ritual are presented and analysed in detail in Brückner 1993.
26. Kalkuda and Kallurti of my third Tuḷu example request Mahādeva to transpose them into the realm of *māya*.

REFERENCES

Blackburn, Stuart H. 1985. Death and Deification: Folk Cults in Hinduism. *History of Religions* 24: 255-74.

———. 1988. *Singing of Birth and Death*. Philadelphia: University of Pennsylvania Press.

———. and Joyce B. Flueckiger. 1989. Introduction. In Stuart H. Blackburn *et al.* (eds.), *Oral Epics in India*. Berkeley: University of California Press.

———. and A.K. Ramanujan (eds.). 1986. *Another Harmony: New Essays on the Folklore of India*. Berkeley: University of California Press.

Bloch, Maurice and Jonathan Parry. 1982. *Death and the Regeneration of Life*. Cambridge: Cambridge University Press.

Brückner, Heidrun. 1993. Kannalāye: The Place of a Tuḷu *Pāḍdana* among Interrelated Oral Traditions. In H. Brückner, L. Lutze, A. Malik (eds.), *Flags of Fame. Studies in Indian Folk Culture*. Delhi: Manohar.

———. 1995. *Fürstliche Feste. Texte und Rituale der Tuḷu-Volksreligion an der Westküste Südindiens*. Wiesbaden: Harrassowitz.

———. 1996. Divinity, Violence, Wedding and Gender in Some South Indian Cults. In Michaels, Axel *et al.* (eds.), *The Wild Goddess in South Asia* (Studia Religiosa Helvetica 2). Bern: Peter Lang.

———. and Narasimha Poti. 1992. 'Dhūmāvati Bhūta:' An Oral Tuḷu Text Collected in the 19th Century. Edition, translation, and analysis. *Studien zur Indologie und Iranistik* 16: 13-63.

Burnell, A.C. 1894-1897. Devil Worship of the Tuḷuvas from the Papers of the Late A.C. Burnell, ed. by Major R.C. Temple. *Indian Antiquary* Vols. 23-6.

Claus, Peter J. 1978. Oral Traditions, Royal Cults and Material for the Reconsideration of the Caste System in South India. *Journal of Indian Folkloristics* 1: 1-25.

———. 1986. Playing Cenne: The Meanings of a Folk Game. In Stuart H. Blackburn and A.K. Ramanujan (eds.), *Another Harmony: New Essays on the Folklore of India*. Berkeley: University of California Press.

———. 1989. Behind the Text: Performance and Ideology in a Tulu Oral Tradition. In Stuart H. Blackburn *et al.* (eds.), *Oral Epics in India*. Berkeley: University of California Press.

Freeman, Richardson J. 1993. Performing Possession: Ritual and Consciousness in the Teyyam Complex of Northern Kerala. In H. Brückner, L. Lutze, A. Malik (eds.), *Flags of Fame. Studies in Indian Folk Culture*. Delhi: Manohar.

Hiltebeitel, Alf (ed.). 1989. *Criminal Gods and Demon Devotees: Essays on the Guardians of Popular Hinduism.* Albany: State University of New York Press.

Männer, August. 1886. *Pāḍdanoḷu.* Mangalore (printed as manuscript).

Nambiar, Balan. 1993. Tāi Paradēvata: A Goddess and Her Ritual Impersonation in the Teyyam Tradition of Kerala. In H. Brückner, L. Lutze, A. Malik (eds.), *Flags of Fame. Studies in Indian Folk Culture.* Delhi: Manohar.

Sontheimer, Günther D. 1981. Dasarā at Dēvaraguḍḍa. Ritual and Play in the Cult of Mailār/Khaṇḍobā. *South Asian Digest of Regional Writing* 10: 1-28.

———. 1989. Between Ghost and God: A Folk Deity of the Deccan. In A. Hiltebeitel (ed.), 1989. *Criminal Gods and Demon Devotees: Essays on the Guardians of Popular Hinduism.* Albany: State University of New York Press.

Kūttāṇṭavar: The Divine Lives of a Severed Head

ALF HILTEBEITEL

Kūttāṇṭavar or Aravāṉ, a Tamil 'village deity' usually represented by a fierce red severed head, has associations with death that extend from the village to the *Mahābhārata.*[1] In the overlapping pantheons of Tamil village gods and epic heroes, he is in each case a relatively inconspicuous figure. My efforts have found only thirty-two Kūttāṇṭavar temples, with concentration decreasing along a belt that extends from South Arcot through North Arcot and Salem Districts to a small but thicker grouping around Coimbatore (see Map). In the *Mahābhārata,* a barely noticeable appearance in Sanskrit versions of the epic unfolds into a richer story in classical Tamil tellings that still gives him only a few new moments of glory.

It is sometimes said that Kūttāṇṭavar is a 'village deity' (*kirāmatēvatai*), whose worship is general to the whole village, rather than a 'clan deity' (*kulateyvam, kulatēvatai*), although the latter terms are also used, particularly in South and North Arcot by some of his main worshippers from the Vaṉṉiyar community,[2] and curiously, by Alis, so-called 'eunuchs', who worship him at certain South Arcot festivals as a deity who helps them increase their *iṉam* (kindred, kind, species).[3] His festival worship is often conjoined with that of village goddesses (especially Māriyammaṉ, Keṅkaiyammaṉ, and Kāḷiyammaṉ), and includes goat and rooster sacrifices—both as general (*potu*) offerings sponsored by the village, and individual offerings—at key points. His fearfulness is often highlighted. At Paṉaimatal (Attur Taluk, Salem District), at the ritual of his eye-opening, no one will stand in front of him for fear of suffering from his glance.[4] At Kuricci (near Coimbatore) the goat sacrifice outside his temple prevents death in the village. At Tailāpuram (Tindivanam Taluk, South Arcot), the four offering stones at the corners of his temple receive offerings to prevent death pollution in the village if a death occurs at his festival. At Vellalūr (near Coimbatore) pieces of his body brought back from the festival protect families from diseases. At Palaiyacūramaṅkalam, he protects children from coughs that are caused by whooping cough (Kakkuvāṉ) Māriyammaṉ. At Vīrāṇantal (Chengam Taluk, North Arcot)

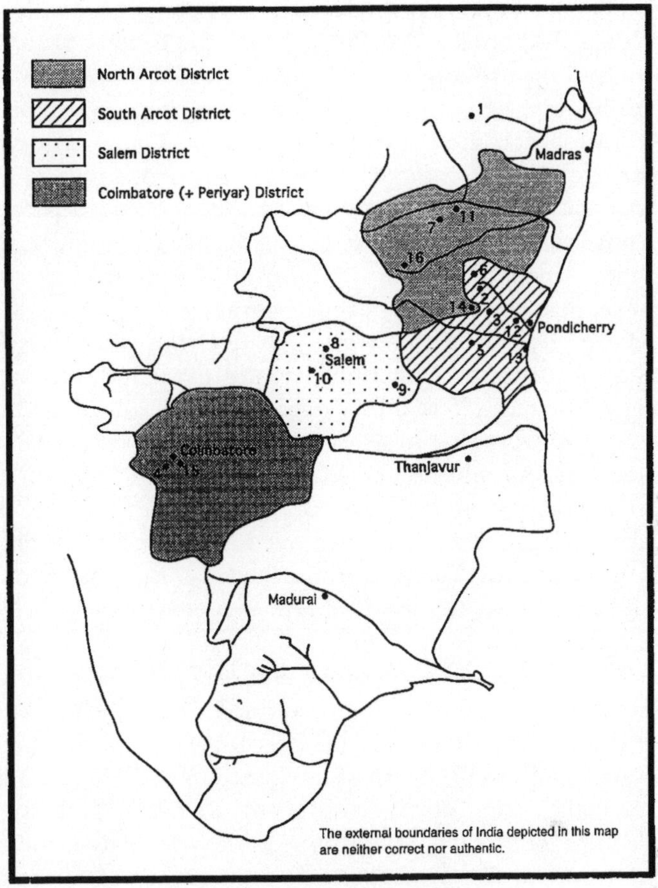

MAP OF SITES MENTIONED

SITES MENTIONED

1. Candragiri, Candragiri Taluk, Chittoor District, Andhra Pradesh
2. Peruntēvaṉār
3. Kōṉalūr, Gingee Taluk, South Arcot District
4. Kuricci, Coimbatore Taluk, Coimbatore District
5. Kūvākkam, Ulunturpet Taluk, South Arcot District
6. Mēl Malaiyaṉūr, Gingee Taluk, South Arcot District
7. Otukkattūr, Vellore Taluk, North Arcot District
8. Palaiyacūramaṅkalam, Salem Taluk, Salem District
9. Paṉaimatal, Attur Taluk, Salem District
10. Pēḷūr, Salem Taluk, Salem District
11. Putūr, Vellore Taluk, North Arcot District
12. Tailāpuram, Tindivanam Taluk, South Arcot District
13. Tēvaṉampaṭṭaṇam, Cuddalore Taluk, South Arcot District
14. Tēvaṉūr, Tiruvannamalai Taluk, North Arcot District
15. Vellalūr, Coimbatore Taluk, Coimbatore District
16. Vīrāṇantal, Chengam Taluk, North Arcot District

and Putūr (Vellore Taluk, North Arcot), he is connected with chicken pox, diarrhoea, and cholera. At Putūr, when his head is brought back from his nightlong procession and swung from a swing, he must be returned to his temple before sunrise or these diseases will afflict the village. At Vīrāṇantal, the guardian deity Pōttu Rāja is sent out from Kūttāṇṭavar's temple to combat cholera if it breaks out. At Tēvaṉūr (Tiruvannamalai Taluk, North Arcot) and Kōṉalūr (Gingee Taluk, South Arcot), he has not only a head that resides in his village temple but an even more ferocious and dangerous one at a hill temple that must not be disturbed except at the opening of his festival.

The *Mahābhārata* would appear to be far from view here, but the festival poster (*pattirikai*) at Tailāpuram is typical in reminding worshippers that this is not the case: 'The one who gave himself in order to end the Pārata war, O God (Aṇṭavar) Aravāṉ, you stood there as a sacrificial body, you come and appear and do goodness for us as Kūttāṇṭavar. . . .' The poster reminds villagers that the god they worship as Kūttāṇṭavar is also the epic hero Aravāṉ, whose sacrifice was for the welfare of the world. The rich unfolding of Tamil traditions about his death, or better deaths, as a hero, clearly ties in with his mastery over death and diseases in villages.

In the Sanskrit *Mahābhārata,* other than a brief account of his birth from his father Arjuna and the serpent woman Ulūpī in the first book, one hears nothing further about him until a single section in the *Bhīṣma Parvan* (Book 6) tells of his death at the hands of the Rākṣasa Alambuṣa on the war's eighth day. Tamil accounts provide him with the new story of his noble self-sacrifice at the beginning of the war. In its earliest telling by the ninth-century Pallava poet Peruntēvaṉār, Aravāṉ agrees to sacrifice himself on the new moon night to Kālī, goddess of the battlefield, so that with Kālī's blessing the 'good' Pāṇḍavas can win the war; and to make it work out right so that Aravāṉ doesn't fulfil a prior agreement to sacrifice himself for Duryodhana and the 'bad' Kauravas, Kṛṣṇa has to make it appear that the new moon night occurs a day early. For his compliance, Aravāṉ obtains a succession of increasingly contradictory boons that accumulate through the development of his story. In Peruntēvaṉār, he asks only to stay alive so that he can die a hero in the eighth day of battle, thus keeping his Sanskrit exit from the story. The (probably) fourteenth-century version of Villipūttūr Āḻvār adds his request to be allowed to watch the entire eighteen-day war with his severed head. And Kūttāṇṭavar and Draupadī cult folk traditions add his appeal for a prewar marriage that will secure him ancestral rites denied to anyone who dies a bachelor. These three Tamil classical accounts are all further elaborated in Kūttāṇṭavar cult ritual and folklore. For present purposes, each of his boons adds something to the problematics of death. In effect, he has three deaths, each of which coincides with one of the three boons.

Deaths	*Boons*
1. battlefield sacrifice (day 1)	1. prewar marriage
2. slain by Alambuṣa (day 8)	2. die a hero
3. of surviving head (day 18)	3. see entire war

In portraying Aravāṉ's prewar sacrifice and his watching of the entire war, Tamil traditions, and the Kūttāṇṭavar cult in particular, virtually cathect the full enormity of death in the *Mahābhārata* into this one figure, and bring it under his singular gaze. Understanding the relation between Kūttāṇṭavar's epic deaths and the mastery over death that extends into his identity as a village deity will be our main concern in this paper.

A. THE EARLY REPORTS

Colonialist ethnography gives us two notices of the cult of Kūttāṇṭavar. J. H. Garstin, in his *Manual of the South Arcot District* (1878: 214), describes a Kūttāṇṭavar festival at Kūvākkam village (Ulunturpet Taluk [formerly Tirukoyilur Taluk], South Arcot) as the 'great Shudra festival in Trikoilur [= Tirukoyilur] taluk. At this festival thousands of sheep and fowls are slaughtered and offered in sacrifice to Kuttandar, a village deity.' W. Francis, in the South Arcot volume of the *Madras District Gazetteers* (1906), expands: 'It is known for its festival of Aravan . . . or Kuttandar, which is one of the most popular feasts with Shudras in the whole district' (376). Although he has just repeated Garstin's line about Śūdras, Francis goes on to specify that it is mainly one caste that is involved:

> The ceremonies are sufficiently curious to deserve some notice, the more so as the deity is not commonly worshiped. The festival occurs in May and for 18 days the *Mahabharata* is recited by a Palli [i.e. Vaṉṉiyar], large numbers of people—especially of that caste—assembling to hear it read. On the eighteenth night a wooden image of Kuttandar is taken to a tope and seated there. This is the signal for the sacrifice of an enormous number of fowls. Everyone who comes brings one or two, and the number killed runs literally into thousands. Such sacrifices are most uncommon in South Arcot. . . . While this is going on, all the men who have taken vows to be married to the deity appear before his image dressed like women, offer to the priest (who is a Palli by caste) a few annas, and give into his hands the talis [*tāli*: necklace denoting marriage] which they have brought with them. These the priest, as representative of the god, ties round their necks. The god is brought back to his shrine that night and when in front of the building he is hidden by a cloth being held before him. This symbolizes the sacrifice of Aravan and the men who have just 'married' to him set up loud lamentations for the death of their 'husband'. (Francis 1906: 376)

From the vantage point of fieldwork on the cult of Kūttāṇṭavar since 1981, and, in particular, on the Kūvākkam Kūttāṇṭavar festival in 1982 and 1990, these descriptions are intriguing both for what they include and what they omit. Garstin's account is typical of late nineteenth-century colonialist ethnography in its lumping together of Śūdras into an undifferentiated mass, its contempt for the local and regional farmer-warrior traditions of landed dominant castes, its evident distaste for animal slaughter, and its total lack of interest in mythic and ritual detail and complexity (Cf. Hiltebeitel 1992). Clearly it is the administrative implications of the size of the festival that prompts him to mention it at all. Francis, however, goes beyond this quantitative impulse to make the valuable observation that 'the deity is not commonly worshipped'. He has clearly done some fieldwork.

Francis also shows more than a glimmer of interest in the ritual proceedings of the festival and the deity's connection with the *Mahābhārata*. Neither he nor Garstin mentions two communities that figure prominently at the Kūvākkam festival today: Paṟaiyars (Untouchables, Harijans) and Alis (Tamil-speaking so-called eunuchs). Alis were probably a much smaller presence at the festival in the period of these descriptions than they are today (Hiltebeitel forthcoming and 1998), but there can be little doubt that the roles that Harijans currently play at the festival are part of its constitution. Francis, however, does identify the Vaṉṉiyars as the main caste involved. He also gives us our first account of a ritual involving one of Kūttāṇṭavar's deaths. On the eighteenth day, the god is taken to a 'tope', seated, and fowls are offered; then he is brought outside his temple, placed behind a cloth to symbolize his sacrifice, and lamented by local farmers dressed as temporary transvestites who regard him as their husband. If we are to believe that Francis is accurate here, then nothing happens any more quite like he tells it. The climactic rituals now occur on the festival's sixteenth day rather than its eighteenth. From Francis's report it is as if Kūttāṇṭavar's multiple ritual deaths have been condensed into one: a cloth held before his icon outside his temple.

Curiously, this is similar to a ceremony performed for Kūttāṇṭavar at his festival in Kuricci (near Coimbatore), and a signal of a more pervasive problem in placing the Kūvākkam festival in the wider context of Kūttāṇṭavar cult traditions elsewhere. Coimbatore is at the far south-western end of the belt of Kūttāṇṭavar cult diffusion from the South Arcot end in which we find Kūvākkam. Garstin and Francis make it clear that the Kūvākkam festival already had a pre-eminence in the cult by the late nineteenth century. One can thus approach the problem from several angles. Is Kūvākkam the source of the cult's dispersal? Is it a concentration point toward which elements from elsewhere converge? Or are parallels that one finds with other Kūttāṇṭavar temples and festivals evidence for surviving traces within Kūvākkam of older features of the festival that have been overlain there with growing complexities? Each of these angles appears to offer insight: some elements have dispersed, some have come in, and, along with the fact that there is no tradition of Kūvākkam as

Kūttāṇṭavar's original temple,[5] there is enough evidence, via parallels with other villages, of old elements beneath the complexities there to make a convincing case that Kūvākkam once had a smaller festival comparable to those found elsewhere.

Francis also gives us our first, and rather intriguing, mythical account of one of Kūttāṇṭavar's deaths.

Aravan was the son of Arjuna. . . . Local tradition (which, though unsupported by the Sanskrit text of the *Mahabharata*, receives some warrant from the Tamil version), says that when the great war was about to begin the Kauravas . . . sacrificed, to bring them success, a white elephant. The Pandavas were in despair of being able to find any such uncommon object with which to propitiate the gods until Arjuna suggested that they should offer up his son Aravan. Aravan agreed to yield his life for the good of the cause, and when eventually the Pandavas were victorious he was deified for the self-abnegation which had thus brought his side success. Since he died in his youth, before he had been married, it is held to please him if men—even though grown up and already wedded—come now and offer to espouse him, and men who are afflicted with serious diseases take a vow to marry him at his annual festival in the hope of being cured. (1906: 375)

Francis shows a familiarity with the Sanskrit *Mahābhārata* and an awareness that Aravāṉ's elaborated story is distinctively Tamil, but the version he tells is striking for its differences from other known Tamil versions. Francis' account is in fact unique on two such points. Nowhere else have I found the Kauravas as the first to offer *kaḷappali* and the Pāṇḍavas' having to reply in kind. Where the Kauravas offer a white elephant in the *Makāpāratam* of Villipūttūr Āḻvār, it is only *after* the Pāṇḍavas' successful offer of Aravāṉ. And nowhere else is Arjuna the instigator of his own son's *kaḷappali* rather than the devious Kṛṣṇa. Indeed, Francis' account also mentions no mythic bride for Aravāṉ. It is as if men undertake their vows of transvestitism to marry a god who is already dead! The marriage theme is not found in the classical Tamil versions of the *Mahābhārata*, but it is pervasive in all four regions of the Kūttāṇṭavar cult, even though the wives Kṛṣṇa provides for Aravāṉ are different from region to region. In these two latter departures, it would seem that Francis' version either reflects or recalls a tradition prior to the development of the marriage story now known in the region, or has been motivated by some interest in removing Kṛṣṇa from that story. The story known at South Arcot Kūttāṇṭavar festivals is that Kṛṣṇa solves the problem of finding Aravāṉ a last-minute bride by transforming himself into Mohinī, the Enchantress. Kṛṣṇa's transformation into Mohinī to marry Aravāṉ is known textually to be at least as early as 1897, so it is certainly possible that two versions could have circulated in this period.[6] It is a major theme in Kūvākkam today, with contending theological explanations: local villagers generally understanding Mohinī as a temporary manifestation by Kṛṣṇa as a woman; the Alis viewing her as Kṛṣṇa's Ali *avatāra* (Hiltebeitel forthcoming and 1998).

Francis also went further to mention that 'similar vows are taken and ceremonies performed' at three other South Arcot Kūttāṇṭavar festivals (all in Chidambaram Taluk, South Arcot; 1906: 376), and left it for Bishop Henry Whitehead to visit them, and other Kūttāṇṭavar temples elsewhere, and retrieve our earliest account of Aravāṉ becoming Kūttāṇṭavar. At Tēvaṉampaṭṭaṇam (Cuddalore Taluk, South Arcot), the Kūttāṇṭavar temple pūcāri (priest) told Whitehead a story that I have not found in circulation anywhere. Indra, having committed Brahmanicide, became incarnated as Kūttāṇṭavar with a curse upon him 'that his body should rot away, leaving only the head'. No one would marry his daughter to him because anyone who married him in the morning would have to cut her *tāli* in the evening. 'Krishna, however, took pity on him, assumed the female form of Mohinī, and consented to be married to him in the morning, and then, as he vanished all but the head, the *tali* was cut in the evening' (1921: 27). Whitehead goes on to say that men dress as women to commemorate this marriage by the sacrifice of fowls and goats to the god 'a little distance in front of the shrine', where there is still today an offering stone on the edge of the beach. This variant, which either de-Mahābhāratizes Kūttāṇṭavar or represents a pre- or non-*Mahābhārata*-linked version of his cult, is curious for its connection of the god with Indra (and Brahmanicide) rather than with a son of Arjuna, Indra's son. Mohinī resolves the predicament. Although Alis are currently said to come to the Tēvaṉampaṭṭaṇam festival in small numbers, Whitehead does not mention them, and there is nothing in his account to indicate that they are part of the ritual or that Mohinī is an Ali in the myth.

Whitehead also mentions a tradition that Kūttāṇṭavar got his name 'from an Asura, or Demon', whom he killed, but does not give the story or locate its source(s). This presented a fieldwork challenge. At Kūvākkam, villagers know the story in localized form, while certain specialists also know it in more elaborate forms that the villagers themselves refer to as *purāṇa*. I found two such informants who circulate in eastern South Arcot. Kō. Eḻumalai (1989: 34) gathered another version at the 1988 Piḷḷaiyārkuppam Kūttāṇṭavar festival in the same area. Otherwise, except for the pūcāri at Tēvaṉūr, who had heard a version but couldn't remember it, I found nothing but likely fragments. Let us now turn to the two 'purāṇic' accounts.

B. THE DEFEAT OF KŪTTĀCŪRAṈ

I cite first the account by the Pāratiyār (*Mahābhārata*-reciter) Muttucāmi Piḷḷai, who performs mainly at southern South Arcot Draupadī festivals, but also, as of 1990, had been the Pāratiyār at the Kūvākkam Kūttāṇṭavar festival for nearly ten years. His version is important for its linking of Kūttāṇṭavar's myth with the Kūvākkam temple and festival.

After the eighteen-day war, Arjuna, Bhīma, and Draupadī began an argument over who actually won the war, each boasting that he or she had won the victory. Kṛṣṇa listened and said, 'We can't come to such conclusions. Let's go to the battlefield to see Aravāṉ, and ask him who finished the Pāratam (war) and who won the battle.' So they all approached Aravāṉ. When Aravāṉ saw all his fathers and uncles and everyone approaching him, he had no strength. He was lying there on the battlefield. Kṛṣṇa asked him, 'Who won the eighteen-day war? And who was the cause of the battle coming to an end?' Aravāṉ replied: 'It is not because of my fathers; the victory didn't come because of them.' Then he looked at Kṛṣṇa and said: 'Ayaṉē, your conch shell held the heads of the *senās* (soldiers, enemies, armies), and your *cakra* (discus) cut their necks. This is what I saw with my eyes.' Bhīma got angry: 'How could Aravāṉ say this? He's just saying it because of Kṛṣṇa.' He raised his mace. Kṛṣṇa, fearing that Aravāṉ would be wounded by Bhīma, called Garuḍa. He ordered Garuḍa to leave Aravāṉ's body in the Carapaṅka River. Garuḍa left Aravāṉ, holding his body between his legs, at the Carapaṅka Nati.

As Aravāṉ was left in the Carapaṅka Nati, a city developed there, which became very famous, called Centirakiri (Candragiri). Being left in the Carapaṅka Nati, having taken the form of a child, he started floating down the river. As the child was floating down the river, the king of Candragiri was in the forest hunting. He came down to the river to quench his thirst. There he saw the floating child. The Candragiri king had never had a child, so he rushed down to the river and held the child in his arms. The child cried 'Kuvā Kuvā'. That is why this (village) is called Kūvākkam. The Candragiri Rāja wondered what to call the child. So it was decided to call him Carapālaṉ. Day by day, hour by hour, he grew into a man.

At that time Kūttācūraṉ made a *digvijaya* [a conquest of the regions]. The king of Candragiri fought against him. Carapālaṉ saw his father being wounded by Kūttācūraṉ, and rushed to the field. He fought so well, everybody admired it; and he defeated Kūttācūraṉ. After defeating him, he came running to the feet of Parācakti: 'You are the supreme mother of the world, Kaṉṉi (maiden) of the world, a good woman (Uttami), Devī Pāñcāli, the undeflowered Pattiṉi (*aḻiyata pattiṉi*: Pattiṉi is the Tamil 'goddess of chastity'), Goddess of the Five (*aivar tēvi*). 'Oṃ Śakti, Icchā Śakti, Kriyā Śakti, Ādi Śakti, Parāśakti. Now I need a temple (*ālayam*) in this world. I should be able to repose (*amara vēṇṭum*) in the temple. I should be able to give my blessing (*aruḷ*) to my devotees (*aṭiyar*). So give me your blessing (*aruḷpotu*), Ammā.' Parāśakti said, 'You have killed the valiant Kūttācūraṉ; so from now on you will be known as Kūttāṇṭavar.' Thus at Kūvākkam they built this holy field (*tiviya kṣettiram*) with a big temple for him.

Clearly, Parāśakti, the goddess who answers Kūttāṇṭavar's prayers to establish his cult at Kūvākkam village, is Draupadī. Only in South Arcot does one find accounts linking Kūttāṇṭavar with Candragiri (see Hiltebeitel forthcoming). And only at Kūvākkam did I find a version linking the myth with Draupadī and the origins of the Kūvākkam temple. More interesting for present purposes are the details of the floating head and its baby's cry, '*kuvā*'. These are among the fragments of the Kūttāṇṭavar myth that recur elsewhere, as far south-west as Salem District. At Paṉaimatal (Salem District), with no apparent linking of the story to Kūvākkam, the pūcāri tells that the child Kūttāṇṭavar came down from a mountain in a basket (*pēṭai*) carried by a flood. When children opened the basket, the child cried, '*kuvā, kuvā*'. Then he played with the children. Here we have not only the head and the river but the mountain: a further theme that we can also anticipate tracing in Kūvākkam.

The second account of Kūttāṇṭavar's rebirth from Aravāṉ's severed head is still richer in themes of death and vitality. It is provided by the *ciṟpi* (icon sculptor and repairer, working in both wood and masonry) N. Dandapani, whose native village neighbours that of Tailāpuram, not far from Kūvākkam, the home of a thriving Kūttāṇṭavar temple and festival. Dandapani weaves together both the local knowledge of Tailāpuram festivals and a wider regional knowledge that comes from working at both village and Brahmanical temples all over northern Tamil Nadu.

Kūttācūraṉ is the reborn spirit (*āvi*) of the demon Tantavakkiraṉ. When Tantavakkiraṉ died, his *āvi* (spirit, ghost) split into two, going to two different worlds. He prayed to Nārada to create a child by bringing those two āvis back together. The two āvis stood together and prayed that they should be united together to form a child (*piḷḷai*). Through Viṣṇu's Tāraka mantra, Nārada made the two āvis into a small *cicu* (child: Sanskrit *śiśu*), and he asked the *cicu* to perform tapas. The tapas was so strong that Īcuvaraṉ (Śiva) appeared before the child, and asked, 'What do you want?' The child explained: 'When I went into the sky in two spirits, Nārada created me and made me into one child, using the Tāraka mantra. Now through my penance I am able to meet you. You should give me a body so that I should be born in such a way that nobody with a complete body (*muḻu uruvam*) should be able to defeat me. Let me not be defeated by anyone except a head from a body that has thirty-two marks (*lakṣaṇas*) that turns into a *cicu*; a person born from water and not from a mother's womb. Give me such a boon. If such a child is born to destroy me, born in the water, from such a head, receiving the grace of god (*kaḍavuḷ anukkirākam*), and grown up just as I was born out of a head, in water, by the grace of god, only such a one should be able to defeat me, a person with such birth, and no one else.'

Dandapani comments, transitioning into the voice of Tantavakkiraṉ: 'Some people say *talaiviti*, 'head fate', is like that. They will say 'I am a *kūṟṟu*' (*nāṉ vantu kūṟṟu*, hypercorrecting from *kūttu* = 'dance' though *kūṟṟu* = 'Death, Yama' to explain *kūṭṭu* = 'joining', as with the two spirits). Everything I do is part of the dance (*kūṟṟu*, but implying *kūttu*). What we dance is *kūṟṟu*. We are all dancing from the order of God (*kaḍavuḷ amaippu*). We do whatever he says. Whatever he wishes we do. That is *kūṟṟu*. Out of this *kūṟṟu* we are born as a child. Because I was born out of this *kūṟṟu*, and because I also originated out of the spirit of an Asura, therefore give me a name. One name Kūṟṟu, another name Cūraṇi, because I originated from an Asura. With both joined together, give me the name Kūttācūraṉ.'

So, with the name Kūttācūraṉ he was ruling. He started torturing the sages. All the gods joined together and cried on the shoulders of Mahāviṣṇu. Kṛṣṇa [i.e. Mahāviṣṇu] said, 'If anyone wants to defeat this child, it must be from the family of the Pāṇḍavas, in which there is one person known as Aravāṉ. Now the war is going to take place. Aravāṉ will be sacrificed, and on the eighth day his head will be severed by Alampācūraṉ (Alambuṣa). Then his head will fall into the *poykai nati*, a "river pond". Thus he will grow into a man. Then only can the Asura be defeated.'

So Aravāṉ goes to the war, does battlefield sacrifice to Kālī, and on the eighth day sets forth to fight Alampācūraṉ. Having become a skeleton, he says, 'I don't want to die without fighting. I'm such a valiant man, son of the man (Arjuna) with thirty-two lakṣaṇas, a great warrior with thirty-two myself. If I die without fighting there is no honor for me. Give me the chance to fight.' Kṛṣṇa gives him about ten to fifteen minutes. But how can a skeleton fight? He starts crying, thinking of his mother Nākakkaṉṉi [Serpent Woman; i.e. Ulūpī]. She comes and asks, 'O son, what do you want?' 'I'm going to fight. I need the strength.' Nākakkaṉṉi thinks of her father Nākarājaṉ. He appears and asks, 'What do you want, my daughter?' So Nākakkaṉṉi tells him, 'My son is going to fight. He needs strength.' So you know all those cobras, snakes, different sizes, suiting different parts of the body—fingers, arms, thighs—came and wound around the different parts of Aravāṉ's body. His skeleton became stiff (*viṟaippu*) now with all the snakes wound around him. He finished off one army division completely in an hour and a half. Kṛṣṇa thought, 'What is this? We won't have anything left for others!' Kṛṣṇa was the illusionist (*māyāvi*) who had come to lift the burden of the earth. So he did another trick (*tantiram*), and called Garuḍa to appear in the sky. When even the shadow of an eagle falls, the cobras will disappear. Alampācūraṉ arrived just at the right time, while the nāgas were falling off from Aravāṉ's body. While Aravāṉ was losing all his strength with the snakes falling off, Alampācūraṉ cut off his head. The head fell into the Carapaṅka River. There it changed its form (*uruvam*). From the *ciracu* (head) a child was born. They gave him a new life (*maṟu uyir uṇṭupaṉṟāṅka*: they gave him a re-life/birth). They gave the child born from the water the name Kūttaṉ. He fought Kūttācūraṉ and killed him. Thus he got the name Kūttāṇṭavar.

Tantavakkiraṉ, Sanskrit Dantavaktra or Dantavakra, is an interesting figure from Sanskrit sources, but something of a mystery even there, not to mention in our present context. He is mentioned briefly in the *Mahābhārata* as an incarnate Krodhavaśa demon (1.61.57-61), and as an ally of Kṛṣṇa's enemy Jarāsandha (2.13.12) he is subdued by the youngest Pāṇḍava Sahadeva on the latter's tour of conquest (2.28.3). The Calcutta edition makes Dantavaktra an incarnation of the Dānava Durjaya (Sörensen [1904] 1963: 234). But Purāṇic accounts make him a brother of Śiśupāla, a son of Vasudeva's sister Śrutadevī or Śrutaśravas (married to Damaghoṣa) and thus a cousin of the Pāṇḍavas and Kṛṣṇa, still allied with Kṛṣṇa's epic enemies (Jarāsandha and Śālva). By the time of the *Bhāgavata Purāṇa*, which has strongly influenced Tamil folk traditions, his slaying by Kṛṣṇa forms a pair with Kṛṣṇa's slaying of Śiśupāla: upon each of their deaths, a ray of light departs from them and enters the person of Kṛṣṇa.[7] As such, Dantavaktra is the least-known of the incarnations of Viṣṇu's doorkeepers Jaya and Vijaya, who turned away a visitation of youthful-seeming Ṛṣis (led by Sanaka Ṛṣi) to Viṣṇu's heavenly palace, and were punished by the Ṛṣis' curse to have to take on three lives each as pairs of demon brothers—Hiraṇyakaśipu and Hiraṇyākṣa, Rāvaṇa and Kumbhakarṇa, Śiśupāla and Dantavaktra—who, even as his great enemies, would remember Viṣṇu when he slew them in his avatārs (*Bhāgavata Purāṇa* 3.15.12-36; 7.1-2).

The folk tradition of Dantavaktra's intermediate state thus finds his spirit (*āvi*) split in two, requiring Nārada's intercession to draw it back together so that he can proceed to a new life. It is not, however, one of resumption of his career as Viṣṇu's gatekeeper, but of another life as a demon. We will see that the notion of reassembling *āvis* after death is also paralleled in a ritual context at Kūvākkam, where it concerns Kūttāṇṭavar himself. Indeed, the parallel between the god and the demon are strikingly evident in their watery, motherless births from spirit-heads and their regeneration of new bodies, probably recapitulating, at least in the case of Aravāṉ, a transmutation of the funerary ritual of s*apiṇḍīkaraṇa*, in which rice balls (*piṇḍas*) representing the head are projected into full bodies for the ancestors to occupy in the after-life.[8] In fact, several of Aravāṉ's myths and rituals evoke rites for the dead: his new moon-night battlefield sacrifice coincides with a time for ancestral offerings, and his last-minute marriage makes him an eligible, if extraordinary, Pitṛ, after whom village children may be named. Aravāṉ's head grows a 'new body', however, not to become a Pitṛ, but to re-enter the world so that he can defeat a demon and protect his devotees. However, we know from Kūttācūraṉ's boon that Aravāṉ's regenerated head cannot turn into a 'full body'. As a reborn 'child's head' (*ciracu kuḻantai*), at the most he grows only into a 'child' (*cicu, kuḻantai*; see n. 7). There is also the probably learned linking of 'dance' (*kūttu*) with 'Yama, Death' (Kūṟṟu, Kūṟṟaṉ), both relating to recurrent folk explanations of Kūttāṇṭavar's name as 'Lord (*aṇṭavar*) of the Dance' and 'Lord of Death', which connect him, respectively, with Śiva and Yama. Then too, there is the intriguing literalization and dramatization of the proverbial sense of *talaiviti*, 'head fate'—the inscription by Brahmā of one's destiny on the forehead. Though they each grow bodies, the opposition of god and demon is essentially a preordained one of 'head-to-head combat'.

C. THE FESTIVAL AT TĒVAṈŪR

Since one purpose of this essay is to glimpse the lives and deaths of Kūttāṇṭavar's severed head not only in the rich proliferation of his myths and rituals at Kūvākkam, but in the surprising manner in which his cult's diffusion of ritual and mythic fragments comprises survivals of his head of yet another (not unrelated) sort through the transmission of his cult, I will choose one festival outside Kūvākkam as an exemplar or archetype of a small-scale village Kūttāṇṭavar festival from which the Kūvākkam festival may have developed by elaborating into some of its more complex forms. My selection is the festival at Tēvaṉūr. It provides on a small scale a rich concentration of elements that one finds in Kūvākkam and elsewhere. And its location geographically in Tiruvannamalai Taluk, North Arcot makes it intermediate between Kūvākkam (and other comparable South Arcot festivals) to the east and the span of North Arcot, Salem, and Coimbatore temples and festivals to the north, west and south. As we shall see, it is not a question of a one-to-one comparison, but of a comparison of two complexes that, together, provide some initial density for a more extended inquiry into the relations between the Kūvākkam festival and other Kūttāṇṭavar festivals.

My information at Tēvaṉūr was obtained during a single visit on a non-festival day, and almost entirely from a single source, the Kūttāṇṭavar temple pūcāri Muniswami Goundar, who was most generous and genial in guiding me to the key festival sites and in digging into his memory as deeply as he could. The account is thus limited by these factors, and by my inability to think of all the questions I should have on one visit.

Kūttāṇṭavar has two temples at Tēvaṉūr. One is found in a large walled compound along with separate temples, all single-room stone structures, for Vināyakar (Gaṇeśa) and Māriyammaṉ. As one enters the compound, Vināyakar's temple is forefronted, freestanding, and to the left; Māriyammaṉ's is central and also freestanding; and Kūttāṇṭavar's (or Aravāṉ's) is set to the rear and built into the temple's back right (northwest) corner. A curved sword or billhook (*arivāl*) of the type that Aravāṉ is said to use for kaḷappali is set point-up, handle in the ground, in front of the entrance. The other Kūttāṇṭavar temple is not a structure at all, but an open-air niche amid trees and rocks, about halfway up a small 'mountain', itself a jagged outcrooping of ledges and boulders that rises about five hundred feet above the plain outside the village. This pattern of double village and hill shrines for Kūttāṇṭavar has already been noted, and provides a suggestive counterpart to other ways in which one finds Kūttāṇṭavar associated with mountains, such as we have begun to notice in his descent at Paṉaimatal in a basket from a mountain flood.

The festival begins on the *āmāvacai* or new moon day of Cittirai (April-May), when flowers and a *karakam* pot are taken to the hill shrine. The first day of the main eighteen-day festival period occurs on the first Sunday after the āmāvacai. 'God-dancers' (*cāmiyāṭis*) assemble at the hill temple and worship a post described as a *cūlam* (literally 'trident', the weapon of Śiva), and called *valiyam* ('strength'). Their worship of this post, a symbol of sacrifice, brings on possession (*āvēcam*). The flowers and karakam from the new moon night are then taken up, and, attended by the possessed cāmiyāṭis, are brought down from the hill temple to the village Kūttāṇṭavar temple in the compound. The karakam is placed before the Kūttāṇṭavar temple, beside the standing sword, and the cāmiyāṭis give oracles that bear upon the welfare of the village (e.g. will it rain?) and the god's pleasure or displeasure in the manner in which his *pūjās* have been conducted over the previous year.

Then the head of Kūttāṇṭavar is brought out from the sanctum of his temple and set in front of the Māriyammaṉ temple. The wooden head is said to be fifteen years old, and to have replaced an older one that was burnt in a fire that spread from the Māriyammaṉ temple. The older one's reduced and weathered remains are still identifiable in the hill temple. The new one will be repainted every fifteen years: a curious coincidence, but one that for now can only be taken at face value. The head is set before the Pāratiyār (*Mahābhārata*-reciter), who begins his eighteen days of *Pāratam* or *Mahābhārata*-recitation with the head as his chief spectator and audience. In this fashion, the Pāratiyār will continue Pāratam in front of the Māriyammaṉ temple for sixteen days, and for the last two days in front of the Kūttāṇṭavar temple. As is still done at other North Arcot Kūttāṇṭavar festivals (see Hiltebeitel 1998), the head used to be placed on a swing (*uñcil*) for its seeing and hearing of Pāratam. But this is no longer done, since the expenses are prohibitive. There are also four hooks in the ceiling of the Kūttāṇṭavar temple for the god to swing from all year, but this has also been discontinued. One finds the deity hung from the ceiling in a wooden box, called a 'basket' (*pēṭai*), at the Palaiyacūramaṅkalam temple in Salem city, Salem District, reminding us that his head descends in a basket from a mountain at another Salem District temple.

From days two through twelve, the thread of the festival consists of the Pāratiyār continuing to sing Pāratam to the head, as he does through all eighteen days. But from the thirteenth on, other activities intensify. On the evenings of the thirteenth, fourteenth, sixteenth, and seventeenth, dramas (*kūttu*) are performed. Aravāṉ's head watches these as well. The pūcāri could recall only that the drama on the night of the sixteenth was a performance by villagers of the 'Slaying of Pakācuraṉ', and that the others were combat scenes. The 'Slaying of Pakācūran (the Asura Baka)', which features the Pāṇḍavas' saving a village from a man-eating demon, in effect launches the heightened participation by villagers in the festival, as it sometimes does in Draupadī festivals in this region (Hiltebeitel 1988: 150-1, 169-82).

The seventeenth is the day for procession (*ūrvalam*) and 'karakam festival' (*karakam tiruviḻā*). The Māriyammaṉ temple is decorated, as is the karakam pot that had been brought down from the mountain with the cāmiyāṭis on the first day, when it was set before the Kūttāṇṭavar temple. The pūcāri takes the karakam on his head on procession through the village streets. That night, local men who have taken vows to do so dress as women with blouses and sarees, and put on tālis. The pūcāri explained: 'They do this so that Aravāṉ should be able to fight for one day and see the Pārata war even after he has offered the thirty-two parts of his body.'

All three boons—first-day marriage, eighth-day fight, and eighteenth-day vigil—are thus condensed. The marriages are celebrated at the Māriyamman̲ temple. The pūcāri added that the marriage was to Mohiṉī and the sacrifice to Kālī. He also knew of Aravāṉ's birth from Nākakkaṉṉi, the 'Serpent Princess', with the added note (new to me, but corresponding to other births of his floating head) that he was 'born in the sea'. It was Muniswami Goundar who had a vague recollection of Kūttācūraṉ in connection with the Carapaṅka River, but could not remember more of that story.

Leaving the Māriyammaṉ temple, everyone is very happy. But when they reach the base of the hill, a burst of firecrackers signals a change of mood toward the imminence of Aravāṉ's death, and everyone starts to weep. The base of the hill—no special spot, just the base—is called the 'weeping ground' (*aḻukaḷam*). The group continues on to the temple of the Ellaitēvatai, the village's 'Boundary Goddess'. They make boiled rice poṅkal, called *kuḻa*, and one man who has bathed offers it to the Boundary Goddess, asking that the dangerous part of the festival will now go smoothly. Thus while Māriyammaṉ is worshipped at her temple in the centre of the village in connection with Kūttāṇṭavar's marriage, the Boundary Goddess, who can be understood as her complement and multiform, is worshipped on the boundary of the village in conjunction with Kūttāṇṭavar's imminent death and his return to the mountain.

The eighteenth day is then the day for Kūttāṇṭavar's head to be embodied. According to Muniswami Goundar, there are thirty-two parts to his body, but only the arms (*pujam*) and chestplate (*mārkkantam*) were mentioned. These are assembled before the Māriyammaṉ temple on a chariot (*tēr*) to provide Kūttāṇṭavar with a standing body. The head is set in place, and garlands are strewn over the arms. A goat is sacrificed, and the chariot is then led in procession. Again, they start from the Māriyammaṉ temple in a happy mood, singing and dancing. But as they approach the base of the hill or aḻukaḷam, they start weeping. Now the cāmiyāṭis come down from the hill shrine once again. This is the moment for the performance of kaḷappali. They 'cut off' Kūttāṇṭavar's garland, remove the parts of his body, and disassemble the rest. The head is removed, and covered with a cloth. Men who have dressed as women now remove their tālis at the aḻukaḷam. A goat is sacrificed, the head going to the pūcāri. The place is then ritually cleaned and appeased (*puṇṇiyavataṉam*: apparently *puṇṇiyākavācaṉam*). Kūttāṇṭavar's head, which never goes beyond the aḻukaḷam to the hill shrine, is then brought back to his village temple.

On the twentieth day, Pāratam is performed—orally, and without any icon facing the Pāratiyār—for the coronation of Yudhiṣthira or Dharma (*tarumarpaṭṭāpicēkam*). And on the twenty-second day, a Sunday, turmeric water play and karakam dancing attend the karakam, covered with coconut and mango leaves, back to the hill temple. This removes all evils and bad omens from the village, since the death of Aravāṉ is borne away in the karakam.

Although it is not articulated, one will notice that there are two destinations for Aravāṉ at the end of the festival. His head goes back to the village temple. But his karakam goes back to the mountain. It is said that the karakam carries his 'death' away. But it is at his mountain shrine that he will possess the cāmiyāṭis at the beginning of the next festival. This raises the possibility that it is not just his death that goes away to the hill temple, but that his true life, or spirit, remains there: not in his head at the village temple but in the hill temple on the mountain. There it has the power to possess people throughout the year. Indeed, when I was at the spot, one man came and got deeply possessed in my presence. Then, as a new festival begins, it is only when the cāmiyāṭis are possessed and accompany the karakam to the village temple that the head can come out of that temple for its own processions and embodiment.

D. THE FESTIVAL AT KŪVĀKKAM: AROUND THE EIGHTEEN-DAY FRAME

Although, like most 'ideal' Kūttāṇṭavar festivals (and also Draupadī festivals [Hiltebeitel 1988: 134-44], Tēvaṉūr's is said to last eighteen days, it could be said more accurately that it spills into an eighteen-day frame at the beginning and overspills that frame at the end. The cāmiyāṭis mark the boundaries of this frame by bringing the god down from the mountain at its beginning and returning him there at its end. The mountain, and the god's temple there, is outside the frame. What occurs inside the frame can to some extent be identified as that which a particular temple and festival brings into relation to the *Mahābhārata*: in particular, the recitation of Pāratam, the eighteen-day war, and myths and rituals that refer, however obliquely or compactly, to Aravāṉ's part within it. This will vary considerably from one temple and festival to the next, and elements that are outside the frame at one festival may be inside it at another. What occurs outside the frame can then to a large extent be identified as the modes through which a particular temple or festival celebrates those features of the god that surpass the eighteen-day frame of his *Mahābhārata*-related manifestations. A shiftable element here is evident at Tēvaṉūr in the case of the 'Coronation of Dharma'. While this occurs at Tēvanūr on the twentieth day, after Kūttāṇṭavar's double adieu, at Kūvākkam it occurs on the eighteenth day itself, with Kūttāṇṭavar himself (that is, his icon) reinstated in his temple and adorned and worshipped as Yudhiṣthira or Dharma: a point to consider later. I pose this metaphor of spilling in and out of frames as a way to get some preliminary sense of the dynamics of diffusion between Kūttāṇṭavar festivals, and also as a way to begin to conceptualize the array, in its varied successions and proliferations, of deaths and revivals that Kūttāṇṭavar festivals call into play.

Turning now to the Kūvākkam festival, I will describe first the sequence of deaths and revivals of Kūttāṇṭavar that occur within the eighteen-day frame, and then take up those that range beyond it. Altogether, it is best to regard their number as beyond count, since for every one that one finds in ritual or myth, there is another that the finding evokes from the next informant—including the Alis, whose variations on the theme I discuss elsewhere (Hiltebeitel forthcoming and 1998). Along the way, we can note how this eighteen-day festival would seem to have changed considerably from the one described, however minimally, by Francis in 1906. Be it noted that the notion of an eighteen-day frame is provided by the Kūvākkam festival organizers, who have printed each year a poster (*pattirikai*) that announces the chief events for each of the eighteen days.

Following the pattirikai's outline description, the first day is sponsored by the Kūvākkam villagers, and consists of a ceremony called *cākai vārttal*, pouring from a brass plate. This refers to a distribution of a gruel made from *irāki* (a grain: *elensine cozacana*) at an open-air Māriyammaṉ temple about fifteen yards in back of the two-room (sanctum and outer maṇḍapa) Kūttāṇṭavar temple. A śakti karakam is prepared for Māriyammaṉ, and after bathing and receiving *kāppu* (a protective wristlet) from the temple pūcāri, the face of the Kūvākkam village washerman (Ēkāli) is thickly smeared with red powder (*kuṅkumum*) to indicate, according to him, 'just the śakti of Māriyammaṉ'. When he gets the goddess's 'grace' (*aruḷ*), he takes up the karakam on his head. Led by two music and drum bands—a Harijan band, the *rāja mēḷam* or 'king's band', in the lead, and a Vaṉṉiyar band, the *kōvil mēḷam* or 'temple band', in train—the Ēkāli carries the śakti karakam around the village's inner square of four streets. Each household is decorated with festoons of margosa leaves (sacred to Māriyammaṉ) in anticipation of his arrival, and at each stop women from the household come forth to offer a plate of food, which he blesses, waving sprigs of margosa, passing the margosa over his reddened face, and returning the plate as *prasādam*.

As the Ēkāli proceeds with the two bands, they are followed by householders, mainly women, who have prepared irāki gruel in their houses, and join the throng once their homes have been visited to bring the gruel to the Māriyammaṉ temple, carrying it in pots on their heads. When all arrive, the karakam is set down there. Village headmen (*nāṭṭāṉmais*), or their representatives, now arrive from about ten other surrounding villages along with additional processions bringing pots of irāki gruel. The gruel can be taken home and kept for about two days. Those who give will not take any home. Vaṉṉiyars can be both givers and receivers; Harijans only receivers. After the gruel is distributed, the pūcāri removes the kāppu from the Ēkāli's wrist.

Different interpretations are given for the karakam procession. One voice from the crowd was the first to offer what seems an impromptu understanding: 'The Ēkāli is Nākakkaṉṉi [Aravāṉ's serpent mother]: the śakti karakam will give birth to Aravāṉ when it reaches the temple.' This was denied by several people, among them the Ēkāli, who said the karakam 'is for Māriyammaṉ; it is śakti only'. The junior temple pūcāri, M. Kaṇṇaṉ Pūcāri, who emerged as one of the most helpful and intriguing informants, said the rite represents Aravāṉ's leave-taking to go to war: 'It is like when we go somewhere from our own village to do work, we go to the Māri temple before leaving, and pray to her—"See, I'm leaving town now, take care of me." The same way Kūttāṇṭavar goes, saying a prayer to Māriyammaṉ before he goes to war. Then only can the eighteen-day war and paṭṭāpicēkam take place.'

The offering of irāki gruel at the beginning of the festival, especially to Harijans, is linked with a local origin myth of the temple known in variants by both Vaṉṉiyars and Harijans. I have gathered versions only from the former, but in groups that included concurrence from members of both communities. Thus, 'Kūttāṇṭavar's head was found in a field of irāki by the Harijans, the 'colony people' (*kālāṉi kuṭimakkaḷ*) who were guarding the fields'; or, 'Kūttāṇṭavar came to a Harijan in a dream: 'I am under a thorny bush, come and get me'. But the Harijan came and told the people in the village. Then the village people [Vaṉṉiyars] went to get it. Thus the colony and village people have equal rights in the worship'; or, tying back into themes developed in the more 'Purāṇic' accounts, 'When the king of Candragiri was ruling this place, the head came floating by down the Carapaṅka River. The river was coming this way in those days. So the head came and stayed on the bank in Nāttaṉ village. While the Harijans were guarding the fields in the night, they were singing some songs because they had bhakti—bhakti songs. Then the head started talking to them. The next day the [Harijan] watchman told the village people, who searched the area, found the head, and brought it here to found the temple'; or 'The head was found on the bank of the Carakōṇi (= Carapaṅka) River under three trees, a *vaṉṉi* [Sanskrit *śamī*], an *ātti* [country fig], and an *āvaram* [a small shrub with a yellow flower]. . . . This place used to be called Candragiri. Only after they built the Kūttāṇṭavar temple did it come to be called Kūvākkam.' The *vaṉṉi*, I confirmed, is the 'thorny bush' mentioned in the second account. The etymology for the village [*kū*+*pākkam*, 'Kū-village'] differs from Muttucāmi Piḷḷai's derivation from the baby's cry, 'Kuvā'.

One senses in these stories, and throughout this opening ceremony, that one is on a boundary of Aravāṉ's identity with Kūttāṇṭavar, and on the margins of the festival's eighteen-day frame. As at Tēvaṉūr, Kūttāṇṭavar is linked with a goddess of the village centre, Māriyammaṉ, who has no immediate connection with the *Mahābhārata*.[9] Kūttāṇṭavar is not even worshipped directly at this point, and *Mahābhārata*-related interpretations of the ceremony are tentative at best. But Kūttāṇṭavar is evoked through his births and deaths, his arrivals and departures, which typify this god, and spill into and out of the frame. The local origin myths differ in whether they accentuate a tree or a river, and, if the latter, how they explain the absence of a river in Kūvākkam today, and connect the village with Candragiri. But, like Muttucāmi Piḷḷai's account, they all explain how the head comes to the Kūvākkam temple.

Kūttāṇṭavar's gradual embodiment and disembodiment through processions then begins on the first night. To music and firecrackers, the head is brought outside the temple to be danced around the village through its inner rectangle of streets. This presents the god in the first of his three types of processions. In the second and third, his head is later carried on a platform (*keṭāyam*), and then joins the god's body on his full chariot (*tēr*). The dancing of the head first occurs after nightfall on the first day, and is repeated through the first six evenings. Nine Vaṉṉiyars, among them Kaṇṇaṉ Pūcāri, dance in relay—only when the Harijan of Paṟaiyar drum band plays. To hold the big wooden head on their own heads, the dancers make a turban from a twenty-five foot-long white cloth, received and gathered up at the temple entrance after it had been extended and stretched out lengthwise from the god's head in the sanctum. Though they are inspired by the Paṟaiyar drummers, the Vaṉṉiyars claim they feel no *āvēcam*, 'possession'. But they are clearly in the role of cāmiyāṭis, since Kūttāṇṭavar does possess people in such circumstances, as we have seen in one case at Tēvaṉūr. At Kūvākkam, one is told that it is Kūttāṇṭavar who dances. The Cāmi is said to be a fearsome or awesome dancer (*cāmi payaṅkaramāka āṭuvār*), and to make the nine Vaṉṉiyars dance spectacularly. *Payaṅkara āṭṭam* is 'fearsome possession dance' that is held to be for real (Blackburn 1988: 230 n. 27). Kūttāṇṭavar's head undergoes a special decoration—called *cattuppiṭi pū alaṅkāram*—with jasmine flowers, which are attached to cut pieces of plantain stalk fixed to his crown, and extend as flower strings that look like wild flying hair. Thus one may suspect that it is the god who is possessed. In any case, his head, brought to life, animates the dancers, who are said to move in the bold strides of medieval Vaṉṉiyar warriors. A contrast with the Tēvaṉūr festival is instructive here. At Tēvaṉūr, possession and descent from the mountain inspire auguries and precede the emergence of the head from the temple. Here the head is brought out before the animated dance so that the nine Vaṉṉiyars can experience themselves in Kūttāṇṭavar's warrior persona. In the one case, inaugural possession occurs outside the festival's *Mahābhārata* frame, in the other it is muted in a way that is appropriate within that frame.

Toward the beginning of the procession, before turning from the initial street to the north to go on the next street to the east, a passageway is made for one of the dancers to dance briefly on a lane that extends further toward the north. This is the passage toward the 'weeping ground' or aḻukaḷam: as at Tēvaṉūr, the site of the lamentation rituals that will take place later in the festival. On the sixteenth day, this will be a site of Kūttāṇṭavar's death: the death that is wept for, which, as we will see, is open to several narrative interpretations, all drawn from the *Mahābhārata*. What is significant is that Kūttāṇṭavar's identity as Aravāṉ is now for the first time highlighted, preparing him for his epic feats, on the opening night of the head's dancing and emergence from his temple. It is not just that Aravāṉ says adieu to Māriyammaṉ. He is now further into the frame of the *Mahābhārata*: even as a head, he is pointed toward his epic destruction. After being danced through Kūvākkam's four main streets, the head is returned late each of the first six nights to the temple.

Whereas the first day is sponsored by the Kūvākkam villagers, the second, says the pattirikai, is sponsored by the Harijans, the Kūvākkam colony people. Along with this, the pattirikai announces that the day's main ceremonies are 'tāli-tying' and 'beginning of Pāratam recitation' (*tāli kaṭṭutal, pāratam ārampam*). In the early afternoon, Harijans come from their hamlet and circle the village in procession with poṅkal preparations, drumming and dancing. Then they go to the side of a dry tankbed west of the temple, make poṅkal (a rice and boiled milk porridge) there, and bring the poṅkal to the Kūttāṇṭavar temple. They do not, however, take the poṅkal into the temple, but worship from outside while the pūcāri offers a waving of lights within. Among the Harijans outside the temple sits the *cāttukkāraṉ*, the one who 'anoints'. He sits on a cloth watching and waiting as the ceremony develops. He is a member of the Harijan family that found the deity in the irāki field. The role of Cāttukkāraṉ is hereditary in his family and analogous to the roles of Harijans in Salem District Kūttāṇṭavar temples (Paṉaimatal and Tēṭavūr) where a Harijan marries Kūttāṇṭavar (Hiltebeitel 1998).

After the poṅkal, later in the afternoon, the double ceremony of tāli-tying and 'beginning of Pāratam' is performed at an open grove of pippal trees known as N. Devanayakar Chettiyar's grove (*tōppu*). This is the site that will come to be known as the aḻukaḷam or 'weeping ground' later in the festival. Tāli-tying refers to the first rites to enact Kūttāṇṭavar's marriage, while the 'beginning of Pāratam' consists of the Pāratiyār briefly recounting the story of Vyāsa, the *Mahābhārata's* composer, getting the elephant-headed Gaṇeśa to be his amanuensis.

On the ground of this grove, these two ceremonies are orchestrated in a space that is repeatedly called *kōvil* or 'temple', and *pantal āti*, 'the base of the pantal'. The notion is that there is not only a 'temple' here, but a pantal or open 'porch' extending from its base. The pantal is called the 'flower pantal' (*pū pantal*). The sanctum of the 'temple' that the pantal extends from to the east is a mound of earth. During the 'marriage' part of this double ceremony, it will be sown with seeds of 'nine grains' (*navatāṉiyam*). The sowing occurs in connection with the tāli-tying: a double wedding in which, first, two male Vaṉṉiyars representing Aravāṉ and Mohinī marry each other within the outdoor 'temple', and then two Harijans representing (at least according to Kaṇṇaṉ Pūcāri and other Vaṉṉiyars) the same two figures, marry each other before a small trident set in the ground just *outside* the putative temple's entrance. The Cāttukkāraṉ, though he was surprised to learn this, is thus, for the Vaṉṉiyars at least, the Harijan bride, or 'Mohinī'. Significantly, the sowing of nine grains takes place in conjunction with his wedding to Kūttāṇṭavar, not during the wedding of the two Vaṉṉiyars. From this second day on, essentially, to the sixteenth day, the day of Kūttāṇṭavar's epic death(s), the Cāttukkāraṉ guards the sprouts that grow on the mound of sown navatāṉiyam from goats and other minor menaces. These sprouts, in their sowing, life, and death, parallel the marriage, epic involvements, and death(s) of Kūttāṇṭavar (Hiltebeitel 1991: 65-71). The Cāttukkāraṉ has also been responsible for constructing the 'flower pantal'. This requires him to gather leaves and twigs from three trees in three different participating villages: *ātti maram* from Kūvākkam itself; and from the two others, a thorny *vaṉṉi* tree (the thorns were emphasized) and an *āvaram*. Let us recall that our fourth source on the origin of Kūttāṇṭavar's head knew these three trees in connection with the site where the head stopped floating. He also explained the use of twigs from these trees for the pantal āti as recalling the finding of the head. Not surprisingly, one also learns that the Cāttukkāraṉ's hereditary role devolves from an ancestor who [was among those who] found the head. The Cāttukkāraṉ would thus seem to construct a 'temple' to commemorate this finding of the god's head by his Harijan ancestors outside the village. Moreover, the ātti is the tree whose twigs, leaves, and branches are gathered at Coimbatore area Kūttāṇṭavar festivals as a source containing the *uyir* or 'life' of Kūttāṇṭavar, must be brought from the forest to the village temple to bring the god into the festival.[10] These animating elements are functionally analogous to the descent from the mountain at Tēvaṉūr. As at Tēvaṉūr, Kūvākkam has both a village temple and an outer temple (the *pantal āti*) for Kūttāṇṭavar. Both the grove and the mountain supply the 'weeping ground'. But on the level plain of Kūvākkam there is not a mountain in sight. The 'flower pantal' cannot be permanent in this setting and must thus be temporarily constructed. The Harijans sponsor this day as one that brings them into the eighteen-day frame that relates the festival to the *Mahābhārata* through the marriage of the Cāttukkāraṉ to Kūttāṇṭavar. But it would also seem that the Vaṉṉiyars bring the Harijans into this frame, attributing their own traditions of epic affinities to them, and, as in the myth of the finding of the head, controlling the compromise in which the two communities have 'equal shares' in the festival.[11]

From days three to twelve, the thread of the festival consists of Pāratam recitation at the village temple, covering epic episodes from the birth of Śāntanu to Kṛṣṇa's embassy to the Kauravas. The only matter of note occurs on the eleventh, when a bamboo post is installed on the axis from the sprouts to the small trident outside the open-air temple, just on the inside (facing the temple) of the trident. Called the *veḷḷikkāl* ('silver leg'), this will be the post at which Alis and transvestite village vow-takers will break their bangles and cut their tālis.

From the thirteenth day onward, preparations are made for the god's fully embodied procession. This marks the period in the festival where Aravāṉ undergoes an increasing concentration of multiple forms of ritualized death and revival.[12] On the thirteenth day, the main ceremony, held in the morning, is *Aravāṉ Pali*, 'the sacrifice of Aravāṉ'. The Pāratiyār recites Aravāṉ's kaḷappali and the opening of the war with the gathering of the armies. But the main ritual activity, called *Kūttāṇṭavar Cāmi Pālāyaṉam*, reflects Aravāṉ's sacrifice only obliquely. *Pālāyaṉam*, a secret mantra (perhaps related to Sanskrit *bāla*, 'youth', or *pāla*, 'protection'), is uttered by an Ācāri carpenter, serving in an hereditary role.[13] This mantra enables the transfer of Kūttāṇṭavar's 'life' (*uyir*) from his head into a *kalacam*, a decorated vessel, through a blade of long, thin *darbha* grass.

The head, now 'mere wood', is then wrapped in red silk, and taken to a shed in the back of the temple. A different carpenter and a painter, both Vaṉṉiyars from a nearby village, who perform this task each year (not every fifteen years, as at Tēvaṉūr), remove Kūttāṇṭavar's jewels and mustache, and peel off all the paint-on-cloth that covers the head. The chief painter has done this for fifteen years, and the right has been in his family for generations. The paint-peeling and mustache-removal are both said to be part of Aravāṉ's death. A white cloth is put over the head and serves as the base of the new painting, the new cloth becoming part of the new face. The beginning of the recovering and repainting starts soon after the head is bared, but the full repainting and final touches await completion at a significant ritual moment two nights hence. The kalacam remains in the sanctum until early on the sixteenth day after midnight (see Plate 9).

On the fourteenth day, the main ceremony is the evening one of *kampam niruttal*, 'the standing of the post'. Again, Ācāris are in charge of the preparations. About twenty feet high, the post is raised upright by these carpenters—with offerings of coconuts, jaggery, betel, and lamp-waving—on a big processional chariot (*tēr*). At around 6 p.m., the Kūvākkam village headman (*nāṭṭāṉmai, nāṭṭār*) plants the post in the *tēr* with the government-appointed HRCE (Hindu Religious and Charitable Endowments Board) Tarumakarttā (chief temple trustee) in attendance. Once this occurs, men who vow to marry Aravāṉ may begin to purchase tālis at two rupees apiece from HRCE officials under the pantal (temporary roof) extending from the front of the *village* temple. They bring the purchased tāli before the pūcāri in the sanctum, who (now representing Aravāṉ) ties it around their necks, along with a protective *kāppu* wristlet around their right wrists. Harijans also sell tālis outside the pantal for fifty paise, mostly to other Harijans, and conduct their marriages to Aravāṉ there. These marriages replicate those of the second day at the open-air temple in the grove. In both cases, the Vaṉṉiyar marriages take place in the temple, the Harijan marriages outside the temple. Now, however, a third group is present: the Alis, who can don the tālis inside the temple, along with the Vaṉṉiyars.

On the fifteenth day, the festive atmosphere builds from the evening on, with the Alis and others coming in increasing numbers. By night-time, it is a carnival. Until well past midnight, the Alis dominate the scene, dancing, singing, letting loose (see Hiltebeitel forthcoming and 1998). After midnight, while many revellers sleep on the ground surrounding the temple, in a ceremony I was not permitted to attend, the final touches are applied to the painting of Kūttāṇṭavar's head. By now it is the sixteenth-day morning. The ceremony is called *cuvāmi tirukkaṇ tiruttal*, 'the opening of the god's holy eyes'. According to an Ācāri assisting in the rite, the deity is first set to face west in the shed behind the temple. At about 3:20 a.m., a Brahman, along with about nine elders, goes to the temple sanctum for the kalacam that had held the god's uyir ('life', 'soul') since the cāmi pālāyaṉam on the thirteenth day. Ten minutes later, the vital vessel is brought into the shed close to the Cāmi's head. The Ācāri recites mantras while connecting the kalacam to the deity's head with a blade of darbha. He then takes a mango leaf, and burns a piece of camphor (*karpūram*). A slight soot forms on the oil of the leaf, which the Brahman takes and holds against Aravāṉ's face. The Brahman then presents the leaf with its oily sooted surface before the deity's face 'like a mirror', to see whether the uyir has transferred from the kalacam to the head. Only the Brahman can tell. Then he takes a blade of darbha, dabs the tip in the soot, and touches the tip only slightly to Aravāṉ's eyes. Thus the Brahman does the actual eye-opening, but the Ācāris follow with a similar rite using a coconut, and touching the deity's pupils with a tip of darbha that extends from one of the three eyes of the coconut. The Ācāri then takes the kalacam back into the temple, to which it belongs as temple property, but it is not returned to the sanctum, since it no longer contains Kūttāṇṭavar's uyir. Once sight and life are restored to the Cāmi's head, only finishing touches—a flower decoration of the head and a refitting of the mustache—remain before the head can be brought out for *darśan* (ritual viewing) and procession.[14]

Meanwhile, outside, between the shed and the temple, excitement mounts. Many jam together in front of the shed to await the god's emergence for his public eye-opening and placement on the portable keṭāyam, which faces north, the direction of his death toward which the procession will begin. The Vaṉṉiyars' *kōvil mēḷam* ('temple band') circumambulates the temple, and then goes off to return with the *tiruvācci*, the flower decoration: an arched scaffold of orange and red flowers, which must be carefully erected at the back of the keṭāyam beneath a royal umbrella, to await the placement of the head in its inner arc. As the parties position themselves for the climactic moment, the Vaṉṉiyar 'temple band' aligns itself in the eastward passageway between the shed and the keṭāyam, while the Paṟaiyar 'king's band' stands ahead of the keṭāyam to precede it north once its procession begins. When opened, the god's eyes will see the Harijans first. The Alis are nowhere in evidence at this moment.

Three series of firecrackers erupt in the fields. Finally the head is brought out from the shed at about 3:40 a.m. The crowd shouts 'Govindā!' as the head is raised onto the keṭāyam, on which five village headmen are perched to receive it. There a cloth is lifted from his eyes for his public eye-opening (see Plate 10). As the procession begins, the Harijan petromax lantern-carriers and Rāja mēḷam lead; the Vaṉṉiyar Kōvil mēḷam with a relay of karakam carriers in its midst comes next; and the Cāmi on the keṭāyam comes last in the position of honor (see Hiltebeitel 1991: 449-50). Once the Cāmi's head has set forth, the keṭāyam is soon flanked by additional platforms, also called *tēr* ('chariot'), one of which bears Kūttāṇṭavar's garland-draped chest-plate (*mār paṭakkam*) and epaulets (*pujam*), which have been brought from one of the nearby villages, and the other his flower karakam, which has been danced through the evening. The mār paṭakkam is so important that is said there can be no festival without it. This train proceeds around the four village streets from about 3:45 to daybreak. Reminding us of Tēvaṉūr, as the Cāmi sets off, it is said that one can see in his face that he is happy (*cantōṣam*) and smiling.

The climax of the festival then begins around 5:30 a.m. Awaiting the completion of the Cāmi's procession around Kūvākkam on the keṭāyam, a vast crowd assembles in the open area among the village temples. On top of the Kūttāṇṭavar temple, cocks are offered: no longer cut, but thrown up onto the temple roof. Only male birds are offered. Finally, the post or kampam on Kūttāṇṭavar's tēr stands ready for the assemblage of his body. Already in place are the wooden horses, forearms, feet bells, and two flags (*koṭicīlai*), all of which come from different surrounding villages, and straw to fill out the frame. The tiruvācci and umbrella (*kuṭai*), removed from the keṭāyam, are danced toward the *tēr* and raised to a support at the top of the kampam. Then the other items, all from neighbouring villages, are also danced through the crowd one-by-one to the *tēr* and raised into place: the umbrella; the winged half-tubular epaulets, which are raised and filled with flowers; the chestplate. Finally, the head, which has been danced around while the other components are positioned, is raised and set on the pole's top. When this happens, it is an amazing scene: a great boom of firecrackers goes off: 200 kilograms of smoky camphor is lit in front (east) of the deity; the entire concourse flings strings of jasmine, spectacularly filling the air before the flowers land on the god's body as 'two lakhs' worth of garlands (200,000 rupees). The Alis contribute much of the camphor, and fling strings of jasmine from their hair. Devotees positioned on the god's frame gather the flowers onto and into his body.

This is the moment when Aravāṉ is framed in his full epic stature: his pose heroic, ready to fight, his frame-and-straw body complete, decorated, draped and filled with flowers. Pulled into motion amid a huge crowd, the giant image sets off as a hero or *vīraṉ* to repeat the march around the village streets. Now, however, he is said to begin looking sad: happy as a head, he is sad as embodied, exhibiting tears and sweat. Thus, as he prepares for the rituals that reenact or recall his battlefield sacrifice and eighth-day fight with Alambuṣa, his embodied state registers his readiness for sacrificial suffering and death. While his *tēr* goes around the village, he takes on an increasingly 'dead look', and when he reaches the southern street where the Alis went, they have a married man with them who provides them with a white saree of a widow. It is here that the Alis begin to ritualize Aravāṉ's death by kaḷappali.

Shortly before noon, having completed the tour of the village, the chariot turns on the unpaved lane to the north, taking the route that was opened up momentarily when the head was danced through the streets on the festival's opening night. Here the Alis let their hair down and start weeping. It is said to be like the point (though it actually inverts it) in an ordinary funeral procession when a pot is broken and the women turn back. According to some (including the Alis), this marks the occasion of Aravāṉ's kaḷappali, his 'battlefield sacrifice'. This would be the moment when he faces north toward Kurukṣetra (Hiltebeitel 1991: 289-94, 301-17), as he does at the Draupadī cult *paṭukaḷam*: the ritual battlefield (lit. 'place of lying down, of death') equivalent to the Kūttāṇṭavar cult 'weeping ground' (ibid.: 208-13, 299-302). Alternately, for others, his march from that point represents his entry of Kurukṣetra on the war's eighth day to fight Alambuṣa. Such informants say that there is no precise ritual enactment of kaḷappali. Rather, it is recalled homonymically as akin to Aravāṉ's 'final sacrifice' (*kaṭaipali*): the dismantling of his body that will take place at the Kālī temple on this evening after nightfall. Both Aravāṉ's kaḷappali and his eighth-day fight are also evoked in the continued procession to the 'weeping ground'. His epic deaths and rebirths thus multiply and interdiffuse. Yet his kaḷappali remains the most universally known mytheme, since it is recalled minimally as the reason that everyone is wearing tālis to marry him.

The tēr now moves through the dried paddy fields away from Kūvākkam toward the 'weeping ground', in N. Devanayakar Chettiyar's grove. In 1982, cocks were still sacrificed as votive offerings before the chariot's wheels as it made this march. On the way, attendants hanging from the heroic giant's arms toss his fading and browning garlands to those below: signs of his loss of vitality and vigour. The widowed Alis, now dishevelled, carry on ritualized women's laments for the god—dead for them, doomed for others—and continue their dirges in approaching the aḻukaḷam. The Alis for the most part then go to the aḻukaḷam long in advance of the slow procession of Kūttāṇṭavar's 'chariot'. There they complete their weeping and, having become Aravāṉ's widows, they sever their tālis' strings and break their bangles at the bamboo veḷḷikkāl. Most of the Alis then go to a bathing tank, don white widow's sarees, and start for home. They are supposed to continue to wear signs of widowhood for thirty days. Most are gone when the chariot arrives at the aḻukaḷam grove in mid-afternoon.

The remainder of the daytime activities involves the huge regionally gathered crowd (up to 20,000 people), and then narrows to the entirely local ceremonies that concern villages around Kūvākkam. The rites at the veḷḷikkāl continue through mid-afternoon. But rather than the Alis, those who now cut their tālis, break bangles, and offer lamp-waving and coconuts at this post are young to middle-aged men from Kūvākkam and its surrounding villages: mostly farmers and traders. Aravāṉ is said to 'watch' these tāli-cuttings, something he cannot do for the Alis, who have left the veḷḷikkāl before his *tēr's* arrival. Ritually, this is Kūttāṇṭavar's last vigil: the completion of the day-long cycle from which his reborn seeing head first went forth around the village happy, only to be saddened as it embodied itself for marriage, kaḷappali, and heroic death in battle.

Clearly, the tāli-cuttings by the villagers before the still 'seeing' deity suggest a compression into the aḻukaḷam rituals of an element of the 'that day tied, that day cut' theme of Aravāṉ's kaḷappali—in other words, his one-day marriage, which occurs (mythically) at the beginning of the war.[15] While still embodied, he can thus continue to watch the war, as promised in his second boon, from beginning to end. But they also foretoken the end of Aravāṉ's war-ending vigil, and coincide with the ritual enactment of his third and last epic death. The clearest evidence of this lies in the Pāratiyār's recitation at the aḻukaḷam of the last two days' battles, culminating in the war-ending death of Duryodhana. This he delivers simultaneously (while hardly anyone listens) with the veḷḷikāl widowing rites of the villagers. Whereas the Alis lament Kūttaṇṭavar only through the half-deaths linked above all with his first death, his kaḷappali, and while the Pāratiyār maintains attention on his second, the villagers undergo their widowing rites at the close of his third, beneath Kūttāṇṭavar's dying eyes. In waiting especially for his third death—at the end of his eighteen-day vigil at the end of the war—to cut their tālis, the villagers' widowhood is analogous to what occurs in rituals for Aravāṉ on the Draupadī cult ritual battlefield. There too Aravāṉ, a surviving head at the end of his eighteen-day vigil, is among the heroes lamented by Draupadī and other women at the paṭukaḷam (Hiltebeitel 1991: 329-31).

The analogy between the lamentation rites at Kūttāṇṭavar and Draupadī cult ritual battlefields is thus significant within the dynamics of village ritual *per se.* Each represents what the villagers do collectively to close their frame on the festival's 'sacrifice of battle'. As 'widowing' rites, they bring vow-taking villagers into their most intimate ritual rapport with the dead *Mahābhārata* heroes. Lamenting male villagers become the wives of those larger-than-life, quasi-demonic heroes—the vīraṉs—who are represented by huge effigies. For the villagers, Kūttāṇṭavar's *real* death comes about with the end of his 'eighteenth-day' vigil. However cumulative or encompassing it may also be of his prior deaths, this is the death that must finally come with the fulfilment of all three of his epic boons. It is the death that frames him as an 'ancestor': a category that clearly cannot pertain to the Alis, but pertains to the villagers with special intensity, and commits them—and them only—to the deity's death rites.

The tangled roots of a great pippal tree behind him, no longer limbed with flowers, the huge figure is said to look skeletal and to be dead (see Plate 11). A large basket of cooked sacrificial rice, called blood rice (*irattacōṟu*), is brought from Kaṇṇan Pūcāri's house, and placed in front of Kūttāṇṭavar's chariot. Supposedly it is sold at twenty-five paise a pinch, and taken as *prasādam.* Actually there is a mêlée, and it goes quickly to those who grab it. Women who eat the rice are enabled to conceive children, who will be called Kūttaṉ if a boy and Kūttammā/Kūttammāḷ if a girl. Aravāṉ is also prominent among Draupadī cult heroes who become ancestors: in his case, again, particularly through rituals involving offerings of 'blood rice' (Hiltebeitel 1991: 292, 296, 298-9). The rice is distributed as on the sixteenth day after a death. Since this is the sixteenth day of the festival, there is not only a collapsing of marriage, death, and sixteen-day waiting period to one day, but an implicit recollection of the opening day of the festival as one of a death that marks the god's entry into his epic life: as evoked on that first day when the head is for the first time danced briefly toward the north.

If we recall Francis' description of the Kūvākkam festival before it attracted large numbers of Alis, we can infer, I think correctly, that the villagers retain what is most basic in honouring Kūttāṇṭavar's cumulative deaths. One might also suspect a solution to the question posed by Whitehead's account from Tēvaṉampaṭṭaṇam, in which Kṛṣṇa becomes

Mohinī to marry Kūttāṇṭavar, alias Indra, to avert the curse 'that his body should rot away, leaving only the head'. Although this too is a one-day marriage, the rotting body seems likely to derive from a rethematizing of the question of what happens to Kūttāṇṭavar's body—as distinct from his head—during his eighteen-day *Mahābhārata* vigil.

After these aḻukaḷam rites, Kūttāṇṭavar's *tēr* is removed from the grove. A cloth is placed over his head—his dead eyes now covered—and the huge chariot, now a 'death bier', is drawn into the open fields between the aḻukaḷam and an open-air Kālī temple by the lakeside (see Plate 12). The lake is considered by some to be the cremation ground, for Aravāṉ's last rites. The *tēr* is backed up and pulled toward the lake bund. Here Kūttāṇṭavar is disaggregated: his umbrella, tiruvācci, mār paṭakkam, epaulets, head, and straw are all removed, in that order, leaving only the post (kampam) and body-scaffolding on the *tēr* (see Plate 13). The removed head, covered with a red cloth, is carried upside-down by a Vaṉṉiyar to a spot near the lake bund, and placed upside-down, because it is dead. At dust and nightfall, a small group of Paṟaiyars holds a vigil by the head. Then after about two hours, it is taken from the corner of the lake bund and carried to the Kālī temple on the south side of the bund. Since the head is dead, the pūcāri will not carry it at these moments, and again it is borne by the same Vaṉṉiyar. The progress of the head is marked by drums, music, and fire-crackers, as at a funeral. Finally, the head is placed near Kāḷiyammaṉ for the ceremony of *uyir perutal,* 'the recovery of life' (see Plate 14). During a small *pūjā* to Kālī, with only about fifteen people in attendance in the dark amid flaming torches, the Pāratiyār recapitulates Aravāṉ's story, in particular his triple-boon-seeking appeal to Kṛṣṇa: 'Give me one day of war to fight. If you give me that, I'll be willing to sacrifice my body. You should give me eyes to see and ears to hear.'

Once Aravāṉ's head has 'recovered life' near the Kālī temple, it is carried horizontally, still covered, back near the aḻukaḷam. The man who carries it must cross three rows of burning straw, which are set alight to keep ghosts (*pēy* and *picācu*) from accompanying Kūttāṇṭavar back to the temple. On the way, the head is set upright in the middle of the street that runs through the village near the aḻukaḷam at a point surrounded by booths still open from the fair. Here it is decorated with the same flower-crown-on-banana-stalk head-dressing as on the opening nights. When the decorations are complete, the head is again danced through the streets of three villages back to the temple.

This dancing return, called *vitaiyātti,* goes on through the night, and is the main event of the festival's seventeenth day, since the full return actually occurs on the seventeenth morning, around 7 a.m. While the head is being returned to Kūvākkam, the other components of Kūttāṇṭavar's full embodiment are returned to the various cooperating villagers. The *tēr* is left by the lake bund so that it can be purified, since it is like a 'death house' with furniture that must be left untouched, or a bier that has been polluted from carrying a body. The people who have returned from the Kālī temple must take a pollution-removing bath to cleanse themselves before going home. Women will have water left outside for them to clean themselves before entering their houses.

Finally, on the eighteenth day the Cāmi's head is decorated and taken around Kūvākkam village only: this time, without dancing. It returns at 6 a.m., with the same nine-man relay of Vaṉṉiyars as on the first six nights. The ritual of Tarumar Pattāpiṣēkam, the coronation of Yudhiṣṭhira (Tarumar-Dharma), with recitation by the Pāratiyār, is performed using Kūttāṇṭavar's head, as if it were his coronation. After that, the head is returned to the sanctum, where it stays, ruling like Dharmarāja, for another year.

E. FROM THE EPIC FRAME TO THE FLUID REALM

The fusion of Kūttāṇṭavar and Tarumar/Dharmarāja-Yudhiṣṭhira into one image in the closing coronation ceremony at Kūvākkam is suggestive. Both Dharma and Kūttāṇṭavar have associations with death through the figure of Yama, who is called both Dharmarāja (like Yudhiṣṭhira) in Sanskrit and Kūṟṟaṉ or Kūṟṟu, 'Death' (one of Kūttāṇṭavar's occasional folk etymologies [e.g. Maṇivaṇṇaṉ 1984: 59]) in Tamil. That the reign of Dharma is in some ways a rule of Death, Yama, is a richly played out theme in Draupadī festivals,[16] where it is characteristic of an understanding, equally pertinent to Kūttāṇṭavar festivals, that a *Mahābhārata* festival brings matters of life and death, as lived in a village, under divine regulation. At Kūvākkam, however, it would seem to place the head of Kūttāṇṭavar that rules now from the temple in a kind of life-death borderland. His head has regained its life (*uyir*) at the Kālī temple, but not, as we shall see, completely. For now, he protects villagers from diseases and deaths only from a kind of limbo of his own.

Here, then, we come to Kūvākkam's version of the reanimation of the deity from beyond the eighteen-day festival frame. Let us recall the ways we have met by which other villages account for such reanimations and transferals: the floating heads, the baby's cry '*kuvā*', the country fig (*ātti*) tree, the boundary-goddess temple rites, possessions, the descent from the mountain. As we have seen already, most of these images and practices already have their evocations or counterparts *within* the eighteen-day epic frame at Kūvākkam, or on its boundaries. Now we can see that some of them also have their fuller development beyond that frame. But to appreciate what goes into the reanimation at Kūvākkam, we must also recall the reassembled 'spirits' (*āvi*) of Kūttāṇṭavar's opponent and double Kūttācūraṉ, and add that at two Salem District Kūttāṇṭavar festivals (at Palaiyacūramaṅkalam and Pēḷūr, both in Salem Taluk),

Kūttāṇṭavar's life (*uyir*) or śakti (both terms are used) is brought into the village at the beginning of the festival on a horse.

As we have seen, on the sixteenth night of his eighteen-day Kūvākkam festival, Kūttāṇṭavar is revived at the Kālī temple by the lake bund and his head is danced back to his own temple to rule from the eighteenth day on as Dharma. But there is a period after this of about three months when it is understood that his spirit (*āvi*) or life (*uyir*) remains elsewhere, and that his head is not yet fully animated. During this time, Kūttāṇṭavar's *tēr*—the chariot that has been his death house or bier—remains by the lake bund either for three months to purify it, or until it is cleansed by strong rains: whichever comes first. Local informants say that in normal cases a death bier is left in the cremation ground, and some say that the lake and the area around the Kālī temple is a cremation ground during this period. One hears about reported sightings of Kūttāṇṭavar's ghost (*pēy*) at these times, dressed in white, walking about on the lake bund.

This three-month period ends on a Tuesday in the month of Āṭi (July-August) with a one-day 'festival' (*viḻā*) called *Muṉṟām Mācam* ('Third Month') and *Kuṭi Aḻaittal* ('Calling [Kūttāṇṭavar] Home'). I signal here only what is essential for this essay and reserve fuller discussion and analysis for a work in progress. I follow for the most part the account and interpretative insights of Kaṇṇaṉ Pūcāri, whose descriptions and reflections, after many interviews, reached a stunning crescendo on the last day we met, 22 May 1990.

A stallion, ideally purchased as a pledge or donation to the temple (*pirattaṉai*) to represent the village Vaṉṉiyars, is adorned at nightfall and taken on procession (mainly by Vaṉṉiyars) from the Kūttāṇṭavar temple to the open-air Kālī temple by the lake bund (the main Kālī temple mentioned above). While one party waits there with the horse, another (mainly Harijans) that has branched off from it goes to the open-air village boundary temple of Ellaikāḷiyammaṉ, 'Kālī of the village boundary'. Here the village headman (Nāṭṭār) sacrifices a tusked pig (*paṉṟi*), whose costs are met by the Paṟaiyar drummers of the Rāja mēḷam. A group of Paṟaiyars then drags the pig's carcass to a grove about thirty feet from the main Kālī temple and leaves it there. Vaṉṉiyars then lead the horse to another tank (*ēri*) or pond (*kuṭṭai*) called Laṭcumaṇattāṉkuṭṭai. Beside this usually dry pond-bed, Kaṇṇaṉ Pūcāri is supposed to sing Tamil mantras to the horse, and a local Pāratiyār should sing *Pāratam* to it. The horse receives a red dhoti on its back to represent the Cāmi's cloth (*tuṇi*), and a sword (the Cāmi's) is tied lengthwise to his right side. Here at the middle of the pond, it is then offered a waving of lamps (*tīpāratanai*), gets possessed, froths at the mouth, and starts shaking (*kulukku*).[17] The Vaṉṉiyars then lead it to the Kālī temple by the lake bund. Here Kālī receives offerings of lamp-waving, and food is distributed to village headmen from Kūvākkam and surrounding villages. Everyone present is feasted, and the horse is garlanded and fed with peanuts, gruel, and horse gram (*koḷḷu*). Now the horse shakes his head and starts running. Accompanied by both *mēḷams* and chased by the Nāṭṭār's son, it runs at great speed around the village, and comes back to the Kūttāṇṭavar temple. Here both the horse and the head in the sanctum receive offerings and lamp-wavings, and the red cloth and sword are removed and left in the sanctum.

All informants agree that the ceremony reanimates the deity, though they use a variety of terms (*uyir, āvi, śakti, aruḷ* [grace]) to describe the process; and they agree that from the middle of the pond on, with the first possession of the horse, it is the Cāmi who rides it. To ride a horse is a conventional trope for possession. Kūttāṇṭavar's reanimation thus already parallels and condenses the traditions we have noticed elsewhere, through which he is drawn back into his head-encapsuled life by rites at boundary goddess temples, trees, emergences from bodies of water, possession rites, dancing, and horses. Kaṇṇan̲ Pūcāri, in a stunning piece of local exegesis, now explains the three locations that tie these themes together. And he takes us to the mountain.

> Aravān̲'s head was removed [sacrificed] for Vīramaṅkāḷi [Kālī]. Three months later this is done to bring him back to life. When Kūttāṇṭavar dies, his spirit (*āvi*) departs. The sacrifice in the Boundary Kālī temple is given for Kūttāṇṭavar. In order to bring him back to life, all these things are done .... The life (*uyir*) is in all three places: the Boundary Kālī temple, the Kālī temple by the lake, and the middle of the pond. So the horse goes into the middle of the pond. People afraid won't go. There it gets the last of the three parts of the uyir. Once the Cāmi's spirit (*āvi*) gets the three parts of the uyir, the horse gets possessed. It has to be brought back, reassembled. The spirit (*āvi*) stays in the Kālī Kōvil. The horse shakes for this reason: Kuṭi Al̲aittal means calling him [Kūttāṇṭavar] home; *kuṭi* means 'family, *kuṭumpam*'. It brings the Cāmi here. Thus the idea is bringing the Cāmi to the temple. It seems Cāmi has left the village; after this—like he has gone to the mountain somewhere. So they bring back the Cāmi from the mountain (*malai*). They don't know which mountain. Kuṭi Al̲aital means inviting him back from the mountain. Why go first to the two goddesses? Once he is given as a sacrifice to Kālī, his uyir goes to Mēl Malaiyan̲ūr. The life of Aravān̲ is brought back from Laṭcumaṇattān̲kuṭṭai; but this equals his being brought back from Mēl Malaiyan̲ūr. That is the mountain!

Let us just recall that it was Kaṇṇan̲ Pūcāri who explained the first-day rites for Māriyamman̲ as a village equivalent to Aravān̲'s leave-taking to go to war. Entering into the eighteen-day epic frame, he suitably leaves the village to go to war; leaving that frame at the end of the war, he leaves the village to go to the mountain.

There was no way to question whether this elegant exegesis was *ex tempore.* All I can say is that while I asked about the mountain and the goddesses, I said nothing of Mēl Malaiyan̲ūr, which never crossed my mind, and that Kaṇṇan̲ Pūcāri seemed deliberate and sincere in this identification of the mountain after another informant suggested Sabarimalai, the mountain pilgrimage site linked with the god Aiyappan in Kerala. To understand this identification, one need know only a few things. *Malai*, 'mountain', is an element of the name of Mēl Malaiyaṉūr: a village no more than thirty miles (as the crow flies) north of Kūvākkam that is famous regionally at the level of Tamil (and especially South Arcot) folk religion for its temple to the goddess Aṅkāḷammaṉ, herself a form of Kālī, and more important, goddess of the cremation ground. Indeed, Mēl Malaiyaṉūr, where a cremation ground is adjacent to her temple, *is* the cremation ground in Aṅkāḷammaṉ's myths and cult (Meyer 1986). In Kūttāṇṭavar's going to and coming from the mountain, the mountain is thus the cremation ground: the ultimate place of death—but also of revival themes in Aṅkāḷammaṉ's cult.[18] Like riding a horse, 'climbing the mountain' is also a trope for possession, as in the phrase *Cāmi malaiyēriyiruccu*, 'Cāmi has climbed the mountain'. This is usually said in the context of possession, whether a person possessed 'climbs the mountain', or whether it refers to something exciting happening at the temple. More commonly, it may also mean that Cāmi leaves somebody he has possessed, leaves him to his natural self, so that in leaving, Cāmi goes back to the mountain: to his divine place. Here, on analogy with the latter meaning but with reference as well to the completion of Aravāṉ's epic deaths, it was used to say that when the festival is over, Cāmi has left Kūvākkam and gone to the mountain, to the cremation ground at Mēl Malaiyaṉūr.[19] If we can take Kaṇṇaṉ Pūcāri at his every word, the Third Month festival then 'calls' Kūttāṇṭavar 'back to his family, to his village'—calls the life he had dispersed to Aṅkāḷammaṉ's cremation-ground 'mountain' back from the temples of her two local forms as Kālī (at the Boundary Temple and the lakeside) and, it would seem, back from a third source as well that is a variant of the watery source that brings forth his head—to reassemble his spirit so that his fluid post-mortem vitality can reanimate the head in his temple making it worthy to receive worship.

At Kūvākkam, then, this reassembling of Kūttāṇṭavar's life spills not into a new eighteen-day cycle directly, but into the one-day festival three months after one *Mahābhārata* festival is over and about eight months before the next one begins. I suspect this may have something to do with the Kūvākkam temple's pre-eminence in the Kūttāṇṭavar cult, both among villagers throughout Tamil Nadu who have Kūttāṇṭavar as their *kulateyvam*, and among Tamil Alis who come from far and wide. Visitors of both kinds do come to the temple at non-festival times to fulfil personal vows. Such visitation patterns could have prompted a desire, probably well before our earliest descriptions by Garstin and Francis, to keep the temple open through most of the year by preponing the most important reanimation rites from the beginning of the festival to the month of Āṭi. However, the three-month period of Aravāṉ's dispersal also has a local explanation. It is the period for arranged marriages in Kūvākkam and its surrounding villages, following a rule that no one in this area arranges a daughter's marriage until Aravāṉ gets married, and then arranged marriages occur only until the month of Āvaṇi (August-September). From Āvaṇi to Cittirai, there will thus be no arranged marriages. 'The idea', it was explained, 'seems to be that Aravāṉ must be married first.' Young women can then follow the model of his bride: and, most curiously, of the men (often their fathers, husbands, and brothers) who have impersonated 'her'. Given Kūttāṇṭavar's 'ancestor' status and the fecundity of his 'blood rice', it may also be that the time of the dispersal of his *uyir* enhances the fertility of these new marriages.

Kūttāṇṭavar's recurrent lives, deaths, and reanimations, in fact, seem to spill into and out of all conventional boundaries, including those Hindu ones that normatively define death, reanimation (the law of *karma*), and the rites of 'establishment' (*pratiṣṭhā*) and 'dismissal' (*visarjana*) whereby deities are invited to enter into icons, enliven them with their breath (*prāṇa*) or Self (*ātman*), and depart from them. But there is little if anything in the Kūttāṇṭavar cult that one can ascribe to tribal or other 'un-Hinduized' influences, and much—beginning with the Vedic conundrum of the severed head and the dismemberment of Puruṣa—that taps deep Hindu sources. It may be that other similar reanimations of specifically wooden icons, like those of the four icons at Puri (see n. 14), will be discovered to push us toward tribalizing or 'proto-Hindu' explanations of the forest-mountain themes and the strains of animate multiplicity. On the other hand, it may only be that the boundaries of life and death have always been fluid in Hindu formulations.

NOTES

1. Alf Hiltebeitel is Professor of Religion at the George Washington University, Washington, D.C.

   This paper benefits from prior preliminary and partial presentations at the Association of Asian Studies Annual Meeting, Washington, D.C.; the École Pratique des Hautes Études, 5th Section, Sciences Religieuses, Paris; the Center for Asian Studies, University of Virginia (all 1992); and the South Asia Seminar, University of Texas, Austin (1993). Fieldwork in 1990 was sponsored by the American Institute of Indian Studies. Writing has been facilitated by support from the George Washington University Committee on Research. I thank E. Sundaramurthy, N. Daivasundaram, Pon Kothandaraman, Lee Weissman, J. Rajasekaran, and Abbie Ziffren for their help with Tamil for this paper. I thank my son Simon Hiltebeitel for his preparation of the map.
2. See Hiltebeitel 1992 for an analysis of this ethnography as it relates to the same issues in the Draupadī cult. Vaṉṉiyars are the most prominent

community in the highest density area of both cults: that is, in South Arcot and adjacent areas.

3. Take up these matters in Hiltebeitel: forthcoming and 1998, where I discuss the roles and contributions of Alis at this and other Kūttāṇṭavar festivals. As of 1990, both local residents and visiting Alis claim that the Alis' big influx occurred in about 1960 or 1970, but that smaller numbers of Alis had come previously.
4. According to Gérard Colas, Vaikhānasa priests say the eye-opening ceremony is always dangerous; immediately on opening, the god has a wide gaze, and should see auspicious things (personal communication, May 1992). At Draupadī festivals, Aravāṉ's eye-opening confronts him with the inauspicious sight of the dying Duryodhana (Hiltebeitel 1991:291). On the 'identity' of Aravāṉ and Kūttāṇṭavar, see below.
5. As there are traditions that Draupadī had her original temple at Gingee, or at Mēlaccēri village outside it (Hiltebeitel 1988: 3-12, 65-100; 1991: 483-9); or even as there are indications that Aṅkāḷammaṉ's original temple would have been at Mēl Malaiyaṉūr (Gingee Taluk, South Arcot) (Meyer 1986: 103, 157).
6. This is the earliest known printing date of a folk drama on this theme (Hiltebeitel 1988: 160). There are different stories of who marries Aravāṉ in Coimbatore and Thanjavur Districts (the latter only in Draupadī cult circles), while in North Arcot, there seem to be cases of transvestitism and marriage rituals without myths on this point. I will take up this matter elsewhere.
7. *Bhāgavata Purāṇa* 10.74.45 (Śiśupāla) and 10.78.10 (Dantavaktra): 'Just as it happened after the slaying of Śiśupāla, a very subtle ray of light emanated from the body of Dantavaktra and entered the person of Kṛṣṇa—a wonderful sight indeed—while all beings witnessed it' (Tagare 1976-8, Part IV: 1772; cf. Part III, p. 887 and n. 2 to 7.1.17 and 7.1.32). There may be some echo of Dantavaktra's connection with Śiśupāla ('protector of children') in Dantavaktra's boon of being reborn as a *cicu*, a Sanskritic word for 'child'.
8. I thank David Gordon White for seeing this connection (personal communication. May 1992). On this ceremony, see Knipe 1977.
9. Actually, to say that Māriyammaṉ has no connection with the epic is misleading, since she is also known as Reṇukā, whose epic identity is most significant. But the primary frame of reference is certainly 'non-epic'. Thus Kaṇṇaṉ Pūcāri adds that 'Māriyammaṉ is also known as Keṅkaiyammaṉ', that is, the river goddess Gaṅgā. One or the other of these goddesses, and sometimes both, are connected with Kūttāṇṭavar from South Arcot or Coimbatore. On Keṅkaiyammaṉ and Kūttāṇṭavar, see for now Hiltebeitel 1998.
10. The preliminary gathering of *ātti* twigs and branches is followed by an extended use of them in connection with the god's life and death at Coimbatore area Kūttāṇṭavar festivals; see for now Maṇivaṇṇaṉ 1984: 45-8, 52-8; Nārullā 1990: 50.
11. Vaṉṉiyars safeguard the purity of the Cāttukkāraṉ or Harijan bride. The latter's vigil over the sprouts is each day broken only by his departure for his morning and evening meals, which he takes at the house of the Vaṉṉiyar

bride, who is also the senior Vaṉṉiyar pūcāri of the temple. His food is prepared by the latter's wife. Before the Cāttukkāraṉ leaves for these meals, he circumambulates the sprouts and then bathes. His wife, meanwhile, also has her special vigil: during the time her husband guards the sprouts, she will eat only one meal a day that must be prepared by a prepubescent girl, and she also keeps a lamp that burns all the time. The Vaṉṉiyar bride's wife, who feeds the Cāttukkāraṉ, keeps no such vow. There are repeated ways throughout the festival by which Vaṉṉiyars supply the god's body while Harijans tender his head (Hiltebeitel forthcoming).

12. From here to the end of this section, this article builds on material also found in a portion of Hiltebeitel forthcoming.
13. Ācāri is a title for the five artisan castes (*pañca kammāḷar*): goldsmiths, braziers, masons, blacksmiths, and carpenters. Ācāris serve as priests in low caste village rituals. Called Visuvapirāmaṇa, the Kūvākkam Ācāris are 'more important than Brahmans' for their ritual expertise.
14. The yearly cycle of death and revival of the icon by repainting, and, at other villages, signs of longer cycles of fifteen (Tēvaṉūr) or twenty years (Putūr; Otukkattūr [Vellore Taluk, South Arcot]), hold similarities to the *Navakalevara* ('new embodiment') ceremony performed at twelve or nineteen-year intervals for the icons of Jagannātha, Balabhadra, Subhadrā, and Sudarśana at Puri. See Tripathi (1978: 229): 'Of importance is only the continuity of the divine substance, . . . and the fact that the new images be constructed exactly in the same manner as the previous ones.' The roles of 'tribals' in searching for the wood and lamenting (ibid., 233, 261), and of Brahmans in the revival (244-61), have analogs in the roles of Paṟaiyars and Brahmans at Kūvākkam. Cf. also Eschmann 1978, who, however, does not succeed in showing that the 'new body' rites are essentially 'tribal'.
15. This refers to the tragedy of cutting the bride's tāli on her wedding day, and is a phrase used also in Coimbatore and Thanjavur districts in connection with Aravāṉ, even though his single-day marriage is in each case to a different woman: a topic to be treated elsewhere.
16. Yudhiṣṭhira's associations with Yama are richly played out in the Draupadī cult (Hiltebeitel 1991: 50-1, 116, 128, 482-5).
17. Cf. Blackburn 1988: 41-6, correlating *tīpāratanai* and possession.
18. As at Kūvākkam, there is no mountain at Mēl Malaiyaṉūr, but the village associates the goddess' coming there with it being ruled by the mythic king Malaiyarācaṉ or Pārvatarājaṉ, i.e. Mount Himavat or Himalaya, and her manifestation there takes the form of a termite hill (Meyer 1986: 27.41).
19. This exegesis was co-formulated by my assistant J. Rajasekaran in continued conversation with Kaṇṇaṉ Pūcāri.

REFERENCES

Blackburn, Stuart H. 1988. *Singing of Birth and Death: Texts in Performance.* Philadelphia: University of Pennsylvania Press.

Eḻumalai, Kō. 1989. *Aravāṉ Tiruviḻā.* Doctoral Dissertation. University of Pondicherry, Kāraikkāl.

Eschmann, Anncharlott. 1978. Prototypes of the Navakalevara Ritual and their Relation to the Jagannātha Cult. In Anncharlott Eschmann, Hermann Kulke, and Gaya Charan Tripathi (eds.), *The Cult of Jagannath and the Regional Tradition of Orissa.* New Delhi: Manohar

Francis, W. 1906. *Madras District Gazetteers: South Arcot.* Madras: Government Press.

Garstin, J.H. 1978. *Manual of the South Arcot District.* Madras: Lawrence Asylum Press.

Hiltebeitel, Alf. 1988. *The Cult of Draupadī,* vol. 1: *Mythologies: From Gingee to Kurukṣetra.* Chicago: University of Chicago Press.

———. 1991. *The Cult of Draupadī,* vol. 2: *On Hindu Ritual and the Goddess.* Chicago: University of Chicago Press.

———. 1992. Colonial Lenses on the South Indian Draupadī Cult. In *Ritual, State, and Society,* Festschrift for Jan Heesterman. Leiden: E. J. Brill.

———. forthcoming. 'Dying before the *Mahābhārata* War: Martial and Transsexual Body-Building for Aravāṉ'.

———. 1998. The Goddess's Mustache. In Alf Hiltebeitel and Barbara D. Miller (eds.), *Hair: its Power and Meaning in Asian Cultures* (tentative title), Albany: State University of New York Press.

Knipe, David M. 1977. *Sapiṇḍīkaraṇa.* The Hindu Rite of Entry into Heaven. In Frank E. Reynolds and Earle H. Waugh (eds.), *Religious Encounters with Death.* University Park: Pennsylvania State University Press.

Maṇivaṇṇaṉ, Celvaṉ P. 1984. *Koṅkunāṭṭil Aravāṉ Vaḻipāḍu.* Doctoral Dissertation, University of Coimbatore.

Meyer, Eveline. 1986. *Aṅkāḷaparamēcuvari: A Goddess of Tamilnadu, Her Myths and Cult.* Wiesbaden: Franz Steiner.

Nārullā, Ār. 1990. *Alikaḷ Vāḻkkai.* Madras: Pūṅkuḻali Accakam.

Sörensen, S. [1904] 1963. *An Index to the Names in the Mahābhārata.* Delhi: Motilal Banarsidass.

Tagare, Ganesh Vasudeo. 1976-78. *The Bhāgavata Purāṇa,* translated and annotated. 5 Parts. Ancient Indian Tradition and Mythology Series, vols. 7-11. Delhi: Motilal Banarsidass.

Tripathi, Gaya Charan. 1978. Navakalevara: The Unique Ceremony of the 'Birth' and 'Death' of the 'Lord of the World'. In Anncharlott Eschmann, Hermann Kulke, and Gaya Charan Tripathi (eds.), *The Cult of Jagannath and the Regional Tradition of Orissa.* New Delhi: Manohar.

Whitehead, Henry. 1921. *The Village Gods of South India.* Calcutta: Association Press.

ILLUSTRATIONS

Plate 1. Bālācaturdaśī—Family groups on Kailāsa hill in the morning after the night of Bālācaturdaśī. (Michaels)

Plate 2. Bālācaturdaśī—Torches (mahādīpa) to be lit in memory of the deceased. (Michaels)

Plate 3. Bālācaturdaśī—Chetrīs (Thāpā) performing *homa.* In white clothes: the chief mourner; with a shawl: the Brahmin priest. (Michaels)

Plate 4. Bālācaturdaśī—Pilgrims taking a (symbolic) bath at the cremation *ghāṭs* (Āryaghāṭ). (Michaels)

Plate 5. Bālācaturdaśī—All the grain collected by Poḍes (sweepers) near the Jayavāgīśvarī temple and Amālkoṭ Kacaharī. (Michaels)

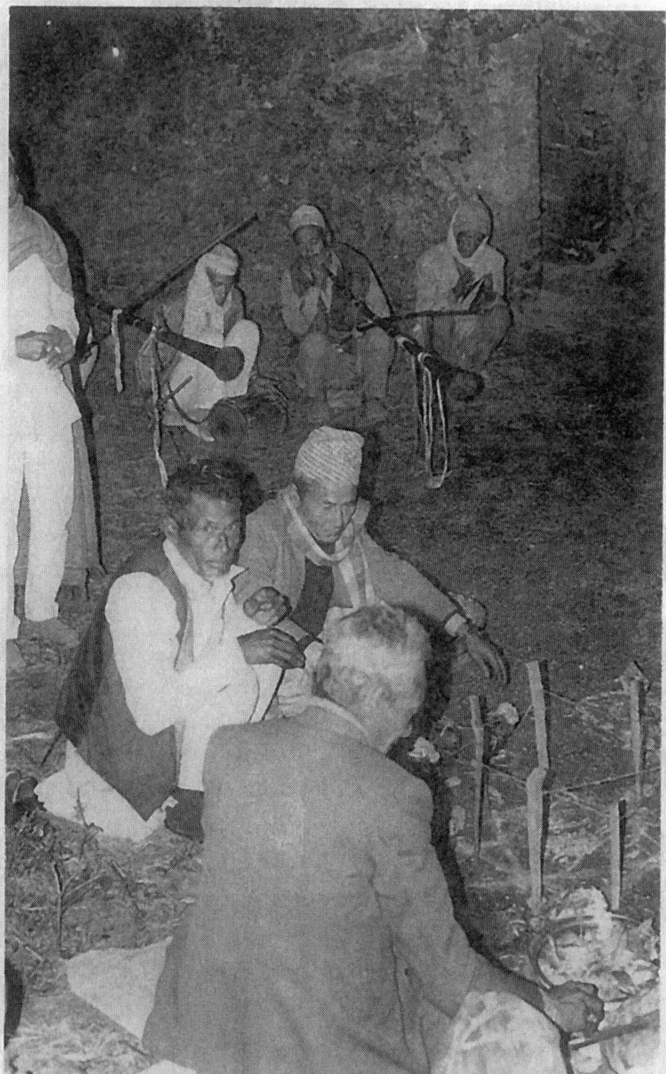

Plate 6. Bālāguṭhīpūjā—To the back: a *kahaḥ* (trumpet) player and the secret entrance into Mṛgasthalī (right side). (Michaels)

Plate 7. Bālāguṭhīpūjā—Sacrificial arena at Dharmeśvara, with places set aside for the *homa* (left; in the middle a *vajra*) and a *kalaśa*, bell and conch. (Michaels)

Plate 8. Bālāguṭhīpūjā—One Mānandhar hands over a basket with two brass fishes and grains to two Rājopādhyāya priests. (Michaels)

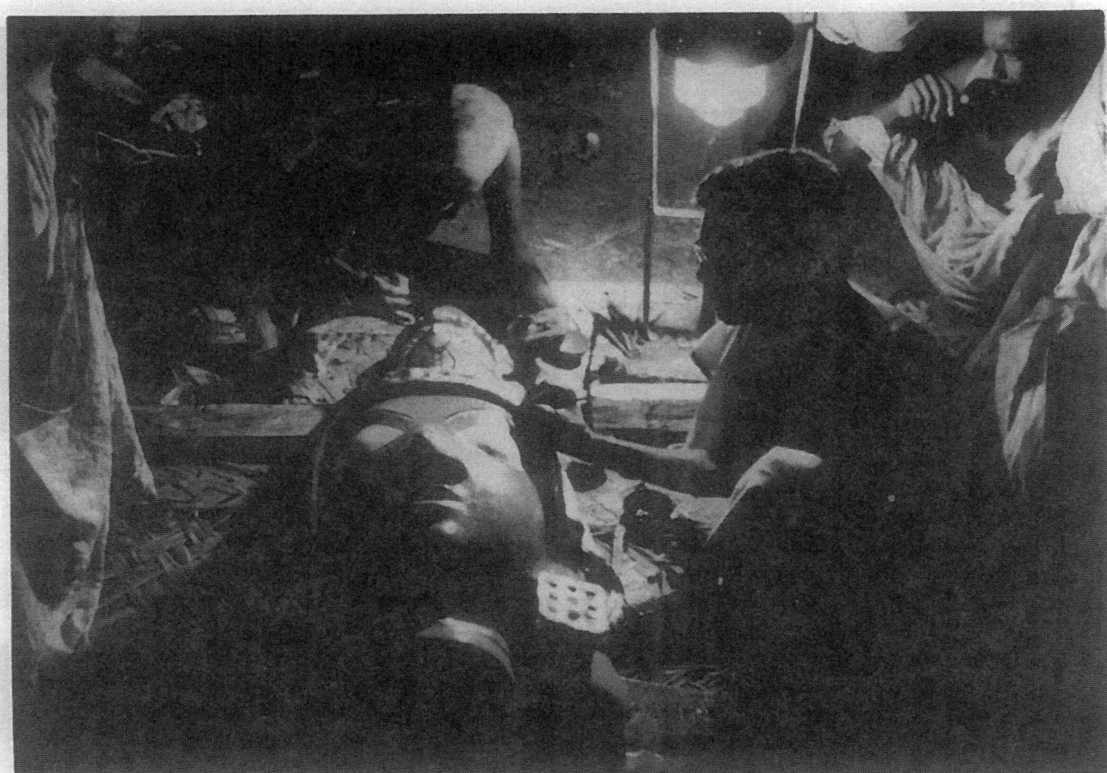

Plate 9. A Vaṉṉiyar carpenter and painter work at night by petromax lantern to repaint Kūttāṇṭavar's head after the previous year's paint has been stripped from it. (Hiltebeitel)

Plate 10. Eye-opening ceremony for Kūttāṇṭavar's newly repainted head, placed for his first viewing on the *keṭāyam*, with village headmen in attendance. (Hiltebeitel)

Plate 11. Kūttāṇṭavar, reduced to a 'skeleton', at the 'weeping ground' (*a̠lukaḷam*) beneath a large peepul tree, overlooking the tali-cutting and bangle-breaking of his devotees. (Hiltebeitel)

Plate 12. Open-air Kāḷiyammaṉ temple by the lake bund, where Kūttāṇṭavar's head regains his 'life' (*uyir*). (Hiltebeitel)

Plate 13. Diaggregation of Kūttāṇṭavar: his head is the last part of his body, other than straw, to be removed from his chariot. The cloth covering it has slipped off the head and is held above it. (Hiltebeitel)

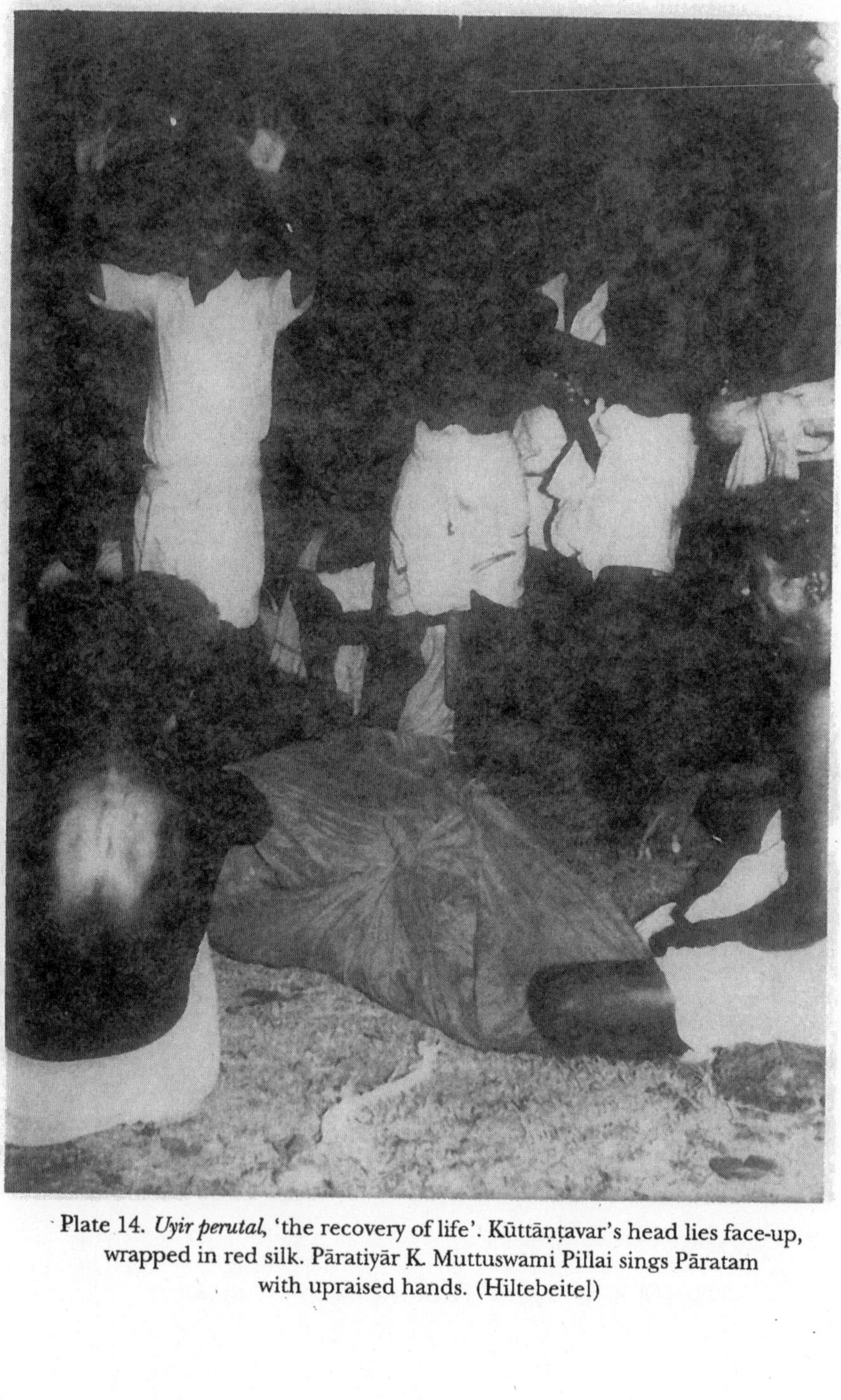

Plate 14. *Uyir perutal*, 'the recovery of life'. Kūttāṇṭavar's head lies face-up, wrapped in red silk. Pāratiyār K. Muttuswami Pillai sings Pāratam with upraised hands. (Hiltebeitel)

Contributors

GEORG BERKEMER is currently research associate in the Department of History, South Asia Institute, Heidelberg University.

HEIDRUN BRÜCKNER is Professor of Indology at the University of Tübingen.

ULRICH DEMMER is currently research associate in the Department of Anthropology, South Asia Institute, Heidelberg University.

ANNE FELDHAUS is Professor of Religious Studies at Arizona State University.

MARTIN GAENSZLE is currently research associate in the Department of Anthropology, South Asia Institute, Heidelberg University.

ALF HILTEBEITEL is Professor in the Religion Department, George Washington University, Washington D.C.

KLAUS-PETER KÖPPING is Professor of Anthropology, Heidelberg University.

CHARLES MALAMOUD is Professor in Studies in Indian Religion at the École pratique des hautes études, Sorbonne, Paris.

ADITYA MALIK is currently research associate in the Department of Modern Indology, South Asia Institute, Heidelberg University.

AXEL MICHAELS is Professor of Classical Indology at the South Asia Institute, Heidelberg University.

SHALINI RANDERIA is Lecturer at the Institute of Sociology, Free University, Berlin.

ELISABETH SCHÖMBUCHER is Lecturer in Anthropology at the South Asia Institute, Heidelberg University.

HUGH VAN SKYHAWK is currently research associate in the Department of Classical Indology, South Asia Institute, Heidelberg University.

CLAUS PETER ZOLLER is currently research associate in the Department of Modern Indology, South Asia Institute, Heidelberg University.